POWERPOINT 2003
PERSONAL TRAINER

POWERPOINT 2003
PERSONAL TRAINER

CustomGuide, Inc.

O'REILLY®

Beijing • Cambridge • Farnham • Köln • Paris • Sebastopol • Taipei • Tokyo

PowerPoint 2003 Personal Trainer
by CustomGuide, Inc.

Copyright © 2005 O'Reilly Media, Inc. All rights reserved.
Printed in the United States of America.

Cover illustration: © 2004 Lou Brooks.

Published by O'Reilly Media, Inc., 1005 Gravenstein Highway North, Sebastopol, CA 95472.

O'Reilly books may be purchased for educational, business, or sales promotional use. Online editions are also available for most titles (*safari.oreilly.com*). For more information, contact our corporate/institutional sales department: (800) 998-9938 or *corporate@oreilly.com*.

Editors	Tatiana Apandi Diaz and Nathan Torkington
Production Editor	Marlowe Shaeffer
Art Director	Michele Wetherbee
Cover Designer	Emma Colby
Cover Illustrator	Lou Brooks
Interior Designer	Melanie Wang

Printing History

November 2004:   First Edition.

Nutshell Handbook, the Nutshell Handbook logo, and the O'Reilly logo are registered trademarks of O'Reilly Media, Inc. *PowerPoint 2003 Personal Trainer* and related trade dress are trademarks of O'Reilly Media, Inc.

Many of the designations used by manufacturers and sellers to distinguish their products are claimed as trademarks. Where those designations appear in this book, and O'Reilly Media, Inc. was aware of a trademark claim, the designations have been printed in caps or initial caps.

While every precaution has been taken in the preparation of this book, the publisher and author assume no responsibility for errors or omissions, or for damages resulting from the use of the information contained herein.

RepKover. This book uses RepKover™, a durable and flexible lay-flat binding.

ISBN: 0-596-00855-4
[C]

CONTENTS

Introduction		xi

Chapter 1 The Fundamentals — 1

LESSON 1.1	Starting PowerPoint	2
LESSON 1.2	What's New in PowerPoint 2003?	4
LESSON 1.3	Understanding the PowerPoint Program Screen	6
LESSON 1.4	Using Menus	9
LESSON 1.5	Using Toolbars and Creating a New Presentation	12
LESSON 1.6	Filling Out Dialog Boxes	15
LESSON 1.7	Keystroke and Right Mouse Button Shortcuts	17
LESSON 1.8	Opening a Presentation	19
LESSON 1.9	Saving and Closing a Presentation and Exiting PowerPoint	22
LESSON 1.10	Creating a New Presentation with the AutoContent Wizard	25
LESSON 1.11	Creating a Blank Presentation and a Presentation from a Template	28
LESSON 1.12	Moving Around in Your Presentations	30
LESSON 1.13	Viewing Your Presentation	33
LESSON 1.14	Printing Your Presentation	36
LESSON 1.15	Getting Help	38
LESSON 1.16	Changing the Office Assistant and Using the "What's This" Button	41
Chapter One Review		43

Chapter 2 Editing a Presentation — 47

LESSON 2.1	Inserting Slides and Text	48
LESSON 2.2	Using the Outline Pane	51
LESSON 2.3	Editing Text	53

Contents

LESSON 2.4	Selecting, Replacing, and Deleting Text		55
LESSON 2.5	Cutting, Copying, and Pasting Text		58
LESSON 2.6	Using Undo, Redo, and Repeat		61
LESSON 2.7	Checking Your Spelling		64
LESSON 2.8	Finding and Replacing Information		66
LESSON 2.9	Viewing a Presentation's Outline		68
LESSON 2.10	Rearranging a Presentation's Outline		71
LESSON 2.11	Inserting Symbols and Special Characters		73
LESSON 2.12	Working in Slide Sorter View		75
LESSON 2.13	Adding Notes to Your Slides		77
LESSON 2.14	Working with Multiple Windows		79
LESSON 2.15	Collecting and Pasting Multiple Items		82
LESSON 2.16	File Management		85
LESSON 2.17	Understanding Smart Tags		88
LESSON 2.18	Recovering Your Presentations		91
Chapter Two Review			94

Chapter 3	**Formatting Your Presentation**		**99**
LESSON 3.1	Formatting Fonts with the Formatting Toolbar		100
LESSON 3.2	Advanced Font Formatting with the Font Dialog Box		103
LESSON 3.3	Using the Format Painter		106
LESSON 3.4	Applying a Template's Formatting		108
LESSON 3.5	Using the Slide Master		110
LESSON 3.6	Choosing a Color Scheme		112
LESSON 3.7	Changing the Background of Your Slides		115
LESSON 3.8	Working with Bulleted and Numbered Lists		118
LESSON 3.9	Changing Paragraph Alignment and Line Spacing		120
LESSON 3.10	Adding Headers and Footers		122
LESSON 3.11	Working with Tabs and Indents		124
LESSON 3.12	Changing the Page Setup		127
Chapter Three Review			129

Contents

Chapter 4 — Drawing and Working with Graphics — 133

LESSON 4.1	Drawing on Your Slides	134
LESSON 4.2	Adding, Arranging, and Formatting Text Boxes	137
LESSON 4.3	Selecting, Resizing, Moving, and Deleting Objects	139
LESSON 4.4	Formatting Objects	142
LESSON 4.5	Inserting Clip Art	145
LESSON 4.6	Inserting and Formatting Pictures	148
LESSON 4.7	Aligning and Grouping Objects	151
LESSON 4.8	Drawing AutoShapes	154
LESSON 4.9	Flipping and Rotating Objects	157
LESSON 4.10	Layering Objects	160
LESSON 4.11	Applying Shadows and 3-D Effects	163
	Chapter Four Review	166

Chapter 5 — Working with Tables and WordArt — 171

LESSON 5.1	Creating a Table	172
LESSON 5.2	Working with a Table	175
LESSON 5.3	Adjusting Column Width and Row Height	177
LESSON 5.4	Inserting and Deleting Rows and Columns	179
LESSON 5.5	Adding Borders to a Table	181
LESSON 5.6	Adding Shading and Fills	183
LESSON 5.7	Inserting a WordArt Object	185
LESSON 5.8	Formatting a WordArt Object	187
	Chapter Five Review	190

Chapter 6 — Working with Graphs and Organization Charts — 193

LESSON 6.1	Creating a Chart	194
LESSON 6.2	Modifying a Chart	197
LESSON 6.3	Selecting a Chart Type	200
LESSON 6.4	Creating an Organization Chart	203
LESSON 6.5	Modifying Your Organization Chart	206
LESSON 6.6	Formatting Your Organization Chart	209
	Chapter Six Review	212

Contents

Chapter 7   Delivering Your Presentation   215

LESSON 7.1	Delivering a Presentation on a Computer	216
LESSON 7.2	Using Slide Transitions	219
LESSON 7.3	Using an Animation Scheme	221
LESSON 7.4	Using Custom Animations	223
LESSON 7.5	Rehearsing Slide Show Timings	225
LESSON 7.6	Creating a Presentation that Runs by Itself	228
LESSON 7.7	Creating a Custom Show	231
LESSON 7.8	Packaging and Copying a Presentation to CD	233
LESSON 7.9	Viewing a Packaged Presentation	236
Chapter Seven Review		238

Chapter 8   Working with Multimedia   243

LESSON 8.1	Inserting Sounds	244
LESSON 8.2	Adding Voice Narration to Your Slides	247
LESSON 8.3	Inserting a Movie Clip	250
LESSON 8.4	Automating the Multimedia in Your Presentation	252
Chapter Eight Review		255

Chapter 9   Working with Other Programs and the Internet   257

LESSON 9.1	Inserting a Slide into a Microsoft Word Document	258
LESSON 9.2	Embedding a Microsoft Excel Worksheet into a Slide	260
LESSON 9.3	Modifying an Embedded Object	262
LESSON 9.4	Inserting a Linked Excel Chart	265
LESSON 9.5	Importing and Exporting an Outline	267
LESSON 9.6	Using Hyperlinks	270
LESSON 9.7	Using Action Buttons	272
LESSON 9.8	Saving a Presentation as a Web Page	275
LESSON 9.9	Viewing a Web-Based Presentation	278
Chapter Nine Review		280

Chapter 10 Advanced Topics — 283

LESSON 10.1	Hiding, Displaying, and Moving Toolbars	284
LESSON 10.2	Customizing PowerPoint's Toolbars	286
LESSON 10.3	Sending Faxes	289
LESSON 10.4	Adding Comments to a Slide	291
LESSON 10.5	Customizing PowerPoint's Default Options	293
LESSON 10.6	File Properties and Finding a File	295
LESSON 10.7	Recording a Macro	298
LESSON 10.8	Playing and Editing a Macro	301
Chapter Ten Review		303

Index — 307

INTRODUCTION

About the Personal Trainer Series

Most software manuals are as hard to navigate as the programs they describe. They assume that you're going to read all 500 pages from start to finish, and that you can gain intimate familiarity with the program simply by reading about it. Some books give you sample files to practice on, but when you're finding your way around a new set of skills, it's all too easy to mess up program settings or delete data files and not know how to recover. Even if William Shakespeare and Bill Gates teamed up to write a book about Microsoft PowerPoint, their book would be frustrating to read because most people learn by doing the task.

While we don't claim to be rivals to either Bill, we think we have a winning formula in the Personal Trainer series. We've created a set of workouts that reflect the tasks you really want to do, whether as simple as resizing or as complex as integrating multimedia components. Each workout breaks a task into a series of simple steps, showing you exactly what to do to accomplish the task.

And instead of leaving you hanging, the interactive CD in the back of this book recreates the application for you to experiment in. In our unique simulator, there's no worry about permanently damaging your preferences, turning all your documents purple, losing data, or any of the other things that can go wrong when you're testing your new skills in the unforgiving world of the real application. It's fully interactive, giving you feedback and guidance as you work through the exercises—just like a real trainer!

Our friendly gym-themed guides can buff up your skills in record time. You'll learn the secrets of the professionals in a safe environment, with exercises and homework for those of you who really want to break the pain barrier. You'll have your PowerPoint 2003 skills in shape in no time!

About This Book

We've aimed this book at PowerPoint 2003. Some features may look different or simply not exist if you're using another version of the program. If our simulator doesn't match your application, check the version number to make sure you're using the right version.

Since this is a hands-on course, each lesson contains an exercise with step-by-step instructions for you to follow.

To make learning easier, every exercise follows certain conventions:

- This book never assumes you know where (or what) something is. The first time you're told to click something, a picture of what you're supposed to click appears in the illustrations at the beginning of the lesson.

- When you see a keyboard instruction like "press Ctrl + B," you should press and hold the first key (Ctrl in this example) while you press the second key (B in this example). Then, after you've pressed both keys, you can release them.

- There is usually more than one way to do something in PowerPoint. The exercise explains the most common method of doing something, while the alternate methods appear throughout the text. Use whatever approach feels most comfortable for you.

Introduction

Our exclusive Quick Reference box appears at the end of every lesson. You can use it to review the skills you've learned in the lesson and as a handy reference when you need to know how to do something fast and don't need to step through the sample exercises.

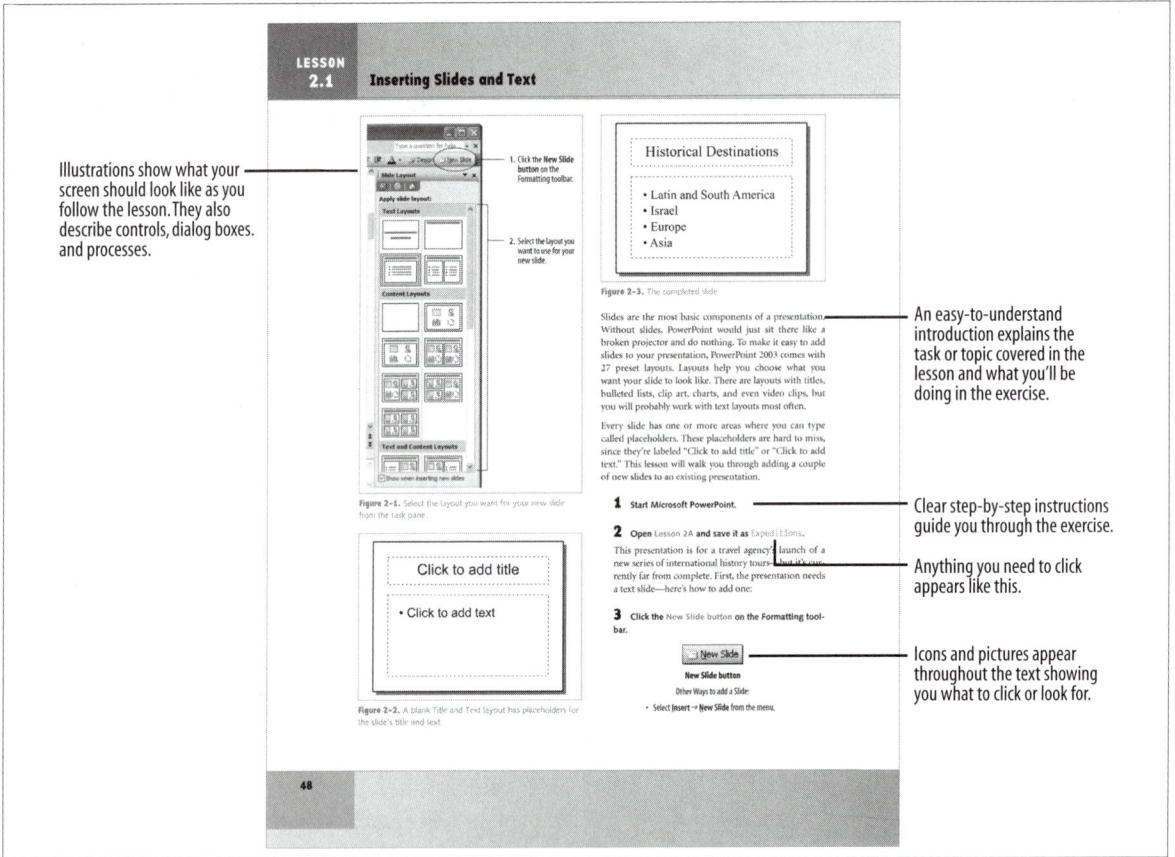

Conventions Used in This Book

The following is a list of typographical conventions used in this book:

Italic

Shows important terms the first time they are presented.

`Constant Width`

Shows anything you're supposed to type.

Color

Shows anything you're supposed to click, drag, or press.

NOTE *Warns you of pitfalls that you could encounter if you're not careful.*

TIP *Indicates a suggestion or supplementary information to the topic at hand.*

Using the Interactive Environment

Minimum Specs

- Windows 98 or better
- 64 MB RAM
- 150 MB Disk Space

Installation Instructions

Insert disc into CD-ROM drive. Click the "install" button at the prompt. The installer will give you the option of installing the "Interactive Content" and the "Practice Files." These are both installed by default. Practice files are also included on the CD in a directory called "Practice Files," which can be accessed without installing anything. If you select the installation item, the installer will then create a shortcut in your start menu under the title "Personal Trainer," which you can use to access your installation selections.

Use of Interactive Content

Once you've installed the interactive content, placing the disc in your drive will cause the program to launch automatically. Then, once it has launched, just make your lesson selections and learn away!

How to Contact Us

We have tested and verified the information in this book to the best of our ability, but you might find that features have changed (or even that we have made mistakes!). As a reader of this book, you can help us to improve future editions by sending us your feedback. Please let us know about any errors, inaccuracies, bugs, misleading or confusing statements, and typos that you find anywhere in this book.

Please also let us know what we can do to make this book more useful to you. We take your comments seriously and will try to incorporate reasonable suggestions into future editions. You can write to us at:

> O'Reilly Media, Inc.
> 1005 Gravenstein Highway North
> Sebastopol, CA 95472
> (800) 998-9938 (in the U.S. or Canada)
> (707) 829-0515 (international or local)
> (707) 829-0104 (fax)

To ask technical questions or to comment on the book, send email to:

> bookquestions@oreilly.com

The web site for *PowerPoint 2003 Personal Trainer* lists examples, errata, and plans for future editions. You can find this page at:

> http://www.oreilly.com/catalog/powerpointpt

For more information about this book and others, see the O'Reilly web site at:

> http://www.oreilly.com

CHAPTER 1
THE FUNDAMENTALS

CHAPTER OBJECTIVES:

Starting Microsoft PowerPoint
Understand the PowerPoint program screen
Using menus and toolbars
Using and filling out dialog boxes
Using keystroke shortcuts and right mouse button menus
Opening and saving presentations
Creating a new presentation
Viewing and printing a presentation
Moving around a presentation
Getting help

CHAPTER TASK: CREATE A SIMPLE PRESENTATION

Prerequisites

- **A computer with Windows 2000 or later, and PowerPoint 2003 installed.**
- **An understanding of basic computer functions (how to use the mouse and keyboard).**

Welcome to your first lesson of Microsoft PowerPoint 2003. PowerPoint is a desktop presentation program that turns your ideas into professional, convincing presentations. If you've ever used an overhead projector, flip chart, or even a blackboard, you're going to love PowerPoint! PowerPoint lets you create slides that include text, graphics, charts, and even digital movies. Once you have created a presentation, you can display it as an electronic slide show on any computer. Or, you can print your slides so that you can display them as transparencies or 35mm slides.

This chapter will introduce you to the PowerPoint "basics"—what you need to know to create, print, and save a presentation. If you've already seen the Microsoft PowerPoint program screen before, you know that it's filled with cryptic-looking buttons, menus, and icons. By the time you've finished this chapter, you will know what most of those buttons, menus, and icons are used for.

LESSON 1.1 Starting PowerPoint

Figure 1-1. The Windows Desktop.

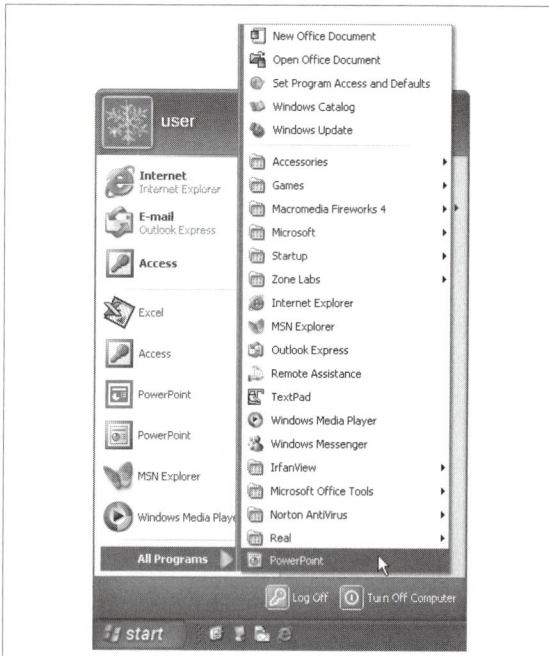

Figure 1-2. Programs located under the Windows Start button.

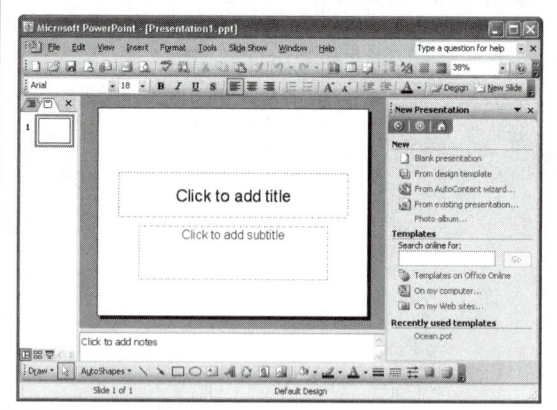

Figure 1-3. The Microsoft PowerPoint program screen.

Before starting PowerPoint 2003 (some people call starting a program opening it or launching it), make sure your computer is on—if it's not, turn it on! You start PowerPoint 2003 the same as you would start any other program on your computer—using the Start button. Because every computer can be set up differently (some people like to rearrange and reorder their program menu), the procedure for starting PowerPoint might be different from the one listed here.

1 Make sure your computer is on and the Windows desktop is open.

Your computer screen should look similar to the one shown in Figure 1-1.

2 Use your mouse to point to and click the Start button, located on the left-hand corner of the Windows taskbar at the bottom of the screen.

Start Button

The Windows Start menu pops up.

3 Move your mouse until the cursor points to All Programs.

A menu similar to the one shown in Figure 1-2 appears to the right of Programs. The programs and menus listed will depend on the programs installed on your computer, so your menu will probably look different from the illustration.

Chapter 1
The Fundamentals

4 On the Programs menu, point to and click **Microsoft Office PowerPoint 2003**.

Depending on how many programs are installed on your computer and how they are organized, it might be a little difficult to find the Microsoft PowerPoint program. Once you click the Microsoft PowerPoint program, your computer's hard drive will whir for a moment while it loads PowerPoint. The PowerPoint program screen appears, as shown in Figure 1-3.

That's it! You are ready to start creating presentations with Microsoft PowerPoint. In the next lesson you will learn what all those funny-looking things on your screen are.

QUICK REFERENCE

TO START MICROSOFT POWERPOINT:

1. CLICK THE WINDOWS **START** BUTTON.

2. SELECT **ALL PROGRAMS** → **MICROSOFT OFFICE POWERPOINT 2003**.

LESSON 1.2 What's New in PowerPoint 2003?

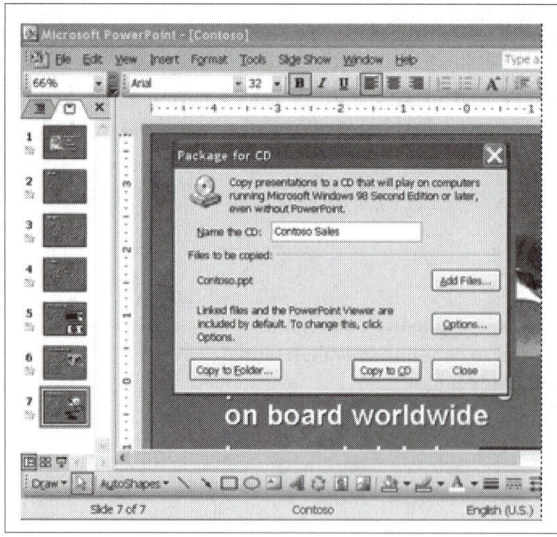

Figure 1-4. Saving your presentation on a CD.

If you're upgrading from a previous version of PowerPoint to PowerPoint 2003, you're in luck—in most respects, PowerPoint 2003 looks and works *almost* the same as previous versions. In fact, the upgrade from PowerPoint 2002 to PowerPoint 2003 probably saw the fewest changes from version to version. Table 1-1 discusses what's new in PowerPoint 2003 (and a review of some features from PowerPoint 2002).

Table 1-1. What's New

Feature	New In	Description
Getting Started task pane	2003	A more advanced Getting Started task pane puts Microsoft Office Online right at your fingertips in PowerPoint 2003. Having such on-demand accessibility to the Internet is like having your very own genie-in-a-bottle, there to aid your every whim. Have a question about a new feature? No problem! Simply enter your question, and voila! Instant access to Microsoft's Online Help database.
Package for CD feature	2003	Allows you to package your presentation to a CD that will automatically begin playing your Slide Show when inserted into the disk drive. The PowerPoint Viewer is included by default, which enables you to play your presentation on a computer that does not have PowerPoint installed.
Slide Show navigation tools	2003	A new Slide Show toolbar gives you easy access to navigation while delivering a presentation without distracting your audience. Notable improvements include a new highlighter tool, and improved ink and pen tools.
Research task pane	2003	Enables you to conduct searches on a topic without leaving your presentation. Choose from a variety of different resources, including online encyclopedias, an online dictionary, and an online translator.
Smart tags	2003	Context-sensitive smart tags are a set of buttons that provide speedy access to relevant information by alerting you to important actions—such as formatting options for pasted information and more.
Improved movie playback	2003	You don't have to keep your movies stuck in a little box on your slide: now you can view them in full screen mode.
Streamlined user interface	2002	Office 2003 has a new look-and-feel that improves the user's Office experience. This includes removing visually competing elements, visually prioritizing items on a page, increasing letter spacing and word spacing for better readability, and defining foreground and background color to bring the most important elements to the front.

Table 1-1. What's New (Continued)

Feature	New In	Description
Task panes	2002	The Task Pane appears on the right side of the screen and lets you quickly perform searches, open or start a new presentation, apply slide formatting, and add animation effects.
Thumbnails of slides in Normal View	2002	You can use the new thumbnail representations of each slide to quickly find the slide you want to work on, or drag a thumbnail to move a slide to a new position in your presentation.
Multiple design templates per presentation	2002	PowerPoint 2003 supports having more than one design template in your presentation. This is great when you want to combine several presentations into one file, but have each section maintain its distinct look.
Automatic layout for inserted objects	2002	As you work, PowerPoint adjusts the slide layout automatically to accommodate pictures, diagrams, charts, and other items you add. When you choose a new slide layout, PowerPoint can automatically rearrange the existing items on the slide to fit the new layout.
Animation effects	2002	PowerPoint has new animation effects, including entry and exit animations, more timing control, and motion paths—pre-drawn paths that items in an animation sequence can follow—so you can synchronize multiple text and object animations.
Animation schemes	2002	Animation schemes let you apply a predesigned set of animation and transition effects to your entire presentation at once.
Better organization charts and new diagram types	2002	Organization charts now use the drawing tools in PowerPoint, resulting in smaller file sizes and easier editing. Also, PowerPoint includes a new gallery of common conceptual diagrams. Choose from diagrams such as Pyramid for showing the building blocks of a relationship, Radial for showing items in relation to a core element, and more.
Document recovery	2002	Document Recovery gives you the option to automatically save your current document, spreadsheet, or presentation at the time an application stops responding, so you don't lose a moment's work. In the event of an error, Office 2003 keeps a backup of your work, giving you the chance to save and recover it so you don't lose valuable time or data.

LESSON 1.3 Understanding the PowerPoint Program Screen

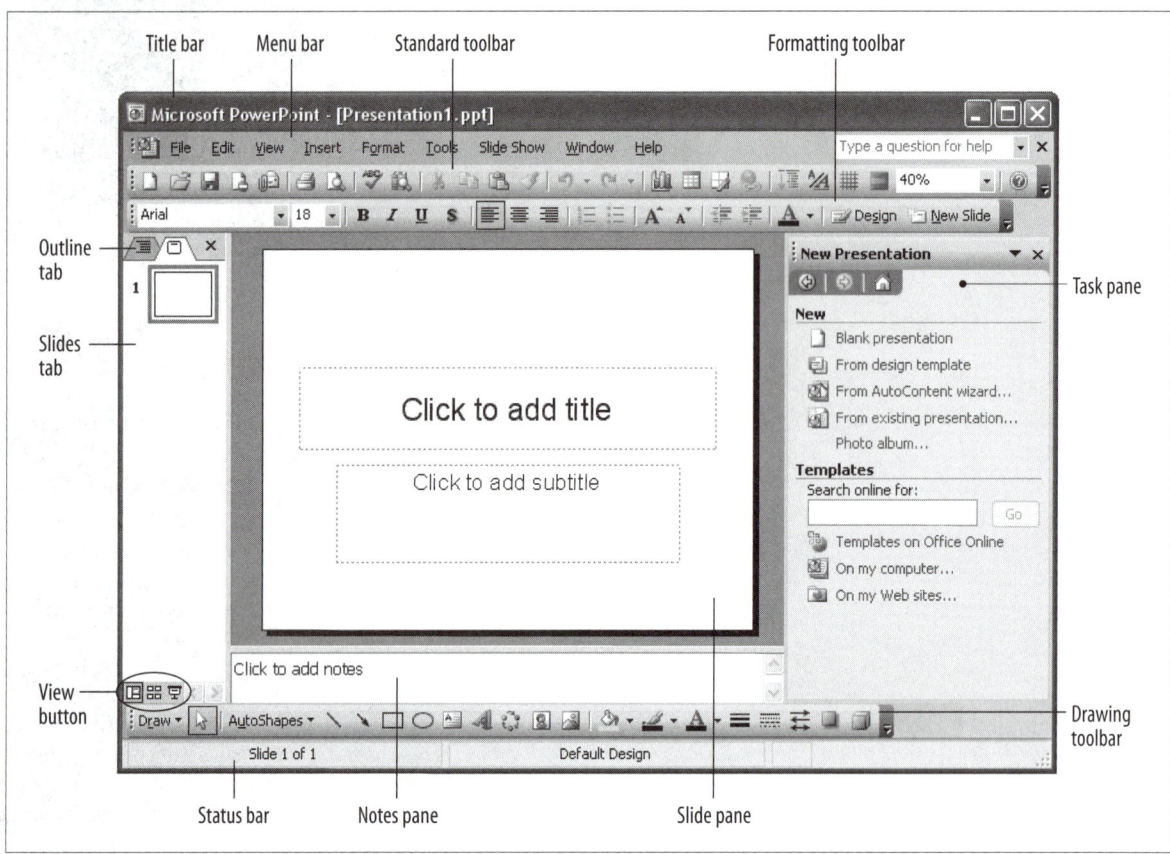

Figure 1-5. Elements of the PowerPoint program screen.

You might find the PowerPoint 2003 program screen a bit confusing and overwhelming the first time you see it. What are all of those buttons, icons, menus, and arrows for? This lesson will help you become familiar with the PowerPoint program screen. There are no step-by-step instructions for this lesson—all you have to do is look at Figure 1-5 then refer to Table 1-2 to see what everything you're looking at means. And most of all, relax! This lesson is only meant to help you get acquainted with the PowerPoint screen; you don't have to memorize anything.

NOTE *PowerPoint 97 users should pay careful attention to how the PowerPoint screen is broken up into three different panes: Outline, Slide, and Notes. Since monitors and resolution sizes have gotten larger in recent years, Microsoft decided to let you view more information about your presentations at once without having to switch between windows.*

Don't worry if you find some of these elements of the PowerPoint program screen confusing at first—they will make sense after you've actually used them, and you will get a chance to use them in the next lesson.

Table 1-2. The PowerPoint Program Screen

Element	What It's Used For
Outline tab	Focuses on the content of your presentation instead of its appearance. Use the Outline tab when you want to develop your presentation and add large amounts of text. You can also use Outline tab to navigate through a presentation by clicking the slide that you want to view.
Slides tab	The Slides tab displays thumbnail representations of each slide in a presentation. You can use Slides tab to navigate through a slide by clicking the slide that you want to view. You can also drag a thumbnail to move a slide to a new position in your presentation.
Title bar	Displays the name of the program you are currently using (Microsoft PowerPoint, of course) and the name of the presentation you are working on. The title bar appears at the top of all Windows programs.
Menu bar	Displays a list of menus that you use to give commands to PowerPoint. Clicking a menu name displays a list of commands—for example, clicking the Format menu name would display different formatting commands.
Standard toolbar	Toolbars are shortcuts—they contain buttons for the most commonly used commands (instead of wading through several menus). The standard toolbar contains buttons for the PowerPoint commands you will use the most, such as saving, opening, and printing presentations.
Formatting toolbar	Contains buttons for the most commonly used formatting commands, such as making text bold or italic.
Drawing toolbar	Contains buttons and menus that you can use to draw lines and shapes, or manipulate existing objects.
View buttons	Allows you to quickly switch between PowerPoint views, which change how your presentation is displayed on the screen.
Slide pane	Displays the slides one at a time, as they will appear when they are printed or displayed in a presentation.
Notes pane	Use Notes View to add notes to each slide that you can use during your presentation so you can remember what to say.
Status bar	Displays messages and feedback.
Task pane	The task pane lists commands that are relevant to whatever you're doing in PowerPoint. You can easily hide the task pane if you want to have more room to view a presentation: simply click the Close button in the upper-right corner of the task pane.

Lesson 1.3
Understanding the PowerPoint Program Screen

QUICK REFERENCE

TO OPEN A MENU:

- CLICK THE MENU NAME WITH THE MOUSE.

OR...

- PRESS **ALT** AND THEN THE UNDERLINED LETTER IN THE MENU.

TO DISPLAY A MENU'S HIDDEN COMMANDS:

- CLICK THE DOWNWARD-POINTING ARROW  AT THE BOTTOM OF THE MENU.

OR...

- OPEN THE MENU AND WAIT A FEW SECONDS.

TO CHANGE HOW MENUS WORK:

1. SELECT **VIEW** → **TOOLBARS** → **CUSTOMIZE** FROM THE MENU AND CLICK THE **OPTIONS TAB**.

2. CHECK OR CLEAR EITHER THE **ALWAYS SHOW FULL MENUS** AND/OR **SHOW FULL MENUS AFTER A SHORT DELAY** OPTIONS, THEN CLICK **CLOSE**.

Using Menus

LESSON 1.4

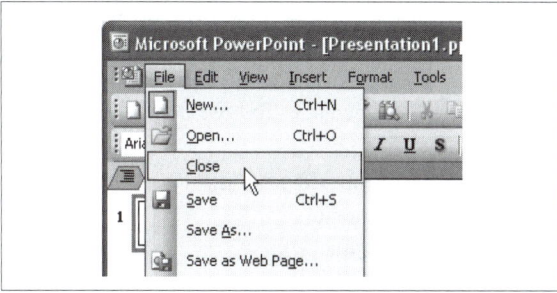

Figure 1-6. The File menu.

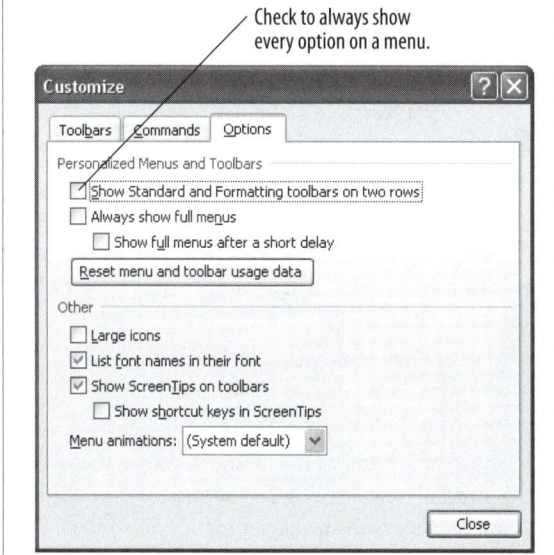

Figure 1-7. The Customize dialog box.

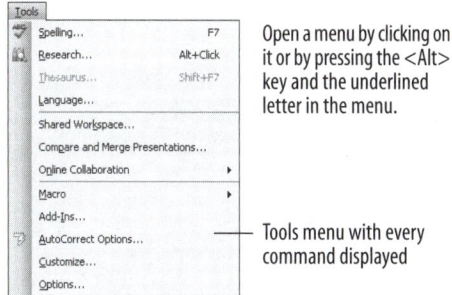

Tools menu with every command displayed

TIP *Open a menu by clicking on it or by pressing the Alt key and the underlined letter in the menu.*

This lesson explains one of the most common ways to give commands to PowerPoint—by using the menus. Menus for all Windows programs can be found at the top of a window, just beneath the program's title bar.

PowerPoint's new personalized menus have some unique characteristics not featured in other Windows programs and previous versions of PowerPoint. Microsoft Power-Point 2003 displays its menu commands on the screen in three different ways:

- By displaying every command possible, like most Windows programs, including earlier versions of Power-Point.
- By hiding the commands you don't use as frequently (the more advanced commands) from view.
- By displaying the hidden commands by clicking the downward-pointing arrows ⯆ at the bottom of the menu or after waiting a couple of seconds.

This lesson explains how to use PowerPoint 2003's new personalized menus.

1 Click the word **File** on the menu bar.

A menu drops down from the word File, as shown in Figure 1-6. The File menu contains a list of file-related commands, such as New, which creates a new file; Open, which opens or loads a saved file; Save, which saves the currently opened file; and Close, which closes the currently opened file. Move on to the next step to try selecting a command from the File menu.

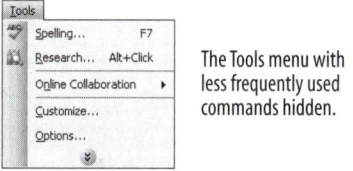

The Tools menu with less frequently used commands hidden.

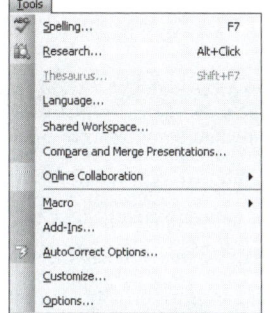

The Tools menu will display less frequently used commands displayed after clicking the downward-pointing arrow (⯆) at the bottom of the menu.

2 Click the word **Close** in the File menu.

The presentation window disappears—you have just closed the current presentation. Notice each of the words in the menu has an underlined letter somewhere in them. For example, the F in the File menu is

9

Lesson 1.4
Using Menus

underlined. Holding down the Alt key and pressing the underlined letter in a menu produces the same effect as clicking on it. For example, pressing the Alt key and then the F key would also open the File menu. Move on to the next step and try it for yourself.

3 Press the **Alt** key then press the **F** key.

The File menu appears. Once you open a menu, you can navigate through the different menus, using either the mouse or the Alt key and the letter that is underlined in the menu name.

4 Press the Right Arrow Key →.

The next menu to the right, the Edit menu, appears. If you open a menu and then change your mind, it is easy to close it without selecting any commands. Click anywhere *outside* the menu, or press the Esc key.

5 Click anywhere outside the menu to close the menu without issuing any commands.

NOTE *The procedure for using menus and the general order/layout of the menu is the same for most Windows programs. So once you master PowerPoint's menus, you can handle just about any Windows-based program!*

6 Click the word **Tools** in the menu.

The most common menu commands appear in the Tools menu. Some people feel intimidated by so many menu options, so the menus don't display the more advanced commands at first. To display a menu's advanced commands either click on the downward pointing arrows ⇩ at the bottom of the menu, or keep the menu open for a few seconds.

7 Click the downward-pointing arrows ⇩ at the bottom of the Tools menu.

The more advanced commands appear shaded on the Tools menu.

If you're accustomed to working with earlier versions of Microsoft Office, you may find that hiding the more advanced commands is disconcerting. If so, you can easily change how PowerPoint's menus work. Here's how:

8 Select **View** → **Toolbars** → **Customize** from the menu.

The Customize dialog box appears, as shown in Figure 1-7. This is where you can change how PowerPoint's menus work. There are two check boxes here that are important:

- **Always show full menus:** Check this box if you want to show all the commands on the menus, instead of hiding the advanced commands.
- **Show full menus after a short delay:** If checked, PowerPoint will wait a few seconds before displaying the more advanced commands on a menu.

9 Click **Close**.

Table 1-3. Menus found in Microsoft PowerPoint

File	Description
File	File-related commands to open, save, close, print, and create new files.
Edit	Commands to copy, cut, paste, find, and replace text in a presentation.
View	Commands to change how the presentation is displayed on the screen.
Insert	Lists items that you can insert into a presentation, such as graphics and more.
Format	Commands to format text, objects, and more.
Tools	You can change PowerPoint's options here.
Slide Show	Slide show related commands.
Window	Commands to display and arrange multiple windows (if you have more than one presentation open).
Help	Get help on using Microsoft PowerPoint.

Chapter 1
The Fundamentals

QUICK REFERENCE

TO OPEN A MENU:

- CLICK THE MENU NAME WITH THE MOUSE.

OR...

- PRESS **ALT** AND THEN THE UNDERLINED LETTER IN MENU.

TO DISPLAY A MENU'S HIDDEN COMMANDS:

- CLICK THE DOWNWARD-POINTING ARROWS  AT THE BOTTOM OF THE MENU.

OR...

- OPEN THE MENU AND WAIT A FEW SECONDS.

TO CHANGE HOW MENUS WORK:

1. SELECT **VIEW** → **TOOLBARS** → **CUSTOMIZE** FROM THE MENU.

2. CHECK OR CLEAR EITHER THE **ALWAYS SHOW FULL MENUS** AND/OR **SHOW FULL MENUS AFTER A SHORT DELAY** OPTIONS, THEN CLICK **CLOSE**.

LESSON 1.5 Using Toolbars and Creating a New Presentation

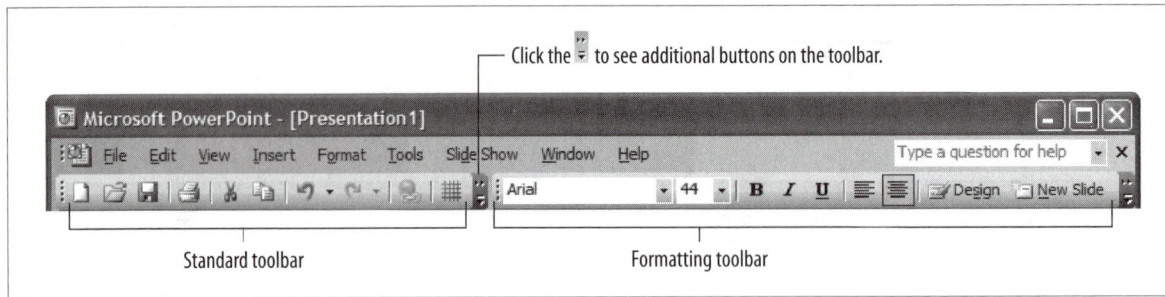

Figure 1-8. The Standard and Formatting toolbars squished together on the same bar.

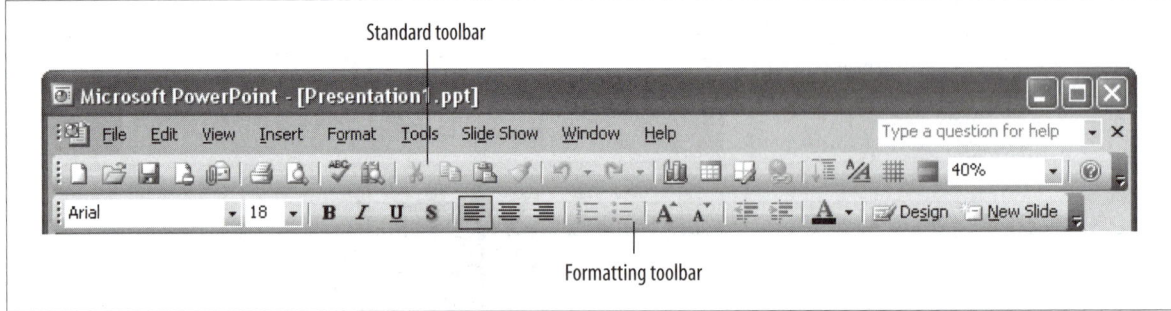

Figure 1-9. The Standard and Formatting toolbars stacked as separate toolbars.

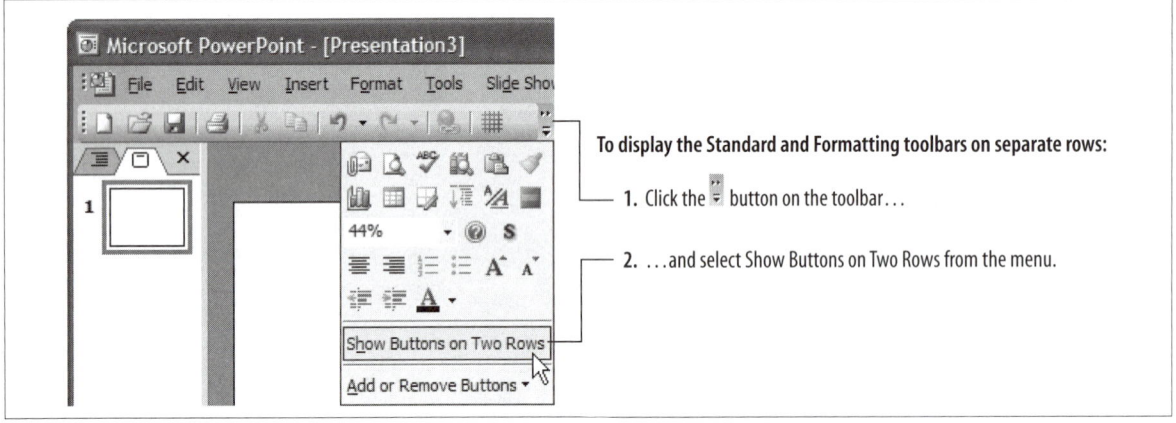

Figure 1-10. The "show more" drop-down menu.

New Presentation button

Other Ways to Create a New Presentation:

- Select **File** → **New** from the menu.

In this lesson, we move on to another common way to give commands in PowerPoint—using toolbars. Toolbars are shortcuts—they contain buttons for the most commonly used commands. Instead of wading through several menus to access a command, you can click a single button on a toolbar. Two toolbars appear when you start PowerPoint by default:

- **Standard toolbar:** Located either to the left or on the top of the screen, the Standard toolbar contains buttons for the commands you'll use most frequently, such as Save and Print.

12

Chapter 1
The Fundamentals

- **Formatting toolbar:** Located either to the right of or below the Standard toolbar, the Formatting toolbar contains buttons for quickly formatting fonts and paragraphs.

1 Position the mouse pointer over the New button on the Standard toolbar (but don't click the mouse yet!).

A ScreenTip appears over the button briefly identifying what the button is, in this case "New". If you don't know what a button on a toolbar does, simply move the pointer over it, wait a second, and a ScreenTip will appear over the button, telling you what it does.

ScreenTip

2 Click the New button on the Standard toolbar.

A new, blank presentation appears—not only have you learned how to use Microsoft PowerPoint's toolbars, but you've also learned how to create a new, blank presentation.

PowerPoint's toolbars also have "show more" arrows, just like menus do. When you click a button, it displays a drop-down menu or a list of the remaining buttons on the toolbar, as well as several toolbar-related options.

3 Click the button on the far right side of the Standard toolbar.

A list of the remaining buttons on the Standard toolbar appears, as shown in Figure 1-10. Just like personalized menus, PowerPoint remembers which toolbar buttons you use most often, and displays them in a more prominent position on the toolbar.

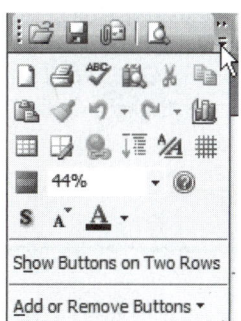

Click the button to see and/or add additional toolbar buttons.

4 Click anywhere outside the toolbar list to close the list without selecting any of its options.

Today, many computers have larger monitors, so Microsoft decided to save space on the screen by squishing both the Standard and Formatting toolbars together on the same bar, as shown in Figure 1-8. While squishing two toolbars together on the same bar gives you more space on the screen, it also makes the two toolbars look confusing—especially if you're used to working with a previous version of Microsoft Office. If you find both toolbars sharing the same bar confusing, you can "un-squish" the Standard and Formatting toolbars and stack them on top of each other, as illustrated in Figure 1-9. Here's how…

5 Click the button on either the Standard or Formatting toolbar.

A list of more buttons and options appear, as shown in Figure 1-10. To stack the Standard and Formatting toolbars on top of one another select the Show Buttons on Two Rows option.

6 Select Show Buttons on Two Rows from the list.

Microsoft PowerPoint displays the Standard and Formatting toolbars on two separate rows. You can display the Standard and Formatting toolbars on the same row using the same procedure.

7 Click the button on either the Standard or Formatting toolbar and select Show Buttons on One Row from the list.

PowerPoint once again displays the Standard and Formatting toolbars on the same row.

13

Lesson 1.5
Using Toolbars and Creating a New Presentation

Should you display the Standard and Formatting toolbars on the same row, or should you give each toolbar its own row? That's a question that depends on the size and resolution of your computer's display and your own personal preference. If you have a large 17-inch monitor, you might want to display both toolbars on the same row. On the other hand, if you have a smaller monitor or are constantly clicking the ⁝ buttons to access hidden toolbar buttons, you may want to consider displaying the Standard and Formatting toolbars on separate rows.

QUICK REFERENCE

TO USE A TOOLBAR BUTTON:

- CLICK THE BUTTON YOU WANT TO USE.

TO DISPLAY A TOOLBAR BUTTON'S DESCRIPTION:

- POSITION THE POINTER OVER THE TOOLBAR BUTTON AND WAIT A SECOND. A SCREENTIP WILL APPEAR ABOVE THE BUTTON.

TO CREATE A NEW PRESENTATION:

- CLICK THE 🗋 NEW BUTTON ON THE STANDARD TOOLBAR.

OR...

- SELECT FILE → NEW FROM THE MENU.

TO STACK THE STANDARD AND FORMATTING TOOLBARS IN TWO SEPARATE ROWS:

- CLICK THE ⁝ BUTTON ON EITHER TOOLBAR AND SELECT SHOW BUTTONS ON TWO ROWS FROM THE LIST.

Filling Out Dialog Boxes

LESSON 1.6

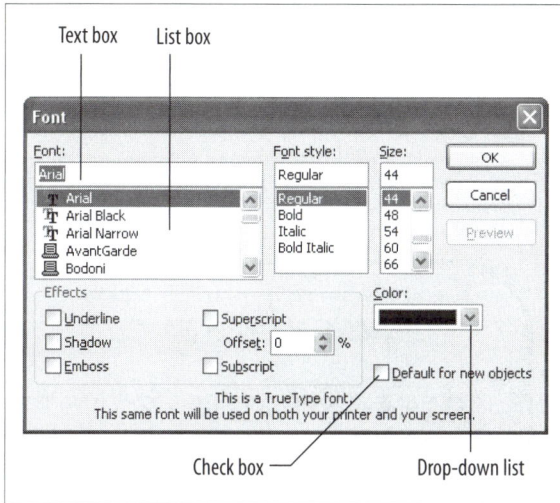

Figure 1-11. The Font dialog box.

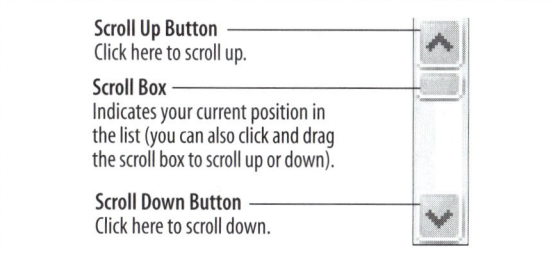

Figure 1-12. Using a Scroll Bar.

Some commands are more complicated than others are. Saving a file is a simple process—you only need to select File → Save from the menu or click the Save button on the Standard toolbar. Other commands are more complex—for example, suppose you want to change the top margin of the current slide to a half-inch. Whenever you want to do something relatively complicated, you must fill out a dialog box. Filling out a dialog box is usually very easy—if you've worked at all with Windows, you've undoubtedly filled out hundreds of dialog boxes. Dialog boxes usually contain several types of controls, including:

Text Box

- Text boxes
- List boxes
- Check boxes
- Drop-down menus (also called combo boxes)

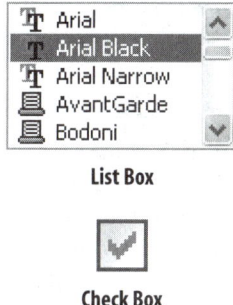

List Box

Check Box

It is important that you know the names of these controls because this book will refer to them in just about every lesson. This lesson gives you a tour of a dialog box and will explain each of these controls to you so that when you run across them, you will know what they are and how to use them.

1 Select **Format** from the menu.

The Format menu appears. Notice the items listed in the Format menu are followed by ellipses (…). The ellipses indicate that there is a dialog box attached to the menu item.

2 Select **Font** from the Format menu.

The Font dialog box appears, as shown in Figure 1-11. The Font dialog box is actually one of the more complex dialog boxes in Microsoft PowerPoint, and it contains several different types of components.

First, let's learn about text boxes. Text boxes are the most common component of a dialog box and are nothing more than simple fill-in-the-blank areas. To use a text box, first select the text box by clicking it, or by pressing the Tab key until the insertion point appears inside it, then simply type the text you want into the text box.

3 Make sure the Font text box is selected, and type **Arial**.

You've just filled out the text box—nothing to it. The next stop in our dialog box tour is the list box. There's a list box located directly below the Font text box you just typed in. A list box is a way of listing several (or many) options into a small box. Sometimes list boxes contain so many options that they can't all be displayed at once, and you must use the list boxes scroll bar, as shown in Figure 1-12, to move up or down the list.

15

Lesson 1.6
Filling Out Dialog Boxes

4 Click and hold the Font list box's Scroll Down button until Times New Roman appears in the list.

5 Click the Times New Roman option in the list.

Our next destination is the Drop-down menu. The drop-down menu is the cousin of the list box—it too displays a list of options. The only difference is that you must click the drop-down menu's downward pointing arrow to display the options.

6 Click the Color drop-down menu's down arrow.

A list of different color options appears below the color drop-down arrow.

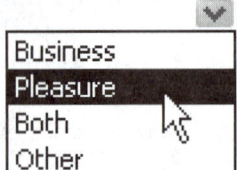

Drop-down menu

7 Select Automatic from the color drop-down menu.

Sometimes you need to select more than one item from a dialog box. For example, what if you want to add Shadow formatting *and* Underline formatting to the selected font? You use the Check box control when you're presented with multiple choices.

8 In the Effects section, click the Shadow check box and click the Underline check box.

The last destination on our dialog box tour is the Button. Buttons found in dialog boxes are used to execute or cancel commands. Two buttons are usually found in every dialog box:

- **OK:** Applies and saves any changes you have made and then closes the dialog box. Pressing the Enter key usually does the same thing as clicking the OK button.
- **Cancel:** Closes the dialog box without applying and saving any changes. Pressing the Esc key usually does the same thing as clicking the cancel button.

9 Click the Cancel button to cancel the changes you made and close the Font dialog box.

Button

QUICK REFERENCE

TO SELECT A DIALOG BOX OPTION:

- CLICK THE OPTION (SUCH AS FONT OR COLOR) WITH THE MOUSE.

OR...

- PRESS TAB TO MOVE TO THE NEXT OPTION IN THE DIALOG BOX OR SHIFT + TAB TO MOVE TO THE PREVIOUS OPTION UNTIL YOU ARRIVE AT THE DESIRED OPTION.

TO VIEW A DIALOG BOX TAB:

- CLICK THE TAB YOU WANT TO VIEW.

TO SAVE YOUR CHANGES AND CLOSE A DIALOG BOX:

- CLICK THE OK BUTTON OR PRESS ENTER.

TO CLOSE A DIALOG BOX WITHOUT SAVING YOUR CHANGES:

- CLICK THE CANCEL BUTTON OR PRESS ESC.

Keystroke and Right Mouse Button Shortcuts

LESSON 1.7

Figure 1-13. Hold down the Ctrl key and press another key to execute a keystroke shortcut.

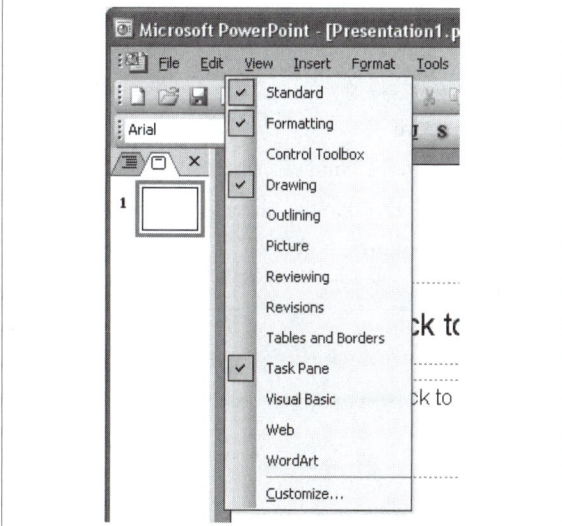

Figure 1-14. Opening a shortcut menu for toolbars.

You are probably starting to realize that there are several methods to do the same thing in PowerPoint. For example, to save a file you can use the menu (select File → Save) or the toolbar (click the Save button). This lesson introduces you to two more methods of executing commands: right mouse button shortcut menus and keystroke shortcuts.

You know that the left mouse button is the primary mouse button, used for clicking and double-clicking, and it's the mouse button you will use over 95 percent of the time when you work with PowerPoint. So what's the right mouse button for? Whenever you *right-click* something, it brings up a shortcut menu that lists everything you can do to the object. Whenever you're unsure or curious about what you can do with an object, click it with the right mouse button. A shortcut menu will appear with a list of commands related to the object or area you right-clicked.

Right mouse button shortcut menus are a great way to give commands to PowerPoint because you don't have to wade through several levels of unfamiliar menus when you want to do something.

1 Click the right mouse button while the cursor is anywhere inside the presentation window.

A shortcut menu will appear where you clicked the mouse. Notice one of the items on the shortcut menu is Copy. This is the same Copy command you can select from the menu (Edit → Copy). Using the right mouse button shortcut method is slightly faster and almost always easier to remember than using PowerPoint's menus.

2 Move the mouse button anywhere outside the menu and click the left mouse button to close the shortcut menu.

Remember that the options listed in the shortcut menu will be different, depending on what you've selected.

3 Position the pointer over either the Standard or Formatting toolbar and click the right mouse button.

A shortcut menu appears that lists all the toolbars you can view, as shown in Figure 1-14.

4 Move the mouse button anywhere outside the menu in the presentation window and click the left mouse button to close the shortcut menu.

On to keystroke shortcuts. Without a doubt, keystroke shortcuts are the fastest way to give commands to PowerPoint, even if they are a little hard to remember. They're great time-savers for issuing common commands that you do all the time. To issue a keystroke-shortcut, press and hold the Ctrl key, press the shortcut key, and release both buttons.

5 Press Ctrl + O (the Ctrl and O keys at the same time).

The Open dialog box appears.

6 Click Cancel to close the open dialog box.

NOTE *Although we won't discuss it in this lesson, PowerPoint's default keystroke shortcuts can be changed or remapped to execute other commands.*

17

Lesson 1.7
Keystroke and Right Mouse Button Shortcuts

7 Click the File menu, and then click the word Close in the File menu.

Table 1-4 lists the shortcut keystrokes you're likely to use the most in PowerPoint.

Table 1-4. Common Keystroke Shortcuts

Keystroke	Description
Ctrl + B	Toggles bold font formatting
Ctrl + I	Toggles italics font formatting
Ctrl + U	Toggles underline font formatting
Ctrl + Spacebar	Returns the font formatting to the default setting
Ctrl + O	Opens a presentation
Ctrl + S	Saves the current presentation
Ctrl + P	Prints the current presentation to the default printer
Ctrl + C	Copies the selected text or object to the Windows clipboard
Ctrl + X	Cuts the selected text or object from its current location to the Windows clipboard
Ctrl + V	Pastes any copied or cut text or object in the Windows clipboard to the current location
Ctrl + Home	Moves the insertion point to the beginning of the presentation
Ctrl + End	Moves the insertion point to the end of the presentation

QUICK REFERENCE

TO OPEN A CONTEXT-SENSITIVE SHORTCUT MENU:
- RIGHT-CLICK THE OBJECT.

TO USE A KEYSTROKE SHORTCUT:
- PRESS CTRL + THE LETTER OF THE KEYSTROKE SHORTCUT YOU WANT TO EXECUTE.

Opening a Presentation

LESSON 1.8

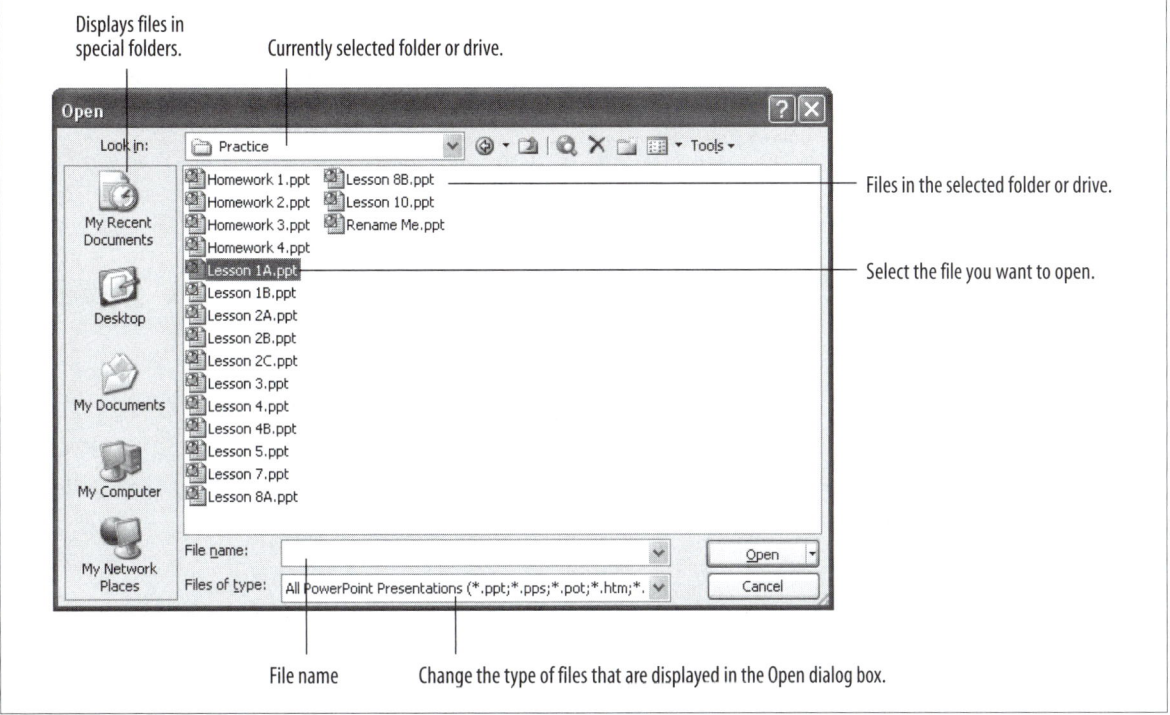

Figure 1-15. The Open dialog box.

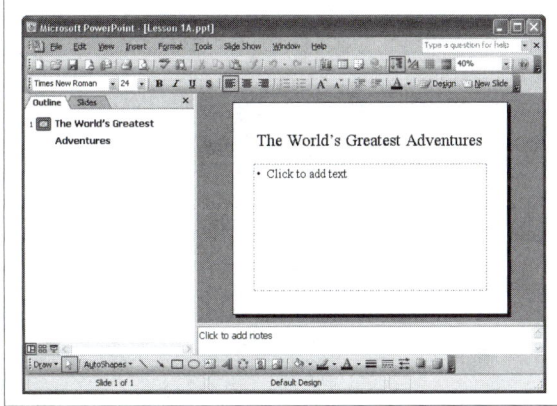

Figure 1-16. The Lesson 1A presentation appears in the PowerPoint program.

Open button

Other Ways to Open a File:
- Select **File → Open** from the menu.
- Press **<Ctrl> + <O>**

When you work with PowerPoint, you will sometimes need to create a new presentation from scratch (something we'll cover in an upcoming lesson), but, oftentimes, you'll want to work on an existing presentation that you or someone else previously saved. This lesson explains how to open, or retrieve, a saved presentation.

1 Click the Open button on the Standard toolbar.

The Open dialog appears, as shown in Figure 1-15. Next, you have to tell PowerPoint where the file you want to open is located.

2 Navigate to and open your practice folder.

Your computer stores information in files and folders, just like you store information in a filing cabinet. To open a file, you must first find and open the folder where it's saved. Normally, new files are saved in a folder named "My Documents" but, sometimes, you will want to save or open files in another folder.

The Open and Save dialog boxes both have their own toolbars that make it easy to browse through your computer's drives and folders. Two controls on this toolbar are particularly helpful:

19

Lesson 1.8
Opening a Presentation

- **Look In List:** Click to list the drives on your computer and the current folder, then select the drive and/or folder whose contents you want to display.
- **Up One Level button:** Click to move up one folder.

3 Click the presentation named **Lesson 1A** in the file list box and click **Open**.

PowerPoint opens the Lesson 1A presentation and displays it in the window, as shown in Figure 1-16.

Table 1-5. Special Folders in the Open and Save As Dialog Boxes

Folder	Description
History	Displays a list of files that you've recently worked on.
My Documents	Displays all the files in the My Documents folder—the default location where Microsoft Office programs save their files.
Desktop	Displays all the files and folders saved on your desktop.
My Computer	Gives access to, and information about, the disk drives and other hardware connected to your computer.
My Network Places	Lets you browse through the computers in your workgroup and the computers on the network.

Chapter 1
The Fundamentals

QUICK REFERENCE

TO OPEN A PRESENTATION:
- CLICK THE  OPEN BUTTON ON THE STANDARD TOOLBAR.

OR...
- SELECT FILE → OPEN FROM THE MENU.

OR...
- PRESS CTRL + O.

LESSON 1.9 — Saving and Closing a Presentation and Exiting PowerPoint

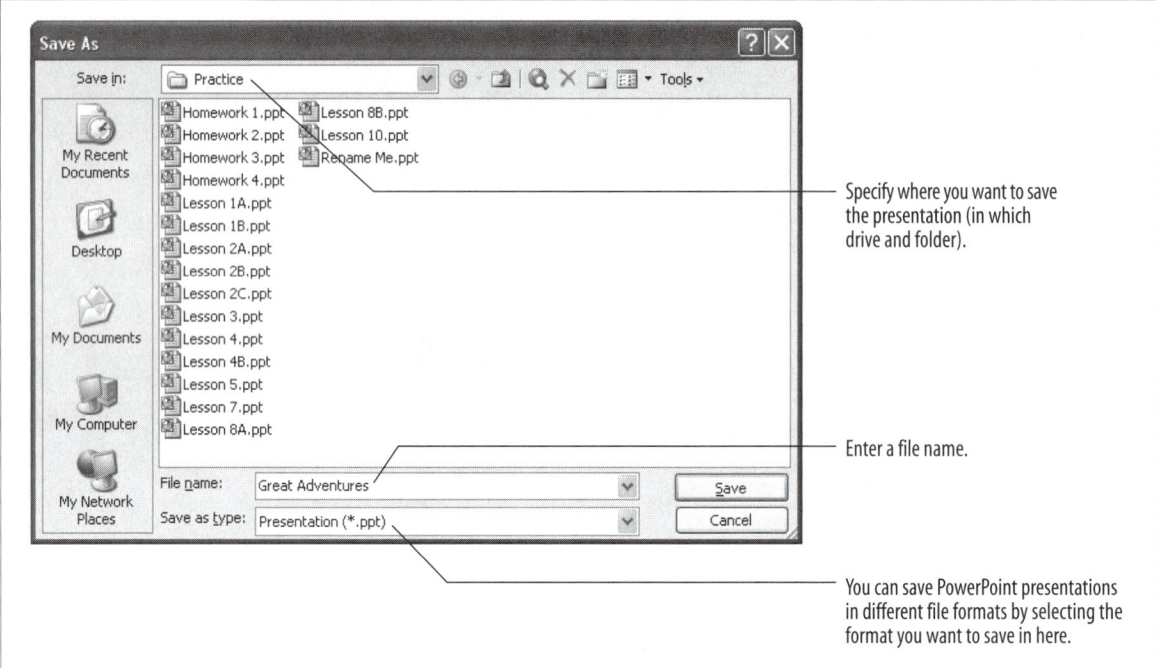

Figure 1-17. The Save As dialog box.

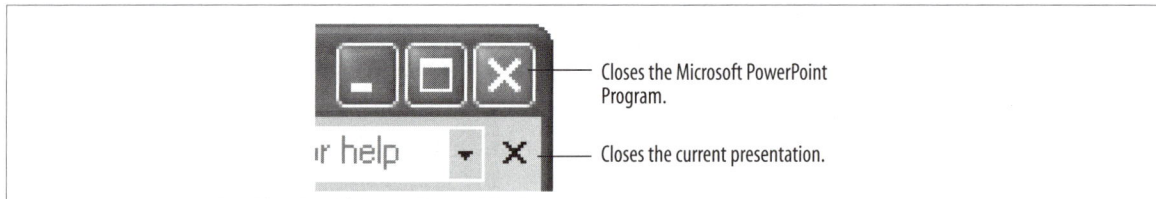

Figure 1-18. The Program and Presentation close buttons.

Save button

Other Ways to Save:

- Select **File** → **Save** from the menu.
- Press **<Ctrl>** + **<S>**

After you've created a presentation, you need to save it if you intend on ever using it again. *Saving* a presentation stores it in a file on your computer's hard disk—similar to putting a file away in a filing cabinet so you can later retrieve it. Once you have saved a presentation for the first time, it's a good idea to save it again from time to time as you work on it. You don't want to lose all your work if the power suddenly went out or if your computer crashed! In this lesson, you will learn how to save an existing presentation with a different name without changing the original presentation. It's often easier and more efficient to create a presentation by modifying one that already exists instead of having to retype a lot of information.

You want to use the information in the Lesson 1A presentation we opened in the previous lesson to create a new presentation. Since you don't want to modify the original presentation, Lesson 1A, save it as a new presentation named "Great Adventures."

1 Select **File** → **Save As** from the menu.

The Save As dialog box appears. Here is where you can save the presentation with a new, different name. If you only want to save any changes you've made to a presentation—instead of saving them in a new file—

click the Save button on the Standard toolbar, or select File → Save from the menu, or press Ctrl + S.

2 In the File name text box, type Great Adventures.

You also have to tell PowerPoint where to save your presentation.

The Save As dialog box has its own toolbar that makes it easy to browse through your computer's drives and folders. Two controls on this toolbar are particularly helpful:

- **Look In List:** Click to list the drives on your computer and the current folder, then select the drive and/or folder whose contents you want to display.
- **Up One Level button:** Click to move up one folder.

3 Click the Save button.

The presentation is saved with the new name, "Great Adventures," and the original presentation, Lesson 1A, closes. Now you can work on your new presentation, "Great Adventures," without changing the original presentation, Lesson 1A.

When you make changes to your presentation, you simply save your changes in the same file. Go ahead and try it.

4 Click the Click to add text box and type Eating three Dairy Queen Blizzards.

Now save your changes.

5 Click the Save button on the Standard toolbar.

PowerPoint saves the changes you've made to the presentation. Congratulations! You've just saved your first PowerPoint presentation.

Make sure you've saved any changes you've made before you close a presentation. Since we've already saved our work in the previous step, we can move on and close the current presentation.

6 Click the presentation Close button. (Make sure you click the presentation Close button, not the PowerPoint program Close button.)

Presentation Close button

Other Ways to Close a Presentation:

• Select **File** → **Close** from the menu.

You will see two close buttons on your screen, as shown in Figure 1-18. Make sure you click the lower close button because clicking the upper close button would close the PowerPoint program entirely. The current presentation closes but not the PowerPoint program. This is what you want to do if you're finished working on a presentation but still want to remain in the PowerPoint program—perhaps to open and work on another presentation. You have now finished this lesson so you want to exit or close the PowerPoint program.

7 Click the Close button on the Microsoft PowerPoint Title Bar.

This time click the Close button in the very far upper-right hand corner of the screen to close PowerPoint. The PowerPoint program window closes and you return back to the Windows desktop.

Program Close button

Other Ways to Exit PowerPoint:

• Select **File** → **Exit** from the menu.

Lesson 1.9
Saving and Closing a Presentation and Exiting PowerPoint

QUICK REFERENCE

TO SAVE A PRESENTATION:
- CLICK THE 💾 SAVE BUTTON ON THE STANDARD TOOLBAR.

OR...
- SELECT FILE → SAVE FROM THE MENU.

OR...
- PRESS CTRL + S.

TO SAVE A PRESENTATION IN A NEW FILE WITH A DIFFERENT NAME:
1. SELECT FILE → SAVE AS FROM THE MENU.
2. TYPE A NEW NAME FOR THE PRESENTATION AND CLICK SAVE.

TO CLOSE A PRESENTATION:
- CLICK THE PRESENTATION WINDOW ✕ CLOSE BUTTON OR SELECT FILE → CLOSE FROM THE MENU.

TO EXIT POWERPOINT:
- CLICK THE POWERPOINT PROGRAM'S CLOSE BUTTON OR SELECT FILE → EXIT FROM THE MENU.

LESSON 1.10

Creating a New Presentation with the AutoContent Wizard

Create a new presentation by selecting and using one of these options:

- **Blank Presentation:** Creates a new, blank presentation using the default settings for text and colors.
- **From Design Template:** Creates a new presentation based on one of the PowerPoint design templates.
- **From AutoContent Wizard:** Creates a new presentation by prompting you for information about content, purpose, style, handouts, and output. The new presentation contains sample text that you can replace with your own information.

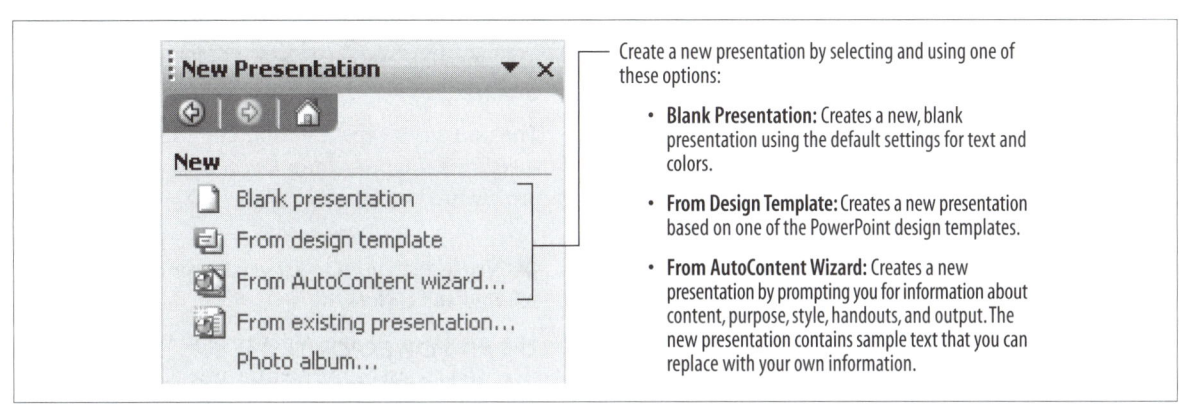

Figure 1-19. The PowerPoint dialog box.

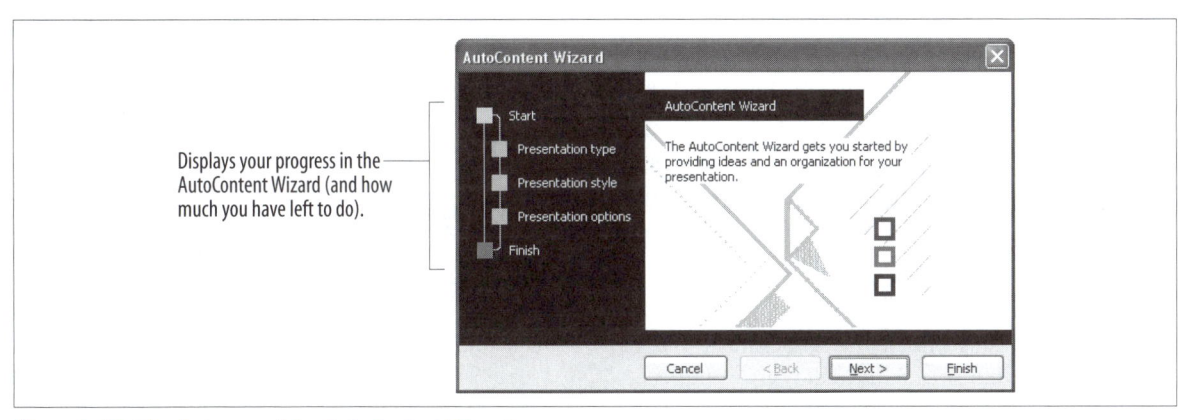

Displays your progress in the AutoContent Wizard (and how much you have left to do).

Figure 1-20. The first page of the AutoContent Wizard.

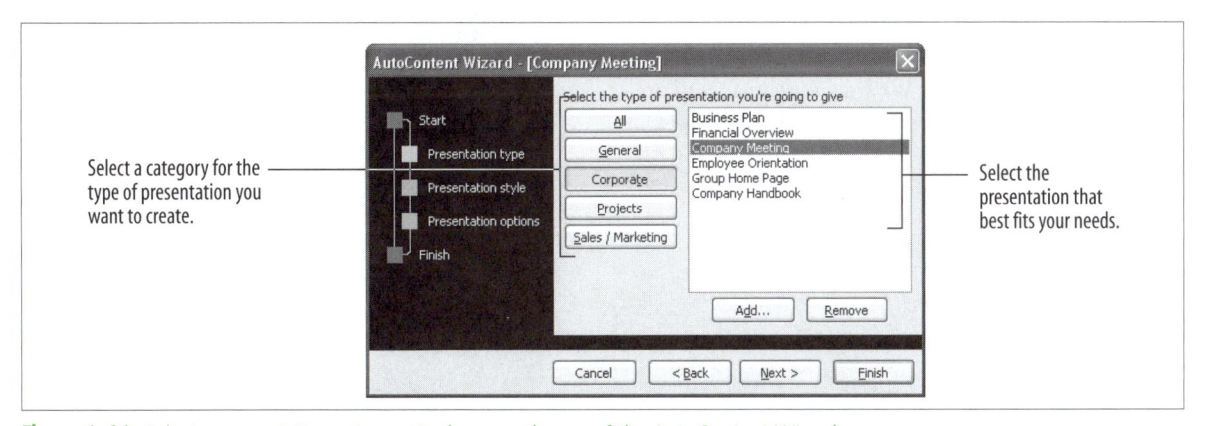

Select a category for the type of presentation you want to create.

Select the presentation that best fits your needs.

Figure 1-21. Select a presentation category in the second page of the AutoContent Wizard.

If you are new to PowerPoint, the easiest way to create a presentation is to use the AutoContent wizard. The AutoContent wizard helps you create a new presentation by asking you about the content, purpose, style, and output of your presentation and makes suggestions about the presentation's content and design. The new presentation contains sample text that you can replace with your own.

1 Start Microsoft PowerPoint and select **Create a new presentation** in the Getting Started task pane.

25

Lesson 1.10
Creating a New Presentation with the AutoContent Wizard

The PowerPoint program starts with a new, blank presentation.

There are actually several different ways that you can create a new presentation. You can create a new presentation by using:

- A Blank Presentation
- A Design Template
- The AutoContent Wizard

Figure 1-19 describes each of these methods in a little more detail. If you're new to PowerPoint, the simplest way to create a new presentation is with the AutoContent Wizard.

2 Select **From AutoContent wizard** in the task pane under New.

The first dialog box of AutoContent Wizard appears, as shown in Figure 1-20. This dialog box walks you through the steps of creating a presentation. The flow chart in the left side of the dialog box shows where you are in the AutoContent Wizard process.

3 Click **Next**.

The second dialog box of the AutoContent Wizard presents you with several different types of presentations to choose from, as shown in Figure 1-21.

4 Click the different category buttons to see which types of presentations are available.

Wow! The AutoContent Wizard gives you a lot of presentation types to choose from, doesn't it? Now that you're a little more familiar with the presentation categories and types that are available in the AutoContent Wizard, let's select one.

5 Click the **Corporate** button, make sure the **Company meeting** presentation in the list is selected, and click **Next**.

The next step of the AutoContent Wizard asks you to specify what type of output you want to use for your presentation.

6 Verify that the **On-screen Presentation** option is selected and click **Next**.

The fifth step of the AutoContent Wizard appears. Here you are asked to enter the title of your presentation and any additional information.

7 Type the following information in the specified fields. Press **Tab** after each entry.

Presentation title	Our Bold Plan For Tomorrow
Footer	North Shore Travel, Inc.

8 Click **Finish**.

You have completed the AutoContent Wizard. PowerPoint creates a new presentation based on your choices, which you can now use as a blueprint to create your own presentation. The new presentation contains sample text that you can replace with your own information.

9 Close the new presentation without saving your changes.

Chapter 1
The Fundamentals

QUICK REFERENCE

TO CREATE A NEW PRESENTATION WITH THE AUTOCONTENT WIZARD:

1. START POWERPOINT AND SELECT FROM AUTOCONTENT WIZARD IN THE TASK PANE.

   OR...

   IF YOU'RE ALREADY IN POWERPOINT, SELECT FILE → NEW FROM THE MENU AND SELECT FROM AUTOCONTENT WIZARD IN THE TASK PANE.

2. CLICK NEXT AND SELECT THE CATEGORY BUTTON THAT BEST FITS THE PRESENTATION YOU WANT TO CREATE.

3. SELECT A PRESENTATION FROM THE PRESENTATION LIST ON THE RIGHT SIDE OF THE DIALOG BOX AND CLICK NEXT.

4. ENTER THE INFORMATION THAT THE PRESENTATION WIZARD PROMPTS YOU FOR, AND FOLLOW ANY ON-SCREEN INSTRUCTIONS.

5. CLICK FINISH WHEN YOU'RE DONE.

6. REPLACE THE PRESENTATION'S SAMPLE TEXT WITH YOUR OWN TEXT.

LESSON 1.11
Creating a Blank Presentation and a Presentation from a Template

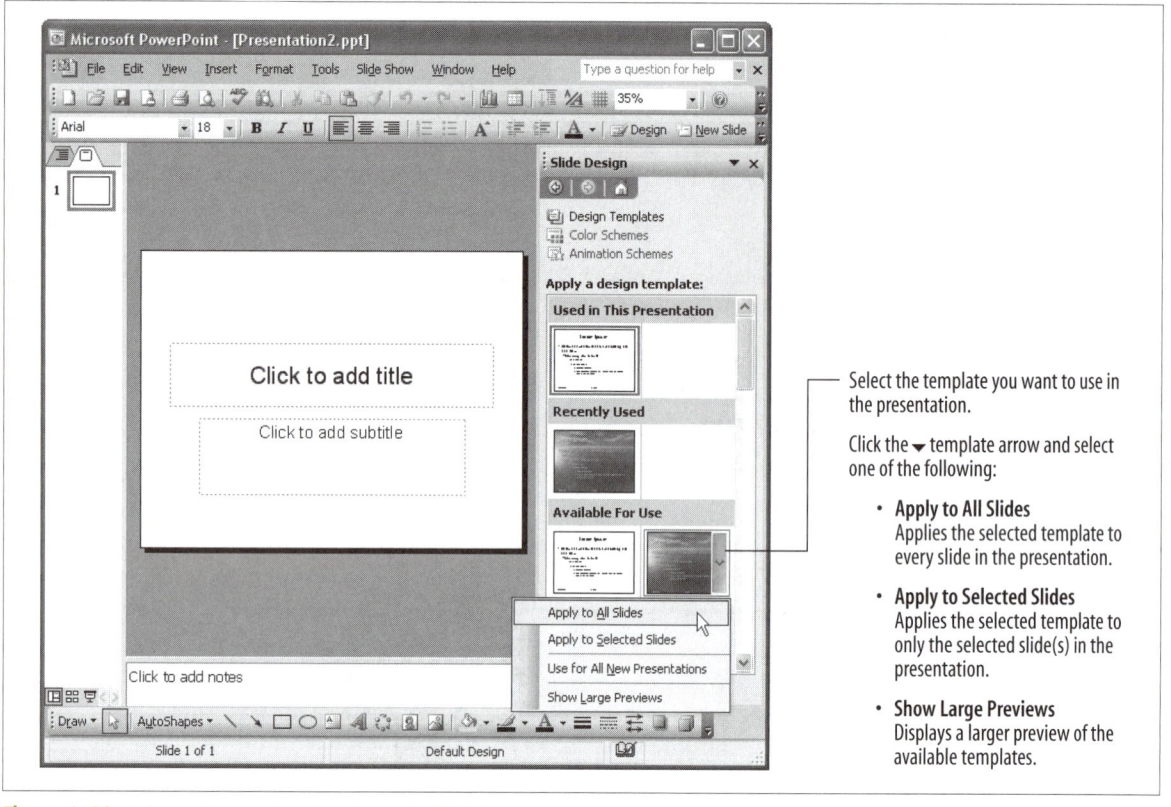

Figure 1-22. Select a Design Template from the Slide Design task pane.

In the previous lesson you learned how to create a PowerPoint presentation using the AutoContent Wizard—and it's a great way to create a presentation if you're new to PowerPoint. Once you've become more familiar with PowerPoint, however, walking through all of the AutoContent Wizard's steps each time you want to create a new presentation may be unnecessary. This lesson explains the two other methods of creating a presentation: creating a blank presentation and creating a presentation from a template.

First off, let's take a look at how to create a new, blank presentation from scratch:

1 Click the New button on the Standard toolbar.

PowerPoint creates a new, blank presentation and inserts a blank title slide to your presentation. Now all you have to do is add some text to the title slide in the provided text placeholders. We'll cover adding text to slides in more depth in another lesson—for now just give your new presentation a title.

New button

Other Ways to Create a new Presentation:
- Select **File → New** from the menu.

2 Click the Click to add title placeholder and type How we managed to misplace 15 million dollars.

Click to add title placeholder

Since we don't need to use this presentation, we can close it without saving our changes.

3 Click the presentation's Close button to close the presentation. Click No to the save changes dialog box.

You can also create a new presentation using one of the professionally designed templates that come with PowerPoint. A template already includes a format and

Chapter 1
The Fundamentals

color scheme—all you have to do is add your own text. Here's how to create a new presentation from a template:

4 Select **File → New** from the menu and click **From Design Template** in the task pane.

The New Presentation task pane appears, as shown in Figure 1-22. Now all you have to do is select the template you want to use to create your new presentation. You can see the name of any template by simply pointing the mouse at a template for a few seconds.

Point the mouse at a template for a few seconds to see its name.

5 Move the mouse pointer over the available templates until you find the **Beam template** (you may have to scroll down the task pane before you find it).

The template previews in the task pane are quite small and difficult to see. You can switch a larger preview of the available templates to get a better look at them. Here's how:

6 Move the pointer over the **Beam template** in the task pane and click the **▼ arrow**, as shown in Figure 1-22. Select **Show Large Previews** from the menu.

PowerPoint displays a larger preview of the available templates in the task pane. Let's turn the Show Large Previews option off for now.

7 Move the pointer over the **Beam template** in the task pane, click the **▼ arrow** and select **Show Large Previews** from the menu.

Okay, let's apply the Beam template to the presentation.

8 Double-click the **Beam template**.

PowerPoint applies the Beam template to the new presentation. Now let's close this presentation without saving any changes.

9 Click the presentation's **Close button** to close the new presentation. Click the **No button** in the Microsoft Office PowerPoint dialog box.

We don't need to display the task pane anymore so...

10 Click the task pane's **Close button**.

Give yourself a pat on the back—in just two short lessons you've learned how to create a new presentation in three different ways—from scratch, using the AutoContent Wizard, and using a template.

QUICK REFERENCE

TO CREATE A BLANK PRESENTATION:

- CLICK THE NEW BUTTON ON THE STANDARD TOOLBAR.

OR...

1. SELECT **FILE → NEW** FROM THE MENU.
2. SELECT **BLANK PRESENTATION** AND CLICK **OK**.

TO CREATE A PRESENTATION FROM A TEMPLATE:

1. SELECT **FILE → NEW** FROM THE MENU.
2. CLICK **FROM DESIGN TEMPLATE** IN THE TASK PANE.
3. DOUBLE-CLICK THE TEMPLATE YOU WANT TO USE (YOU MIGHT HAVE TO SELECT IT FROM ONE OF THE TABBED CATEGORIES).

TO DISPLAY LARGE TEMPLATE PREVIEWS:

- MOVE THE POINTER OVER ANY TEMPLATE IN THE TASK PANE, CLICK THE **▼ ARROW**, AND SELECT **SHOW LARGE PREVIEWS** FROM THE MENU.

LESSON 1.12 Moving Around in Your Presentations

Click the slide you want to view on either the Outline tab or Slides tab.

Scroll Up Button — Click to scroll up.

Scroll Box — Indicates your current position in the presentation (you can also click and drag the scroll box to scroll up or down).

Scroll Down Button — Click here to scroll down.

Previous Slide — Move up to the previous slide.

Next Slide — Move down to the next slide.

The Status bar displays your current position in the presentation.

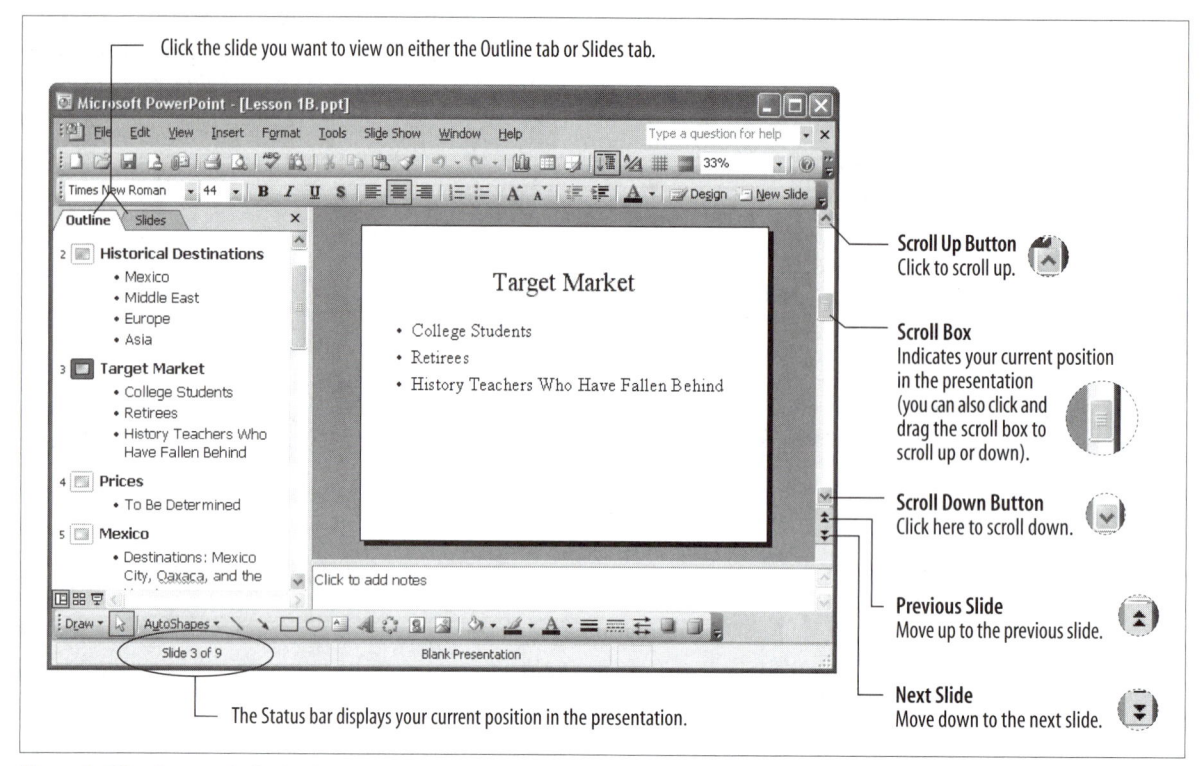

Figure 1-23. Along with the keyboard, the horizontal scroll bar is one of the main ways to move around in your presentations.

This lesson explains how to move from slide to slide in your presentation. Getting around in PowerPoint is very easy, so this lesson should be a breeze for you.

One way to get around in a presentation is by using PowerPoint's scroll bars. The vertical scroll bar is located along the right side of the window and is used to move up and down in a presentation. The horizontal scroll bar is located along the bottom of the window and is used to move from left to right when a presentation doesn't fit entirely on the screen—most likely you will rarely, if ever, have to use the horizontal scroll bar.

The procedures for getting around in a PowerPoint presentation can differ slightly, so this lesson will show you how to get around in a presentation no matter which view you're using.

Scroll down arrow

1 Open the **Lesson 1B** presentation.

One way to get around a presentation is by using the scroll bar to move up or down.

2 Click the **Scroll Down button** on the Slide pane scroll bar (the one to the far right of the screen).

PowerPoint moves to the next slide when you click the slide pane's scroll bar.

3 Click the **Next Slide button** on the Slide pane scroll bar.

Next Slide button

Other Ways to Move to the Next Slide:
- Press **<Page Down>** key.

You jump to the next slide in the presentation.

Chapter 1
The Fundamentals

PowerPoint's scroll bars let you see more of a slide's content and are no different than the scroll bars in just about every other Windows program. Scrolling works a bit differently in the Outline pane, however.

4 Click the Scroll Down button on the Outline pane's scroll bar (the scroll bar located to the right of the Outline pane).

Clicking the Outline pane's Scroll Down button causes the outline to scroll down one line at a time.

Slide 3 of 7 — The Status Bar (located at the very bottom of the screen) displays the current slide and how many slides are in your presentation.

5 Click and hold the Scroll Down button on the Outline pane's scroll bar.

This causes the pane to move downward more rapidly.

You can also use the keyboard to get around in a presentation. It's easier to demonstrate this in Normal View, so let's return to that.

6 Press the Page Down key.

Move to the next slide.

7 Press Ctrl + End.

That's one of the keystroke shortcuts we talked about earlier. Press and hold down the Ctrl key, press the End key, and then release both keys. When you do, PowerPoint jumps to the very end of the presentation.

Table 1-6 lists the most common keyboard shortcuts for quickly navigating through a presentation.

Table 1-6. Keyboard Shortcuts for Moving Around in a Presentation

Press	To Move
Home	Start of line (used when editing text)
End	End of line (used when editing text)
Page Up	Move up to the previous slide
Page Down	Move down to the next slide
Ctrl + Home	Go to the beginning of the presentation
Ctrl + End	Go to the end of the presentation

Lesson 1.12
Moving Around in Your Presentations

QUICK REFERENCE

TO MOVE UP:
- Click the SCROLL UP BUTTON in the scroll bar.
- Press PAGE UP.
- Click the PREVIOUS SLIDE BUTTON.

TO MOVE DOWN:
- Click the SCROLL DOWN BUTTON in the scroll bar.
- Press PAGE DOWN.
- Click the NEXT SLIDE BUTTON.

TO MOVE TO THE BEGINNING OF A PRESENTATION:
- Click and drag the SCROLL BOX to the top of the scroll bar.
- Press CTRL + HOME.

TO MOVE TO THE END OF A PRESENTATION:
- Click and drag the SCROLL BOX to the bottom of the scroll bar.
- Press CTRL + END.

Viewing Your Presentation

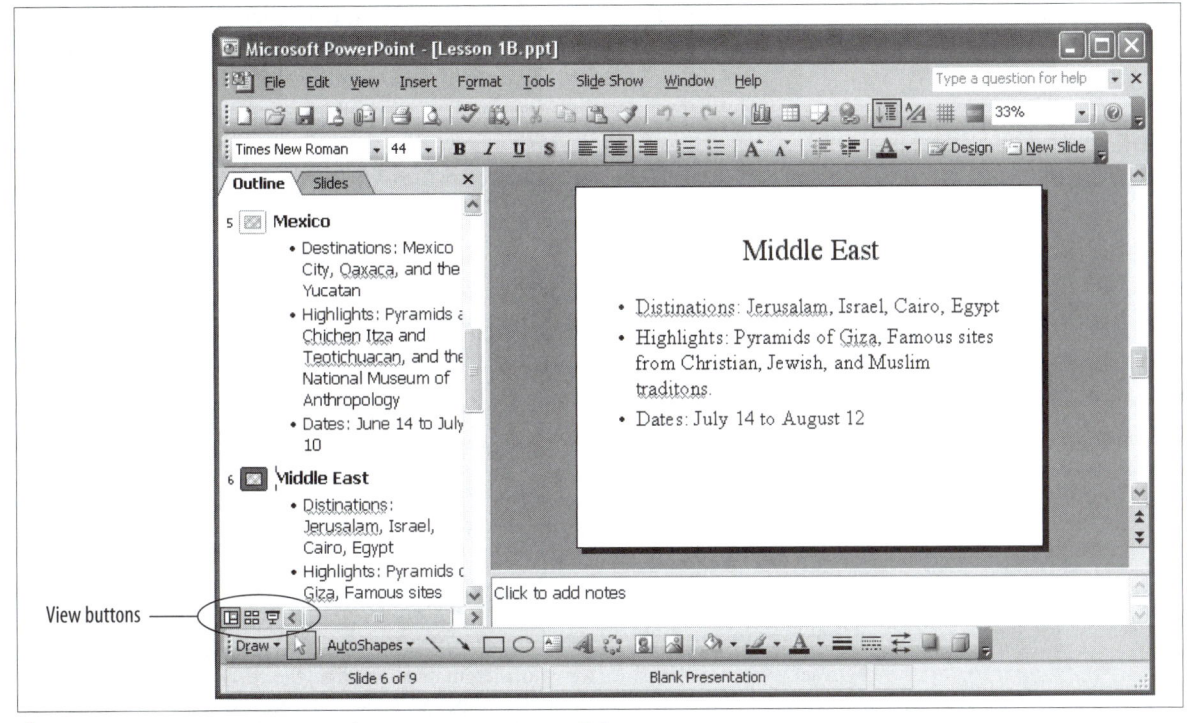

LESSON 1.13

Figure 1-24. PowerPoint displaying the presentation in Normal View.

Because there are several phases of developing a presentation, PowerPoint provides several different views: Normal, Slide Sorter, and Slide Show. Each view displays your presentation in a different way and allows you to work with your presentation differently. In this lesson you'll be introduced to each of these three views and learn how to quickly switch between them.

You'll also pick up another viewing trick in this lesson: how to zoom in and out of a presentation.

If you are continuing from the previous lesson, you can skip the first step of this exercise; otherwise, you will need to open the Lesson 1B file.

1 If necessary, open the presentation named **Lesson 1B** in your Practice folder.

Here's how to switch views in PowerPoint.

2 Click the **Normal View button**, as shown in Figure 1-24.

PowerPoint displays the presentation in Outline View.

Normal View button

3 Refer to Table 1-7, switch between each of the PowerPoint Views, and read about their descriptions.

Don't worry if you find the purpose of some of these views a little confusing right now—they will make more sense to you later on when you actually get a chance to use them. Let's move on to how to zoom in and out of a presentation. First though, you need to make sure you're in Normal View.

4 Switch to Normal View by clicking the **Normal View button**.

View buttons

Other Ways to Switch Views:

- Select **View** from the menu. Then select the View you want to use.

Lesson 1.13
Viewing Your Presentation

Normal View is the best place to see how zooming works. The button is located to the left of the Slide Sorter View button.

5 Click the Zoom list arrow.

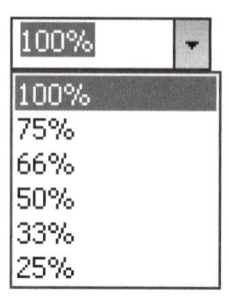

Zoom List arrow

A list of various zoom or magnification levels appears below the zoom list arrow at the far right of the Standard toolbar. Normally, you'll want to use a zoom factor so that each slide is displayed in its entirety. Sometimes, however, the text or object may be too small to see and you will need to change the zoom factor.

6 Select 50% from the Zoom list.

PowerPoint displays the slide at 50 percent. Now let's switch back so that the entire slide appears on the screen.

7 Click the Zoom list arrow and select 100%.

PowerPoint changes the zoom to 100 percent.

Table 1-7. PowerPoint Views

View	Description
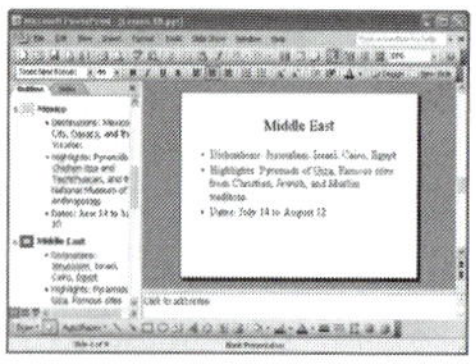  Normal View	**Normal View** includes panes for your presentation's outline, the current slide, and any notes for that slide. You will spend more time in Normal View than in any other view.
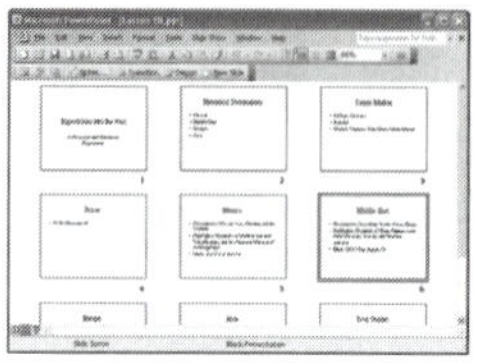  Slide Sorter View	**Slide Sorter View** displays all the slides in your presentation as *thumbnails* (itty-bitty pictures). Use Slide Sorter View when you want to rearrange the slides in your presentation and add transition effects between them.
   Slide Show View	**Slide Show View** displays your presentation as an electronic slide show. Use Slide Show View when you want to deliver your presentation.

Chapter 1
The Fundamentals

Table 1-7. PowerPoint Views (Continued)

View	Description
 Notes Page View	**Notes Page View** displays a small version of the slide and all the notes that go along with it. Use this view to add charts, pictures, tables, or other illustrations to a slide's notes. (This must be accessed through the View menu.)

QUICK REFERENCE

TO SWITCH BETWEEN VIEWS:

- CLICK THE VIEW BUTTON ON THE HORIZONTAL SCROLL BAR FOR THE VIEW YOU WANT.

OR...

- SELECT VIEW FROM THE MENU BAR AND SELECT THE VIEW YOU WANT (REQUIRED FOR NOTES PAGE VIEW).

TO CHANGE THE ZOOM LEVEL OF A PRESENTATION:

- SELECT THE ZOOM LEVEL FROM THE ZOOM LIST ARROW ON THE STANDARD TOOLBAR.

OR...

- SELECT VIEW → ZOOM FROM THE MENU, SELECT THE ZOOM LEVEL YOU WANT, AND CLICK OK.

35

LESSON 1.14 Printing Your Presentation

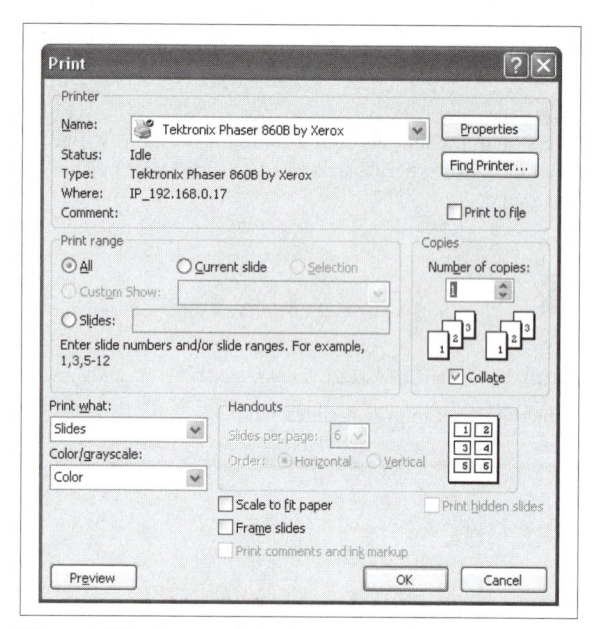

Figure 1-25. The Print dialog box.

After you finish your presentation, you're probably going to want to print it. This lesson will show you how to send your presentation to the printer. Printing is another very, very easy task.

Before you print a presentation, it is usually a good idea to preview it on screen before sending it to the printer—just in case you find something that needs to be changed.

NOTE *If you've worked with other Microsoft Office programs, such as Word or Excel, you might be wondering: "Hey! Where's my Print Preview command?!" PowerPoint doesn't have a Print Preview command because Normal View is already an exact representation of your presentation.*

1 Switch to Normal View (if you're not already there).

Normal View displays how your presentation will appear when printed.

2 Select File → Print from the menu.

The Print dialog box appears, as shown in Figure 1-25. The print dialog box contains various print options such as how many copies you wish to make, which printer you wish to use, and which slides you wish to print. See Table 1-8 for a description of the available print options.

NOTE *If you don't want to specify any printing options, you can print your presentation a lot faster by simply clicking the Print button on the Standard toolbar, or by pressing Ctrl + P.*

3 In the Number of copies box, type 2.

This will print two copies of your presentation. It's up to you if you actually want to print out your presentation.

4 If you actually want to print your presentation, click OK; otherwise, click Cancel to close the Print dialog box without printing anything.

5 Close the presentation without saving any of your changes.

Table 1-8 explains some of the other print options you can use when printing a presentation—how to print a specific page or a range of pages, for example.

Table 1-8. Print Dialog Box Options

Print Option	Description
Name	Used to select which printer to send your presentation to when it prints (if you are connected to more than one printer). The currently selected printer is displayed.
Properties	Displays a dialog box with options available for your specific printer, such as what paper size you're using, if your presentation should be printed in color or black and white, etc.
Print to file	Prints the presentation to a file instead of sending it to the printer.

Table 1-8. Print Dialog Box Options (Continued)

Print Option	Description
Page range	Allows you to specify which pages you want printed. There are several options here: **All:** Prints the entire presentation. **Current slide:** Prints only the page of the slide you're currently on. **Selection:** Prints a custom slide show (a presentation within a presentation) that you click in the Custom Show list. **Slides:** Prints only the slides you specify. Select a range of slides with a hyphen (like 2-5) and separate single pages with a comma (like 3,7).
Number of copies	Specify the number of copies you want to print.
Print what	Select the component of your presentation that you want to print—slides, handouts, notes pages, or the presentation's outline. Several check boxes appear in this section. Here's what each of them does: **Black and white:** Optimizes the look of color slides for printing on a black and white printer. **Pure black and white:** Prints the entire presentation in only black and white. Changes all shades of gray to either black or white. **Scale to fit paper:** Reduces or enlarges slide images so that they fill the printed page. This only affects how the presentation is printed; it doesn't change the dimension of slides in your presentation. **Frame slides:** Adds a thin frame around the border of printed slides, handouts, and notes pages.
Options	Lets you specify other printing options, such as printing a presentation in reverse order (from the last page to the first).

QUICK REFERENCE

TO PRINT A PRESENTATION:

- CLICK THE PRINT BUTTON ON THE STANDARD TOOLBAR.

OR...

- SELECT FILE → PRINT FROM THE MENU.

OR...

- PRESS CTRL + P.

FOR ADVANCED PRINTING OPTIONS:

1. SELECT FILE → PRINT FROM THE MENU.
2. REFER TO TABLE 1-8 FOR INFORMATION ON VARIOUS PRINTING OPTIONS.

LESSON 1.15 Getting Help

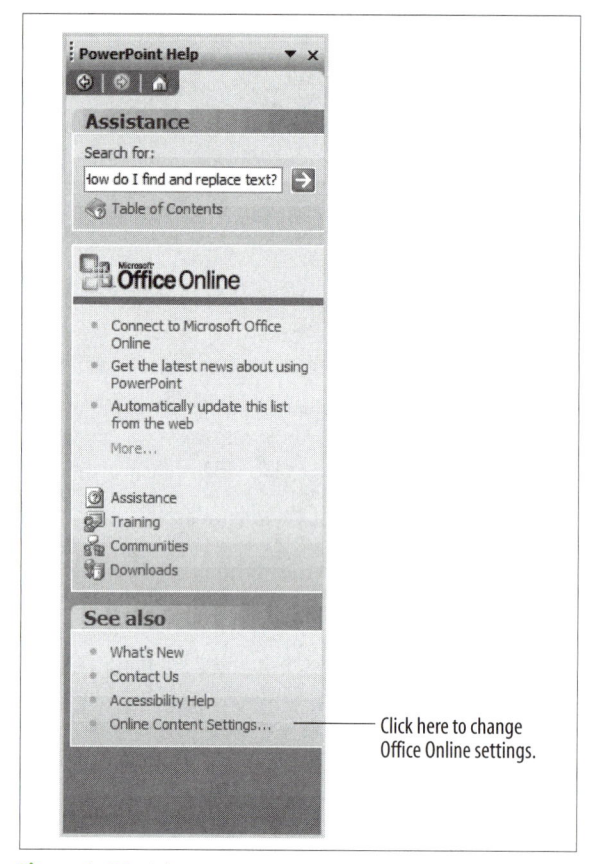

Figure 1-26. Asking a question in PowerPoint Help.

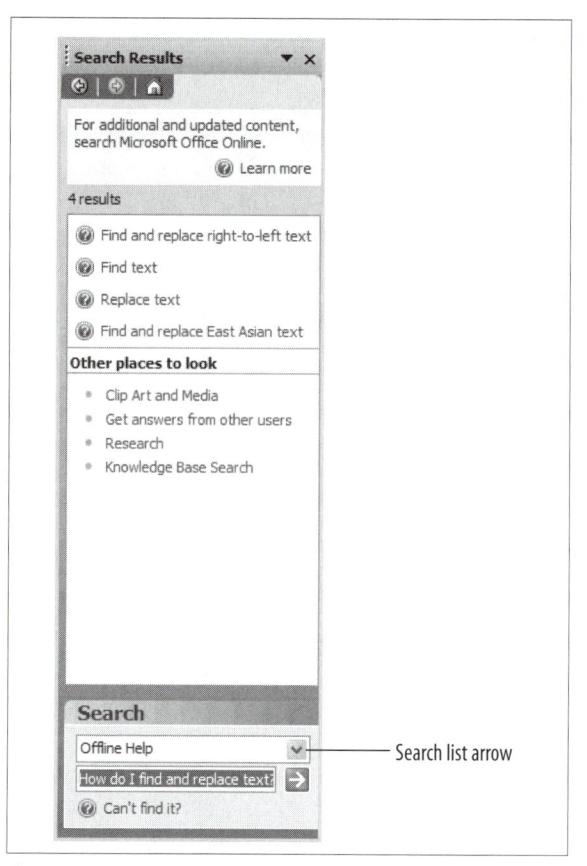

Figure 1-27. Offline Help Search results.

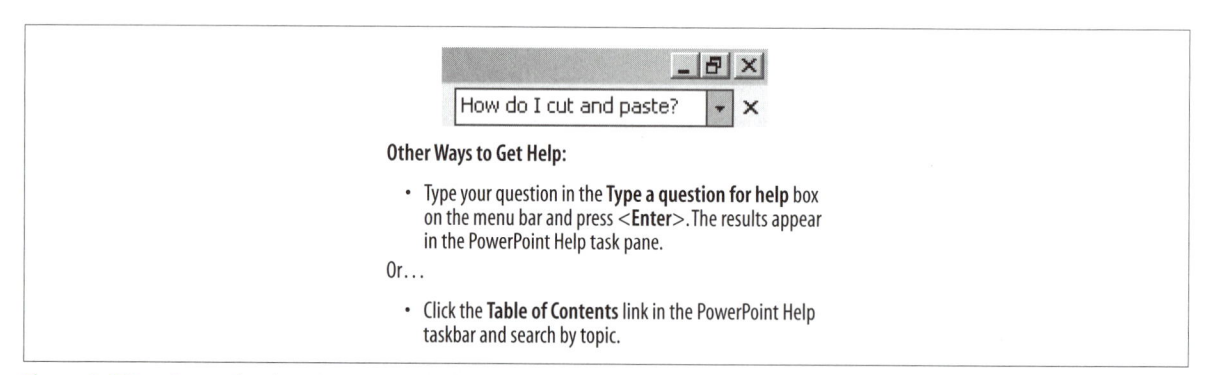

Figure 1-28. Help text for the selected topic.

Other Ways to Get Help:

- Type your question in the **Type a question for help** box on the menu bar and press **<Enter>**. The results appear in the PowerPoint Help task pane.

Or...

- Click the **Table of Contents** link in the PowerPoint Help taskbar and search by topic.

When you don't know how to do something in Windows or a Windows-based program, don't panic, just look up your question in the PowerPoint Help files. The PowerPoint Help files can answer your questions, offer tips, and provide help for all of PowerPoint's features. Many PowerPoint users forget to use Help, and this is unfortunate, because the Help files know more about PowerPoint than most reference books do!

You can make the PowerPoint Help files appear by pressing the F1 key. Then all you have to do is ask your question in normal English. This lesson will show you how you can get help by asking the Help files a question about a specific PowerPoint feature.

TIP *The F1 key is the help key for all Windows-based programs.*

Chapter 1
The Fundamentals

1 Press the F1 key.

The PowerPoint Help task pane appears, as shown in Figure 1-26.

2 Type How do I find and replace text? in the Search for: text box, as shown in Figure 1-26.

You can ask PowerPoint Help questions in normal English, just as if you were asking a person instead of a computer. The program identifies keywords and phrases in your questions like "find," "replace," and "text."

NOTE *Microsoft has totally changed the way Help works in Office 2003 with Office Online. Instead of searching for help in the files already stored on your computer, Office Online searches for the topic in its online database. The purpose of this feature is to provide current, up-to-date information on search topics. In their efforts to provide information on more advanced topics, however, they forget the most basic and important ones, like finding and replacing text.*

3 Click the ➡ Start searching button.

Office Online finds results like "Find and replace East Asian text," but nothing that will simply help you replace "Acme" with "Apex" in your presentation. We have to look in the trusty old Offline Help files for that.

NOTE *Fortunately, you can change your settings to perform Help searches without Office Online. Go to the "See also" section at the bottom of the PowerPoint Help task pane. Click the "Online Content Settings" option. Uncheck the "Search online content when connected" option and click OK.*

4 Click the Search list arrow in the Search area at the bottom of the task pane. Select Offline Help from the list and click the ➡ Start searching button.

The Offline Help search results appear, as shown in Figure 1-27.

TIP *Office Online will refer to Offline Help files if a connection to the Internet is not detected.*

5 Click the Replace text help topic.

PowerPoint displays information on how to replace text, as shown in Figure 1-28.

Notice that the Microsoft Office PowerPoint Help window has a toolbar that looks like some of the buttons you might have seen on a web browser. This lets you navigate through each help topic just as if you were browsing the Web.

6 Click the Microsoft Office PowerPoint Help window's Close button to close the window.

The Help window closes.

Table 1-9. Help Buttons

Button	Description
⬅	Moves back to the previous help topic.
➡	Moves forward to the next help topic.
🖶	Prints the current help topic.
▯▯	Tiles the PowerPoint program window and the Help window so you can see both at the same time.

Lesson 1.15
Getting Help

QUICK REFERENCE

TO GET HELP:

1. PRESS THE **F1** KEY.
2. TYPE YOUR QUESTION IN THE POWERPOINT HELP TASK BAR AND CLICK THE **START SEARCHING BUTTON** OR PRESS **ENTER**.
3. CLICK THE HELP TOPIC THAT BEST MATCHES WHAT YOU'RE LOOKING FOR (REPEAT THIS STEP AS NECESSARY).

TO TURN OFF OFFICE ONLINE:

1. CLICK THE **ONLINE CONTENT SETTINGS** OPTION IN THE POWERPOINT HELP TASK PANE.
2. UNCHECK THE **SEARCH ONLINE CONTENT WHEN CONNECTED** OPTION AND CLICK **OK**.

LESSON 1.16

Changing the Office Assistant and Using the "What's This" Button

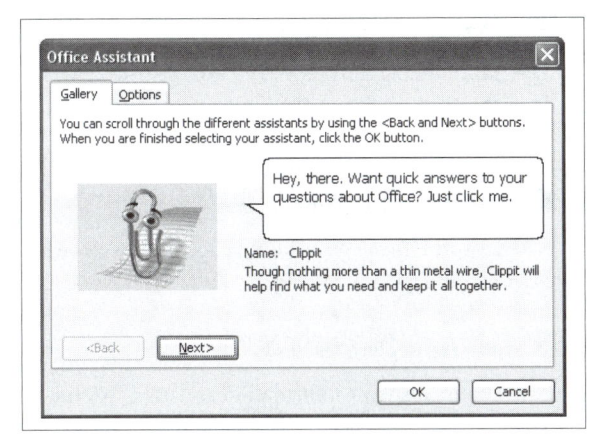

Figure 1-29. Choosing a new Office Assistant.

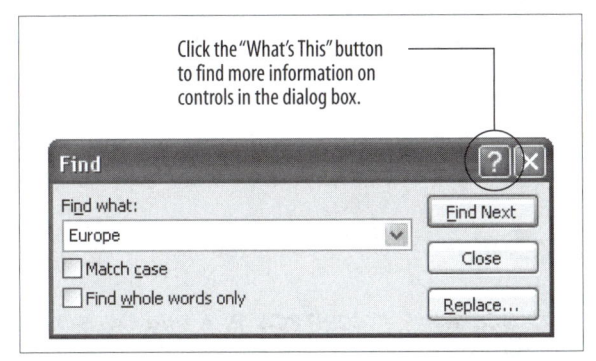

Figure 1-30. Click the "What's This" button [?] to view a brief description of all the controls in a dialog box.

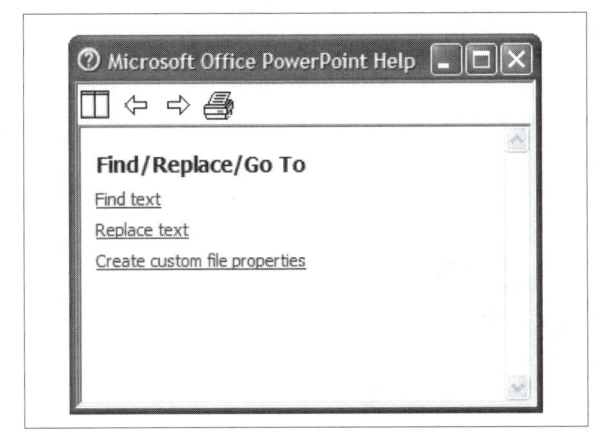

Figure 1-31. Click a link to find more information about the controls in the tab.

The Office Assistant is a cute animated character (a paper clip by default) that can answer your questions, offer tips, and provide help for all of PowerPoint's features. Many PowerPoint users don't use the Office Assistant, but it can be a very helpful tool. If you like using the Office Assistant but want a change of pace from Clippit's antics, you can choose one of eight different Office Assistants to guide you through PowerPoint. Of course, if you really hate the Office Assistant, you can always shut it off.

To hide the Office Assistant altogether, right-click the Office Assistant and click Hide.

The other topic covered in this lesson is how to use the "What's This" button. During your journey with PowerPoint, you will undoubtedly come across a dialog box or two with a number of confusing controls and options. To help you find out what the various controls and options in a dialog box are for, many dialog boxes contain a "What's This" [?] button that explains the purpose of each of the dialog box's controls. This lesson will show you how to use the "What's This" button, but first, let's start taming the Office Assistant.

1 Select **Help → Show the Office Assistant** from the menu.

The Office Assistant appears.

2 Right-click the Office Assistant and select **Choose Assistant** from the shortcut menu.

The Office Assistant dialog box appears, as shown in Figure 1-29.

3 Click the **Back** or **Next** button to see the available Office Assistants.

The Office Assistant you select is completely up to you. They all work the same—they just look and act different.

Lesson 1.16
Changing the Office Assistant and Using the "What's This" Button

4 Click OK when you find an Office Assistant that you like.

If you find the Office Assistant annoying (as many people do) and want to get rid of it altogether, here's how:

5 Right-click the Office Assistant.

A shortcut menu appears.

6 Select Hide from the shortcut menu.

You can always bring the Office Assistant back whenever you require its help.

Now, let's move on to how to use the "What's This" button to discover the purpose of confusing dialog box controls.

7 Select Edit → Find from the menu.

The Find dialog box appears. Notice the "What's This" button located in the dialog box's title bar just to the left of the dialog box's close button.

8 Click the "What's This" button.

A Microsoft Office PowerPoint Help window appears, as shown in Figure 1-31.

9 Click the Replace text link.

PowerPoint displays information on how to replace text.

10 Click the Close button to close the Microsoft Office PowerPoint Help window, and close the Find dialog box.

QUICK REFERENCE

TO CHANGE OFFICE ASSISTANTS:

1. IF NECESSARY, SELECT HELP → SHOW THE OFFICE ASSISTANT FROM THE MENU.
2. RIGHT-CLICK THE OFFICE ASSISTANT AND SELECT CHOOSE ASSISTANT FROM THE SHORTCUT MENU.
3. CLICK THE NEXT OR BACK BUTTONS UNTIL YOU FIND AN OFFICE ASSISTANT YOU LIKE, THEN CLICK OK.

TO HIDE THE OFFICE ASSISTANT:

- RIGHT-CLICK THE OFFICE ASSISTANT AND SELECT HIDE FROM THE SHORTCUT MENU.

TO SEE WHAT A CONTROL IN A DIALOG BOX DOES:

1. CLICK THE DIALOG BOX "WHAT'S THIS" BUTTON (LOCATED RIGHT NEXT TO THE CLOSE BUTTON).
2. FIND THE CONTROL DESCRIPTION IN THE MICROSOFT OFFICE POWERPOINT HELP WINDOW.

Chapter One Review

Lesson Summary

Starting PowerPoint

Start PowerPoint by clicking the Start button, selecting Programs, and selecting Microsoft PowerPoint.

Understanding the PowerPoint Screen

Be able to identify the main components of the PowerPoint program screen.

Using Menus

To Use a Menu: Either click the menu name with the mouse pointer, or press the Alt key and the letter that is underlined in the menu name.

PowerPoint 2003's new personalized menus hide more advanced commands from view. To display a menu's hidden commands, click the downward-pointing arrows at the bottom of the menu, or open the menu and wait a few seconds.

To Change How Menus Work: Select View → Toolbars → Customize from the menu, select the Options tab, check or clear either the Always Show Full Menus and/or Show Full Menus After a Short Delay option, then click Close.

Using Toolbars

To See a Description of a Toolbar Button: Leave the pointer over the button to display a ScreenTip of what the button does.

To Stack the Standard and Formatting Toolbars in Two Separate Rows: Click the button on either toolbar and select Show Buttons on Two Rows from the list.

Filling Out Dialog Boxes

Be able to identify and use text boxes, list boxes, drop-down menus, check boxes, and sheet tabs.

Click the control you want to use, or press Tab to move to the next control in the dialog box and Shift + Tab to move back to the previous control.

To Save Your Changes and Close a Dialog Box: Click the OK button or press Enter.

To Close a Dialog Box Without Saving Your Changes: Click the Cancel button or press Esc.

Keystroke and Right Mouse Button Shortcuts

Keystroke Shortcuts: Press Ctrl and the letter that corresponds to the shortcut command at the same time.

Right Mouse Button Shortcut Menus: Whenever you're unsure or curious about what you can do with an object, click it with the right mouse button to display a list of commands related to the object.

Opening a Presentation

To Open a Presentation: Click the Open button on the Standard toolbar, or select File → Open from the menu, or press Ctrl + O.

Saving and Closing a Presentation and Exiting PowerPoint

To Save a Presentation: Click the Save button on the Standard toolbar, or select File → Save from the menu, or press Ctrl + S.

To Save a Presentation in a New File with a Different Name: Select File → Save As from the menu and enter a different name for the presentation.

To Close a Presentation: Click the presentation window close button or select File → Close from the menu.

To Exit PowerPoint: Click the PowerPoint program's close button or select File → Exit from the menu.

Creating a New Presentation with the AutoContent Wizard

To Create a New Presentation with the AutoContent Wizard: Start PowerPoint and select From AutoContent Wizard in the task pane, or, if you're already in PowerPoint, select File → New from the menu, and select From AutoContent Wizard in the task pane. Click Next and select the Category button that best fits the presentation you want to create. Select a presentation from the presentation list on the right side of the dialog box and click Next. Enter the information that the Presentation Wizard prompts you for and follow any on-screen instructions. Click Finish when you're done.

Chapter 1
Chapter One Review

Creating a Blank Presentation and a Presentation from a Template

To Create a Blank Presentation: Click the New button on the Standard toolbar, or select File → New from the menu, select Blank Presentation, and click OK.

To Create a Presentation from a Template: Select File → New from the menu, click From Design Template in the task pane, then find and double-click the template you want to use (you may have to select it from one of the tabbed categories).

To Display Large Template Previews: Move the pointer over any template in the task pane, click the ▾ arrow, and select Show Large Previews from the menu.

Moving Around in Your Presentations

Page Up moves up one screen, Page Down moves down one screen.

Ctrl + Home moves to the beginning of a presentation.

Ctrl + End moves to the end of a presentation.

Viewing Your Presentation

You can view a presentation in Normal, Slide Sorter, and Slide Show Views. Change views by clicking on the View buttons located on the horizontal scroll bar, or by selecting them from the View menu.

Normal View displays the slides one at a time, as they will appear when they are printed or displayed in a presentation.

Slide Sorter View displays all the slides in your presentation as small pictures or thumbnails. Use Slide Sorter View when you want to rearrange the slides in your presentation and add transition effects between them.

Slide Show View displays your presentation as an electronic slide show.

Notes Page View displays a small version of the slide and all the notes that go along with it.

Change the zoom level by using the 100% Zoom box on the Standard toolbar.

Printing Your Presentation

To Print a Presentation: Click the Print button on the Standard toolbar, or select File → Print from the menu, or press Ctrl + P.

To Specify Additional Printing Options: Select File → Print from the menu. You can specify the number of copies and which pages to print.

Getting Help

To Get Help: Press the F1 key. Type your question in the PowerPoint Help task pane and click the Start Searching button or press Enter. Click the help topic that best matches what you're looking for (repeat this step as necessary).

To Turn Off Office Online: Click the Online Content Settings option in the PowerPoint Help task pane. Uncheck the Search online content when connected option and click OK.

Changing the Office Assistant and Using the "What's This" Button

To Change Office Assistants: If necessary, select Help → Show the Office Assistant from the menu. Right-click the Office Assistant and select Choose Assistant from the shortcut menu. Click the Next or Back buttons until you find an Office Assistant you like, then click OK.

To Hide the Office Assistant: Right-click the Office Assistant and select Hide from the shortcut menu.

To Get Help Regarding the Content of an Individual Dialog Box: Click the "What's This" button (located right next to the close button). Find the control description in the Microsoft Office PowerPoint Help window.

44

Chapter 1
The Fundamentals

Quiz

1. Microsoft PowerPoint is a:
   A. Word processing program
   B. Database program
   C. Spreadsheet program
   D. Presentation program

2. Right-clicking something in PowerPoint:
   A. Deletes the object
   B. Opens a shortcut menu listing everything you can do to the object
   C. Selects the object
   D. Nothing—the right mouse button is there for left-handed people

3. Which of the following is NOT a way to create a new presentation?
   A. From scratch (create a blank presentation)
   B. Using a template
   C. Using the Scan-In Slides feature
   D. Using the AutoContent Wizard

4. Which of the following is NOT one of PowerPoint's Views?
   A. Normal View
   B. Presentation View
   C. Slide Show View
   D. Slide Sorter View

5. A keystroke combination is:
   A. Pressing two or more keys at the same time, for example pressing the Shift and Tab keys at the same time.
   B. A way to lock your computer to prevent unauthorized access. To unlock the computer, simply retype your keystroke combination.
   C. Using the keyboard in conjunction with the mouse.
   D. A type of mixed drink.

6. PowerPoint automatically creates a blank presentation when you first start the program. (True or False?)

7. Which of the following is NOT a technique for moving around in a presentation?
   A. Pressing Ctrl + Home to move to the first slide in a presentation.
   B. Pressing Page Down to move to the next slide in a presentation.
   C. Selecting Edit → Move from the menu and specify the slide you want to go to.
   D. Using the vertical scroll bar to move forward or backward through the slides in your presentation.

8. To save a presentation you: (Select all that apply.)
   A. Press Ctrl +F5.
   B. Select File → Save from the menu.
   C. Click the Save button on the Standard toolbar.
   D. Click Save on the Windows Start button.

9. The Print dialog box, which can be found by selecting File → Print from the menu, lets you print multiple copies of a presentation and print specific slides. (True or False?)

Homework

1. Start Microsoft PowerPoint by clicking the Windows Start button, pointing to Programs, and clicking Microsoft PowerPoint.
2. Click the Open button on the Standard toolbar and navigate to your Practice folder. Find and click the Homework 1 file and click Open.
3. Press the Page Down key to move to the second slide in the presentation.
4. Switch to Outline View by clicking the Outline tab on the left side of the screen.
5. Switch back to Slide View by clicking the Slides View tab on the left side of the screen.

Chapter 1
Chapter One Review

6. Select 100% from the Zoom List on the Standard toolbar. Readjust the zoom level again by selecting Fit from the Zoom List.

7. Save the presentation as "Flea Circus": select File → Save As from the menu, navigate to your Practice folder, type "Flea Circus" in the file name box, and then click Save.

8. Open the Print dialog box by selecting File → Print from the menu. Do you know how to print only the first slide of the presentation? How would you print more than one copy of the presentation? Click Cancel to close the dialog box without printing anything.

Extra Credit: Use the AutoContent Wizard to create a sample presentation on whatever topic you want.

Quiz Answers

1. D. PowerPoint is a presentation program. Hopefully you got this question right!

2. B. Right-clicking an object displays a shortcut menu for the object.

3. C. There isn't a Scan-In Slides feature anywhere in PowerPoint!

4. B. PowerPoint doesn't have a Presentation View.

5. A. A keystroke combination is when you press two or more keys at the same time, for example Ctrl + Home.

6. False. When you first start the PowerPoint program, a dialog box where you can create a new presentation or open an existing presentation greets you.

7. C. There isn't an Edit → Move command on the menu. All the others are valid navigation techniques.

8. B and C.

9. True. Selecting File → Print from the menu opens the Print dialog box where you can specify exactly what you want to print.

CHAPTER 2
EDITING A PRESENTATION

CHAPTER OBJECTIVES:

Inserting new slides and entering text
Working in the outline pane—promoting and demoting slides
Editing, selecting, replacing, and deleting text
Cutting, copying, and pasting text
Finding and replacing text
Using undo, redo, and repeat
Checking the spelling in a presentation
Reorganizing a presentation in the outline pane
Copying, moving, and deleting slides in Slide Sorter View
Adding notes to your slides
Working with more than one presentation and window
Managing your files
Understanding smart tags
Recovering your presentations

CHAPTER TASK: REVISE AND EDIT A SIMPLE PRESENTATION

Prerequisites

- Know how to start Microsoft PowerPoint.
- Know how to use menus, toolbars, dialog boxes, and shortcut keystrokes.
- Move the mouse pointer and navigate between the slides in a presentation.
- Open and save a presentation.

Now that you're familiar with the PowerPoint basics, you're ready to move on to editing your slides. This chapter focuses on adding slides and text to your presentation. Most presentations take a lot of time and thought to put together and are often edited and revised several times before they're finished. Toward that end, this chapter covers just about every trick you will need to know about editing—how to add, edit, cut, copy, and paste text; how to check for spelling errors; and how to undo any mistakes you might make.

LESSON 2.1

Inserting Slides and Text

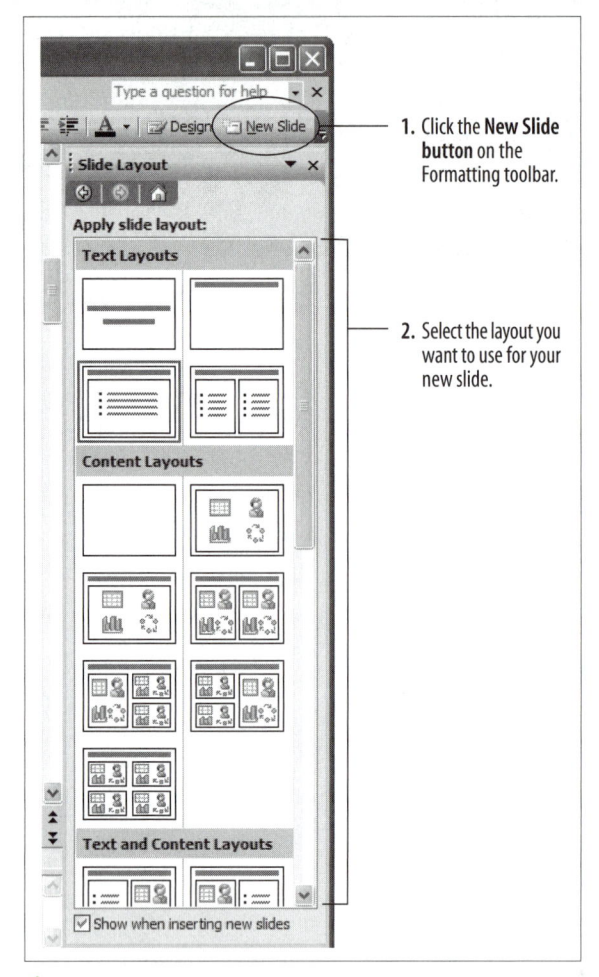

Figure 2-1. Select the layout you want for your new slide from the task pane.

1. Click the **New Slide** button on the Formatting toolbar.
2. Select the layout you want to use for your new slide.

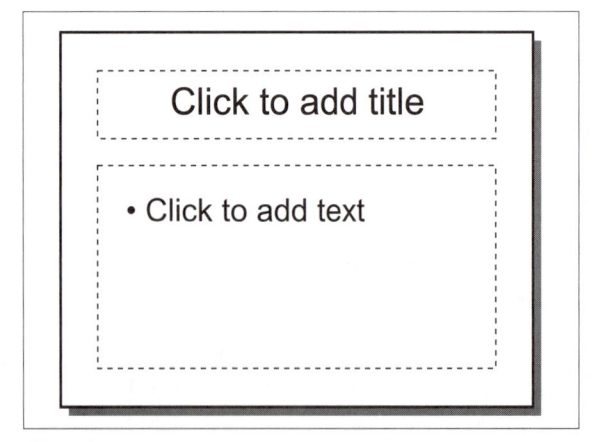

Figure 2-2. A blank Title and Text layout has placeholders for the slide's title and text.

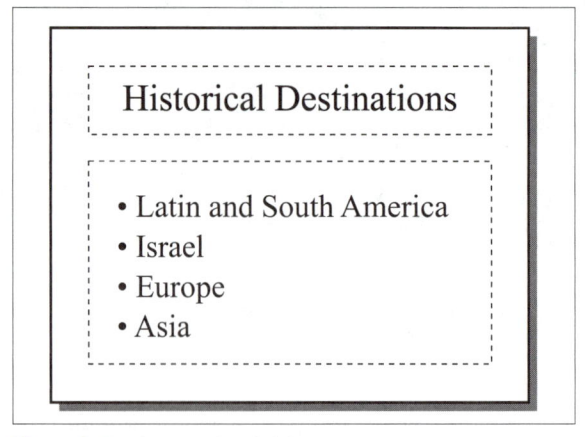

Figure 2-3. The completed slide.

Slides are the most basic components of a presentation. Without slides, PowerPoint would just sit there like a broken projector and do nothing. To make it easy to add slides to your presentation, PowerPoint 2003 comes with 27 preset layouts. Layouts help you choose what you want your slide to look like. There are layouts with titles, bulleted lists, clip art, charts, and even video clips, but you will probably work with text layouts most often.

Every slide has one or more areas where you can type called placeholders. These placeholders are hard to miss, since they're labeled "Click to add title" or "Click to add text." This lesson will walk you through adding a couple of new slides to an existing presentation.

1 Start Microsoft PowerPoint.

2 Open **Lesson 2A** and save it as **Expeditions**.

This presentation is for a travel agency's launch of a new series of international history tours—but it's currently far from complete. First, the presentation needs a text slide—here's how to add one:

3 Click the **New Slide button** on the Formatting toolbar.

New Slide button

Other Ways to add a Slide:

- Select **Insert** → **New Slide** from the menu.

Chapter 2
Editing a Presentation

The Slide Layout task pane appears as shown in Figure 2-1. The Slide Layout task pane lets you select from numerous layouts that determine what you want to appear on the new slide. We want to add a Title and Text Slide.

4 Click the Title and Text layout, as shown in Figure 2-1.

A new slide appears after the current slide in your presentation as shown in Figure 2-2. Notice there are two placeholders on this slide: one for the title of the slide and the other for the bulleted list. To add text to a placeholder, all you have to do is click and type.

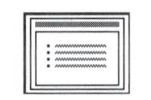

Title and text layout

5 Click the title placeholder (where it says: "Click to Add Title").

An insertion point (|) appears in the placeholder, indicating that you can add text to the placeholder.

6 Type Historical Destinations.

Now let's add some text to the bulleted list placeholder.

7 Click the bulleted list placeholder, type Latin and South America, and press Enter.

PowerPoint adds another bullet to the list when you press the Enter key.

TIP *Placeholders grow and shrink to accommodate any text that you enter.*

8 Type Israel, press Enter, type Europe, press Enter, and type Asia.

Your completed slide should look like the one in Figure 2-3.

9 Click the Slide Layout pane's Close button.

If you are not planning to use the Slide Layout pane again for a while, it is usually a good idea to close it so you can have extra viewing space for your presentation.

In this exercise you added a slide using a Title and Text layout, but there are many more types of layouts you can use to add different types of slides. Table 2-1 describes some of the things you can insert into your slides. If you ever add a new slide and want to change its layout, click the *New Slide button* on the Formatting toolbar and select the layout you want to apply to the slide.

Table 2-1. Slide Layout Placeholders

Symbol	Placeholder Type	Description
	Title	Inserts a title or heading
	Text	Inserts a bulleted list of related points
	Contents	Allows you to select the type of content you want to insert in the slide: Table, Chart, Clip Art, Picture, Diagram or Organizational Chart, or Media Clip
	Table	Inserts a table
	Chart	Inserts a chart
	Diagram or Organizational Chart	Inserts an organizational chart

49

Lesson 2.1
Inserting Slides and Text

Table 2-1. Slide Layout Placeholders (Continued)

Symbol	Placeholder Type	Description
	Clip Art	Inserts clip art
	Media Clip	Inserts music, sound, or a video clip

QUICK REFERENCE

TO INSERT A SLIDE INTO A PRESENTATION:

1. CLICK THE NEW SLIDE BUTTON ON THE FORMATTING TOOLBAR.

   OR...

   SELECT INSERT → NEW SLIDE FROM THE MENU.

2. SELECT THE SLIDE LAYOUT YOU WANT TO USE FOR THE SLIDE AND CLOSE THE TASK PANE.

TO ADD TEXT TO A SLIDE:

- CLICK THE APPROPRIATE TEXT PLACEHOLDER AND TYPE THE TEXT.

Using the Outline Pane

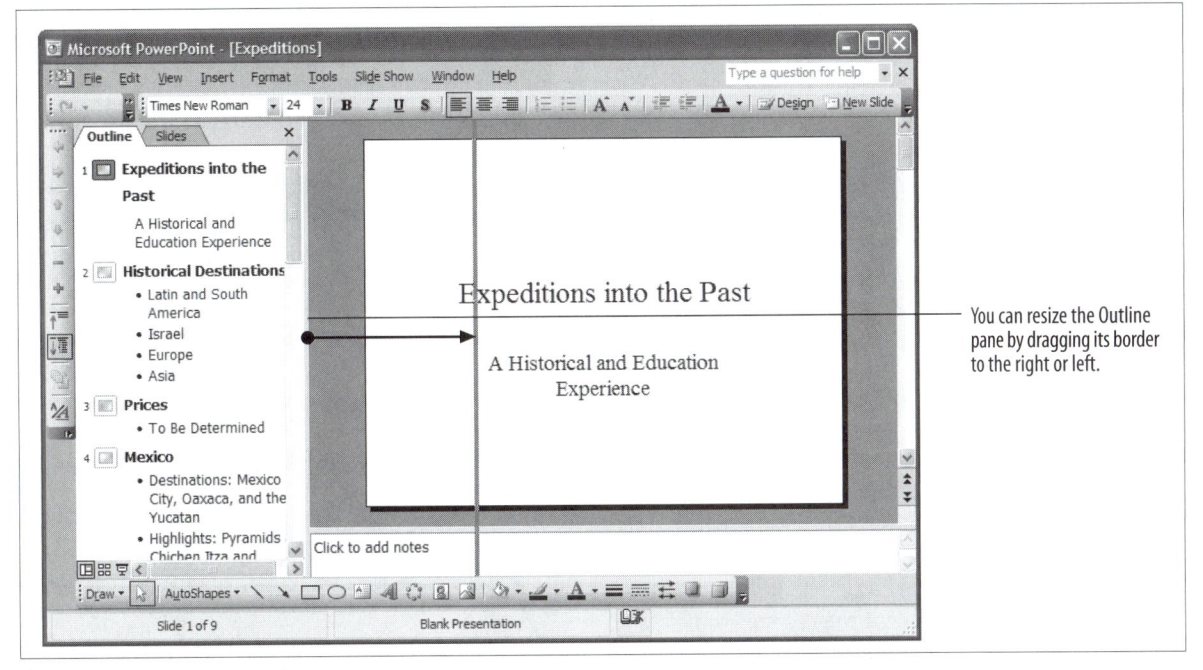

LESSON 2.2

Figure 2-4. Resizing the Outline pane.

You've probably already noticed that most of the slides in PowerPoint contain nothing more than headings and bulleted lists. This might seem simple—perhaps a bit boring—but it's an extremely effective method for getting your point across. Since most presentations are highly structured, containing many points and subpoints, it makes sense to work with them as outlines—and that's the purpose of PowerPoint's Outline pane.

The Outline pane displays the title and text of each slide. This lesson will introduce you to the Outline pane.

Here are a few more notes about the Outline pane before we start:

- A numbered heading represents each slide in the outline. Notice each slide also has a ▣ symbol next to it indicating that it's a slide.
- Each slide's body text appears as an indented heading under the slide's main title heading.

1 Click the **Outline tab**.

The Outline pane appears, as shown in Figure 2-4. Now you can easily view the content of the entire presentation. If you're going to be working with a presentation's outline for any length of time you should probably resize the Outline pane so that you can see more of the outline at once.

2 Click and drag the Outline pane's right border to the middle of the PowerPoint screen, as shown in Figure 2-4.

Now you have enough room to view and work with your presentation's outline.

TIP *You can demote a paragraph by clicking the* ➡ *Demote button on the Outlining toolbar, or by clicking the point you want to demote and dragging the mouse to the right.*

3 Click anywhere in the **Outline pane** and press **Ctrl + End** to move to the very end of the presentation.

This is where we want to add another slide.

4 Press **Ctrl + Enter** to add a new slide to the presentation.

A brand new slide appears on the page—notice its slide icon ▣. By default, any new slides you add in the Outline pane after the title slide will be Title and Text slides, like the one you created in the previous lesson.

5 Type `Target Market`.

This will be the title of your new slide.

Lesson 2.2
Using the Outline Pane

TIP *You can promote a paragraph by clicking the Promote button on the Outlining toolbar, or by clicking the point you want to promote and dragging the mouse to the left.*

6 Press **Enter**.

Whenever you press the Enter key in the Outline pane, it adds a new line just like the one before it. Because the preceding line is a slide, pressing Enter adds a new slide. Since we don't want to add a new slide, we can demote the current line to a bullet by pressing the Tab key.

7 Press **Tab**.

You've just demoted the current line and moved it down one level in the outline. The current paragraph now appears as a subpoint under the "Target Market" heading. You demote paragraphs by selecting them and pressing the Tab key, or, if you're a toolbar fanatic, you can also click the Demote button on the Outlining toolbar.

Let's add the subpoints to the "Target Market" slide.

8 Type **College Students**.

This will be the first bulleted item on the slide.

9 Press **Enter**.

PowerPoint adds another subpoint paragraph.

10 Type **Retirees** and press **Enter**.

We want to add several subpoints under the "Retirees" point.

11 Press **Tab** to demote the new paragraph, type **Archeologists**, press **Enter**, and type **Professors**.

To *promote* a paragraph means to move it up one level in the outline. You promote paragraphs by selecting them and pressing the Shift + Tab keys or by clicking the *Promote button* on the Outlining toolbar.

12 Press **Enter** to add a new paragraph, and press **Shift** + **Tab** twice to promote the paragraph to Level 1 of the outline, making it a title for a new slide.

Let's finish this lesson by adding the text for the new slide.

13 Type **Dates**, press **Enter** to add a new paragraph, press **Tab** to demote the paragraph, and type **To be determined**.

Because the Outline pane focuses on the content of a presentation rather than on appearance or layout, new slides added in the Outline pane are always the basic Title and Text layout. You can always change the layout of a new slide by clicking the *New Slide button* on the Formatting toolbar.

QUICK REFERENCE

TO DEMOTE A PARAGRAPH:
- SELECT THE PARAGRAPH(S) AND PRESS THE **TAB** KEY, OR CLICK THE **DEMOTE BUTTON** ON THE OUTLINING TOOLBAR.

TO PROMOTE A PARAGRAPH:
- SELECT THE PARAGRAPH(S) AND PRESS **SHIFT** + **TAB**, OR CLICK THE **PROMOTE BUTTON** ON THE OUTLINING TOOLBAR.

TO ADD A NEW SLIDE IN THE OUTLINE TAB:
- PRESS **CTRL** + **ENTER**, OR PROMOTE A SELECTED PARAGRAPH TO THE HIGHEST LEVEL ON THE OUTLINE.

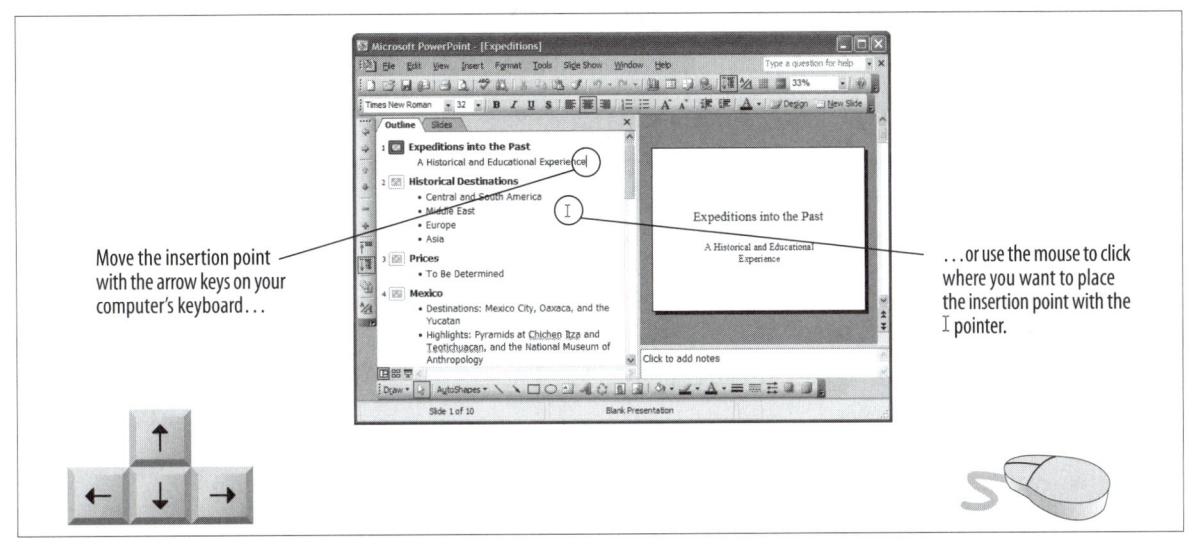

LESSON 2.3

Editing Text

Figure 2-5. Moving the insertion point in a presentation.

Often, after typing a presentation, you will discover that you need to make some changes to your text—perhaps you want to rephrase or even delete a sentence. Or maybe you inherited your boss's feeble attempt at creating a PowerPoint presentation and have to make a lot of changes. Editing a presentation by inserting and deleting text is very simple. To insert text, you move the insertion point (the blinking bar) to where you want to insert the text. You move the insertion point using the arrow keys on the keyboard or by using the mouse to click where you want to move the insertion point, as shown in Figure 2-5. Once the insertion point is where you want, just start typing.

There are a couple ways to delete text. One way to delete text is to place the insertion point to the right of the text you want to delete and press the Backspace key. Another way to delete text is to place the insertion point to the left of the text you want to delete and press the Delete key.

If you have already used a word processing program, you undoubtedly already know how to edit text, and since this lesson will be kid stuff to a pro like you, you'll probably want to skip it. If not, this lesson will give you some practice inserting and deleting text.

1 Press **Ctrl** + **Home** to move to the beginning of the presentation.

Placing the Insertion Point

You jump to the very beginning of the presentation. Notice the insertion point—the blinking | that appears before the word "Expeditions." Anything you type appears wherever the insertion point is located—just move the insertion point, using the mouse or keyboard, to where you want to enter some text, and then type the text.

2 Press the Down Arrow Key ↓ button.

The insertion point moves down one line. If the cursor is not at the beginning of the current line, move it there now.

3 Press and hold the Right Arrow Key → button until the insertion point is located immediately after the word **Education**.

4 Type `al`.

The text is inserted at the insertion point, so that the word "Education" now says "Educational." You've just learned how to insert text into a slide—pretty easy, huh?

Lesson 2.3
Editing Text

5 Move the insertion point to the very beginning of the Latin and South America line.

Here you need to delete some text—the word "Latin."

6 Press the Delete key several times, until the word Latin is deleted.

The Delete key deletes one space to the right, or after the insertion point.

7 Type Central.

You've just deleted the word "Latin" and inserted the word "Central" to take its place.

You can also use the mouse to move the insertion point instead of the arrow keys. Simply move the mouse until the I pointer is placed where you want it to be and then click the left mouse button.

8 Click immediately after the word Israel in the fifth line of the presentation with the I pointer.

The insertion point appears immediately after the word Israel—right where you clicked the mouse button.

You can also use the Backspace key to delete text. Like the Delete key, the Backspace key also deletes text, but in a slightly different way. The Backspace key deletes text before, or to the left of the insertion point, while the Delete key deletes text after, or to the right of the insertion point.

9 Press the Backspace key.

The Backspace key deletes text before, or to the left of the insertion point.

10 Press and hold the Backspace key until you have deleted the rest of the word Israel. Don't delete too far—we still need an empty line here!

Great! You've learned how to delete text using the Backspace key.

11 Type Middle East.

Now that you've revised the presentation, you need to save your changes.

12 Save your changes and close the current presentation.

QUICK REFERENCE

TO MOVE THE INSERTION POINT:

- USE THE ARROW KEYS.

OR...

- CLICK WHERE YOU WANT TO PLACE THE INSERTION POINT WITH THE I POINTER.

TO INSERT TEXT (INTO AN EXISTING TEXT BOX):

- CLICK IN THE TEXT BOX, MOVE THE INSERTION POINT WHERE YOU WANT TO INSERT THE TEXT, AND THEN TYPE THE TEXT YOU WANT TO INSERT.

TO DELETE TEXT:

- THE BACKSPACE KEY DELETES TEXT BEFORE, OR TO THE LEFT OF THE INSERTION POINT.

- THE DELETE KEY DELETES TEXT BEHIND, OR TO THE RIGHT OF THE INSERTION POINT.

Selecting, Replacing, and Deleting Text

LESSON 2.4

8 ☐ Tour Guides • Ricardo Perez - Mexico • George Montenegro - Middle East • Kolja Richter - Europe	1. Position the insertion point before or after the text that you want to select.
8 ☐ Tour Guides • [Ricardo Perez] - Mexico • George Montenegro - Middle East • Kolja Richter - Europe	2. Click and hold down the left mouse button, drag the mouse across the text you want to select, then release the mouse button.
8 ☐ Tour Guides • Luis Gonzales - Mexico • George Montenegro - Middle East • Kolja Richter - Europe	3. If you want to replace the selected text, simply type in the new text – it will overwrite the selected text.

Figure 2-6. Selecting and replacing text.

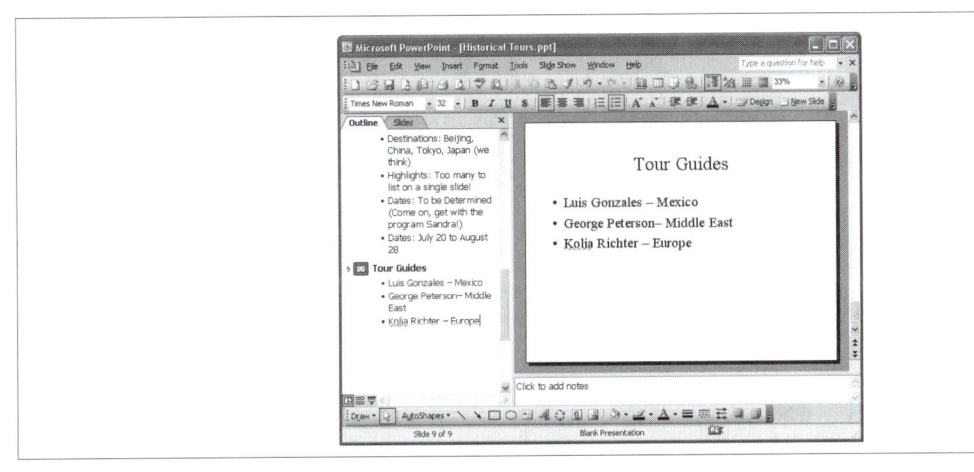

Figure 2-7. The updated presentation.

Whenever you want to edit more than one character at a time, you must *select* it first. A lot of editing techniques—such as formatting, cutting, copying, and pasting text—require that you select the text you want to modify. There are probably hundreds of reasons to select text in PowerPoint, so it pays off if you're an expert at doing it.

1 Open **Lesson 2B** and save it as **Historical Tours**.

Move on to the next step and resize the Outline pane.

2 Click and drag the Outline pane's right border to the middle of the PowerPoint screen.

Now you have more room to view and edit the presentation's outline.

3 Press **Ctrl + End** to move to the very end of the presentation and make sure that the insertion point appears at the end of the line **Sandra Wu – Asia**.

Actually, you can place the insertion point before or after the text you want to select.

4 Click and hold down the mouse button and drag the mouse to the left across the entire line **Sandra Wu – Asia** (the words should be highlighted). Release the mouse button when you're finished.

The words Sandra Wu – Asia should be highlighted in black. Selecting text with the mouse can be a little tricky at first, especially if you're still a novice at using it. Once you have selected a block of text, you can

55

Lesson 2.4
Selecting, Replacing, and Deleting Text

delete it by pressing either the Delete key or the Backspace key.

5 Press Delete **to delete the selected text.**

As you've probably guessed, you can delete anything you select—a word, a sentence, a slide, even the entire presentation! Let's try something else…

6 Select the words Ricardo Perez **on the last slide (see Figure 2-6).**

When you select text, anything you type while the text is selected will replace the selected text.

7 Type Luis Gonzales**.**

The name "Luis Gonzales" replaces the selected text "Ricardo Perez."

TIP *Double-click a word to select it.*

8 Double-click the word Montenegro**.**

9 Type Peterson**.**

The word "Peterson" replaces the word "Montenegro". You can also use the keyboard to select text if you don't like using the mouse. To select text using the keyboard, move the insertion point before or after the text you want to select, press and hold down the Shift key while you use the arrow keys to select the text. See Table 2-2 for a list of shortcuts to select text.

10 Move the insertion point to the very end of the line Dates: July 20 to August 28 **in** Slide 8**.**

Try selecting text with the keyboard in the next step.

11 Press and hold down the Shift **key and press and hold down the left arrow key** ← **until you have selected the text** July 20 to August 28**.**

It's easy to deselect text if you change your mind—just click anywhere on the screen.

12 Click anywhere in the Outline pane to deselect the text.

The dates are no longer selected. Figure 2-7 shows the updated presentation.

Table 2-2. Shortcuts for Selecting Text

To Select This	Do This
A word	Double-click the word.
A line	Click next to the line in the left margin.
A sentence	Press and hold Ctrl and double-click the sentence.
A slide (in the Outline pane)	Click next to the slide icon in the left margin.
The entire presentation	Select Edit → Select All from the menu, or press Ctrl + A.

Chapter 2
Editing a Presentation

QUICK REFERENCE

TO SELECT A STRING OF TEXT:

1. MOVE THE INSERTION POINT TO THE BEGINNING OR END OF THE TEXT YOU WANT TO SELECT.
2. CLICK AND HOLD THE LEFT MOUSE BUTTON AND DRAG THE INSERTION POINT ACROSS THE TEXT, THEN RELEASE THE MOUSE BUTTON ONCE THE TEXT IS SELECTED.

   OR...

   PRESS AND HOLD DOWN THE SHIFT KEY WHILE USING THE ARROW KEYS TO SELECT THE TEXT YOU WANT.

TO SELECT A SINGLE WORD:

- DOUBLE-CLICK THE WORD YOU WANT TO SELECT.

TO REPLACE TEXT:

- REPLACE TEXT BY FIRST SELECTING IT, THEN TYPING THE NEW TEXT YOU WANT.

TO DESELECT TEXT:

- CLICK ANYWHERE ON THE COMPUTER SCREEN.

TO DELETE SELECTED TEXT:

1. SELECT THE TEXT.
2. PRESS THE DELETE KEY.

57

LESSON 2.5   Cutting, Copying, and Pasting Text

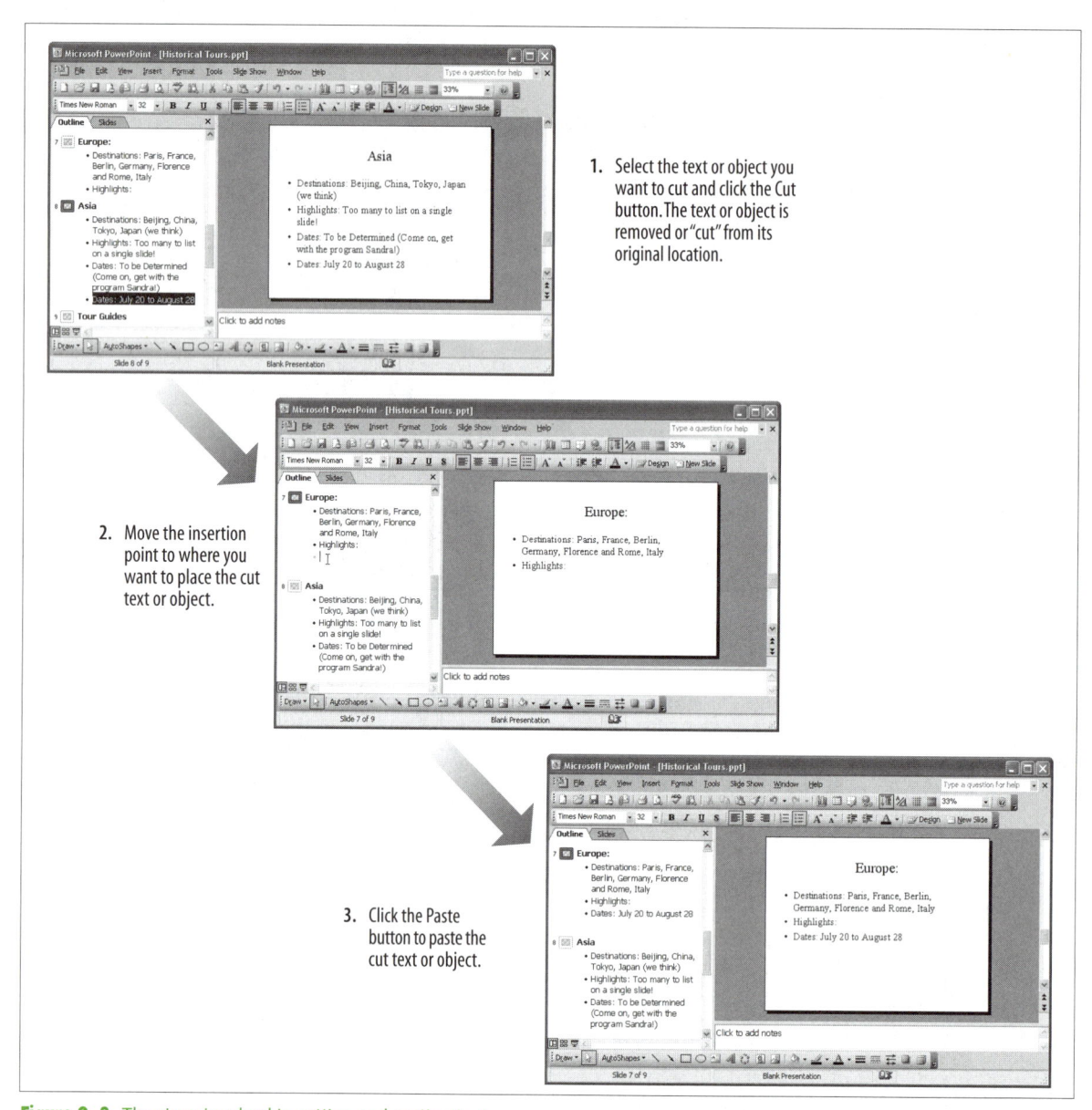

Figure 2-8. The steps involved in cutting and pasting text.

1. Select the text or object you want to cut and click the Cut button. The text or object is removed or "cut" from its original location.

2. Move the insertion point to where you want to place the cut text or object.

3. Click the Paste button to paste the cut text or object.

By now, you should already know how to select text in a presentation. Once text is selected, you can move it to another place in the presentation by cutting or copying it and then pasting it elsewhere. Cutting, copying, and pasting text is one of the more common tasks you will do in PowerPoint. Anything you cut is placed in a temporary storage area called the Windows Clipboard. The Clipboard is available to any Windows program, so you can cut and paste text between different programs.

1 Go to **Slide 8** and select the entire last line—**Dates: July 20 to August 28**.

Remember how to select a line in PowerPoint? Just click next to the line in the left margin. Someone accidentally put the date on the wrong slide—you need to cut the selected text to the Windows Clipboard and paste it elsewhere in the presentation.

2 Click the Cut button on the Standard toolbar.

Cut button

Other Ways to Cut:

- Select **Edit** → **Cut** from the menu.
- Press **<Ctrl>** + **<X>**.

The selected text disappears and is placed in the Windows Clipboard, ready to be moved to a new location.

3 Move the insertion point to the end of the Highlights: line on Slide 7 (the Europe slide) and press Enter to add a new line.

This is where you want to paste the dates that you cut.

4 Click the Paste button on the Standard toolbar. Press the Backspace key twice if a blank line appears after the dates to delete it.

Poof! The cut text, the dates, appears at the insertion point.

Copying information is very similar to cutting information. Both commands put your selected information in the Clipboard where you can then paste it to a new location. The only difference between the two commands is that the Cut command deletes selected information when it copies it to the clipboard, while the Copy command copies the selected information to the clipboard without deleting it.

5 Select the text Too many to list on a single slide! on Slide 8 (the Asia slide).

Now you can copy the selected text to the clipboard.

6 Click the Copy button on the Standard toolbar.

Copy button

Other Ways to Copy:

- Select **Edit** → **Copy** from the menu.
- Press **<Ctrl>** + **<C>**.

Nothing appears to happen, but the selected text has been copied to the clipboard.

7 Place the insertion point after Highlights: in the Europe slide.

First you need to add a space here.

8 Press the Spacebar button to add a space.

You're ready to paste the copied text.

9 Click the Paste button on the Standard toolbar.

Paste button

The copied text is pasted at the insertion point.

10 Save your work.

You can also copy, cut, and paste text between two different Windows programs—for example, you could copy text from a Word document and then paste it in a PowerPoint presentation. The cut, copy, and paste commands (the toolbar buttons, menus, and/or keyboard shortcuts) you learned in PowerPoint will work with most Windows applications.

Lesson 2.5
Cutting, Copying, and Pasting Text

QUICK REFERENCE

TO CUT SOMETHING:

1. SELECT THE TEXT OR OBJECT YOU WANT TO CUT.
2. CLICK THE **CUT BUTTON** ON THE STANDARD TOOLBAR.

   OR...

   SELECT **EDIT** → **CUT** FROM THE MENU.

   OR...

   PRESS **CTRL + X**.

TO COPY SOMETHING:

1. SELECT THE TEXT OR OBJECT YOU WANT TO COPY.
2. CLICK THE **COPY BUTTON** ON THE STANDARD TOOLBAR.

   OR...

   SELECT **EDIT** → **COPY** FROM THE MENU.

   OR...

   PRESS **CTRL + C**.

TO PASTE CUT OR COPIED TEXT OR OBJECTS:

1. PLACE THE INSERTION POINT WHERE YOU WANT TO PASTE THE TEXT OR OBJECT.
2. CLICK THE **PASTE BUTTON** ON THE STANDARD TOOLBAR.

   OR...

   SELECT **EDIT** → **PASTE** FROM THE MENU.

   OR...

   PRESS **CTRL + V**.

LESSON 2.6

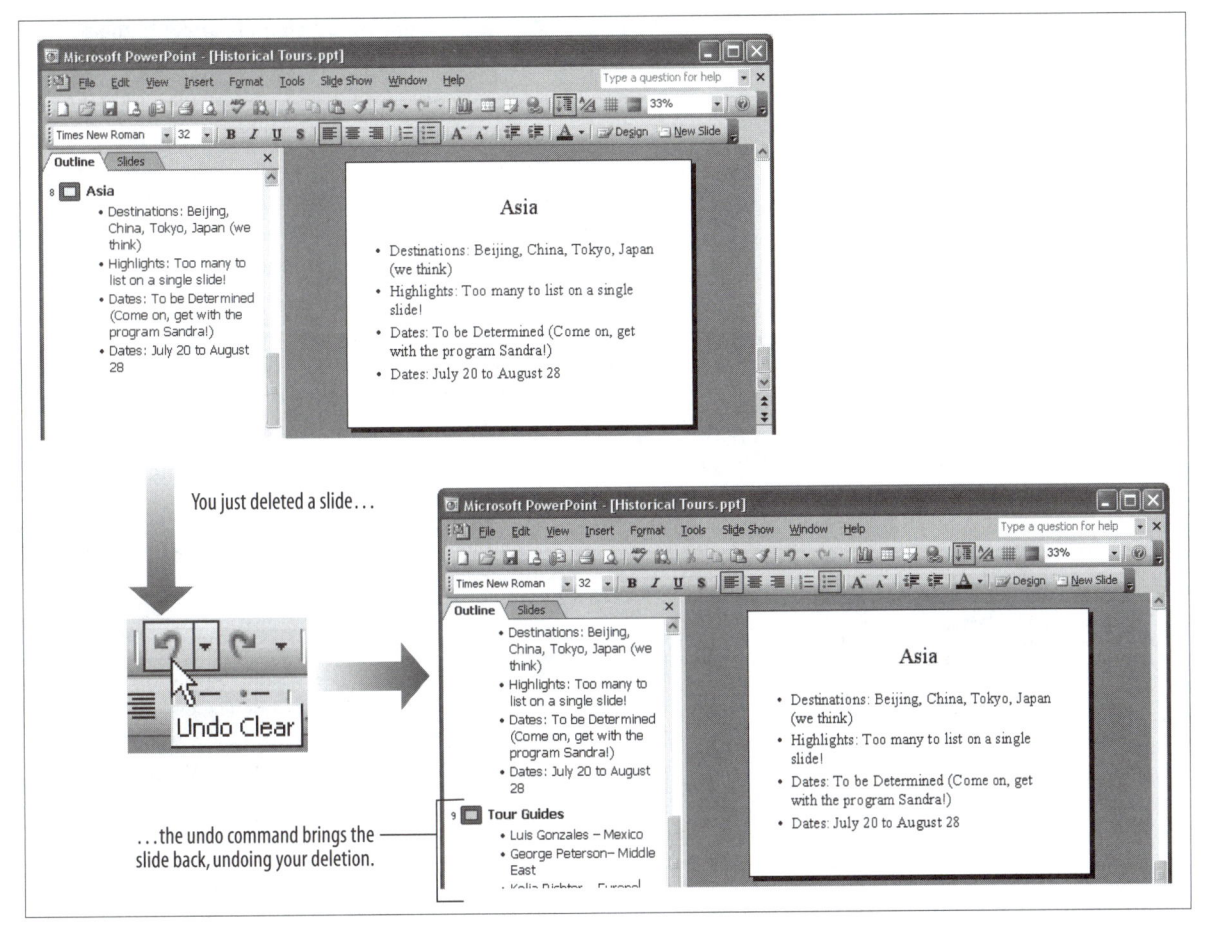

Using Undo, Redo, and Repeat

Figure 2-9. Undoing a slide deletion.

You may not want to admit this, but you're going to make mistakes when you use PowerPoint. You might accidentally delete a paragraph or slide you didn't mean to delete, or paste something you didn't mean to paste. Fortunately, PowerPoint has a wonderful feature called undo that does just that—undoes your mistakes and actions, making them as though they never happened. This lesson explains how you can undo both single and multiple mistakes, and how to redo your actions in case you change your mind.

1 Select **Slide 9** (the Tour Guides slide) by clicking to the left of the ▭ symbol, and then delete the selected slide by pressing the **Delete** key.

The selected slide disappears. Whoops! You didn't really want to delete that! Watch how you can undo your "mistake."

2 Click the **Undo button**.

Undo button

Other Ways to Undo:

- Select **Edit** → **Undo** from the menu.
- Press **<Ctrl>** + **<Z>**.

Poof! The deleted "Tour Guides" slide is back again. Hmmm…maybe you did want to delete the slide after all. Anything that can be undone can be redone if you change your mind or want to "undo an undo." Here's how you can redo the previous delete command.

3 Click the **Redo button**.

The "Tour Guides" slide disappears again.

Lesson 2.6
Using Undo, Redo, and Repeat

Redo button

Other Ways to Redo:

- Select **Edit** → **Redo** from the menu.
- Press <**Ctrl**> + <**Y**>.

Often, you will probably make not one, but several, mistakes, and it may be a minute or two before you've even realized you've made them. Fortunately, the programmers at Microsoft thought of this when they developed PowerPoint, because the undo feature is multileveled—meaning you can undo more than one mistake or action. The next few steps will show you how you can undo multiple errors.

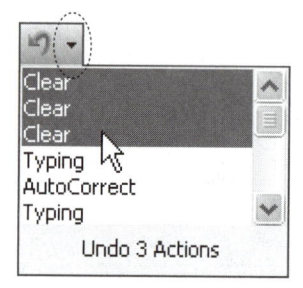

Multilevel Undo

4 On **Slide 8** (the Asia slide) click to the left of the **Highlights: Too many to list on a single slide!** line to select it and press the **Delete** key.

The selected line is deleted—your second mistake (the first was deleting the "Tour Guides" slide).

5 Press **Ctrl** + **End** to move to the end of the presentation.

Let's add another paragraph here—another "mistake."

6 Press **Ctrl** + **Enter** to add a new slide and type `This slide needs a lot of work!`

You've made enough mistakes now to see how multilevel undo works. Here's how to undo all of your mistakes.

7 Click the downward pointing arrow to the right of the undo button.

A list of your recent actions appears beneath the Undo button. Notice that there are more actions listed than just your three most recent "mistakes." If you wanted, you could undo any of the commands and actions you've made since you opened the current presentation. You don't want to undo everything—just the last three mistakes.

8 Select the second word **Clear** from the undo list (it should be the fourth action on the list).

The last three changes you made to the presentation—deleting a slide, a line, and adding a new paragraph—are all undone.

The opposite of the Undo command is the Repeat command, which repeats your last command or action, if possible. Here's how to use it.

9 Select **Slide 8** (the Asia slide) by clicking to the left of the ▦ symbol, and then delete the selected slide by pressing the **Delete** key.

You've just deleted the Asia slide. Now let's see how you can repeat your last command…

10 Select **Side 7** (the Europe slide) by clicking to the left of the ▦ symbol, and press **Ctrl** + **Y**.

PowerPoint repeats your last command and deletes the current slide.

11 Click the **Undo button** on the Standard toolbar twice to undo your deletions, and then save your work.

62

Chapter 2
Editing a Presentation

QUICK REFERENCE

TO UNDO:
- CLICK THE UNDO BUTTON ON THE STANDARD TOOLBAR.

OR...
- SELECT EDIT → UNDO FROM THE MENU.

OR...
- PRESS CTRL + Z.

TO REDO:
- CLICK THE REDO BUTTON ON THE STANDARD TOOLBAR.

OR...
- SELECT EDIT → REDO FROM THE MENU.

OR...
- PRESS CTRL + Y.

TO REPEAT AN ACTION:
- SELECT EDIT → REPEAT FROM THE MENU.

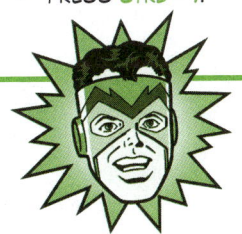

OR...
- PRESS CTRL + Y.

LESSON 2.7

Checking Your Spelling

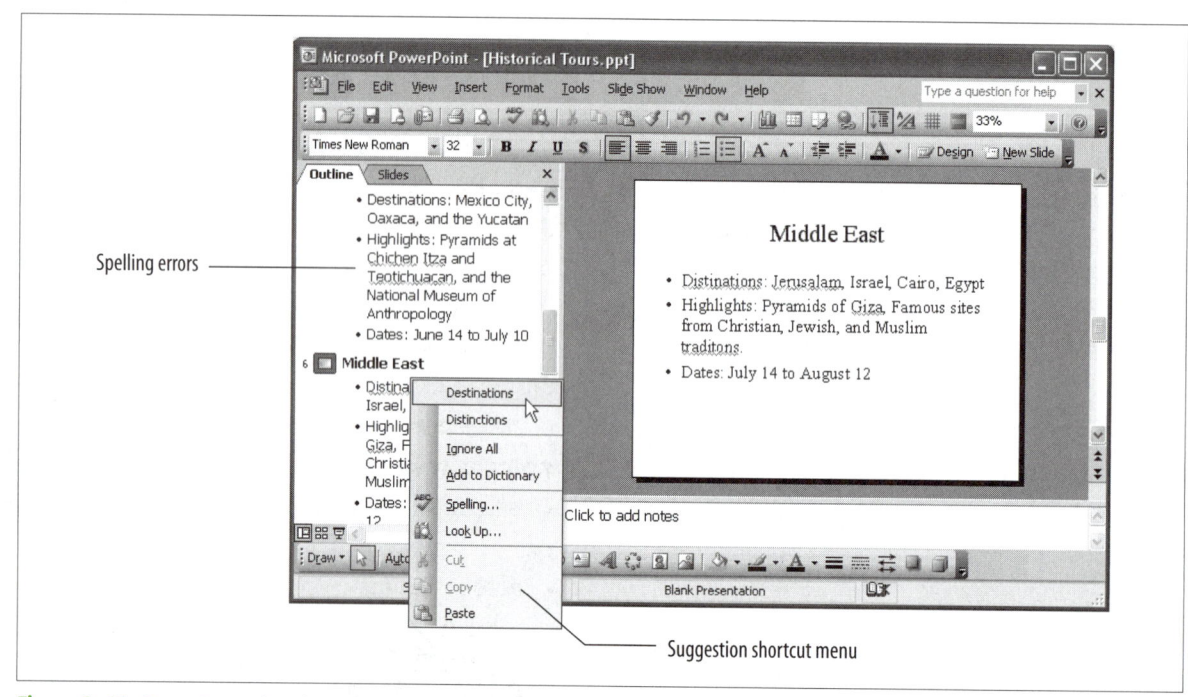

Figure 2-10. PowerPoint identifies spelling errors by underlining them in red.

Spell checking used to be a feature only available in word processing programs—but no more! You can use PowerPoint's spell checker to find and correct any spelling errors that you might have made in your presentations. PowerPoint's spell checker is shared and used by the other programs in the Microsoft Office suite. Any words you add to the custom spelling dictionary in one Microsoft Office program will be available in all the other programs. What's more, PowerPoint checks for spelling errors as you type, highlighting them with a squiggly red underline. Of course, you could fix spelling errors the hard way and manually retype them, but if you're not a spelling bee champion, it's much easier to right-click a spelling error and select one of PowerPoint's suggested spelling corrections.

This lesson will show you how you can correct the spelling in your slides, and how to tell PowerPoint to ignore words that it thinks are misspelled.

If you don't like on-the-fly spell checking, you can correct your spelling by clicking the **Spelling button** on the Standard toolbar or by selecting **Tools → Spelling** from the menu.

1 Right-click the red-underlined word **Distinations** on **Slide 6**.

Remember that a right-click is when you click something with the right mouse button.

A shortcut menu appears with suggestions for the correct spelling and several other options, as shown in Figure 2-10. Luckily, the correct spelling, "destinations" is one of the corrections listed.

NOTE *The correct spelling for a word usually appears in the list of corrections. If it doesn't, that either means spell checker doesn't have the word in its dictionary (names can sometimes cause this to happen), or else you've butchered the spelling of the word so badly that the spell checker doesn't recognize it.*

2 Click **Destinations** on the shortcut menu with the left mouse button.

PowerPoint makes the spelling correction. The next spelling error in the presentation is the very next word: "Jerusalam".

3 Right-click the red-underlined word Jerusalam.

Another shortcut menu appears, this time displaying any possible spelling corrections for the word "Jerusalam." There's only one suggested spelling correction listed here—and it's the one we're looking for.

4 Select Jerusalem from the shortcut menu.

The next spelling error in the presentation is on the next line—the word "Giza". Wait a second, "Giza" IS spelled correctly. Whenever the spell checker sees a word that it doesn't recognize, even if it is spelled correctly, it marks it as a spelling error. Names of people, places, and products are often flagged as spelling errors.

There are two things you can do when the spell checker doesn't recognize a correctly spelled word:

- **Ignore All:** Leaves the spelling as it is, and ignores it throughout the rest of your presentation.
- **Add to Dictionary:** Adds the word to the spelling dictionary so that PowerPoint won't nag you about it during future spell checks. Use this option for nonstandard words you use often.

5 Right-click the red-underlined word Giza, then select Ignore All from the shortcut menu.

The spell checker ignores the word "Giza" and its annoying, red underline disappears. There's still one more spelling error nearby.

6 Right-click the red-underlined word traditons located on the next line.

7 Select traditions from the shortcut menu.

PowerPoint makes the correction.

No doubt about it, the spell checker is a great tool to assist you in creating accurate slides. It's important to note, however, that PowerPoint will not catch all of your spelling errors. For example, if you mistyped the word "had" as "hat" PowerPoint won't catch it because "hat" is a correctly spelled word.

QUICK REFERENCE

TO CORRECT A SPELLING ERROR:

- RIGHT-CLICK THE SPELLING ERROR AND SELECT THE CORRECTION FROM THE SHORTCUT MENU.

OR...

- CORRECT THE SPELLING ERROR BY RETYPING IT.

TO IGNORE A SPELLING ERROR:

- RIGHT-CLICK THE SPELLING ERROR AND SELECT IGNORE ALL FROM THE SHORTCUT MENU.

TO ADD A WORD TO THE SPELLING DICTIONARY:

- RIGHT-CLICK THE WORD YOU WANT TO ADD AND SELECT ADD TO DICTIONARY FROM THE SHORTCUT MENU.

LESSON 2.8
Finding and Replacing Information

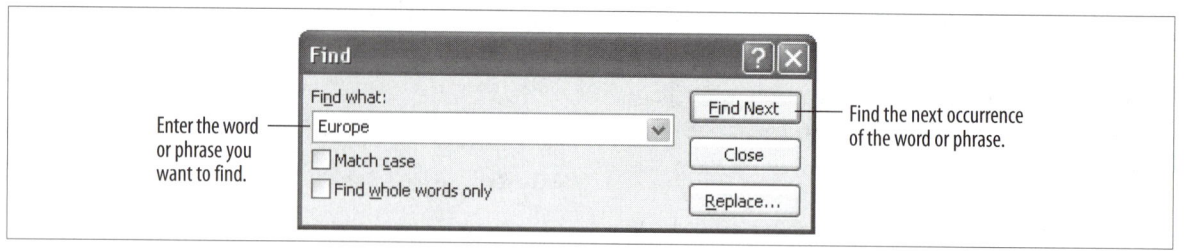

Figure 2-11. The Find dialog box.

- Enter the word or phrase you want to find.
- Find the next occurrence of the word or phrase.

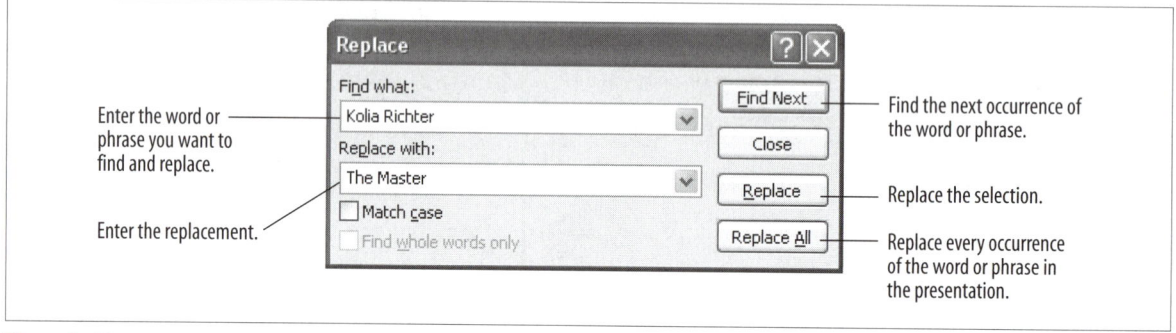

Figure 2-12. The Replace dialog box.

- Enter the word or phrase you want to find and replace.
- Enter the replacement.
- Find the next occurrence of the word or phrase.
- Replace the selection.
- Replace every occurrence of the word or phrase in the presentation.

For reasons known only to him, Kolia Richter has legally changed his name to "The Master." Great—now you'll have to go back to your presentation and find and replace every occurrence of "Kolia Richter" with "The Master." You don't even remember where his name was used—it could take you forever to go through all those slides. Or it could take you less than a minute if you use PowerPoint's Find and Replace function.

This lesson explains how to find specific words, phrases, and values in your presentation, and how to automatically replace those words, phrases, and values.

1 If you have been skipping around lessons, find and open the Lesson 2C presentation and save it as Historical Tours.

2 Press Ctrl + Home to move to the beginning of the presentation.

You don't have to move to the beginning of a presentation to find or replace something—but this will put us on the same page for this exercise.

3 Select Edit → Find from the menu.

The Find dialog box appears, as shown in Figure 2-11.

TIP Another way to find information is to press Ctrl + F.

4 In the Find what box type Europe.

You want to find every occurrence of the word "Europe" in the presentation.

5 Click the Find Next button.

PowerPoint jumps to the first occurrence of the word "Europe" it finds in the presentation—on Slide 2.

6 Click the Find Next button.

PowerPoint jumps to the next occurrence of the word "Europe" in the presentation, found on Slide 7.

7 Click Close to close the Find dialog box.

The Find dialog box closes. You can also replace information in a presentation, such as changing every occurrence of "Kolia Richter" in the presentation to "The Master."

8 Select Edit → Replace from the menu.

The Replace dialog box appears, as shown in Figure 2-12.

Chapter 2
Editing a Presentation

TIP *Another way to find and replace information is to press Ctrl + H.*

9 In the **Find what** text box type **Kolia Richter**.

You want to replace every occurrence of the phrase "Kolia Richter" with the phrase "The Master."

10 Select the **Replace with box** by clicking it or by pressing the **Tab** key, and type **The Master**.

11 Click **Replace All**.

The Replace dialog box disappears, and you're back to your presentation. Notice how all the occurrences of the word "Kolia Richter" (there's only one on Slide 9) have been replaced with "The Master."

PowerPoint finds all the occurrences of the phrase "Kolia Richter" in the presentation and replaces them with "The Master."

NOTE *Think before you use the Replace All button—you might not want it to replace every instance of a word or phrase! You can find and replace each individual occurrence of a label or value by clicking Find Next and then Replace.*

12 Click **Close**.

QUICK REFERENCE

TO FIND INFORMATION IN A PRESENTATION:

1. SELECT **EDIT** → **FIND** FROM THE MENU.
   OR...
   PRESS **CTRL** + **F**.
2. ENTER THE TEXT YOU WANT TO SEARCH FOR IN THE FIND WHAT BOX.
3. CLICK THE **FIND NEXT BUTTON**.
4. REPEAT STEP 3 UNTIL YOU FIND THE SPECIFIC TEXT THAT YOU ARE LOOKING FOR.

TO FIND AND REPLACE INFORMATION:

1. SELECT **EDIT** → **REPLACE** FROM THE MENU.
   OR...
   PRESS **CTRL** + **H**.
2. ENTER THE TEXT YOU WANT TO SEARCH FOR IN THE FIND WHAT BOX.
3. ENTER THE TEXT YOU WANT TO REPLACE IT WITH IN THE REPLACE WITH BOX.
4. CLICK THE **FIND NEXT BUTTON**.
5. CLICK THE **REPLACE BUTTON** TO REPLACE THE TEXT.
6. REPEAT **STEPS 4 AND 5** IF THERE IS MORE THAN ONE OCCURRENCE THAT YOU WANT TO REPLACE.
   OR...
   CLICK **REPLACE ALL** TO REPLACE EVERY OCCURRENCE OF TEXT IN THE PRESENTATION.

LESSON 2.9

Viewing a Presentation's Outline

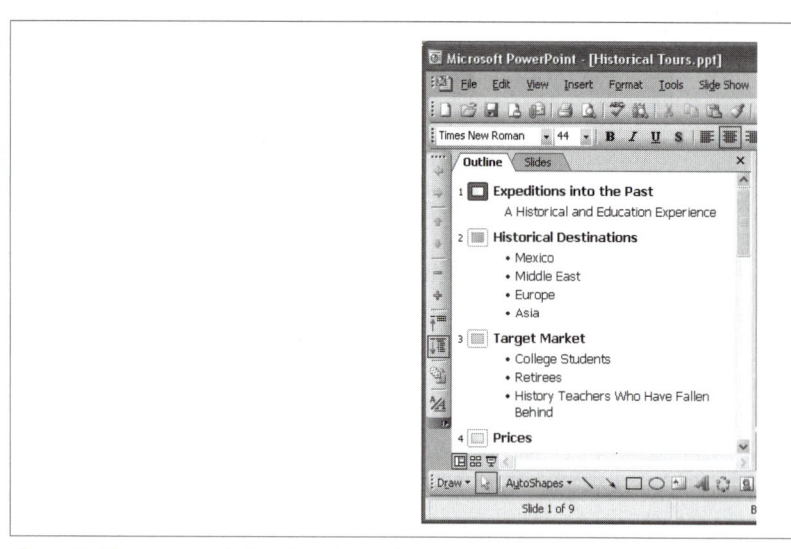

Figure 2-13. An expanded outline shows all the presentation's details.

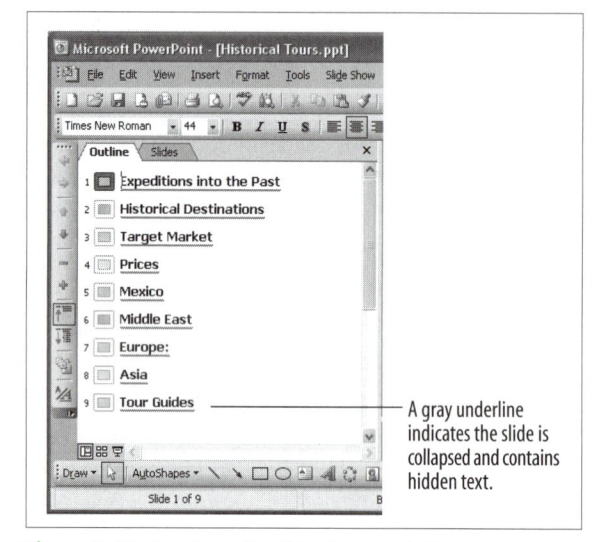

Figure 2-14. A collapsed outline shows only the presentation's slide titles.

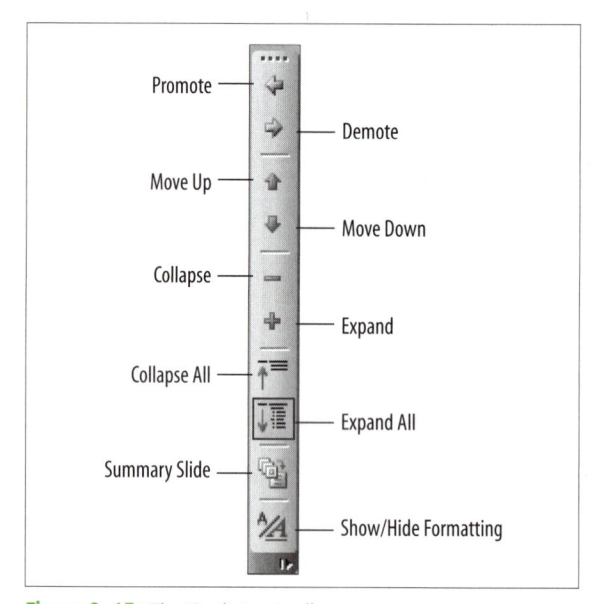

A gray underline indicates the slide is collapsed and contains hidden text.

Figure 2-15. The Outlining toolbar.

If your presentation has a lot of slides, it can become increasingly difficult to see its overall structure. Fortunately, PowerPoint's Outline pane can tame even the longest, wildest presentations and let you separate "the forest from the trees." The Outline pane lets you decide how much of your presentation you want to see. You can choose to view only the first main heading levels of your slide, several levels of headings and subheadings, or the entire presentation.

In this lesson you'll learn how to collapse an outline so that only the slide titles are shown and how to expand an outline so that you can once again see the slide details. First you'll need to summon the Outlining toolbar…

1 If it is not already displayed, select **View → Toolbars → Outlining** from the menu to display the Outlining toolbar.

The Outlining toolbar appears, as shown in Figure 2-15. Here's how to collapse a slide.

68

Chapter 2
Editing a Presentation

Collapse button

2 Double-click on the slide icon for Slide 2.

PowerPoint collapses the slide and only displays its title. A gray line appears underneath the slide title, indicating that it contains hidden details. Here's how to expand a slide to see any hidden details.

Expand button

3 Double-click on the slide icon for Slide 2 again.

The subpoints under Slide 2 reappear.

You can collapse individual slides, as you just did, or all the slides in a presentation.

4 Click the Collapse All button on the Outlining toolbar.

Collapse All button

PowerPoint collapses the entire presentation so that only the slide titles are displayed.

The Outline pane was designed to hide the appearance of a presentation so that you can concentrate on its content. You can even remove the text formatting from your outline if you find it somewhat distracting.

5 Click the Show Formatting button on the Outlining toolbar.

Show Formatting button

PowerPoint displays the outline without any text formatting. Don't worry—the text formatting is still there; it's just hidden from view. To redisplay a presentation's text formatting, simply click the Show Formatting button again.

Let's expand the entire outline—see if you can guess how to do it without looking at the next step. No peeking!

6 Click the Expand All button on the Outlining toolbar.

Expand All button

PowerPoint expands the presentation and displays all the slides' text.

Table 2-3. Buttons on the Outlining Toolbar

Button	Description
Promote	Promotes the paragraph to a higher level on the outline.
Demote	Demotes the paragraph to a lower level on the outline.
Move Up	Moves the paragraph up.
Move Down	Moves the paragraph down.
Collapse	Collapses the selected slide and displays only the slide heading.
Expand	Expands the selected slide and displays all of its content.

Lesson 2.9
Viewing a Presentation's Outline

Table 2-3. Buttons on the Outlining Toolbar (Continued)

Button	Description
Collapse All	Collapses an entire presentation and displays only the slide headings.
Expand All	Expands an entire presentation.
Summary Slide	Creates a summary slide from any selected slides.
Show Formatting	Show or hides text formatting.

QUICK REFERENCE

TO SHOW/HIDE THE OUTLINING TOOLBAR:
- SELECT VIEW → TOOLBARS → OUTLINING FROM THE MENU.

TO COLLAPSE A SLIDE:
- MAKE SURE THE INSERTION POINT IS IN THE SLIDE AND CLICK THE COLLAPSE BUTTON ON THE OUTLINING TOOLBAR.

TO EXPAND A SLIDE:
- MAKE SURE THE INSERTION POINT IS IN THE SLIDE AND CLICK THE EXPAND BUTTON ON THE OUTLINING TOOLBAR.

TO SHOW OR HIDE A PRESENTATION'S TEXT FORMATTING:
- CLICK THE SHOW FORMATTING BUTTON ON THE OUTLINING TOOLBAR.

Rearranging a Presentation's Outline

LESSON 2.10

1. Select the slide you want to move by clicking the slide icon.

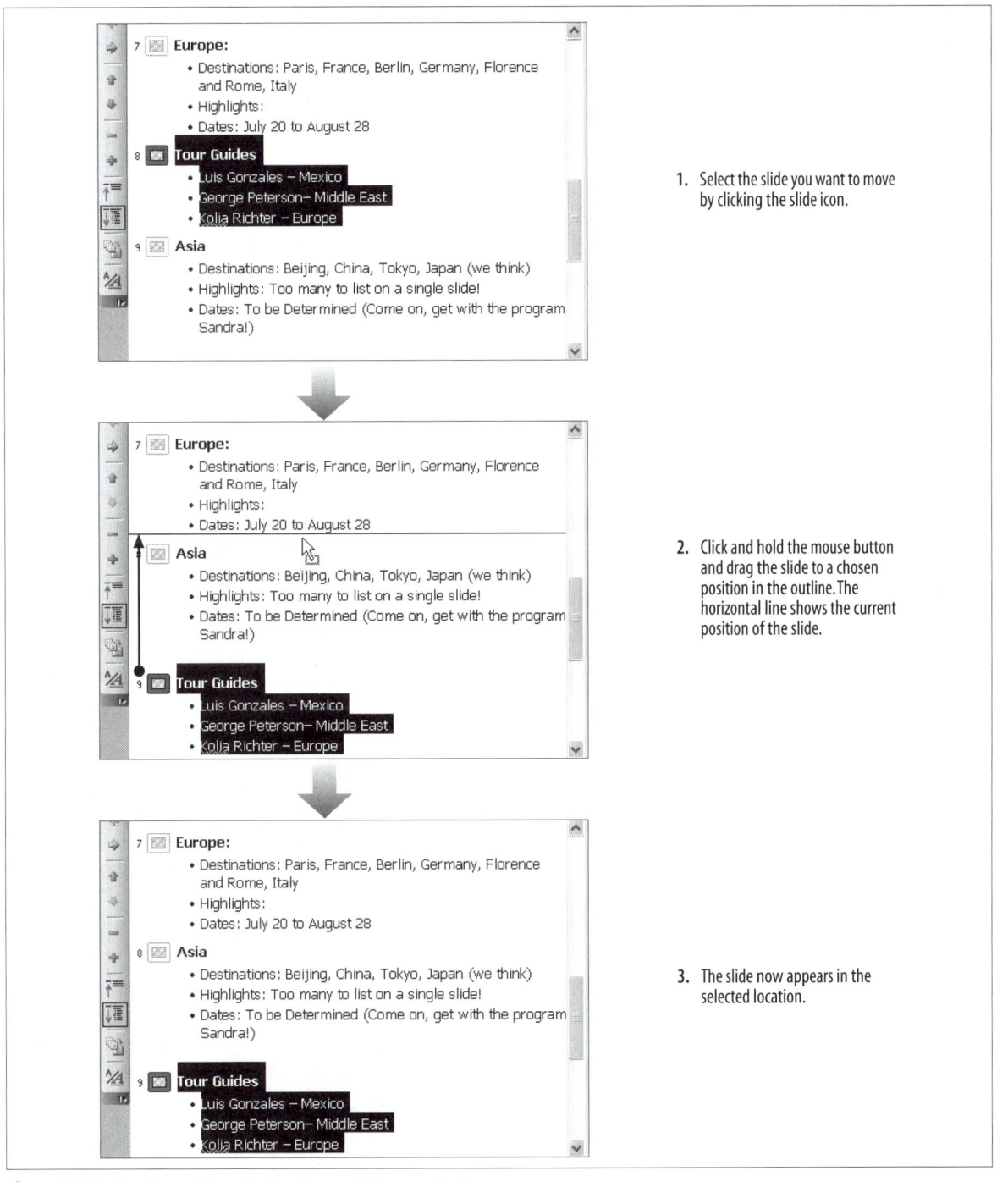

2. Click and hold the mouse button and drag the slide to a chosen position in the outline. The horizontal line shows the current position of the slide.

3. The slide now appears in the selected location.

Figure 2-16. Moving a slide with the drag and drop method.

71

Lesson 2.10
Rearranging a Presentation's Outline

Another benefit of working in the Outline pane is how easy it is to modify your presentation's content. You can change the order of points on a slide, or you can even rearrange the order of the slides themselves. This lesson will give you some practice rearranging the order of points and slides in your presentation's outline.

1 **If the Outlining toolbar isn't displayed, summon it by selecting View → Toolbars → Outlining from the menu.**

Now let's try rearranging the order of slides in the presentation.

2 **Click the Slide 9 slide icon.**

Make sure you've selected the entire slide and not just the "Tour Guides" heading. We want to move the entire slide, not just the slide heading.

NOTE When you want to move a slide in the Outline pane, make sure you select the entire slide by clicking the slide icon.

3 **Click the Move Up button on the Outlining toolbar.**

Move Up button

The selected "Tour Guides" slide moves up the outline, appearing beneath the "Dates: To Be Determined" subheading.

4 **Click the Move Up button on the Outlining toolbar four more times, until it appears above the Asia slide.**

The "Tour Guides" slide moves up the outline, one line at a time, and appears below the "Dates: July 20 to August 28" paragraph of the "Europe" slide.

Although it's easy, using the Move Up and Move Down buttons to move a slide or paragraph can be slow, especially if the destination is on the other side of a long presentation. Fortunately, as with so many other procedures, there is more than one way to move paragraphs and slides in PowerPoint—the drag and drop method.

5 **Hold the cursor over the Tour Guide slide icon, until the pointer changes to a ✥.**

To move a slide, click and hold the mouse button and drag the slide up or down to the desired position in the outline.

6 **Click and drag the slide above the Mexico slide, then release the mouse button.**

A horizontal line appears as you drag the slide, indicating where the slide will be moved.

You can now hide the Outlining toolbar since we're finished using it.

7 **Select View → Toolbars → Outlining from the menu to hide the Outlining toolbar.**

Using the drag and drop technique can be a little tricky if you're still a novice with the mouse. However, if you make a mistake and don't like where you moved a slide, you can always undo it by clicking the Undo button on the Standard toolbar, or by pressing Ctrl + Z.

QUICK REFERENCE

TO REARRANGE AN OUTLINE:

- SELECT THE SLIDE(S) OR PARAGRAPH(S) YOU WANT TO MOVE AND CLICK EITHER THE MOVE UP BUTTON OR MOVE DOWN BUTTON ON THE OUTLINING TOOLBAR.

OR...

- SELECT THE SLIDE(S) OR PARAGRAPH(S) YOU WANT TO MOVE AND DRAG THEM TO A NEW LOCATION IN THE OUTLINE.

LESSON 2.11

Inserting Symbols and Special Characters

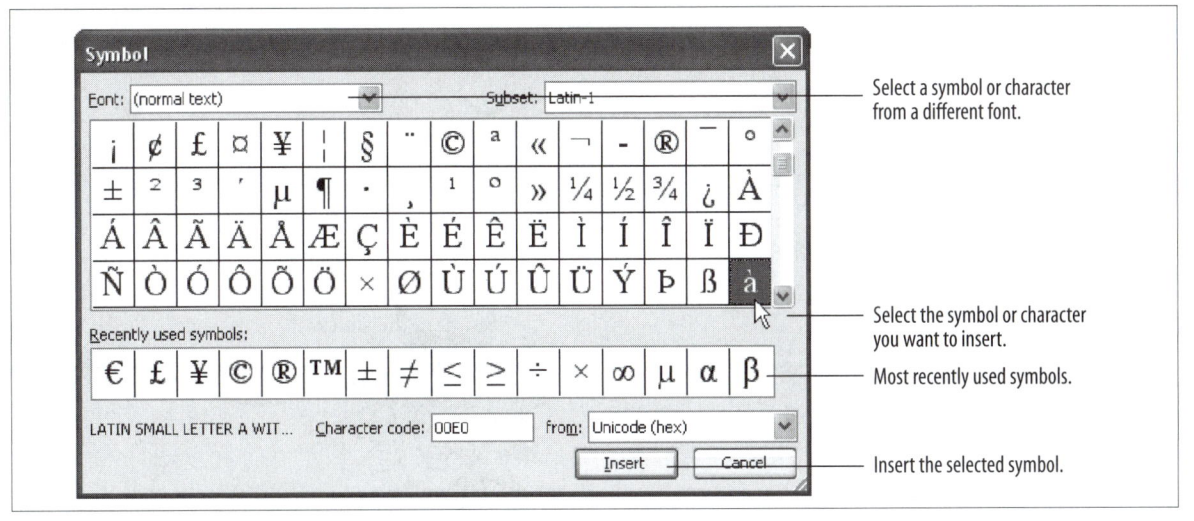

Figure 2-17. The Symbol dialog box.

Believe it or not, you can enter many more characters and symbols in a slide that cannot be found on the keyboard. For example, you can insert the copyright symbol (©), accented and foreign characters (Æ), silly characters (☺), and many, many more. In this lesson you will learn how to insert several of these special symbols into a slide.

1 If necessary, find and open the Lesson 2D presentation and save it as Historical Tours.

2 Move to the Mexico slide and move the insertion point immediately after the word Itza in Chichén Itza.

You were watching a special about Mexico last night on PBS and realized, to your horror, that the "a" in Itza is accented (á). After a sleepless night, you rush to the office to fix the problem. First you'll have to erase the incorrect, non-accented "a."

TIP *The symbols that appear depend on which fonts are installed on your computer.*

3 Delete the a from the word Itza.

Now that the offending character has been deleted, we can add a properly accented "á" in its place.

4 Select Insert → Symbol from the menu.

The Insert Symbol dialog box appears, as shown in Figure 2-17.

5 Verify that (normal text) appears in the Font list box. If it doesn't, click the Font list arrow and select (normal text).

Let's see if we can find the " á " character.

6 Find and click the letter á symbol.

You'll probably spend a few minutes looking for the tiny "á" symbol before you find it. Figure 2-17 will give you a better idea of where it is. Find it?

There is a list of the most recently used symbols on the bottom of the dialog box to make it easier if you have to return and insert the same symbol later.

7 Click Insert.

The " á " symbol is inserted, completing the proper spelling of Chichén Itzá. Whew! Now you will be able to sleep tonight!

8 Click Close to close the Symbol dialog box.

Lesson 2.11
Inserting Symbols and Special Characters

QUICK REFERENCE

TO INSERT A SYMBOL OR SPECIAL CHARACTER:
1. PLACE THE INSERTION POINT WHERE YOU WANT TO INSERT THE CHARACTER.
2. SELECT INSERT → SYMBOL FROM THE MENU.
3. SELECT THE SYMBOL YOU WANT AND CLICK INSERT.

LESSON 2.12

Working in Slide Sorter View

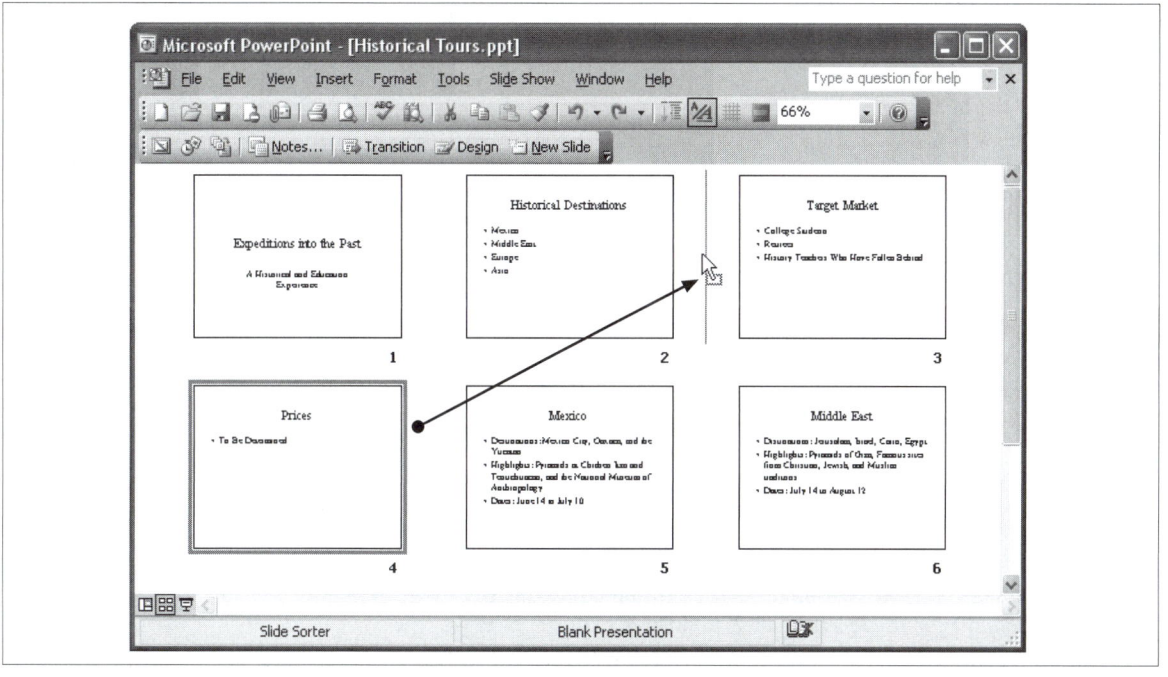

Figure 2-18. Rearranging the slide order by dropping and dragging in Slide Sorter View.

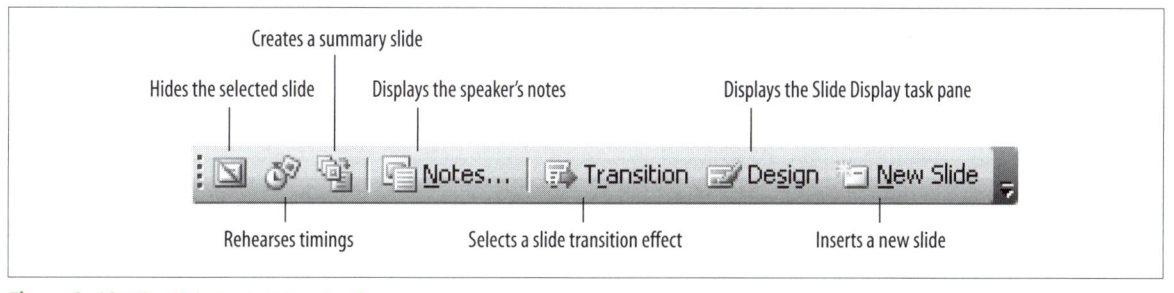

Figure 2-19. The Slide Sorter View toolbar.

Normal View is what you'll use the most when you create a PowerPoint presentation, but this view has a serious limitation: it doesn't let you view all the slides in your presentation at the same time. That's where Slide Sorter View comes in.

Slide Sorter View button

Other Ways to Switch to Slide Sorter View:

- Select **View** → **Slide Sorter** from the menu.

When you put pictures into a photo album, you probably lay all the pictures out on a table or floor so that you can look at all of them and decide in which order they should go. Slide Sorter View works on the same principle—it allows you to see thumbnails of all the slides in your presentation so that you can:

- Sort your slides into an order that works best for your presentation.
- Delete any slides.
- Hide slides that you don't want to include in a presentation or show any hidden slides (more on this in another lesson).
- Add animation and control how the slides appear and disappear (known as slide transitions—more on this in another lesson).
- Determine how long a slide should be displayed on the screen if you're creating an automated, standalone show (more on this in another lesson).

75

Lesson 2.12
Working in Slide Sorter View

As you can see, a lot of the power behind Slide Sorter view has to do with delivering your presentation—and that's the topic of a later chapter. In this lesson, you'll learn how to use Slide Sorter View to rearrange your slides, duplicate an entire slide, and delete a slide.

1 Switch to Slide Sorter View by clicking the Slide Sorter View button on the horizontal scroll bar.

TIP *You can also duplicate a slide by selecting the slide you want to duplicate and pressing Ctrl + D, or by copying and pasting the slide using standard copy and paste procedures.*

PowerPoint displays the presentation in Slide Sorter View, as shown in Figure 2-18. To move a slide in Slide Sorter View, click and drag it to new location. Move to the next step to give it a try.

2 Click Slide 4 (the Prices slide), hold down the mouse button, drag the slide immediately after Slide 2 (the Historical Destinations slide), and then release the mouse button, as shown in Figure 2-18.

You've just changed the order of your presentation, so that the Price slide will appear as the third slide in the presentation instead of the fourth slide.

Since Slide Sorter View lets you view all the slides in your presentation at once, there are several other slide-related chores that are easier to perform here than in Normal View, such as duplicating a slide. Duplicating a slide copies everything on the slide—text, formatting, you name it. Duplicating is useful when you need to churn out several slides that have the same title, images, and formatting.

3 Select Slide 1 (the title slide) and select Edit → Duplicate from the menu.

PowerPoint creates an exact duplicate of the selected title slide. In case you're wondering, duplicating a slide is really a one-step process for selecting, copying, and pasting a slide.

We don't really need the duplicated slide in our presentation, so this is a good place to learn how to delete a slide in Slide Sorter View.

4 Select the duplicate title slide and press the Delete key.

Wow! That was easy!

Let's delete another slide while we're at it:

5 Select the Asia slide and delete it by pressing the Delete key.

Deleting slides in Slide Sorter View is easy—almost too easy. If you accidentally delete a slide you didn't really want to delete, you can always undo your acting with the trusty Undo command: by clicking the Undo button on the Standard toolbar or by pressing Ctrl + Z.

QUICK REFERENCE

TO SWITCH TO SLIDE SORTER VIEW:
- CLICK THE ▦ SLIDE SORTER VIEW BUTTON ON THE HORIZONTAL SCROLL BAR.

OR...
- SELECT VIEW → SLIDE SORTER FROM THE MENU.

TO MOVE A SLIDE (IN SLIDE SORTER VIEW):
1. CLICK THE SLIDE THAT YOU WANT TO MOVE. TO SELECT AND MOVE MULTIPLE SLIDES, HOLD DOWN THE SHIFT KEY AS YOU SELECT EACH SLIDE.
2. DRAG THE SLIDE(S) TO A NEW LOCATION AND RELEASE THE MOUSE BUTTON.

TO DELETE A SLIDE (IN SLIDE SORTER VIEW):
- CLICK THE SLIDE AND PRESS THE DELETE KEY.

TO DUPLICATE A SLIDE (IN SLIDE SORTER VIEW):
- CLICK THE SLIDE AND PRESS CTRL + D.
- SELECT EDIT → DUPLICATE FROM THE MENU.

LESSON 2.13

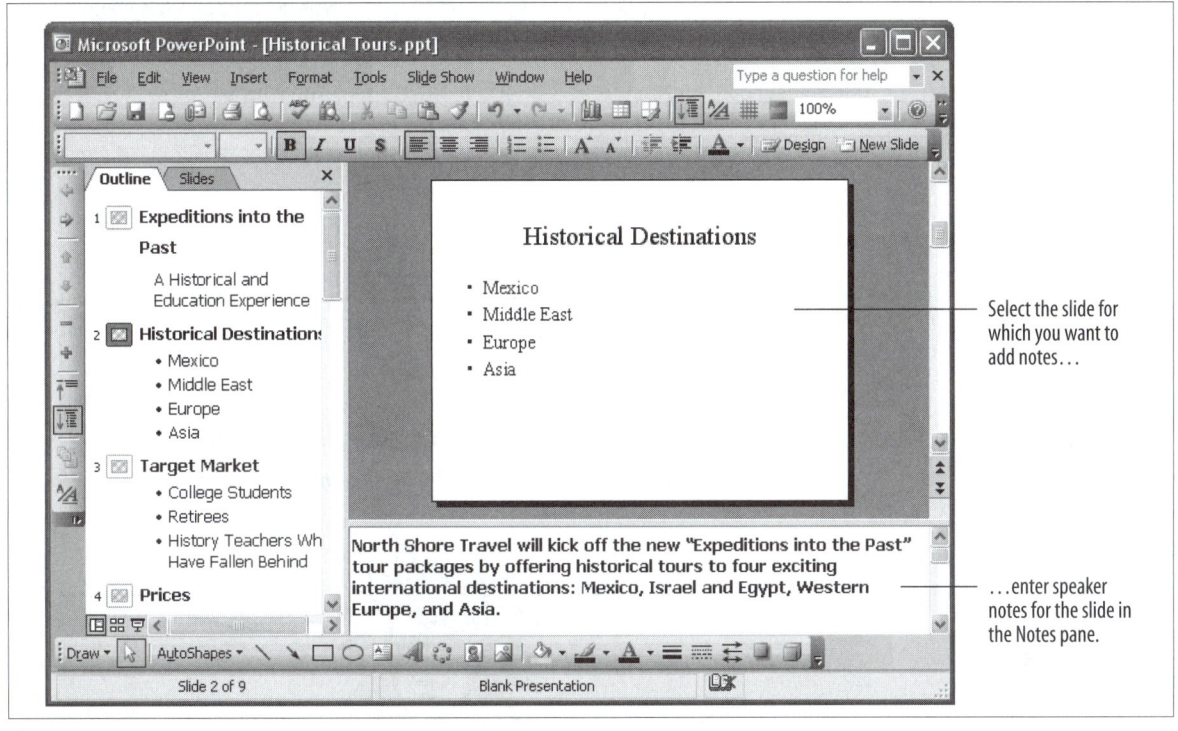

Adding Notes to Your Slides

Figure 2-20. Enter notes for each slide in the Notes pane.

Unless you have a perfect memory, you're going to need notes to help you remember what to say about each slide when you deliver a presentation. PowerPoint's notes are like the cue cards you use during a speech, reminding you to tell a joke, make eye contact, and about any key points you want to make. Notes don't appear on the slide show presentation itself, but they can be printed so that you can use them when you deliver your presentation.

1 If necessary, find and open the Lesson 2E presentation and save it as Historical Tours.

2 Click the Normal View button and select slide 2 from the Slides tab.

PowerPoint returns to Normal View. To add speaker notes to a slide, all you have to do is click the Notes pane as shown in Figure 2-20 and begin typing.

3 Click in the Notes pane and type the following paragraph:

North Shore Travel will kick off the new "Expeditions into the Past" tour packages by offering historical tours to four exciting international destinations: Mexico, Israel and Egypt, Western Europe, and Asia. Each tour will explore the region's most important and interesting historical sites. For example, those who enroll in the Middle East tour will be visiting Jerusalem, Cairo, the Egyptian pyramids at Giza, and many famous sites from Christian, Jewish, and Muslim traditions. Let's take a closer look at each of the new "Expeditions into the Past" tour packages. (I should really try to tell some witty joke here to keep my audience awake!)

Compare your slide to the one shown in Figure 2-20.

77

Lesson 2.13
Adding Notes to Your Slides

You can also use Notes Page View to enter or view notes. This view is especially convenient because it displays the slide and its notes on a full page. It also has a larger area in which to enter your notes, and you can add images or tables in the notes area.

4 Select **View** → **Notes Page** from the menu.

PowerPoint displays the slide and its notes.

You can zoom in on the page to work with the notes more easily.

5 Save your work.

QUICK REFERENCE

TO ADD NOTES TO A SLIDE:
- MAKE SURE YOU'RE IN NORMAL VIEW AND BEGIN TYPING YOUR NOTES IN THE **NOTES PANE**.

TO USE NOTES PAGE VIEW:
- SELECT **VIEW** → **NOTES PAGE** FROM THE MENU.

Working with Multiple Windows

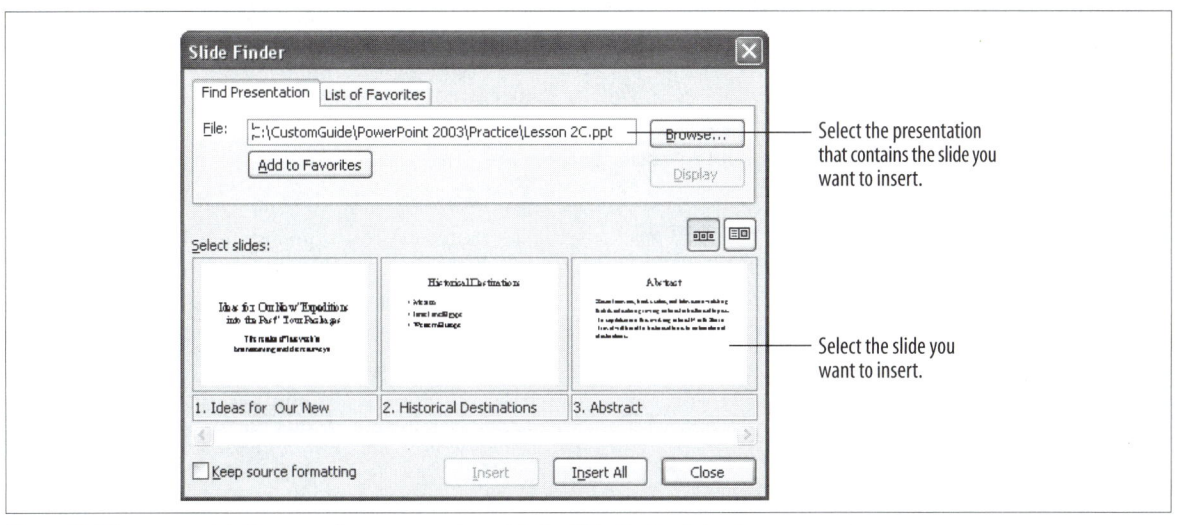

LESSON 2.14

Figure 2-21. Insert a slide from another presentation with the Slide Finder dialog box.

Select the presentation that contains the slide you want to insert.

Select the slide you want to insert.

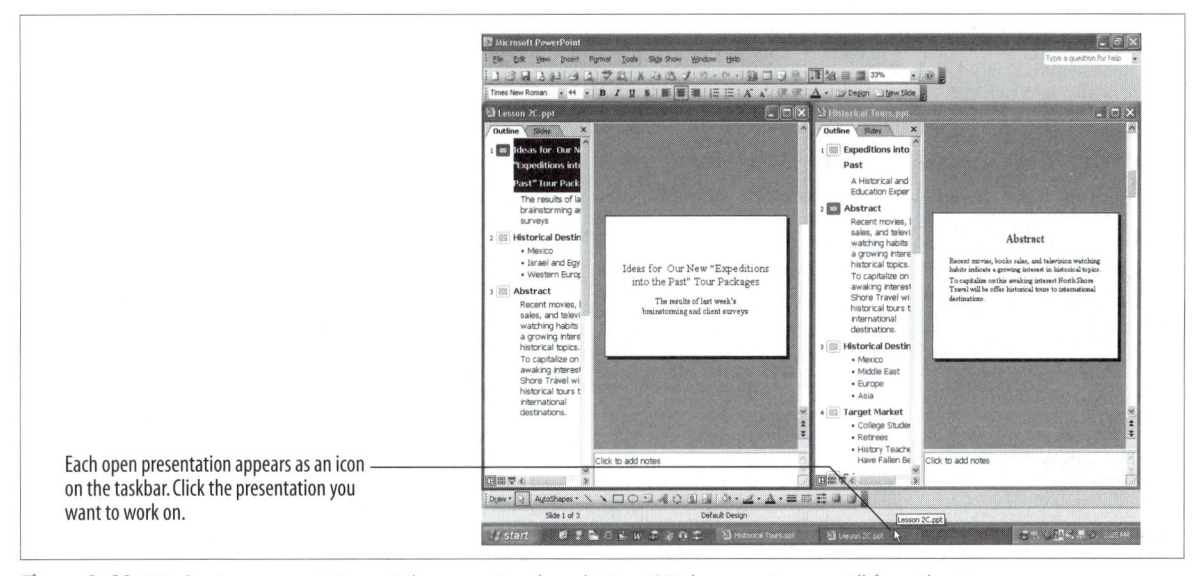

Each open presentation appears as an icon on the taskbar. Click the presentation you want to work on.

Figure 2-22. Display two presentations at the same time by selecting Window → Arrange All from the menu.

One of the many benefits of the Windows operating system is that you can open and work with several files at the same time, and PowerPoint is no exception to this rule. Each presentation you open in PowerPoint is displayed in its own separate window. This lesson explains how to open and work with more than one presentation. First though, let's take a look at how to insert a slide from another presentation.

TIP *Use the Window menu to switch between any open presentations.*

1 Press **Ctrl** + **Home** to move to the beginning of the presentation, then select **Insert** → **Slides from Files** from the menu.

The Slide Finder box appears. You need to specify the name and location of the presentation that contains the slide(s) you want to insert.

79

Lesson 2.14
Working with Multiple Windows

2 Click the Browse button, navigate to your practice folder or disk, then find and double-click the Lesson 2F presentation.

Next you need to display the slides in the Lesson 2F presentation and select the slide(s) you want to insert.

3 Click the Display button if the Slide Finder does not automatically display thumbnails of the slides in the presentation.

The Slide Finder dialog box displays thumbnails of all the slides in the presentation, as shown in Figure 2-21—now all you have to do is select the slide(s) you want to insert.

4 Select the third slide (Abstract) in the Lesson 2F presentation, click Insert and then click Close.

PowerPoint inserts the selected slide immediately after the current slide. Now let's look at how to work with several open presentations. First we'll need to open another presentation...

5 Without closing the current Historical Tours presentation, open the Lesson 2F presentation.

There's the Lesson 2F presentation, but where did our Historical Tours presentation go? Don't worry, it's still there in a window behind the Lesson 2F presentation.

6 Select Window from the menu.

The Window menu displays all the presentations that are currently open. Simply select the presentation you want to work on.

7 Select Historical Tours from the Window menu.

The Historical Tours presentation appears. Instead of selecting an open presentation from the Windows menu, you can also select an open presentation by clicking its icon on the Windows taskbar. The Lesson 2F presentation is still open, but you can't see it because it's located behind the Historical Tours presentation window.

8 Select Window → Arrange All from the menu.

Both presentations—the Lesson 2F and Historical Tours—appear in the PowerPoint window, as shown in Figure 2-22. Sometimes it's useful to look at more than one presentation at a time—especially if you want to copy text or objects from one presentation to the other.

9 Maximize the Historical Tours window by clicking its Maximize button.

The Historical Tours presentation once again fills the entire PowerPoint window. See Table 2-4 for descriptions of the three window states.

10 Save your work.

Table 2-4. The Three Window Sizes

Window State	Description
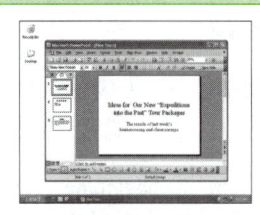	A presentation window in a **Maximized** state fills the entire PowerPoint window, or the desktop, allowing you to see as much of a presentation as possible. PowerPoint normally opens presentations in Maximized windows.
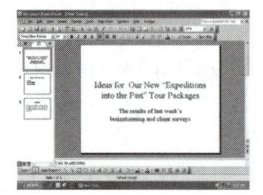	A presentation window with a **Restore** button usually fills the entire screen and can be restored to a smaller size.

Chapter 2
Editing a Presentation

Table 2-4. The Three Window Sizes (Continued)

Window State	Description
	A **Minimized** window appears only as an icon on the Windows taskbar. Minimize a presentation when you need to put it away for the time being and work on something else. You can restore a minimized window by selecting the presentation from the taskbar.

QUICK REFERENCE

TO SWITCH BETWEEN MULTIPLE OPEN PRESENTATIONS:

- CLICK THE PRESENTATION ON THE WINDOWS TASKBAR.

OR...

- SELECT **WINDOW** FROM THE MENU BAR AND SELECT THE NAME OF THE PRESENTATION YOU WANT TO VIEW.

TO VIEW MULTIPLE WINDOWS AT THE SAME TIME:

- SELECT **WINDOW** → **ARRANGE ALL**.

TO MAXIMIZE A WINDOW:

- CLICK THE WINDOW'S **MAXIMIZE BUTTON**.

TO RESTORE A WINDOW:

- CLICK THE WINDOW'S **RESTORE BUTTON**.

TO MANUALLY RESIZE A WINDOW:

1. POSITION THE MOUSE POINTER OVER THE EDGE OF THE WINDOW.
2. HOLD DOWN THE MOUSE BUTTON AND DRAG THE MOUSE TO RESIZE THE WINDOW.
3. RELEASE THE MOUSE BUTTON.

TO MOVE A WINDOW:

- DRAG THE WINDOW'S TITLE BAR TO THE LOCATION WHERE YOU WANT TO POSITION THE WINDOW.

81

LESSON 2.15 Collecting and Pasting Multiple Items

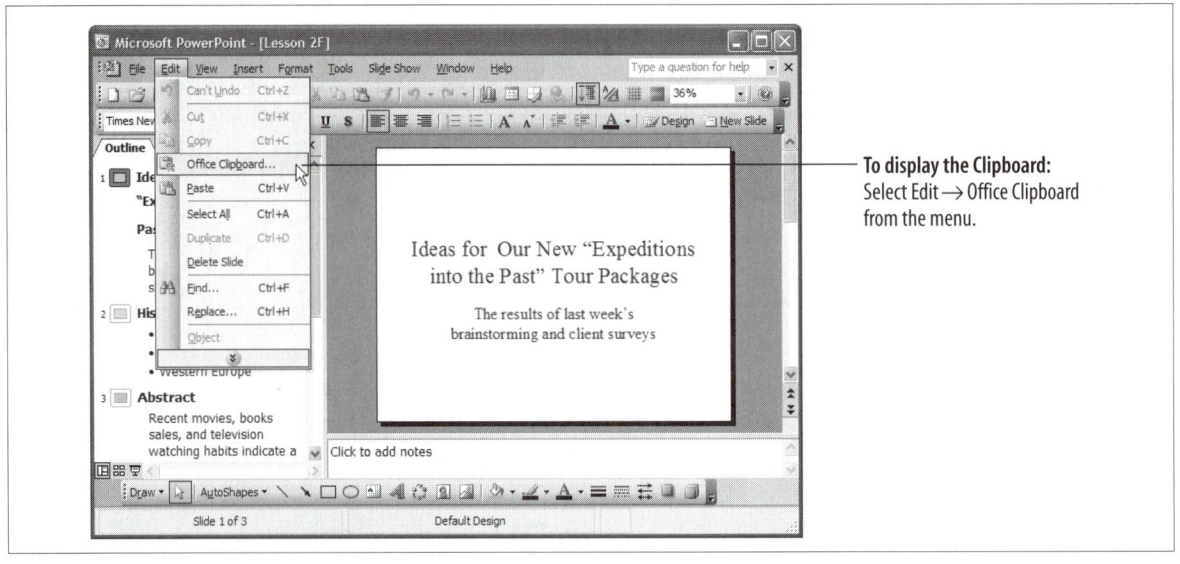

Figure 2-23. The Clipboard task pane displays the cut or copied objects you've collected.

To display the Clipboard: Select Edit → Office Clipboard from the menu.

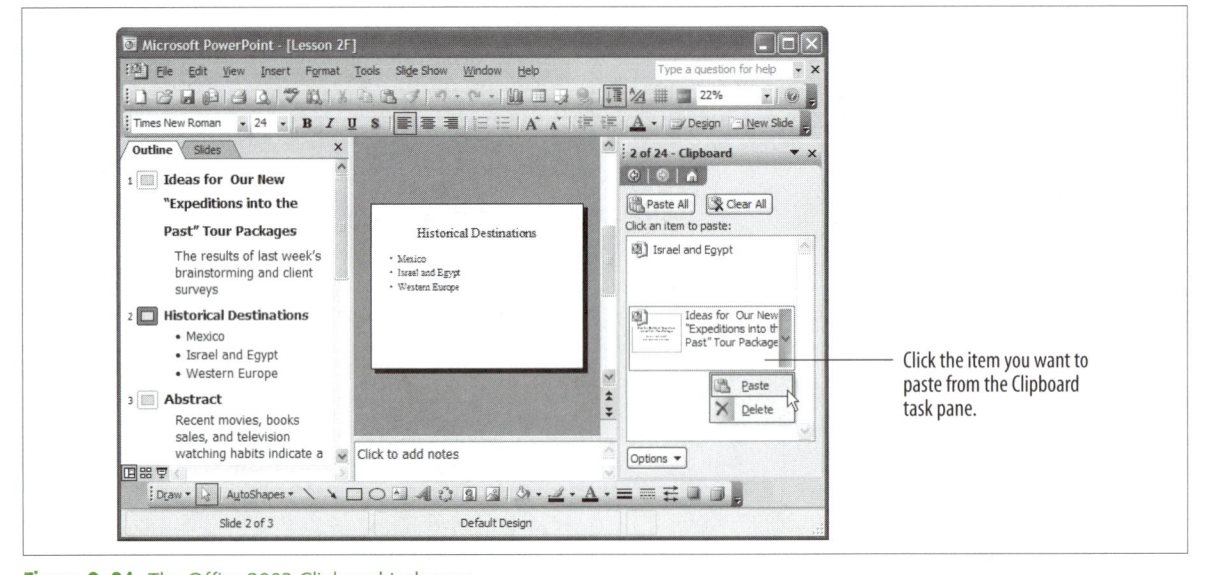

Figure 2-24. The Office 2003 Clipboard task pane.

Click the item you want to paste from the Clipboard task pane.

If you do a lot of cutting, copying, and pasting, you will probably appreciate PowerPoint 2003's new and improved Office 2003 clipboard, which holds 24 cut or copied objects.

You can use the Office Clipboard to collect and paste multiple items. For example, you can copy text in a Microsoft Word document, switch to Excel and copy a drawing object, switch to PowerPoint and copy a bulleted list, switch to Access and copy a datasheet, and then switch back to Word and paste the collection of copied items.

1 Switch to the **Lesson 2F** presentation.

This presentation contains several items that need to be copied and pasted into the "Historical Destinations" presentation. Instead of switching between the two presentations to copy and paste the items, you can use the Office 2003 Clipboard to copy and/or cut several items and then paste them all at once. In order to "collect and paste" multiple items you need to display the Clipboard task pane.

Chapter 2
Editing a Presentation

2 Select **Edit → Office Clipboard** from the menu.

The Office 2003 Clipboard task pane appears, as shown in Figure 2-24. Anything you cut or copy (up to 24 items) will appear on the Clipboard.

3 Click the **slide 1 icon** in the Outline pane, then copy the selected slide by clicking the **Copy button** on the Standard toolbar.

PowerPoint copies the slide to the Office clipboard and a Microsoft PowerPoint icon appears on the Clipboard pane to indicate the copied slide. Instead of switching back to the "Historical Destinations" presentation to paste the copied text, here's how you can copy (or cut) several things to the Office 2003 clipboard.

4 Select the line **Israel and Egypt** on Slide 2 and click the **Copy button** on the Standard toolbar.

Copy button

Other Ways to Copy:
- Select **Edit → Copy** from the menu.
- Press **<Ctrl>** + **<C>**.

PowerPoint copies the selected text to the Clipboard and another PowerPoint icon appears in the task pane. Don't worry if your Clipboard has several more icons—they represent any text you may have cut or copied earlier.

The type of clipboard icon indicates which program the object was collected from, as described in Table 2-5.

5 Switch to the **Historical Destinations** presentation by clicking its icon on the Windows taskbar.

To paste an object from the Office clipboard, simply click the icon you want to paste.

6 Place the insertion point immediately after the text **A Historical and Educational Experience** on Slide 1 in the Outline pane, and click the **Ideas For Our New "Expeditions into the Past" Tour Packages** icon in the Clipboard task pane.

PowerPoint pastes the selected contents of the Office clipboard. This creates a new slide.

7 Select the **Middle East** line in Slide 4, then click the **Israel and Egypt** icon in the Clipboard task pane.

Move on to the next step and close the Clipboard task pane.

8 Click the Clipboard task pane's **Close button**.

You won't need either of these presentations anymore, so…

9 Save your work and close all open presentations.

Table 2-5. Icons in the Clipboard Task Pane

Clipboard Icons	Description Contents
	Object cut or copied from a Microsoft Access 2003 database
	Object cut or copied from a Microsoft Excel 2003 workbook
	Object cut or copied from a Microsoft PowerPoint 2003 presentation
	Object cut or copied from a Microsoft Word 2003 document

Lesson 2.15
Collecting and Pasting Multiple Items

Table 2-5. Icons in the Clipboard Task Pane (Continued)

Clipboard Icons	Description Contents
	Web page contents cut or copied from Microsoft Internet Explorer
	Cut or copied graphic object
	Object cut or copied from a program other than Microsoft Office 2003

QUICK REFERENCE

TO DISPLAY THE CLIPBOARD TASK PANE:

- SELECT EDIT → OFFICE CLIPBOARD FROM THE MENU.

TO ADD ITEMS TO THE OFFICE CLIPBOARD:

- COPY AND/OR CUT THE ITEMS AS YOU NORMALLY WOULD, OR CONSECUTIVELY.

TO VIEW THE CONTENTS OF A CLIPBOARD ITEM:

- POINT TO THE ITEM ON THE CLIPBOARD TASK PANE.

TO PASTE FROM THE OFFICE CLIPBOARD:

- DISPLAY THE CLIPBOARD TASK PANE AND THEN CLICK THE ITEM YOU WANT TO PASTE. CLICK THE PASTE ALL BUTTON TO PASTE EVERYTHING.

LESSON 2.16

File Management

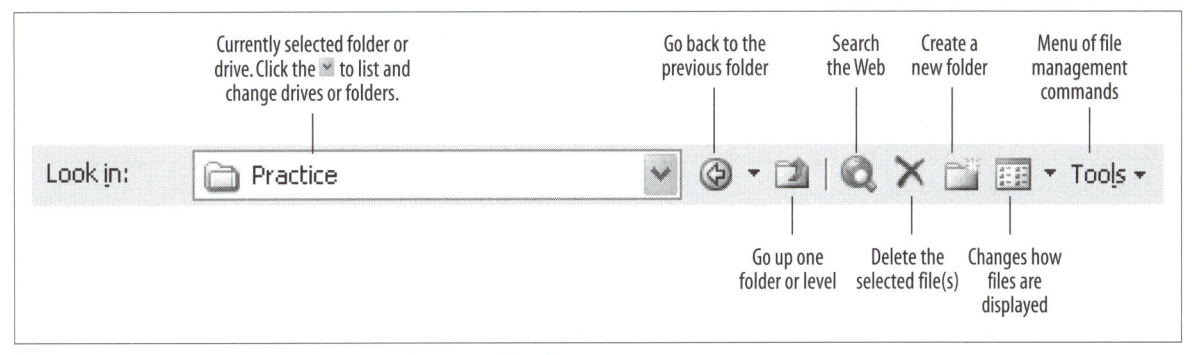

Figure 2-25. The Open and Save As dialog boxes' toolbar.

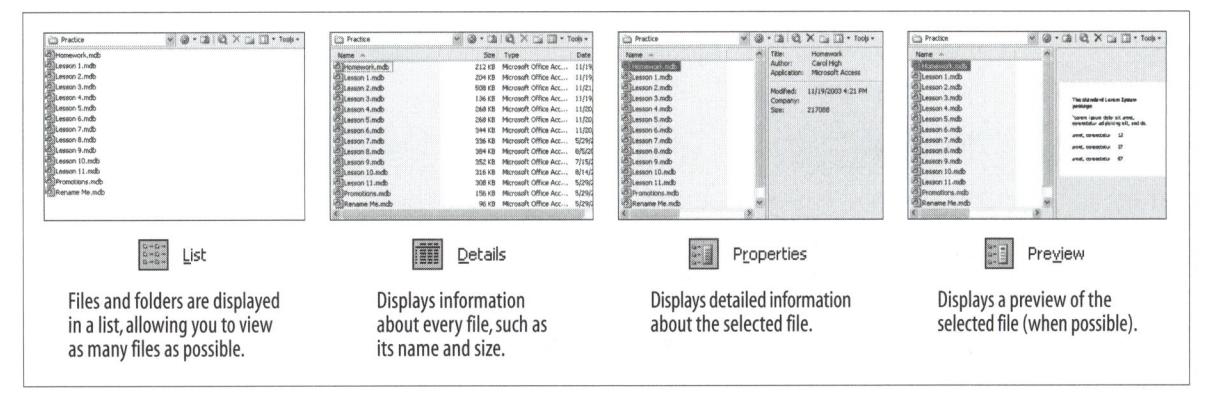

Toolbar labels:
- Currently selected folder or drive. Click the ⌄ to list and change drives or folders.
- Go back to the previous folder
- Search the Web
- Create a new folder
- Menu of file management commands
- Go up one folder or level
- Delete the selected file(s)
- Changes how files are displayed

List — Files and folders are displayed in a list, allowing you to view as many files as possible.

Details — Displays information about every file, such as its name and size.

Properties — Displays detailed information about the selected file.

Preview — Displays a preview of the selected file (when possible).

Figure 2-26. The Views button lets you change how files are displayed in the Open or Save As dialog boxes.

File management includes moving, copying, deleting, and renaming the files you've created. Although it's a little easier to work with and organize your files using Windows Explorer or My Computer, you can also perform a surprising number of file management chores right from inside Microsoft PowerPoint 2003—especially with its new and improved Open and Save dialog boxes.

1 Click the Open button on the Standard toolbar.

Open button

The Open dialog box appears. The Open dialog box is normally used to open files, but you can also use it to perform several file management functions. There are two different ways to access file management commands from inside the Open or Save As dialog boxes:

- Select a file and then select the command you want from the dialog box's Tools menu.
- Right-click a file and select the command you want from the shortcut menu.

2 Right-click the Rename Me file.

A shortcut menu appears with a list of available file management commands for the selected file.

3 Select Rename from the shortcut menu, type Home Budget, and press Enter.

You have just changed the name of the selected file from "Rename Me" to "Home Budget". Instead of right-clicking the file, you could have selected it and then selected Rename from the Tools menu. Move on to the next step to learn how to delete a file.

4 Click the Home Budget file to select it and press the Delete key.

A dialog box appears, asking you to confirm the deletion of the Home Budget file.

85

Lesson 2.16
File Management

5 Click **Yes**.

The Home Budget file is deleted. If you work with and create numerous files, you may find it difficult to remember what you named a file. In order to find the file(s) you're looking for, it can help to preview your files without opening them.

6 Click the **Views button arrow** and select **Preview**.

The Open dialog box changes the display of PowerPoint files in the Practice folder or disk from List View to Preview View. To see the contents of a file, select it in the file list on the left side of the dialog box, and it will appear in the Preview area on the right side of the dialog box. Try previewing the contents of a file without opening it now.

7 Click the **Lesson 2A** file.

The Lesson 2A file is selected, and a preview of its contents appears in the Preview section. Change back to List mode to display as many files in the window as possible.

8 Click the **Views button arrow**, select **List** to display the files in list view, then close the dialog box by clicking **Cancel**.

Table 2-6. File Shortcut Menu Commands

Command	Description
Open	Opens the selected file.
Open With . . .	Opens the presentation using the program of your choice.
Scan with Norton Antivirus	Choose this option when you are receiving a presentation via email to make sure it does not contain a virus.
Select	Selects the file you have highlighted; works the same as double-clicking.
New	Creates a new slide.
Print	Sends the selected file to the default printer.
Show	Displays the slide show.
Send To	Depending on how your computer is set up, it lets you send the selected file to the desktop, a printer, to an email recipient, to a fax, or to a floppy drive.
Cut	Used in conjunction with the Paste command to move files. Cuts or removes the selected file from its current folder or location.
Copy	Used in conjunction with the Paste command to copy files. Copies the selected file.
Make Available Offline	Makes the presentation available offline.
Create Shortcut	Creates a shortcut—a quick way to a file or folder without having to go to its permanent location—to the file.
Delete	Deletes the selected file or files.
Rename	Renames the selected file.
Properties	Displays the properties of the selected file, such as when the file was created or last modified, or how large the file is.

Chapter 2
Editing a Presentation

QUICK REFERENCE

BASIC FILE MANAGEMENT IN THE OPEN DIALOG BOX:

1. OPEN THE OPEN OR SAVE AS DIALOG BOXES BY SELECTING OPEN OR SAVE AS FROM THE FILE MENU.

2. RIGHT-CLICK THE FILE AND REFER TO TABLE 2-6 FOR A LIST OF THINGS YOU CAN DO TO THE SELECTED FILE, OR SELECT THE FILE AND SELECT A COMMAND FROM THE TOOLS MENU.

TO CHANGE HOW FILES ARE DISPLAYED:

- CLICK THE VIEW BUTTON LIST ARROW AND SELECT A VIEW.

LESSON 2.17 Understanding Smart Tags

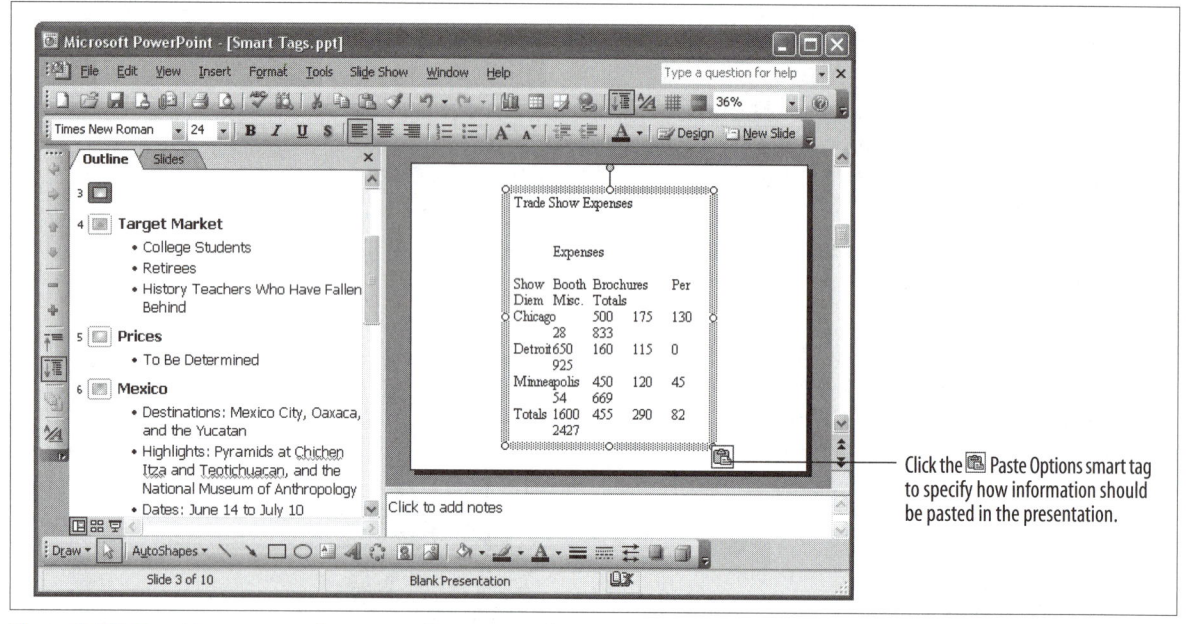

Figure 2-27. Smart tags appear when you perform a particular task or when PowerPoint recognizes certain types of information.

Click the 📋 Paste Options smart tag to specify how information should be pasted in the presentation.

Smart tags appear when you can choose from more than one option regarding a task, for example, how information is pasted.

Click the Paste Options button arrow to display a list of actions that you can take.

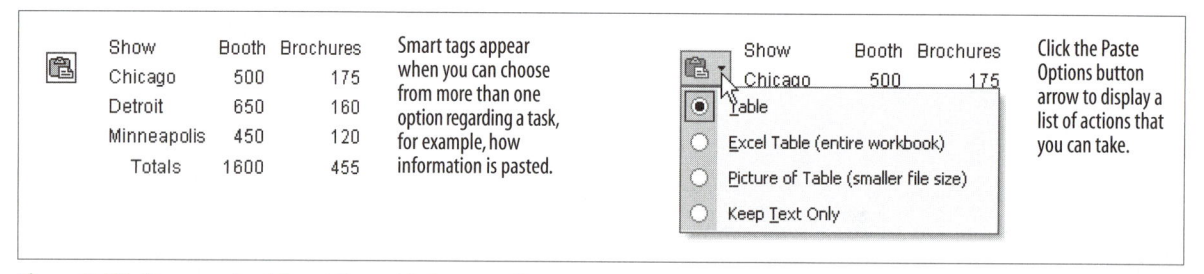

Figure 2-28. An example of Smart Tags with the Paste function.

Smart tags are one of the biggest additions to Microsoft Office 2003, and they make working with PowerPoint a lot easier. Smart tags are similar to right-mouse button shortcuts—you click smart tags to perform actions on various items. Smart tags appear when you perform certain actions, such as when you paste information or format text. PowerPoint marks these items with 📋 and ⊞ indicators. Clicking a smart tag indicator displays a list of things that you can do to the smart tag, such as paste information in a different format.

In this lesson you will learn what smart tags look like and how to use them.

1 Open the Lesson 2C presentation, save it as Smart Tags, and place the insertion point after the word "Asia" in slide 2.

2 Add a blank slide to the current presentation by clicking the New Slide button on the Formatting toolbar and selecting the Blank Slide layout from the task pane.

PowerPoint adds a blank slide to your presentation.

For this exercise we will cut and paste information from a Microsoft Excel workbook into this slide, so we will have to start the Microsoft Excel program.

3 Click the Start button and select Programs → Microsoft Excel.

You probably already know that the procedure for opening a file in Microsoft Excel is no different from opening a file in Microsoft PowerPoint.

Chapter 2
Editing a Presentation

4 Click the Open button on the Standard toolbar, browse to your practice folder or disk, then find and open the Trade Show Chart file.

Next you need to select and copy the information in this workbook.

5 Click the Sheet1 tab. Select the cell range A1:F8 by clicking cell A1, holding down the mouse button and dragging to cell F8.

Now you can copy the selected cells to the Clipboard.

6 Click the Copy button on the Standard toolbar.

The information is copied to the Clipboard.

7 Close Microsoft Excel.

You should be back in Microsoft PowerPoint, looking at the blank slide we added. Let's paste the copied information.

8 Click anywhere on the blank slide, then click the Clipboard task pane and click the Expense text.

PowerPoint pastes the copied information into the presentation. Notice the button appears next to the pasted text. Click this button to specify how information is pasted.

9 Position the pointer over the Paste Options button.

A drop-down arrow appears on the Paste Options button. Click this arrow to display a list of various options for how information is pasted into your presentation.

10 Click the Paste Options button and select Excel Table (entire workbook) from the list.

PowerPoint pastes the Excel information into the slide as an embedded worksheet.

Table 2-7. Smart Tags and Buttons

Smart Tag Button	Description
Paste Options	The Paste Options button appears after you paste something. Click the Paste Options button to specify how information is pasted into your presentation. The available options depend on the type of content you are pasting, the program you are pasting from, and the format of the text where you are pasting.
AutoCorrect Options	The AutoCorrect Options button appears after AutoCorrect identifies what could be a formatting error. You can click the AutoCorrect Options button to have PowerPoint automatically resize text to fit in its placeholder.

Lesson 2.17
Understanding Smart Tags

QUICK REFERENCE

UNDERSTANDING SMART TAGS:
- As you enter information in a presentation, 📋▾ smart tag buttons will appear. Click these buttons to do something to the specified information.

TO USE A SMART TAG:
- Click the **SMART TAG** and select the desired action or option.

Recovering Your Presentations

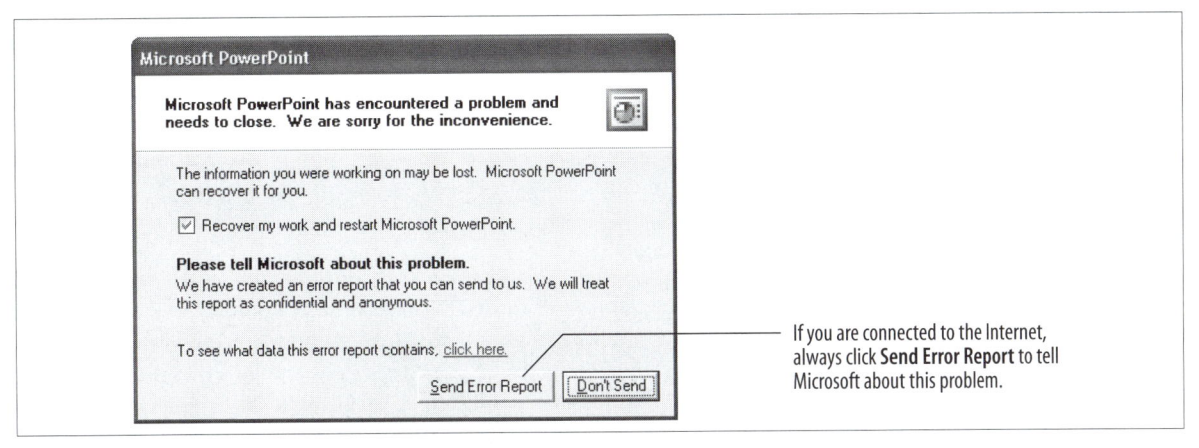

LESSON 2.18

Figure 2-29. Oops! There goes tomorrow's presentation!

If you are connected to the Internet, always click **Send Error Report** to tell Microsoft about this problem.

The Document Recovery task pane displays any recovered documents. To see the status of a recovered document, simply point to it for a few seconds with the mouse.

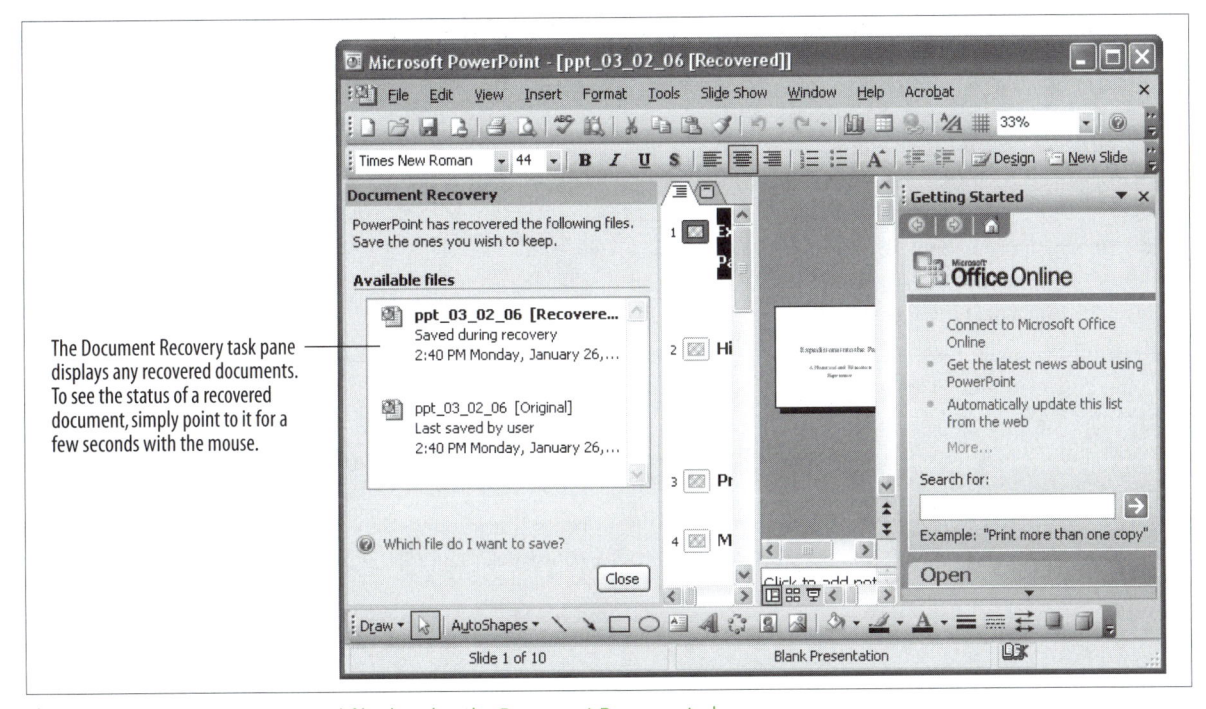

Figure 2-30. Review the recovered files listed in the Document Recovery task pane.

If you haven't found this out already, sooner or later you're going to discover that computers don't always work the way they're supposed to. Nothing is more frustrating than when a program, for no apparent reason, decides to take a quick nap, locks up, and stops responding to your commands—especially if you lose that precious presentation you've been working on!

Fortunately, after more than 10 years and roughly 9 software versions, Microsoft has finally realized that people might want to recover their presentations if Microsoft PowerPoint locks up or stops responding. If PowerPoint 2003 encounters a problem and stops responding, after you finish swearing and hitting your computer's monitor, you can restart Microsoft PowerPoint or your computer and try to recover your lost presentations. Sometimes PowerPoint will display a dialog box similar to the one shown in Figure 2-29 and automatically restart itself.

In this lesson, you will learn how to use Microsoft PowerPoint's new presentation recovery features, should disaster strike.

Lesson 2.18
Recovering Your Presentations

1 If necessary, restart your computer and/or Microsoft PowerPoint.

NOTE *You may not need to restart your computer or PowerPoint at all—often PowerPoint will display the dialog box shown in Figure 2-29 and automatically restart itself when it encounters a problem.*

When you have restarted Microsoft PowerPoint hopefully the Document Recovery pane will appear, as shown in Figure 2-30. If the Document Recovery pane doesn't appear, unfortunately, you're out of luck—PowerPoint did not recover any of your presentations. Hope you made a backup!

Sometimes PowerPoint will display several recovered presentations in the Document Recovery task pane (see Table 2-8), such as the original presentation that was based on the last manual save and a recovered presentation that was automatically saved during an AutoRecover save process. You can see the status of any recovered presentation simply by pointing at the recovered presentation for a second or two.

2 To view details about any recovered presentation, simply point at the presentation in the Document Recovery task pane for a few seconds.

Hopefully you will find a version of your presentation—either original or recovered—that isn't missing too much of your work.

Here's how to select and save a recovered presentation…

3 Click the desired recovered presentation from the task pane.

The presentation appears in PowerPoint's slide window.

4 Select **File → Save As** from the menu and save the presentation.

You can further protect your work by using the AutoRecover feature to periodically save a temporary copy of the presentation you're working on. To recover work after a power failure or similar problem, you must have turned on the AutoRecover feature before the problem occurred. You can set the AutoRecover save interval to occur more frequently than every 10 minutes (its default setting). For example, if you set it to save every 5 minutes, you'll recover more information than if you set it to save every 10 minutes. Here's how to change the AutoRecover save interval…

5 Select **Tools → Options** from the menu and click the **Save tab**.

The Save tab of the Options dialog box appears.

6 Ensure that the **Save AutoRecovery info box** is checked and specify the desired interval, in minutes, in the **minutes box**. Click **OK** when you're finished.

Even with Microsoft Office 2003's new document recovery features, the best way to ensure that you don't lose much information if your computer freezes is to save your work regularly.

Table 2-8. Status Indicators in the Document Recovery Task Pane

Status Indicator	Description
Original	Original file based on last manual save.
Recovered	File recovered during recovery process, or file saved during an AutoRecover save process.
Repaired	PowerPoint encountered problems while recovering the presentation and has attempted to repair them. Make sure that you double-check your presentation to make sure that there isn't any corruption.

QUICK REFERENCE

TO RECOVER A PRESENTATION:

1. RESTART MICROSOFT POWERPOINT (IF IT DOESN'T RESTART BY ITSELF).
2. FIND AND THEN CLICK THE BEST-RECOVERED PRESENTATION IN THE DOCUMENT RECOVERY TASK PANE.
3. SAVE THE PRESENTATION BY SELECTING FILE → SAVE AS FROM THE MENU.

TO CHANGE THE AUTORECOVERY SETTINGS:

1. SELECT TOOLS → OPTIONS FROM THE MENU AND CLICK THE SAVE TAB.
2. ENSURE THAT THE SAVE AUTORECOVERY INFO BOX IS CHECKED, AND SPECIFY THE DESIRED INTERVAL, IN MINUTES, IN THE MINUTES BOX. CLICK OK WHEN YOU'RE FINISHED.

Chapter Two Review

Lesson Summary

Inserting Slides and Text in Normal View

To Insert a Slide: Click the New Slide button on the Formatting toolbar or select Insert → Slide from the menu. Select the slide layout you want to use for the slide and close the task pane.

To Add Text to a Slide: Click the appropriate text placeholder and type the text.

Using the Outline Pane

The Outline pane lets you work on the overall content of a presentation without being distracted by formatting or graphical objects. It's also easy to reorganize your presentation using the Outline pane.

To Demote a Paragraph: Select the paragraph(s) and press the Tab key or click the Demote button on the Formatting or Outlining toolbar.

To Promote a Paragraph: Select the paragraph(s) and press Shift + Tab or click the Promote button on the Formatting or Outlining toolbar.

To Add a New Slide in the Outline Tab: Press Ctrl + Enter or promote a selected paragraph to the highest level on the outline.

Editing Text

Move the insertion point by pressing the appropriate arrow key or by clicking where you want to place the insertion point with the I pointer.

To Insert Text (Into an Existing Text Box): Click in the text box, move the insertion point where you want to insert the text and then type the text you want to insert.

To Delete Text: Press the Backspace key to delete text before, or to the left of, the insertion point. Press the Delete key to delete text after, or to the right of, the insertion point.

Selecting, Replacing, and Deleting Text

To Select a String of Text (Using the Mouse): Move the insertion point to the beginning or end of the text you want to select, click and hold the left mouse button and drag the insertion point across the text, then release the mouse button once the text is selected.

To Select a String of Text (Using the Keyboard): Move the insertion point to the beginning or end of the text you want to select, then press and hold down the Shift key while using the arrow keys to select the text.

To Select a Single Word: Double-click the word you want to select.

To Replace Text: Select the text and then type the new text.

To Deselect Text: Click anywhere on the computer screen.

To Delete Selected Text: Select the text and press the Delete key.

Cutting, Copying, and Pasting Text

To Cut Something: Select the text or object you want to cut and do any of the following:

- Click the Cut button on the Standard toolbar.
- Select Edit → Cut from the menu.
- Press Ctrl + X.

To Copy Something: Select the text or object you want to copy and do any of the following:

- Click the Copy button on the Standard toolbar.
- Select Edit → Copy from the menu.
- Press Ctrl + C.

To Paste a Cut or Copied Object: Place the insertion point where you want to paste the text or object and do any of the following:

- Click the Paste button on the Standard toolbar.
- Select Edit → Paste from the menu.
- Press Ctrl + V.

Using Undo, Redo, and Repeat

To Undo a Mistake or Action: Do any of the following:

- Click the Undo button on the Standard toolbar.
- Select Edit → Undo from the menu.
- Press Ctrl + Z.

Chapter 2
Editing a Presentation

To Redo an Undo: Do any of the following:

- Click the Redo button on the Standard toolbar.
- Select Edit → Redo from the menu.
- Press Ctrl + Y.

To Repeat an Action: Do any of the following:

- Press Ctrl + Y.
- Select Edit → Repeat from the menu.

Checking Your Spelling

PowerPoint flags any spelling errors with red squiggly underlines.

To Correct a Spelling Error: Right-click the spelling error and select the correction from the shortcut menu, or simply retype the misspelled word.

To Ignore a Spelling Error: Right-click the spelling or grammar error and select Ignore All from the shortcut menu.

To Add a Word to the Spelling Dictionary: Right-click the word you want to add and select Add from the shortcut menu.

Finding and Replacing Information

To Find Information in a Presentation: Select Edit → Find from the menu or press Ctrl + F. Enter the text you want to search for in the Find what box and click the Find next button. Keep clicking the Find next button until you find the text that you are looking for.

To Find and Replace Information: Select Edit → Replace from the menu or press Ctrl + H. Enter the text you want to search for in the Find what box and the text you want to replace it with in the Replace with box. Click the Find next button to find each occurrence of the text, and click the Replace button as needed to replace the text. Click Replace All to replace every occurrence of text in the presentation.

Viewing a Presentation's Outline

To Show/Hide the Outlining toolbar: Select View → Toolbars → Outlining from the menu.

You can hide or display your presentation's subtopics by expanding and collapsing your presentation's headings.

To Collapse a Heading: Make sure the insertion point is in the heading and click the Collapse button on the Outlining toolbar.

To Expand a Heading: Make sure the insertion point is in the heading and click the Expand button on the Outlining toolbar.

To Show or Hide a Presentation's Text Formatting: Click the Show Formatting button on the Outlining toolbar.

Rearranging a Presentation's Outline

To Rearrange an Outline (Using the Outlining toolbar): Select the slide(s) or paragraph(s) you want to move and click either the Move Up button or Move Down button on the Outlining toolbar.

To Rearrange an Outline (Using Drop and Drag): Select the slide(s) or paragraph(s) you want to move and drag them to a new location in the outline.

Inserting Symbols and Special Characters

To Insert a Symbol or Special Character: Place the insertion point where you want to insert the character, select Insert → Symbol from the menu, select the symbol you want, and click Insert.

Working in Slide Sorter View

Slide Sorter View displays all the slides in your presentation as small pictures, or thumbnails. Use Slide Sorter View when you want to rearrange the slides in your presentation and add transition effects between them.

To Switch to Slide Sorter View: Click the Slide Sorter View button on the horizontal scroll bar or select View → Slide Sorter from the menu.

To Move a Slide (in Slide Sorter View): Click the slide that you want to move. To select and move multiple slides hold down the Shift key as you click each slide you want to select. Drag the slide(s) between two other slides in Slide Sorter View and release the mouse button.

To Delete a Slide (in Slide Sorter View): Click the slide you want to delete and press the Delete key.

To Duplicate a Slide (in Slide Sorter View): Click the slide you want to copy and press Ctrl + D.

Chapter 2
Chapter Two Review

Adding Notes to Your Slides

To Add Notes to a Slide: Make sure you're in Normal View and begin typing in your notes in the Notes pane.

Working with Multiple Windows

To Switch between Multiple Open Presentations: Click the presentation icon on the Windows taskbar or select Window and select the name of the presentation you want to view.

To View Multiple Windows at the Same Time: Select Window → Arrange All.

To Maximize a Window: Click the window's Maximize button.

To Restore a Window: Click the Window's Restore button.

To Manually Resize a Window: Position the mouse pointer over the edge of the window, hold down the mouse button and drag the mouse to resize the window. Release the mouse button when the window reaches the desired size.

To Move a Window: Drag the window's title bar to the location where you want to position the window.

Collecting and Pasting Multiple Items

To Display the Clipboard Task Pane: Select Edit → Office Clipboard from the menu.

To Add Items to the Office Clipboard: Copy and/or cut the items as you would normally.

To Paste from the Office Clipboard: If necessary, display the Clipboard task pane, then click the item you want to paste. Click the Paste All button to paste all collected items.

File Management

You can perform most file management functions, such as delete, rename, and copy, from the Open File dialog box. Open the Open File dialog box by clicking the Open button on the Standard toolbar or selecting File → Open.

Right-click a file and select a file command from the shortcut menu.

Understanding Smart Tags

As you enter information in a presentation, smart tag buttons will appear. Click these buttons to do something to the specified information.

To Use a Smart Tag: Click the Smart Tag arrow and select the desired action or option.

Recovering Your Presentations

To Recover a Presentation: Restart Microsoft PowerPoint (if it doesn't restart by itself after a crash). Find and then click the best-recovered presentation in the Document Recovery task pane. Save the presentation by doing a File → Save As from the menu.

To Change the AutoRecovery Settings: Select Tools → Options from the menu and click the Save tab. Ensure that the Save AutoRecovery info box is checked and specify the desired interval, in minutes, in the minutes box. Click OK when you're finished.

Quiz

1. Which is the best view for organizing your thoughts on a presentation's content?

   A. Normal View

   B. Slide Sorter View

   C. Outline pane

   D. Notes View

2. Which of the following statements is NOT true?

   A. Pressing the Tab key in the Outline pane demotes the selected paragraph.

   B. Pressing Ctrl + Enter in the Outline pane adds a new slide to the paragraph.

   C. Pressing the Shift + Tab key in the Outline pane promotes the selected paragraph.

   D. The Outline pane is the best view for adding and working with graphics on your slides.

Chapter 2
Editing a Presentation

3. Which key deletes text before, or to the left, of the insertion point?

   A. Page Up
   B. Page Down
   C. Delete
   D. Backspace

4. Which of the following is not a way to cut text?

   A. Select the text and press Ctrl+X.
   B. Select the text and click the cut button on the toolbar.
   C. Select the text and press the delete button.
   D. Select the text and select Edit → Cut from the menu.

5. Once a block of text is selected, you can replace the selected text with new text by:

   A. Simply typing the new text.
   B. Selecting File, then Insert New Text from the menu.
   C. You can't replace selected text with new text.
   D. Clicking the Replace Text button on the Standard toolbar.

6. To view a list of suggestions for a misspelled word:

   A. Select the misspelled word and select Tools → Suggestions from the menu.
   B. Press Ctrl + S.
   C. Select the misspelled word and click the Spelling Suggestion button on the Standard toolbar.
   D. Right-click the misspelled word.

7. Notes Page View displays a notes page for the selected slide, where you can create speaker notes for the slide. (True or False?)

Homework

1. Open the Homework 2 presentation, located in your Practice folder or disk, and save it as "Fleas."

   Three-Ring Flea Circus!
   - Date and Time:
   - June 8, 3:00 to 5:00
   - Location: 7-11 Parking Lot
   - Cost:
     - Adults: $16.50
     - Children: $16.50
   - Please: NO DOGS!

2. Go to Slide 2 and change the cost from $16.50 to $4.00 for both adults and children.

3. Switch to the Outline pane by clicking the Outline tab.

4. Place the insertion point anywhere in the "June 8, 3:00 to 5:00" paragraph. Demote the paragraph by pressing the Tab key.

5. Place the insertion point anywhere in Slide 2's "Three-Ring Flea Circus" slide title. Hide the sub-topics of Slide 2 by clicking the Collapse button on the Outlining toolbar.

6. Display Slide 2's collapsed subtopics by clicking the Expand button on the Outlining toolbar.

7. Switch to Normal View, go to Slide 2, and add a new slide to the presentation by clicking the New Slide button on the Standard toolbar, selecting the Title and Text layout, and clicking OK.

8. Copy the slide title from Slide 2 and paste it in the slide title area of the newly added Slide 3.

9. Click in the Notes Panel area to enter notes. Type in whatever you want—be creative!

10. Switch to Slide Sorter View by clicking the Slide Sorter View button on the horizontal scroll bar, located at the bottom of the screen.

11. Delete Slide 3 by clicking Slide 3 to select it and then pressing the Delete key.

12. Undo the slide deletion by clicking the Undo button on the Standard toolbar.

13. Save your work and exit PowerPoint.

Chapter 2
Chapter Two Review

Quiz Answers

1. C. The Outline pane is the best place for drafting a presentation.

2. D. You can't even see graphics in the Outline pane!

3. D. The Backspace key deletes text to the left of the insertion point.

4. C.

5. A. Typing replaces any selected text.

6. D. Right-click a misspelled word to display a list of suggestions.

7. True.

CHAPTER 3
FORMATTING YOUR PRESENTATION

CHAPTER OBJECTIVES:

Formatting fonts
Using the format painter to copy and apply formatting
Applying a template's design to a presentation
Using slide masters
Working with color schemes
Changing the slide background
Creating and formatting bulleted lists
Changing paragraph alignment and line spacing
Adding headers and footers
Working tabs and indents, and changing the page setup

CHAPTER TASK: FORMAT AN EXISTING PRESENTATION

Prerequisites

- **Windows basics: know how to use menus, toolbars, dialog boxes, and shortcut keystrokes.**
- **Move the mouse pointer and navigate between the slides in a presentation.**
- **Open and save a presentation.**
- **Select text and objects.**

A presentation is always more effective when it's attractively designed and formatted. Think about it: people would rather buy expensive name-brand cereals in flashy boxes than much more affordable cereals in plain, generic boxes—even though they are really the same cereal!

This chapter explains how to format your presentations to give them more impact and make them more visually appealing. You will learn how to change the appearance, size, and color of the text in your presentations and how to change your color scheme and background. You will also learn the ins and outs of aligning text to the left, right, and center of a text box; using tabs; and indenting paragraphs. This chapter also describes how to add headers and footers to your presentations.

LESSON 3.1

Formatting Fonts with the Formatting Toolbar

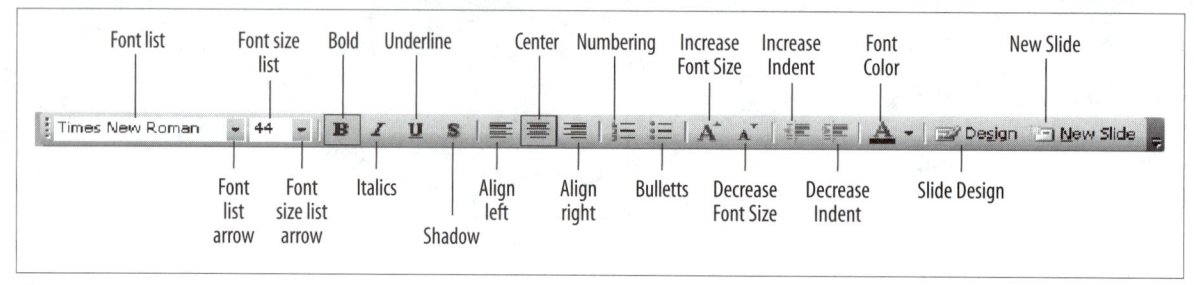

Figure 3-1. The Formatting toolbar.

Labels: Font list, Font size list, Bold, Underline, Center, Numbering, Increase Font Size, Increase Indent, Font Color, New Slide, Font list arrow, Font size list arrow, Italics, Shadow, Align left, Align right, Bullets, Decrease Font Size, Decrease Indent, Slide Design

1. Select the text you want to format.

2. Click the Size List arrow (▼) and select the font size.

   Click here to scroll down the list.

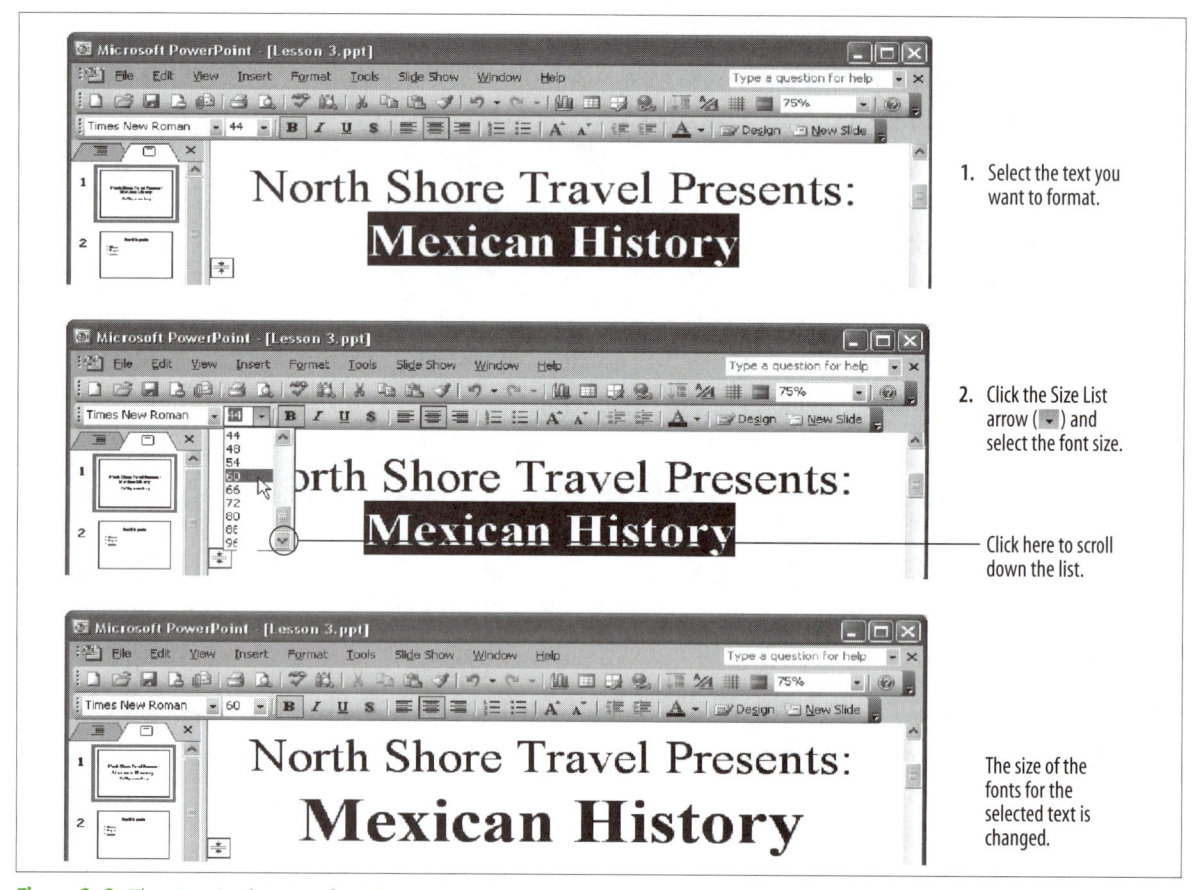

   The size of the fonts for the selected text is changed.

Figure 3-2. The steps in changing font size.

You can emphasize text in a presentation by making the text darker and heavier (**bold**), slanted (*italics*), larger, or in a different typeface (or font). One of the easiest methods of applying character formatting is to use the Formatting toolbar. The Formatting toolbar includes buttons for applying the most common character and paragraph formatting options.

1 Start Microsoft PowerPoint.

2 Open the presentation named `Lesson 3A` and save it as `History of Mexico`.

First, let's make the title of the presentation, "Mexican History", stand out by making it bold. Still remember how to select text? Good, because you have to select text to format it.

100

3 Select the Mexican History text in the Slide pane and click the Bold button on the Formatting toolbar.

Bold button

Other Ways to Bold:

- Select **Format** → **Font** from the menu, select **Bold** from the Font Style box, then click **OK**.
- Press <Ctrl> + <B>.

The selected text "Mexican History" appears in boldface (although it may not appear to change very much since you're using such a large font). Hmm…since applying bold didn't really do much for the presentation's title, let's try changing the size and style of the font.

4 Keeping the title selected, click the Font list arrow on the Formatting toolbar.

Font List

A list appears with all the fonts that are available on your computer, listed in alphabetical order. Since there isn't enough room to display all the font types at once, you may have to scroll up or down the list until you find the one you want.

5 Scroll up the Font list until you see the Arial font, then click the Arial font.

The title is formatted using Arial font. You can also change the font size, making text appear larger or smaller.

6 Keeping the title selected, click the Font Size list arrow on the Formatting toolbar and then click 60.

Font Size List

The selected text "Mexican History" appears in a larger font size (60 point type instead of the previous 44 point type). Wow! That really makes the heading stand out from the rest of the slide, doesn't it? Font sizes are measured in points (pt.) that are 1/72 of an inch. The larger the number of points, the larger the font.

Next, let's change the font formatting for the "North Shore Travel Presents" heading.

7 Select the text North Shore Travel Presents and click the Italics button on the Formatting toolbar.

Italics button

Other Ways to Italics:

- Select **Format** → **Font** from the menu, select **Italic** from the Font Style box, then click **OK**.
- Press <Ctrl> + <I>.

The selected text appears in italics. Move on to the next step and reduce the size of the selected text.

8 Keeping the same text selected, click the Font Size list arrow on the Formatting toolbar and then click 36.

The selected text "North Shore Travel Presents" appears in a smaller font size.

9 Save your work by clicking the Save button on the Standard toolbar.

Table 3-1. Examples of Common Font Types and Sizes

Common Font Types	Common Font Sizes
Arial	Arial 8 point
Comic Sans MS	Arial 10 point

Lesson 3.1
Formatting Fonts with the Formatting Toolbar

Table 3-1. Examples of Common Font Types and Sizes (Continued)

Common Font Types	Common Font Sizes
Courier New	Arial 12 point
Times New Roman	Arial 14 point

QUICK REFERENCE

TO BOLDFACE TEXT:
- CLICK THE **B** BOLD BUTTON ON THE FORMATTING TOOLBAR OR PRESS CTRL + B.

TO ITALICIZE TEXT:
- CLICK THE *I* ITALICS BUTTON ON THE FORMATTING TOOLBAR OR PRESS CTRL + I.

TO UNDERLINE TEXT:
- CLICK THE U UNDERLINE BUTTON ON THE FORMATTING TOOLBAR OR PRESS CTRL + U.

TO CHANGE FONT SIZE:
- SELECT THE PT. SIZE FROM THE [24] FONT SIZE LIST ON THE FORMATTING TOOLBAR.

TO CHANGE FONT TYPE:
- SELECT THE FONT FROM THE [Times New Roman] FONT LIST ON THE FORMATTING TOOLBAR.

Lesson 3.2

Advanced Font Formatting with the Font Dialog Box

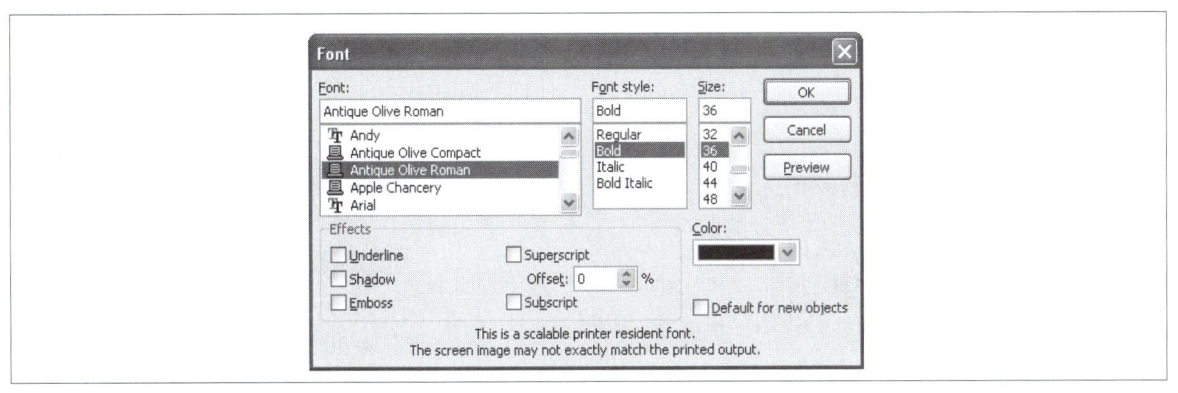

Figure 3-3. The Font dialog box.

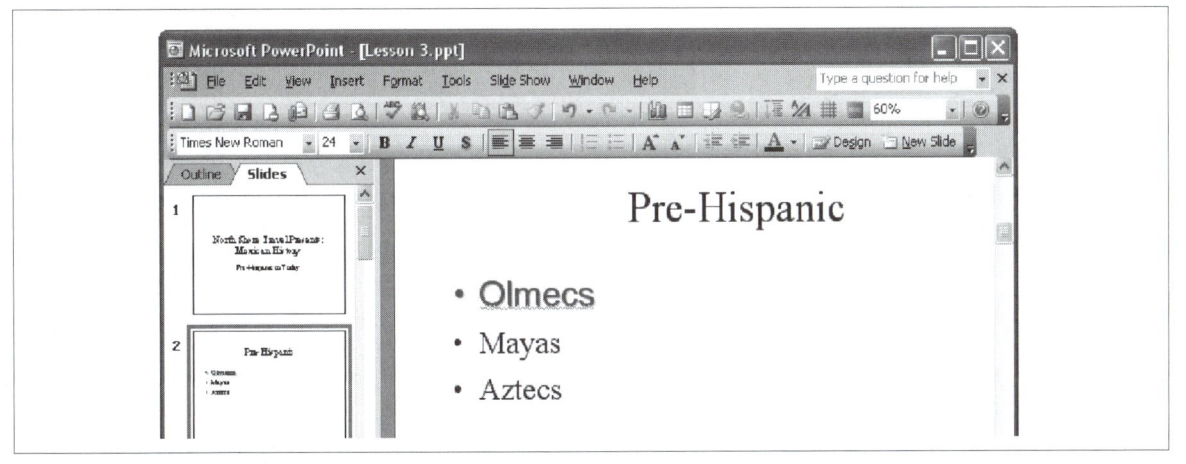

Figure 3-4. The reformatted presentation.

The Formatting toolbar is great for quickly applying the most common formatting options to text, but it doesn't offer every available formatting option. To see and/or use every possible character formatting option, you need to use the Font dialog box, which can be found by selecting Format → Font from the menu or by right-clicking and selecting Font from a shortcut menu. This lesson looks at how to format characters with the Font dialog box. See Table 3-2 for a list of font formatting options.

1 Press the Page Down key to move to Slide 2.

Whether you format text using toolbars, dialog boxes, or the keyboard, you always have to select what you want to format, first.

2 Select the Olmecs bulleted text item and select Format → Font from the menu.

The Font Window appears, as shown in Figure 3-3, you can adjust all of the settings of the selected text, such as its size, font type, style, and color.

3 Scroll up the Font list and select Arial.

This will change the font type, just like selecting it from the Font List in the Formatting toolbar.

4 Add a check to the Shadow box by clicking it.

This will add a shadow behind your text, which can make it stand out against its background.

103

Lesson 3.2
Advanced Font Formatting with the Font Dialog Box

5 Click the **Color list arrow**.

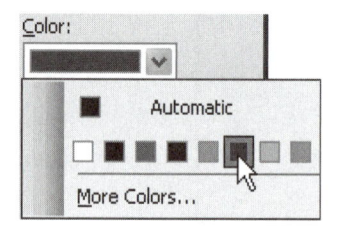

Font Color List

A list of colors you can apply to the selected text appears.

NOTE *Unlike Microsoft Word or Excel, in PowerPoint the Font Color list initially displays only eight colors. These eight colors are determined by the color scheme that you are currently using. A color scheme determines the background, text, lines, shadows, and fill colors in your presentation. Instead of having to choose from more than 16 million colors, you can use a coordinated color scheme that was carefully put together by design professionals. We'll talk more about color schemes later on in the chapter.*

6 Select the **blue color**.

The Colors dialog box closes and we return to the Font dialog box. Just one more font formatting change to make before we move on…

Font Color button

7 Select **36** from the **Size** list.

This will change the size of the selected text to 36 points.

8 Click **OK** and deselect the text to see the changes.

The Font dialog box closes and the formatting options you have chosen are applied to the selected text.

9 Save your work.

Table 3-2. Font Formatting Options

Option	Description
Font	Displays all fonts installed on your computer and allows you to change the font that you are currently using.
Font style	Formats the style of the font: Regular (no emphasis), Bold, Italic, and Bold Italic.
Size	Displays and allows you to increase or decrease the size of the font.
Color	Displays and allows you to change the font color.
Effects	Allows you to add special effects to fonts as follows: Underline Shadow Emboss ^{Super}script $_{Sub}$script
Default for new objects	Makes the current font formatting the default font formatting (be **very** careful about using this option!).
Preview	Previews the current font settings.

Chapter 3
Formatting Your Presentation

QUICK REFERENCE

TO OPEN THE FONT DIALOG BOX:
- SELECT FORMAT → FONT FROM THE MENU.

TO CHANGE A FONT'S COLOR:
- CLICK THE FONT COLOR BUTTON ARROW ON THE DRAWING TOOLBAR AND SELECT THE COLOR.

LESSON 3.3

Using the Format Painter

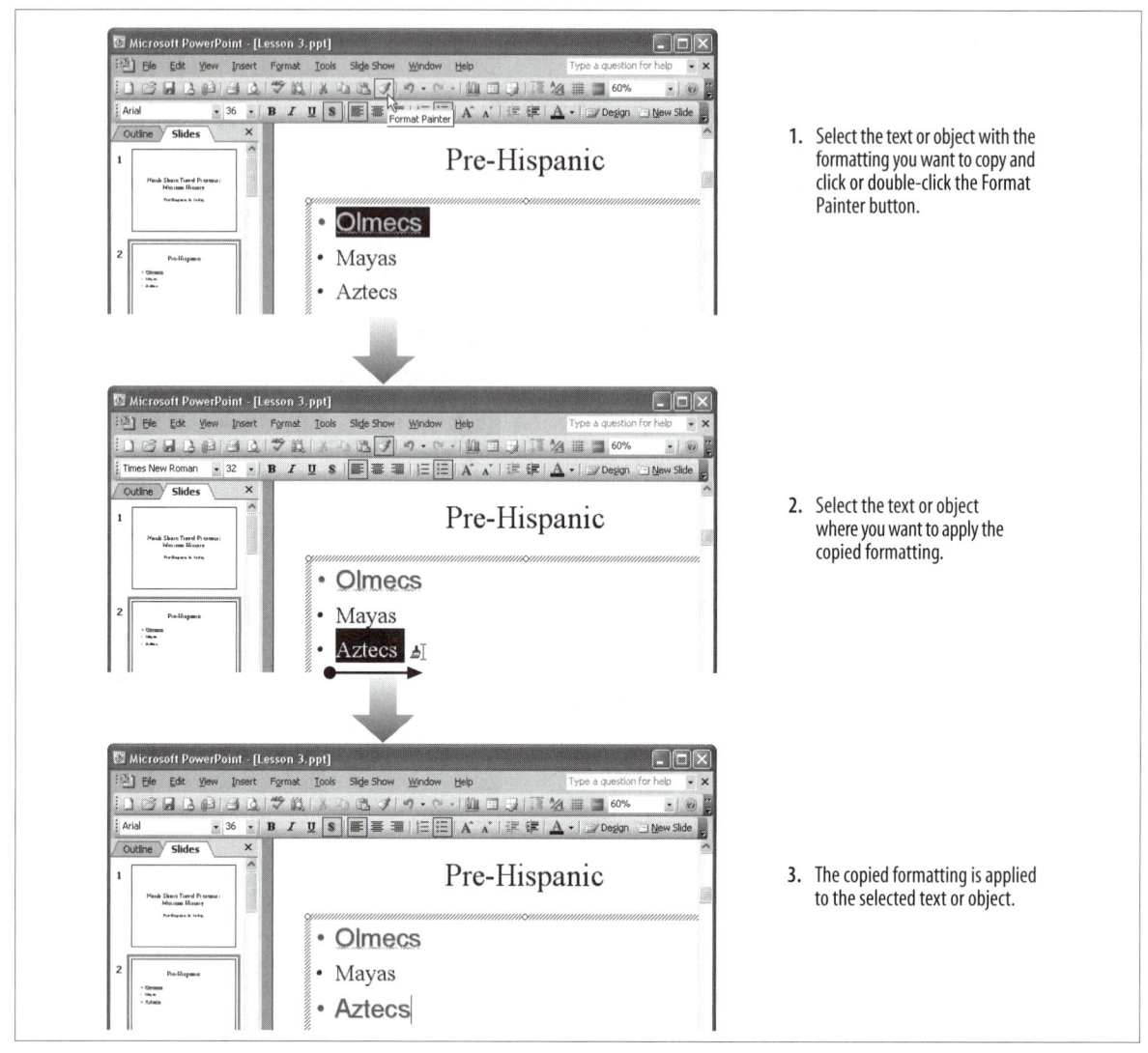

Figure 3-5. Use the Format Painter to copy formatting to other text and objects.

1. Select the text or object with the formatting you want to copy and click or double-click the Format Painter button.

2. Select the text or object where you want to apply the copied formatting.

3. The copied formatting is applied to the selected text or object.

Remember how we used the Font dialog box to format text in the previous lesson? It wasn't exactly grueling mental work, but it did require a number of steps to change the font type, size, color, and style. Now you want to format all of your bulleted text like the text you formatted on Slide 2. This could take a while—even if you are able to remember the exact format and color options. When you want to copy formatting from text or objects and apply it elsewhere in your presentation, the Format Painter is the tool you need. The Format Painter tool copies how text or objects are formatted and then pastes or applies that formatting to other text or objects. The Format Painter makes it easy to keep your slides looking consistent.

The Format Painter tool is a feature that is easier to demonstrate than explain, so let's get started!

1 Make sure you're on Slide 2 and then select the Olmecs bulleted text.

First you need to select the text or object that contains the formatting you want to apply elsewhere in the presentation. You should be rather familiar with selecting text by now, so let's move on to the next step.

2 Double-click the Format Painter button on the Standard toolbar.

106

Chapter 3
Formatting Your Presentation

Format Painter button

Click the Format Painter button once to apply formatting once. Double-click the Format Painter button to apply formatting several times.

Notice the pointer changes to a ▱. All you have to do is select the text or object that you want to apply the formatting to with the format painter ▱ tool.

3 Select the Aztec bulleted text with the ▱ tool.

Like other mouse-intensive operations, this one can be a little tricky for some people the first time they try it. The font formatting from the first bullet is now applied to the third bullet.

4 Now select the Mayas bulleted text with the ▱ tool.

The font formatting is now applied here as well. Now let's deactivate the Format Painter.

5 Click the Format Painter button once again to deactivate the Format Painter.

6 Save your work.

In addition to text formatting, the Format Painter can also pick up the formatting or attributes of other objects on your slides, such as the color and size of a drawing object, and apply them elsewhere.

QUICK REFERENCE

TO COPY FORMATTING WITH THE FORMAT PAINTER:

1. SELECT THE TEXT OR PARAGRAPH WITH THE FORMATTING OPTIONS YOU WANT TO COPY.
2. CLICK THE FORMAT PAINTER BUTTON ON THE STANDARD TOOLBAR.
3. SELECT THE TEXT OR OBJECT WHERE YOU WANT TO APPLY THE COPIED FORMATTING WITH THE FORMAT PAINTER POINTER.

TO COPY SELECTED FORMATTING TO SEVERAL LOCATIONS:

1. SELECT THE TEXT OR PARAGRAPH WITH THE FORMATTING OPTIONS YOU WANT TO COPY.
2. DOUBLE-CLICK THE FORMAT PAINTER BUTTON.
3. SELECT THE TEXT OR OBJECT WHERE YOU WANT TO APPLY THE COPIED FORMATTING WITH THE FORMAT PAINTER POINTER.
4. CLICK THE FORMAT PAINTER BUTTON WHEN YOU'RE FINISHED.

LESSON 3.4 Applying a Template's Formatting

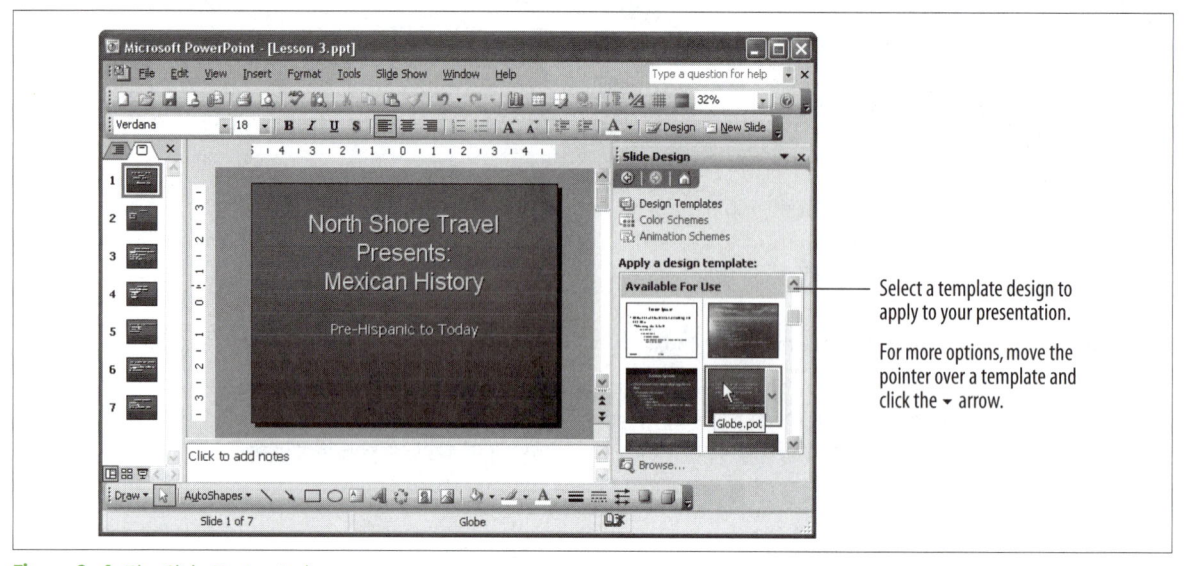

Figure 3-6. The Slide Design task pane.

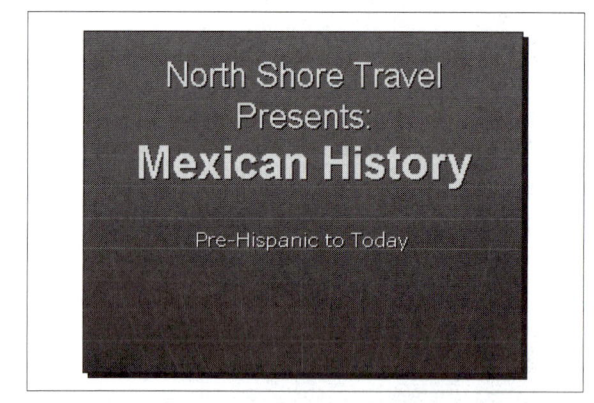

Figure 3-7. Slide 1, once the Globe template has been applied.

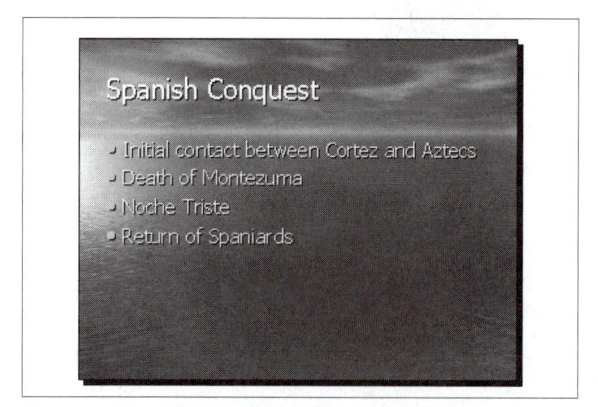

Figure 3-8. Slide 3, once the Ocean template has been applied.

If you're halfway through creating a presentation and you suddenly realize that you hate how it looks, don't worry, you can always assign a new design template to a presentation at any time. This lesson explains how.

1 If necessary, find and open the Lesson 3B presentation and save it as History of Mexico.

2 Press Ctrl + Home to move to the Title slide in the presentation.

You can apply a design template anywhere in a presentation, but, for this exercise, we are going to start at the beginning.

3 Click the Design button on the Formatting toolbar.

Design button

Other Ways to Apply a Design Template:

- Double-click the name of the template on the status bar, located at the bottom of the PowerPoint screen.

The Slide Design task pane appears as shown in Figure 3-6. The task pane can only display a few templates at a time, so you will probably have to scroll down until you find the template you want to apply. Once you have found a suitable template, simply click it to apply the template to all the slides in your

Chapter 3
Formatting Your Presentation

presentation. You can view more template options by moving the pointer over the template in the task pane and clicking the ▾ arrow.

4 Take some time to scroll down the task pane and look at the various templates.

Move the pointer over a design template, click the ▾ arrow and select one of the following:

- **Apply to All Slides:** Applies the selected template to every slide in the presentation.
- **Apply to Selected Slides:** Applies the selected template to only the selected slide(s) in the presentation.
- **Show Large Previews:** Displays a larger preview of the available templates.

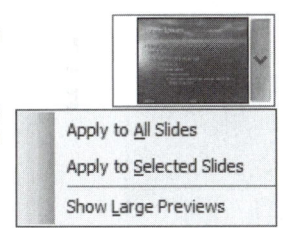

Move on to the next step when you've seen enough of PowerPoint's available templates.

5 Click the Globe template in the task pane.

The Globe template is applied to all the slides in your presentation. Notice how the colors of the text and background have changed in order to appropriately match the new design.

6 Press Page Down to move to Slide 2.

PowerPoint has cleverly changed the text to a color that matches the new design.

7 Press Page Down to move to Slide 3.

PowerPoint 2003 supports having more than one design template in your presentation—a major improvement over previous versions of PowerPoint, which supported only one design template. Using more than one template is great when you want to combine several presentations into one file, and you want each section to maintain its distinct look.

8 Scroll down the task pane until you find the Ocean template.

Here's how to apply a template to a single slide…

9 Move the pointer over the Ocean template in the task pane and click the ▾ arrow. Select Apply to Selected Slides from the menu.

PowerPoint applies the Ocean template to the selected slide. Let's make sure the other slides in the presentation haven't been affected…

10 Press Page Up until you are back at Slide 1.

The remaining slides in the presentation still use the Globe template, while Slide 3 uses the Ocean template.

You can close the task pane since we're finished using it.

11 Click the task pane's ✕ Close button.

QUICK REFERENCE

TO APPLY A DESIGN TEMPLATE TO A PRESENTATION:

1. CLICK THE [Design] DESIGN BUTTON ON THE FORMATTING TOOLBAR.
2. CLICK THE TEMPLATE YOU WANT TO APPLY TO THE PRESENTATION.

TO APPLY A DESIGN TEMPLATE TO SELECTED SLIDE(S):

1. CLICK THE [Design] DESIGN BUTTON ON THE FORMATTING TOOLBAR.
2. MOVE THE POINTER OVER THE TEMPLATE IN THE TASK PANE, CLICK THE ▾ ARROW, AND SELECT APPLY TO SELECTED SLIDES FROM THE MENU.

LESSON 3.5

Using the Slide Master

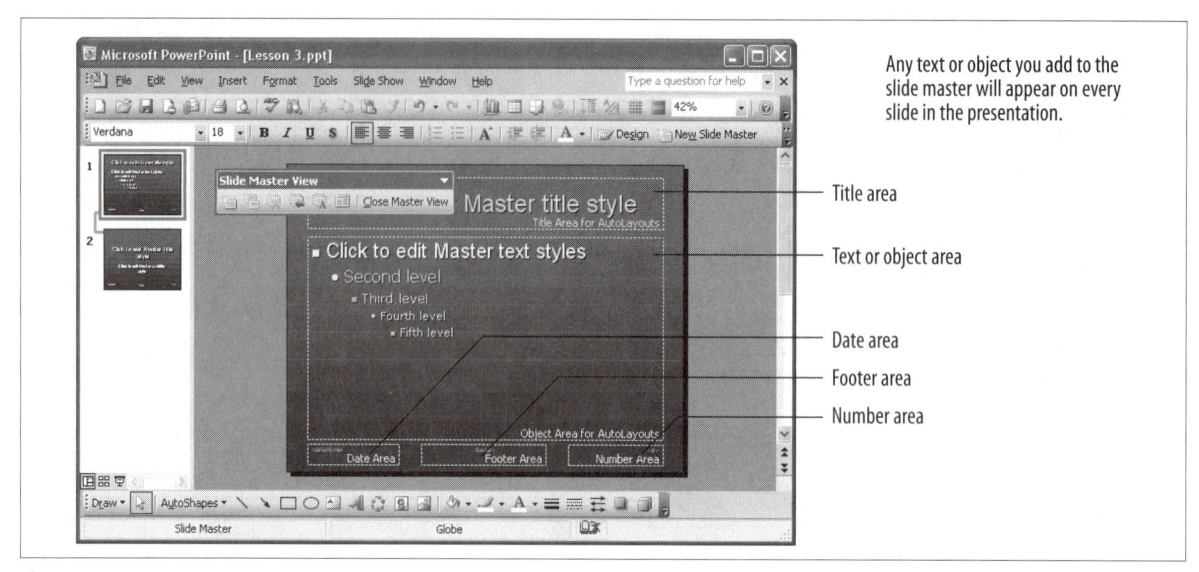

Figure 3-9. Slide Master View

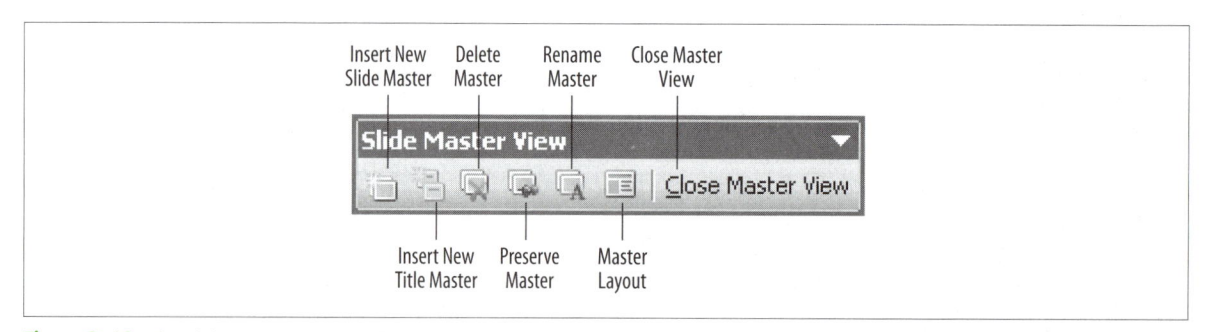

Callouts on figure:
- Any text or object you add to the slide master will appear on every slide in the presentation.
- Title area
- Text or object area
- Date area
- Footer area
- Number area

Figure 3-10. The Slide Master View toolbar

Callouts on toolbar:
- Insert New Slide Master
- Delete Master
- Rename Master
- Close Master View
- Insert New Title Master
- Preserve Master
- Master Layout

Do you want something to appear on every slide in your presentation (except the title slide), such as your company's name and logo? Do you want to change how the text on all your slides is formatted? Using the Slide Master is the fastest and easiest way to set up the appearance of all slides in a presentation. The Slide Master controls all aspects of a slide's appearance, including its background color, font style, and any reoccurring text or pictures. Changing the Master changes every slide in your presentation—adding a candy-striped background to the Master adds a candy-striped background to every single one of your slides.

Each presentation has two types of Masters:

- **Slide Master:** Governs the appearance of your slides.
- **Title Master:** Governs the appearance of your presentation's title slide.

This lesson introduces you to these Masters and how to use them to fine-tune the look of your presentation.

1 Go to Slide 2 and select View → Master → Slide Master from the menu.

The Slide Master appears, as shown in Figure 3-9. Notice the Slide Master includes placeholders for the slide title and body. Also, notice that the Slide Master has three additional placeholders at the bottom of the slide for the Date, Footer, and Slide Number. These areas are used by the Header and Footer command, which we'll talk about later on in this chapter.

2 Select the Click to edit Master text styles text in the body area.

Now that we've selected the text, we can format it.

Chapter 3
Formatting Your Presentation

3 Change the size of the selected font to **36 pt.** and the font type to **Arial**.

Remember that when you format something in the Slide Master, you're formatting each and every one of your slides. You can also add text or graphics that you want to appear in all of your slides to the Slide Master.

4 Click the **Text Box button** on the Drawing toolbar.

Text Box button

The pointer changes to a ↧, indicating you can use it to insert a text box. We'll discuss text boxes further in a future lesson—for now, all you need to know is that they allow you to add text anywhere on your slides.

5 Click near the bottom middle of the body placeholder with the ↧ pointer.

A text box appears where you click—now all you have to do is type the text you want to appear in the text box.

6 Type **North Shore Travel's History Expeditions**.

Don't worry if your text overlaps some of the text on the slide master, because text on the slide master is only meant to act as a guideline. The text you just added, however, will appear on all the slides in your presentation. Now we're finished making changes to the Slide Master, so let's close it and return to our slides.

7 Click the **Close Master View button** on the Slide Master View toolbar.

The Slide Master view closes and you've returned to your beloved slides. Let's take a look and see what's changed and what hasn't.

8 Press **Ctrl** + **Home** to move to the first slide in your presentation.

Hey! There aren't any changes here? Where's the "North Shore Travel's History Expeditions" text we added? Why isn't the text formatted differently? The first slide in a presentation is the Title Slide and it has its own special master called the *Title Master*. To make changes to the Title Master, you would have to first go to the title slide and then repeat Step 1. Okay, so nothing has changed here. Let's move on.

9 Press **Ctrl** + **End** to move to the last slide in your presentation.

Here are the changes we've made—both the "North Shore Travel's History Expeditions" text we added and the formatting we applied to the slide's title.

You can always override a master—simply go to the slide you want to override and format the text or background however you want. The formatting changes you make will apply only to the selected slide. To illustrate how the Slide Master's formatting can be overridden, take a look at a previously formatted slide.

10 Press the **Page Up** key until you reach **Slide 2**.

Notice some of the text formatting on this slide differs from the slide master. That's because you previously formatted this slide, and any formatting changes you make to an individual slide overrides the Slide Master.

QUICK REFERENCE

YOU CAN EDIT, FORMAT, OR INSERT SOMETHING ON EVERY SLIDE IN YOUR PRESENTATION WITH THE SLIDE MASTER.

TO EDIT THE SLIDE MASTER:

1. SELECT VIEW → MASTER → SLIDE MASTER FROM THE MENU.
2. EDIT AND FORMAT THE SLIDE MASTER AS NEEDED.
3. CLICK THE CLOSE MASTER VIEW BUTTON ON THE SLIDE MASTER VIEW TOOLBAR.

TO OVERRIDE THE SLIDE MASTER:

- EDIT AND FORMAT THE SLIDE YOU WANT TO OVERRIDE.

LESSON 3.6

Choosing a Color Scheme

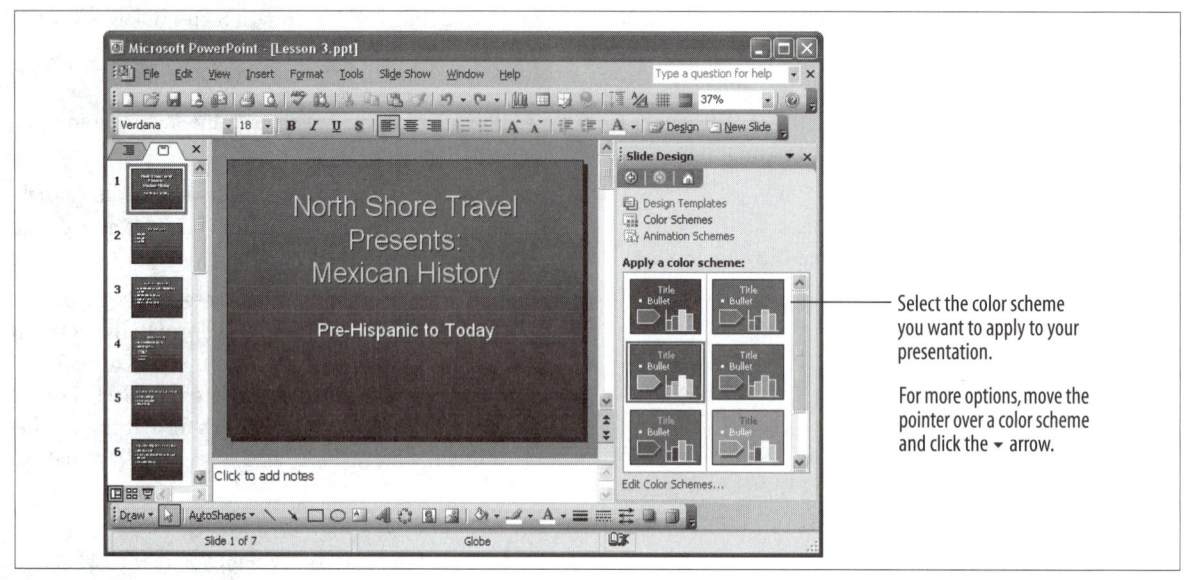

Figure 3-11. Select a color scheme in the Slide Design task pane.

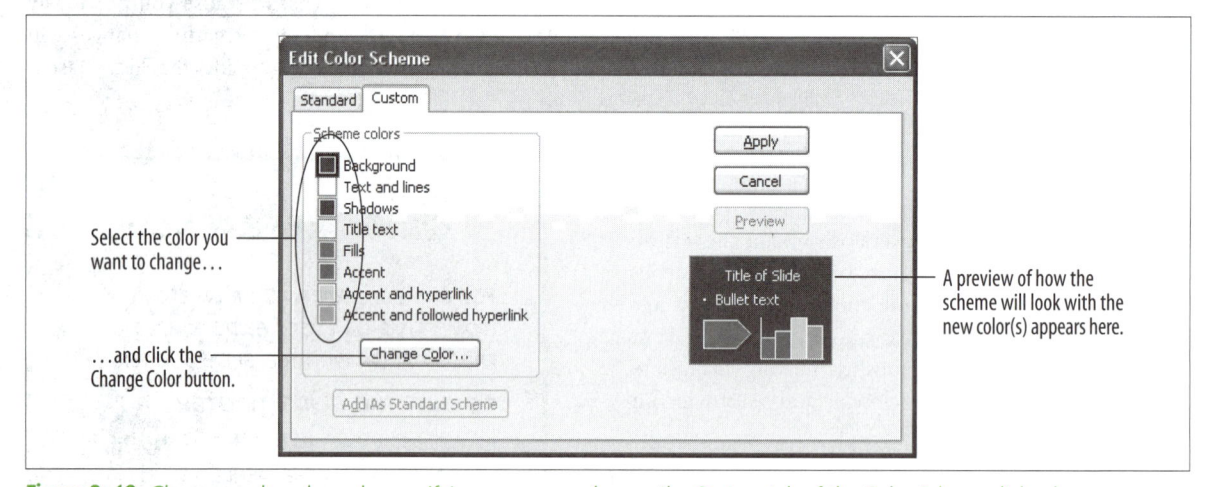

Figure 3-12. Change a color scheme by specifying your own colors on the Custom tab of the Color Scheme dialog box.

Does your presentation look a little dreary? If so, you're in luck! This lesson shows you how to add vibrant color to your presentations by using a color scheme—PowerPoint's very own interior designer. A color scheme is a set of eight coordinated colors you can use as the main colors in your presentation. A color scheme determines the background, text, line, shadow, and fill colors in your presentation. Color schemes are the neatest thing to come along since sliced bread. Instead of having to choose from more than 16 million colors, you can use a coordinated color scheme, carefully put together by design professionals.

If you think you have better taste in color than Microsoft, you can always change one or more of the colors used in a color scheme, or you can create your own custom color schemes altogether. PowerPoint stores color schemes in the template the presentation is based on, including several alternate color schemes that have been customized to work with the template's design.

1 Click the **Design button** on the Formatting toolbar and click **Color Schemes** in the task pane.

The Slide Design task pane appears as shown in Figure 3-11. The task pane can only display a few

Chapter 3
Formatting Your Presentation

color schemes at a time, so you will probably have to scroll down until you find the color scheme that you want.

2 Click the **rust colored** color scheme in the task pane.

Pointer over a Color Scheme, Click the ▾ arrow and select one of the following:

- **Apply to All Slides:** Applies the selected color scheme to every slide in the presentation.
- **Apply to Selected Slides:** Applies the selected color scheme to only the selected slide(s) in the presentation.
- **Show Large Previews:** Displays a larger preview of the available color schemes.

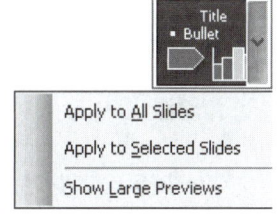

PowerPoint applies the color scheme to all the slides in the presentation.

So what happens if you like most of the colors in a color scheme, but one particular color really bothers you? Not a problem—you can easily change one or more of the colors in a color scheme with your own colors.

3 Click **Edit Color Schemes** at the bottom of the task pane.

The Edit Color Scheme dialog box appears, as shown in Figure 3-12.

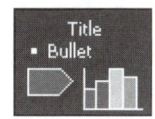

Color Scheme

4 Select the **Title text color** and click the **Change Color** button.

The Color dialog box appears—all you have to do here is select a new color.

5 Select a **yellow color** and click **OK**.

The Title text color will now be changed to the brighter yellow color you selected.

6 Click **Apply** to close the dialog box and return to Normal View.

The Color Scheme dialog box closes, and all slides are updated with the color scheme changes.

7 Click on any of the slides' text and then click the **Font Color list arrow** on the Drawing toolbar.

The eight colors displayed in the Font Color list are the coordinating colors used in the current color scheme. Changing color schemes is like a painter changing paint palettes—you have eight different colors to work with each time.

8 Click anywhere outside the Font Color list to close the list without selecting any colors.

Table 3-3. The Eight Colors of a Color Scheme

Color	Description
Background	The color of your slide's background. It's usually a good idea to use a dark color for overhead slides and a light color for handouts.
Text and lines	The color applied to bulleted text, text blocks, and to any lines drawn onto the slide. Use a Text and Line color that is the opposite of the background so that it shows up well.
Shadows	The color of shadow effects used in text and drawing formatting. You will usually want to use a dark color for shadows.
Title text	The color applied to your slide's title. Use a color that really stands out.
Fills	Any shapes you draw with the Drawing toolbar will be filled in by this color.

Lesson 3.6
Choosing a Color Scheme

Table 3-3. The Eight Colors of a Color Scheme (Continued)

Color	Description
Accent	The color applied to odds and ends in your slides, such as charts.
Accent and hyperlink	The color of hyperlinks on your slides. Hyperlinks are usually blue.
Accent and followed hyperlink	The color of hyperlinks after they have been clicked on or followed. Followed hyperlinks are usually purple.

QUICK REFERENCE

A COLOR SCHEME IS A SET OF EIGHT COORDINATED COLORS YOU USE AS THE MAIN COLORS IN YOUR PRESENTATION.

TO CHANGE THE SLIDE COLOR SCHEME:

1. CLICK THE **DESIGN BUTTON** ON THE FORMATTING TOOLBAR AND CLICK **COLOR SCHEMES** IN THE TASK PANE.
2. SELECT A COLOR SCHEME FROM THE TASK PANE.

   OR...

   MOVE THE POINTER OVER THE TEMPLATE IN THE TASK PANE, CLICK THE ▾ ARROW, AND SELECT A COLOR SCHEME OPTION FROM THE LIST.

TO CHANGE A COLOR IN A COLOR SCHEME:

1. CLICK THE **DESIGN BUTTON** ON THE FORMATTING TOOLBAR.
2. CLICK **EDIT COLOR SCHEMES** IN THE TASK PANE.
3. SELECT THE COLOR YOU WANT TO CHANGE, CLICK THE **CHANGE COLOR BUTTON**, SELECT THE COLOR YOU WANT TO USE, AND CLICK **OK**.
4. CLICK **APPLY**.

Changing the Background of Your Slides

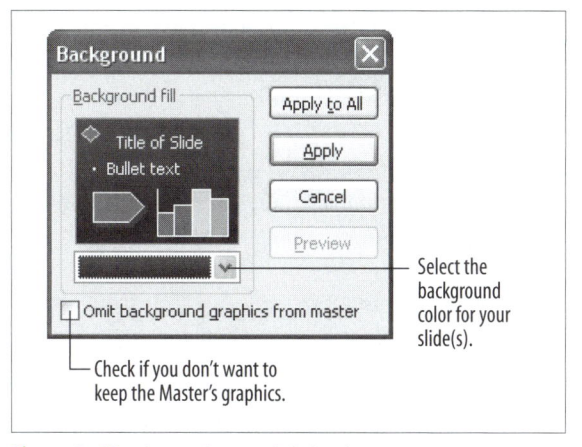

LESSON 3.7

Figure 3-13. The Background dialog box.

Select the background color for your slide(s).

Check if you don't want to keep the Master's graphics.

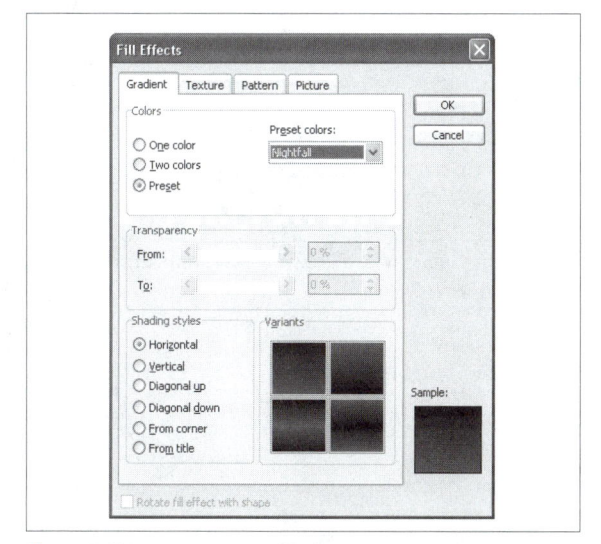

Figure 3-14. The Gradient tab of the Fill Effects dialog box.

Figure 3-15. The presentation with a preset Nightfall gradient background.

Now that we know how to format color schemes, it's time to move on to something a little more complicated: changing the slide's background. Choosing an appropriate background for your slides is like picking out wrapping paper—it's the first thing people notice about your presentation; therefore, you want it to be visually appealing and tasteful. This lesson will explain background fill patterns and how they can be used in your slides to produce dramatic, eye-catching effects.

1 If necessary, find and open the Lesson 3C presentation and save it as History of Mexico.

2 Press the Page Up key until you get to the Title Slide, then select Format → Background from the menu.

The Background dialog box appears, as shown in Figure 3-13.

3 Click the background fill list arrow.

Now you have to specify how you want to change the background. Here are your choices:

- **Color palette:** Fills the background with one of the eight colors from the slides' current color scheme.
- **More colors:** Fills the background with one of the hundreds of rainbow colors from the Color dialog box.
- **Fill Effects:** Fills the background with more dramatic-looking effects. There are four types of fill effects: gradient, texture, pattern, and picture. Table 3-4 describes each of them.

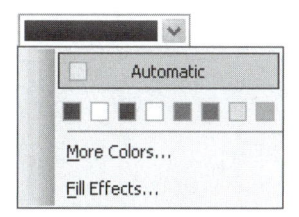

Background Fill List

4 Select Fill Effects from the background fill list.

The Fill Effects dialog box opens with the Gradient tab in front, as shown in Figure 3-14.

115

Lesson 3.7
Changing the Background of Your Slides

5 Ensure the Gradient tab is in front and then click the Preset option in the Colors section.

This indicates that you want to fill the background using a Preset Color. PowerPoint comes with numerous professionally designed background gradients.

6 Click the Preset Color list arrow and select Nightfall from the list.

A preview of the Nightfall color scheme appears in the Sample window, found in the bottom right of the dialog box. Compare your Fill Effects dialog box with the one in Figure 3-14.

7 Click OK to close the Fill Effects dialog box.

We're back at the Background dialog box. When you're changing a slide's background, you have to decide whether or not you want to keep the Slide Master's graphics and text. Check the "Omit background graphics from master" box if you don't want to keep the Master's graphics.

8 Click the Preview button.

PowerPoint temporarily applies the background to your presentation so you can see how it will look.

9 Click Apply to All.

The slides are formatted with the gradient you selected.

Believe it or not, by learning how to use fill patterns, you've learned a formatting trick that probably less than five percent of all PowerPoint users know. You should feel proud of yourself!

Table 3-4. Types of Fill Effects

Fill Pattern Tab	Example	Description
Gradient		Fills the background or objects with a gradient that gradually changes from one color to another color.
Texture		Fills the background or objects with a texture.
Pattern		Fills the background or objects with a pattern.
Picture		Fills the background or objects with a graphic or picture file.

Chapter 3
Formatting Your Presentation

QUICK REFERENCE

TO CHANGE THE SLIDE BACKGROUND:

1. SELECT **FORMAT → BACKGROUND** FROM THE MENU.
2. SELECT A COLOR FROM THE DROP-DOWN COLOR LIST. IF YOU WANT TO USE A MORE VIBRANT BACKGROUND, FOLLOW THE NEXT STEPS; OTHERWISE, CLICK **APPLY** OR **APPLY TO ALL**.

TO USE FILL EFFECTS FOR THE BACKGROUND:

1. FOLLOW THE PREVIOUS STEPS TO OPEN THE BACKGROUND DIALOG BOX.
2. SELECT THE **FILL EFFECTS** OPTION FROM THE DROP-DOWN COLOR LIST.
3. CLICK THE FILL EFFECTS TAB (GRADIENT, TEXTURE, PATTERN, OR PICTURE) AND SPECIFY HOW YOU WANT THE FILL EFFECT TO APPEAR.

117

Lesson 3.8 Working with Bulleted and Numbered Lists

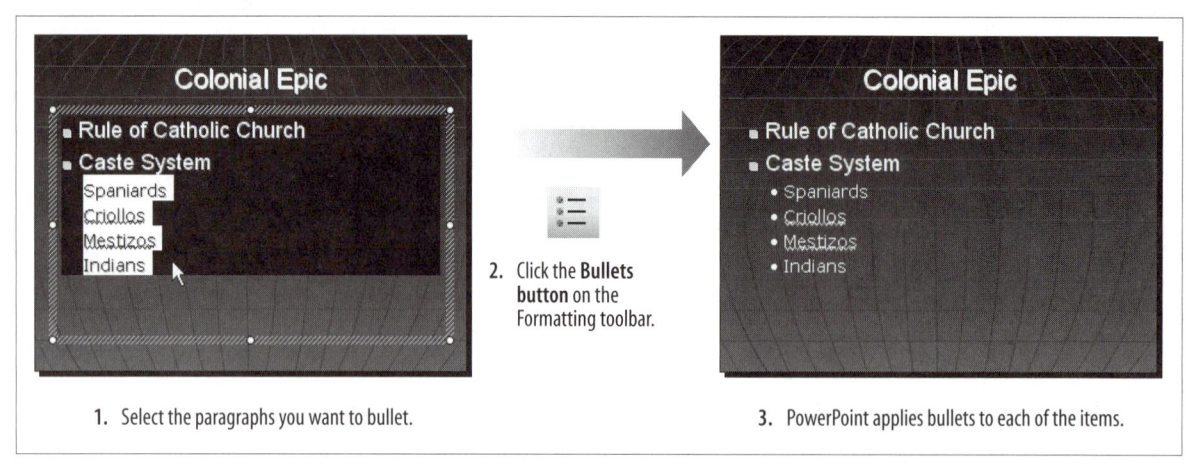

Figure 3-16. Adding bullets to a series of paragraphs.

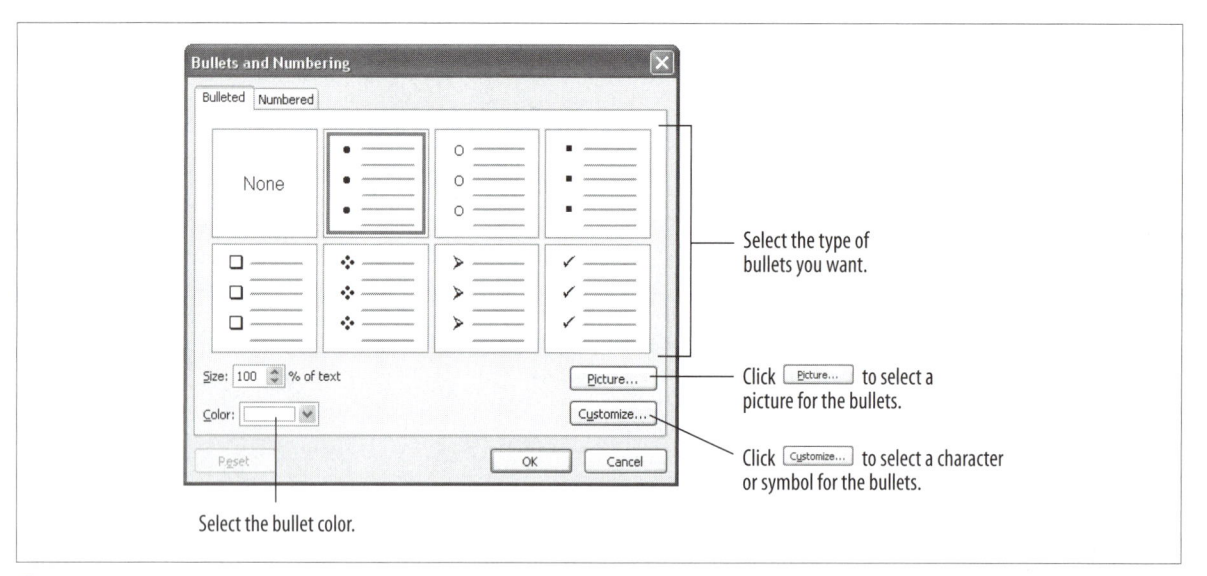

1. Select the paragraphs you want to bullet.
2. Click the **Bullets button** on the Formatting toolbar.
3. PowerPoint applies bullets to each of the items.

Figure 3-17. The Bullets and Numbering dialog box.

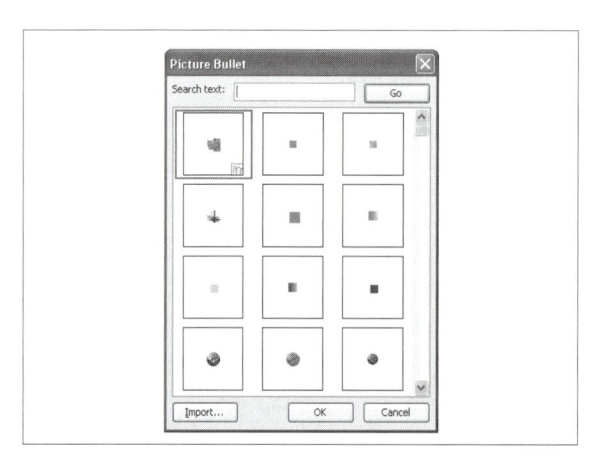

- Select the type of bullets you want.
- Click **Picture...** to select a picture for the bullets.
- Click **Customize...** to select a character or symbol for the bullets.
- Select the bullet color.

Figure 3-18. The Picture Bullet dialog box.

You've probably already noticed that most presentations include several bulleted lists—a list of items accented by a special character known as a bullet. By default, Power-Point uses a no-nonsense • character as a bullet, but you can use any character you want as a bullet, such as ✓, ❀, or even *.

This lesson explains how to add bullets to several paragraphs and how to change the character used as the bullet.

1 Go to Slide 4 (the Colonial Epic slide).

This slide contains a series of paragraphs that need to be bulleted. Here's how to add bullets to a paragraph or series of paragraphs:

118

Chapter 3
Formatting Your Presentation

2 Highlight the paragraph beginning with Spaniards and ending with Indians, as shown in Figure 3-16.

Now that you've selected the paragraphs, you can add bullets to them.

3 Click the Bullets button on the Formatting toolbar.

Bullets button

PowerPoint adds a bullet to each of the selected paragraphs.

The Bullets button is really a toggle switch—clicking it once adds bullets, clicking it again removes them. Therefore, to remove bullets from a bulleted list, simply select the list and click the Bullets button.

If you think the bullets PowerPoint uses are rather dull, you can choose a different bullet character. Here's how:

4 With the bulleted list still selected, select Format → Bullets and Numbering from the menu.

The Bullets and Numbering dialog box appears, as shown in Figure 3-17. Here you can specify which character to use for your bullet, the color of the bullet, or the size of the bullet compared to the paragraph, if you like any of the characters displayed.

5 Click the Customize button.

The Bullet dialog box is updated to display all the characters in the Wingding font set. Symbol, Wingdings, and Webdings are three fonts that contain many interesting characters suitable for bullets. We don't want to use any of these for our bullet at this time, so…

6 Click Cancel.

A new feature in PowerPoint 2003 is the ability to use any picture or graphical object as a bullet.

7 Click the Picture button.

In this window, as shown in Figure 3-18, you can see a variety of pictures that you can use as a bullet. Let's find one appropriate for our slide.

8 Scroll down until you find the picture of a small brown x (hint: it's in the first column). Click the picture and then click OK.

The Bullet dialog box closes and the selected bullet replaces the existing ones.

QUICK REFERENCE

TO CREATE A BULLETED LIST:

1. SELECT THE PARAGRAPH THAT YOU WANT TO BULLET.
2. CLICK THE BULLET BUTTON ON THE FORMATTING TOOLBAR.

TO CHANGE OR FORMAT THE BULLET SYMBOL:

1. SELECT FORMAT → BULLETS AND NUMBERING FROM THE MENU.
2. CLICK CUSTOMIZE TO USE A SYMBOL AS THE BULLET(S), OR CLICK PICTURE TO USE A PICTURE OR GRAPHIC AS THE BULLET(S).
3. IF YOU SELECT CUSTOMIZE, SELECT THE SYMBOL YOU WANT TO USE AND CLICK OK. IF YOU SELECT PICTURE, SELECT THE PICTURE YOU WANT TO USE, CLICK THE PICTURE, AND THEN CLICK OK.

LESSON 3.9
Changing Paragraph Alignment and Line Spacing

Left Aligned

Centered

Right Aligned

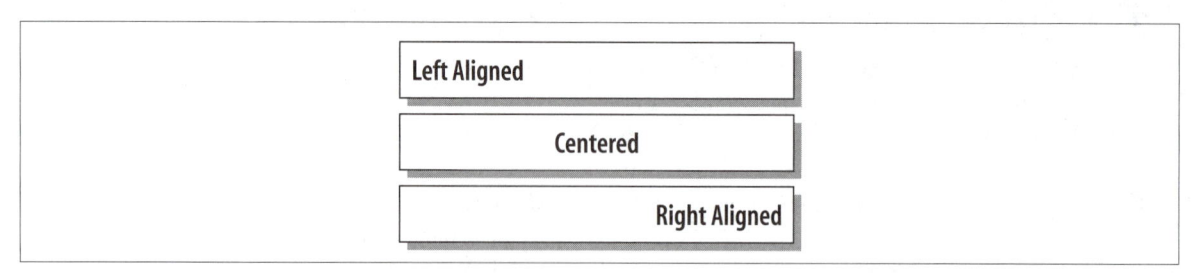

Figure 3-19. Examples of left aligned, centered, and right aligned text.

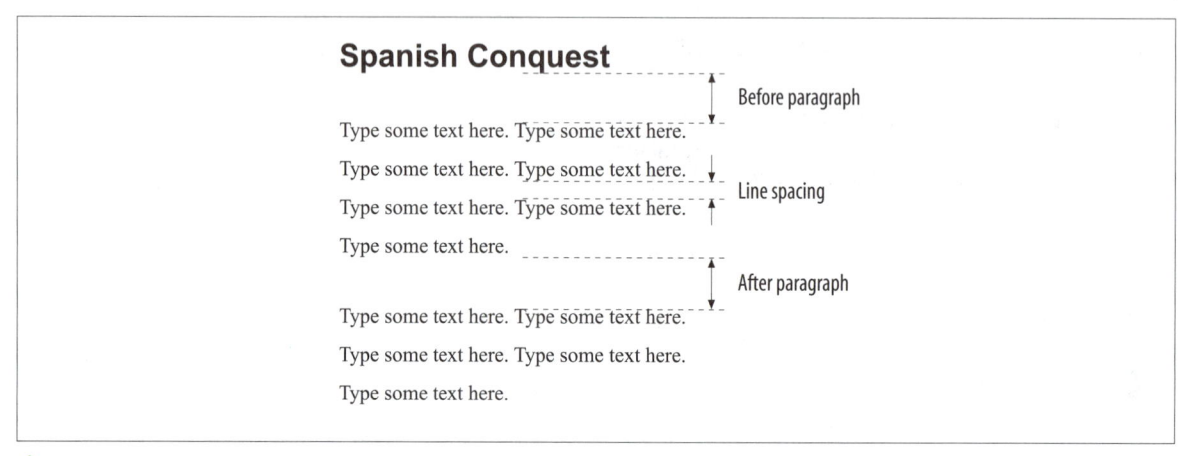

Spanish Conquest

Type some text here. Type some text here. — Before paragraph
Type some text here. Type some text here.
Type some text here. Type some text here. — Line spacing
Type some text here.
— After paragraph
Type some text here. Type some text here.
Type some text here. Type some text here.
Type some text here.

Figure 3-20. Examples of line spacing and spacing before and after a paragraph.

Line Spacing dialog box:

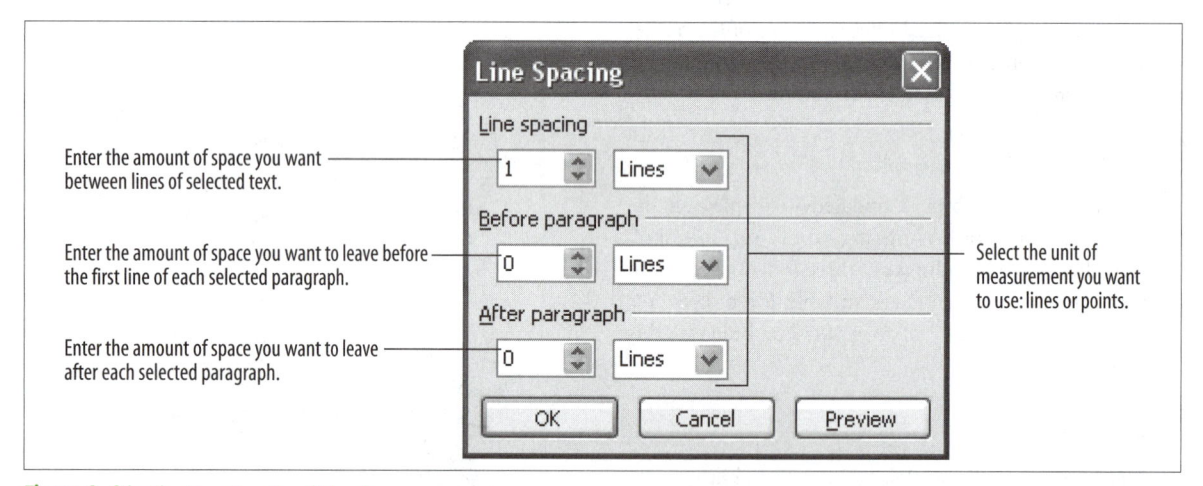

- Enter the amount of space you want between lines of selected text.
- Enter the amount of space you want to leave before the first line of each selected paragraph.
- Enter the amount of space you want to leave after each selected paragraph.
- Select the unit of measurement you want to use: lines or points.

Figure 3-21. The Line Spacing dialog box.

This lesson explains how to align the paragraphs in your slides to the left, center, or right. Figure 3-19 gives a better idea of what the various paragraph alignments look like. Actually, paragraphs in PowerPoint are aligned inside the text boxes that contain the text, so if you center a paragraph, it will appear centered inside its text box, not necessarily centered exactly on the slide.

Do you need more room before or after a paragraph? Would you like to tighten up the amount of space that appears between the lines of text on your slides? This lesson also explains how you can adjust the amount of space that appears before and after a paragraph, and how much space appears between the lines of text in a paragraph—for example, if you want to double-space a paragraph.

120

Look at Figure 3-20 for a visual reference of the different areas where you can adjust a paragraph's line spacing.

1 Press the Page Up key until you're back to Slide 1. Place the insertion point anywhere in the subtitle "Pre-Hispanic to Today" and click the Align Left button on the Formatting toolbar.

Left Align button

PowerPoint left aligns the text.

2 With the insertion point still in the subtitle click the Center button on the Formatting toolbar.

Center button

The slide title is once again centered inside the text box.

There's nothing to this paragraph alignment stuff, is there? Now let's move on to line spacing.

Since PowerPoint is presentation software, you probably won't need to adjust how much space appears before, after, or inside a paragraph as much as you might need to in a word processing program. Still, if your paragraphs feel too cramped or too far apart, here's how to adjust paragraph line spacing:

3 Go to slide 4 and select the four bulleted subtopics, beginning with "Spaniards" and ending with "Indians".

We'll adjust the line spacing for these paragraphs.

4 Select Format → Line Spacing from the menu.

The Line Spacing dialog box appears, as shown in Figure 3-21. There are three boxes where you can specify how much space appears between the lines in a paragraph, how much space appears above a paragraph, and how much space appears below a paragraph. Notice the combo boxes to the right of each of these boxes—they allow you to select between two different units of measurement: lines and points.

5 Type 1.5 in the Line spacing box and click OK.

The Line Spacing dialog box closes and PowerPoint adjusts the line spacing for the selected text to one and a half lines.

6 Save your work.

> ## QUICK REFERENCE
>
> **TO CHANGE PARAGRAPH ALIGNMENT:**
>
> - SWITCH TO NORMAL VIEW.
>
>   LEFT: CLICK THE ALIGN LEFT BUTTON ON THE FORMATTING TOOLBAR OR PRESS CTRL + L.
>
>   CENTER: CLICK THE CENTER BUTTON ON THE FORMATTING TOOLBAR OR PRESS CTRL + E.
>
>   RIGHT: CLICK THE ALIGN RIGHT BUTTON ON THE FORMATTING TOOLBAR OR PRESS CTRL + R.
>
> OR...
>
> - SELECT FORMAT → PARAGRAPH FROM THE MENU AND SELECT THE PARAGRAPH ALIGNMENT FROM THE ALIGNMENT LIST.
>
> **TO CHANGE LINE SPACING:**
>
> 1. SWITCH TO NORMAL VIEW.
> 2. SELECT THE PARAGRAPHS WHOSE LINE SPACING YOU WANT TO CHANGE.
> 3. SELECT FORMAT → LINE SPACING FROM THE MENU, ADJUST THE LINE SPACING SETTINGS IN THE DIALOG BOX, AND CLICK OK.

LESSON 3.10
Adding Headers and Footers

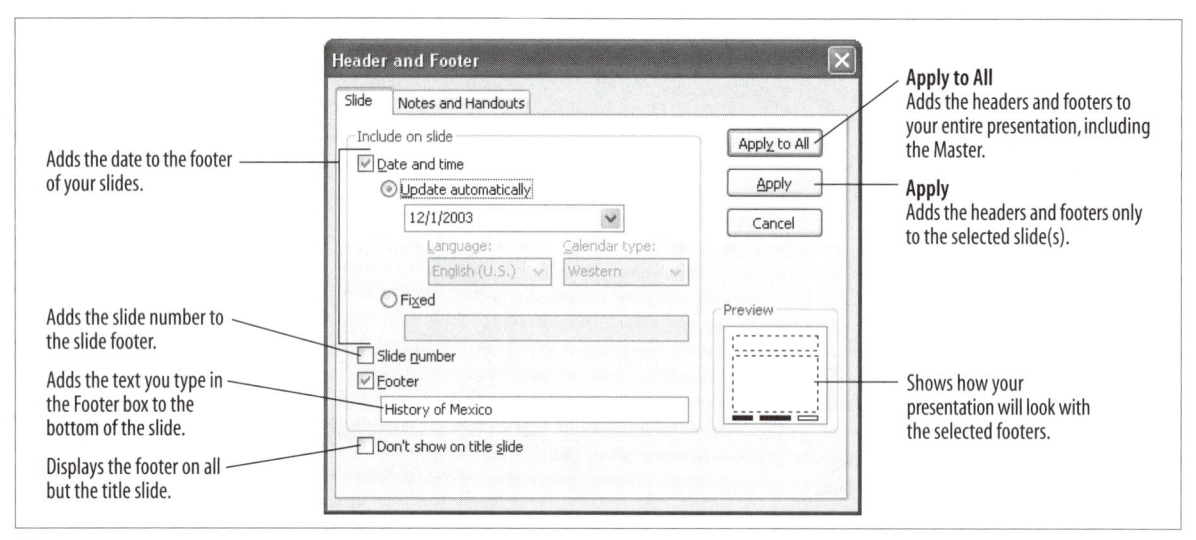

Figure 3-22. The Slide tab of the Header and Footer dialog box.

- Adds the date to the footer of your slides.
- Adds the slide number to the slide footer.
- Adds the text you type in the Footer box to the bottom of the slide.
- Displays the footer on all but the title slide.
- **Apply to All** — Adds the headers and footers to your entire presentation, including the Master.
- **Apply** — Adds the headers and footers only to the selected slide(s).
- Shows how your presentation will look with the selected footers.

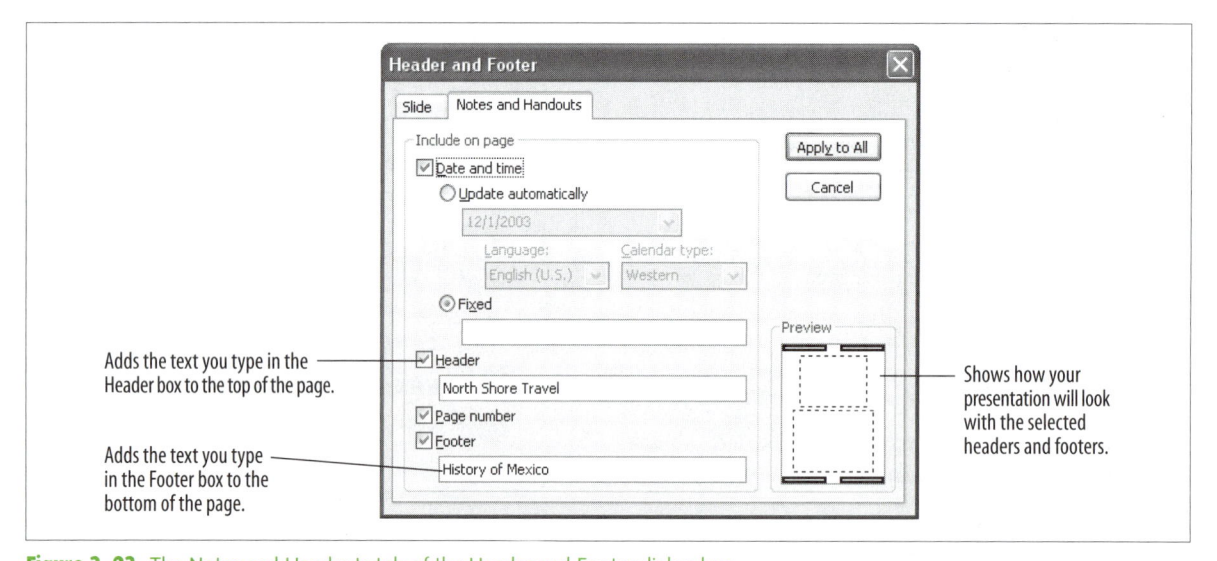

Figure 3-23. The Notes and Handouts tab of the Header and Footer dialog box.

- Adds the text you type in the Header box to the top of the page.
- Adds the text you type in the Footer box to the bottom of the page.
- Shows how your presentation will look with the selected headers and footers.

Presentations that are several slides long often have information—such as the slide number, the slide's title, or the date—located at the top or bottom of every slide. Text that appears at the top of every slide is called a *header*, while text appearing at the bottom of each slide is called a *footer*. In this lesson, you will learn how to add headers and footers to your slides and handouts.

1 If necessary, find and open the Lesson 3D presentation and save it as History of Mexico.

2 Select View → Header and Footer from the menu.

The Header and Footer dialog box appears, as shown in Figure 3-22. This is where you can add a footer that appears at the bottom of all the slides in your presentation.

Notice the Header and Footer dialog box has two tabs: a Slide tab and a Notes and Handouts tab. Because PowerPoint produces two types of output (slides and handouts), each gets its own separate set of headers and footers.

122

3 Make sure the Date and Time box is checked.

Checking the Date and Time box adds the date in the bottom left corner of your slides. There are two different ways to add the date:

- **Update Automatically:** Displays and automatically updates the current date. For example, if you create a presentation on Saturday and then deliver it on a Wednesday, Wednesday would appear on the footer.
- **Fixed:** You type the date and time you want to appear in the Fixed box. The date is not updated.

4 Select the Fixed option and type today's date in the Fixed box.

This will add the date you enter to your slide footer. You can also add your own text to the footer.

5 Make sure the Footer box is checked and then type History of Mexico in the Footer box.

Now that we're finished specifying what we want to appear on our slides' footer, let's take a look at the header and footer for our presentation's notes and handouts.

6 Click the Notes and Handouts tab.

The Notes and Handouts tab of the Header and Footer dialog box appears, as shown in Figure 3-23. At first, the Notes and Handouts tab looks identical to the Slides tab, but look closely—there's also a place to add a header to your presentation's notes and handouts. Move on to the next step and let's add a header to our presentation's notes and handouts.

7 Make sure the Header box is checked and then type North Shore Travel in the Header box.

The text "North Shore Travel" will appear in the header of your presentation's notes and handouts. Let's add the date to the notes and handouts header.

8 Make sure the Date and Time box is checked, select the Fixed option, and type today's date in the Fixed box.

Last, but not least, we need to add the presentation's title to the footer.

9 Make sure the Footer box is checked and then type History of Mexico in the Footer box.

Like so many other formatting options, you can apply the header and footer to the current slide only or to all the slides in your presentation.

10 Click Apply to All to add the header and footer to all the slides in your presentation.

The Header and Footer dialog box closes and you can see the headers and footers on your screen.

11 Save your work.

QUICK REFERENCE

TO INSERT A HEADER OR FOOTER:

1. SELECT VIEW → HEADER AND FOOTER FROM THE MENU.

   FILL IN ANY OF THESE BOXES:

   DATE: DISPLAYS THE DATE AND TIME.

   NUMBER: DISPLAYS THE SLIDE NUMBER.

   FOOTER: DISPLAYS TEXT THAT APPEARS ON EACH AND EVERY ONE OF YOUR SLIDES.

2. CLICK APPLY (TO APPLY THE HEADER AND/ OR FOOTER TO THE CURRENT SLIDE) OR APPLY TO ALL (TO APPLY THE HEADER AND/ OR FOOTER TO THE ENTIRE PRESENTATION).

LESSON 3.11

Working with Tabs and Indents

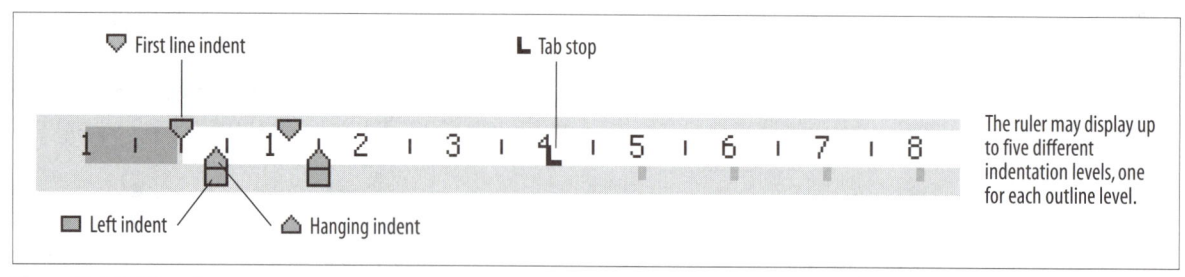

Figure 3-24. The ruler.

- First line indent
- Tab stop
- Left indent
- Hanging indent

The ruler may display up to five different indentation levels, one for each outline level.

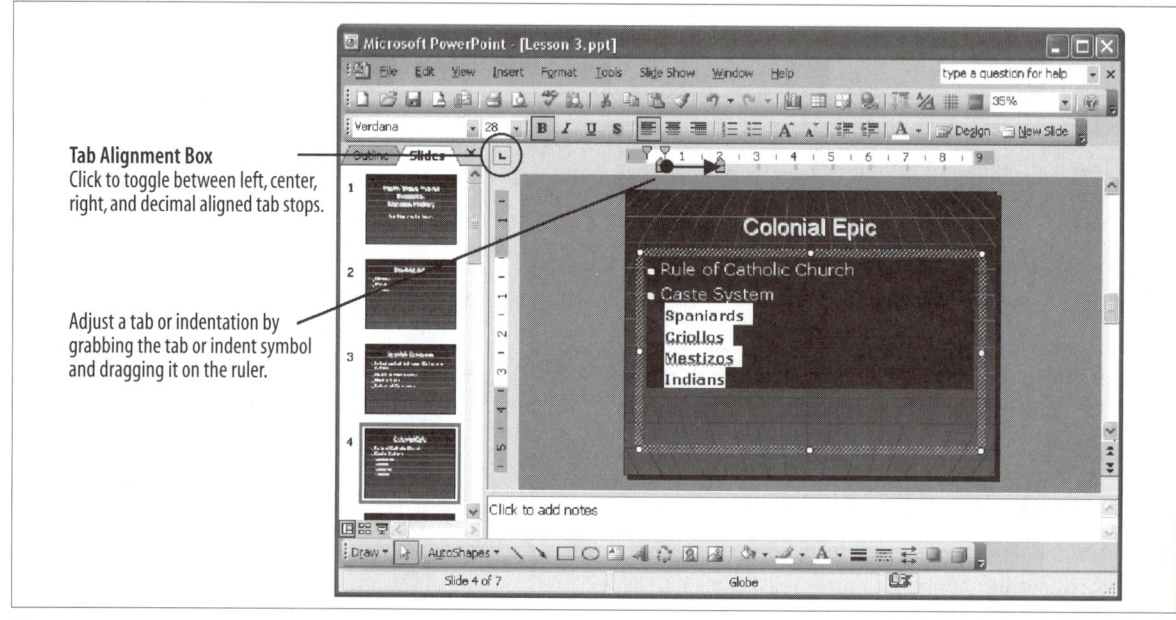

Figure 3-25. How to set and modify tab stops.

Tab Alignment Box
Click to toggle between left, center, right, and decimal aligned tab stops.

Adjust a tab or indentation by grabbing the tab or indent symbol and dragging it on the ruler.

This lesson is completely optional—PowerPoint is a presentation program, not a word processor, so there is little reason to mess with your presentation's tab or indent settings. PowerPoint already indents each paragraph according to its position in the outline, and the template determines the amount of indentation you can use.

If you still want to learn about adding tabs and indents to your slides, here's how:

1 Display the ruler by selecting **View** → **Ruler** from the menu.

The ruler appears above the presentation window and displays the tab and indent settings for the selected text box, as shown in Figure 3-25.

NOTE *You need to be in Normal View if you want to make changes to your slide's tabs and indents. You can't adjust tabs and indents in Outline View, and although you can adjust tabs and indents in Notes View, it's much easier to do in Normal View.*

Next, you need to select the text box whose tabs and indents you want to change.

2 On Slide 4, select the four bulleted subtopics, beginning with "Spaniards" and ending with "Indians."

Notice several symbols appear on the ruler, such as a ▽ or even a △. These are indention markers. You adjust a slide's indentation by grabbing and dragging the appropriate indention marker. Figure 3-24 illustrates the three types of indentation markers—each indents text on your slide in a different way.

124

Chapter 3
Formatting Your Presentation

NOTE *The ruler may display up to five different indentation levels—one for each outline level on the current slide. The illustration in Figure 3-24 has two indention levels.*

Ready to try indenting the text in the text box? Then move on to the next step.

Left Indent marker

3 Click and drag the second ▽ **First Line Indent marker** on the ruler to the right, to the **2-inch mark**.

The subtopics move further away from their bullets. If you're curious, you can try dragging the other indent markers on the ruler to see how each one indents text.

Once the ruler is visible, it is incredibly easy to add tab stops to your slides—simply click the ruler where you want to add a tab stop.

4 Click the **5-inch mark** on the ruler.

You've just added a left tab stop ⌞ at the five-inch mark. Let's see how it works.

5 Place the insertion point after **Spaniards**, press the **Ctrl** + **Tab** key, and type `Highest Caste`.

Sure enough, the tab stops right at the five-inch tab stop you added.

NOTE *If you don't add any tab stops to a slide, PowerPoint uses default tab stops, which are located at each inch on the ruler.*

Adjusting and removing tab stops is almost as easy as adding them. To adjust a tab stop, simply grab it and drag it to a new position on the ruler, just like you did with the indent markers. To remove a tab stop, simply drag it off the ruler.

6 Remove the tab stop you added in Step 4 by dragging it off the ruler.

Since we're done using the ruler, let's hide it so that we have move room to view and work with our slides.

7 Delete the "Highest Caste" text and then select **View** → **Ruler** from the menu.

The ruler disappears and we're back in Normal View.

By clicking the Tab Alignment box (see Figure 3-25) you can toggle which type of tab stop is added when you click the ruler. Table 3-5 describes the four different types of tabs you can add.

Table 3-5. Types of Tabs

Alignment	Mark	Example	Description
Left	⌞	100.00	Aligns the left side of text with the tab stop.
Center	⊥	100.00	Aligns the text so that it is centered over the tab stop.
Right	⌟	100.00	Aligns the right side of text with the tab stop.
Decimal	⊥·	100.00	Aligns text at the decimal point. Text and numbers before the decimal point appear to the left, text and numbers after the decimal point appear to the right.

125

Lesson 3.11
Working with Tabs and Indents

QUICK REFERENCE

TO SET A TAB STOP USING THE RULER:

1. Click the [L] TAB SELECTOR BOX on the ruler until you see the type of tab you want to use (left, center, right, and decimal).

2. Click on the ruler where you want to set the tab stop.

LESSON 3.12

Changing the Page Setup

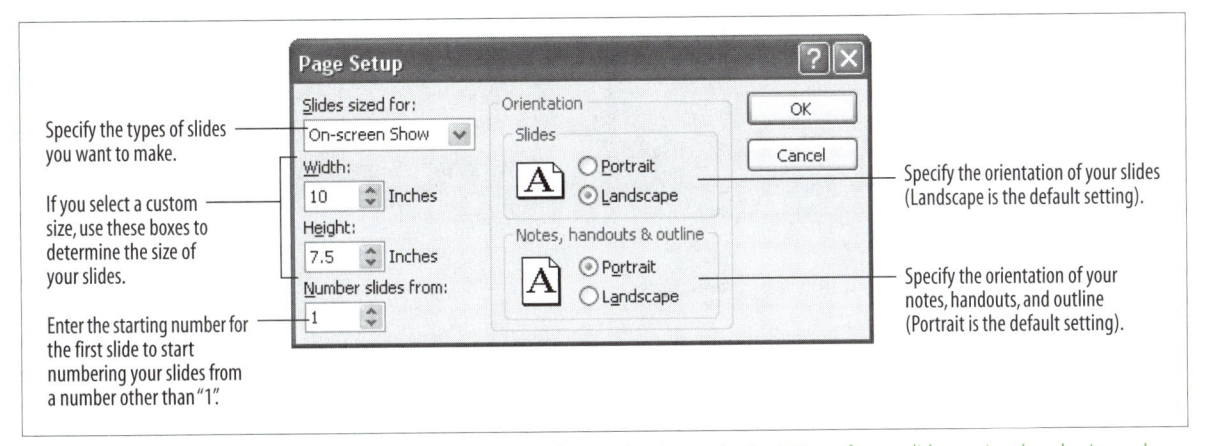

Figure 3-26. The Page Setup dialog box is where you can change the size and orientation of your slides, notes, handouts, and outlines.

Callouts in figure:
- Specify the types of slides you want to make.
- If you select a custom size, use these boxes to determine the size of your slides.
- Enter the starting number for the first slide to start numbering your slides from a number other than "1".
- Specify the orientation of your slides (Landscape is the default setting).
- Specify the orientation of your notes, handouts, and outline (Portrait is the default setting).

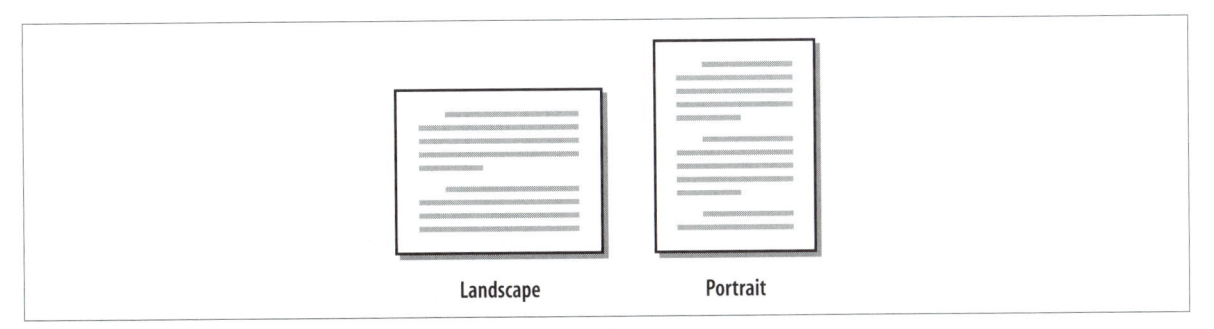

Figure 3-27. Comparison of portrait and landscape page orientations.

Most people deliver their PowerPoint presentations on their computer screen or on an overhead projection unit connected to a computer, so changing the page setup—the height, width, and orientation of the page—is not nearly as important as it is in other programs, such as Microsoft Word or Microsoft Excel. However, if you want to deliver your presentation on printed paper, transparencies, or 35mm slides, you need to specify the types of slides you want to make in the Page Setup dialog box.

This lesson also explains how to change the page orientation. Everything you print uses one of two different types of paper orientations: Portrait and Landscape. In Portrait orientation, the paper is taller than it is wide—like a painting of a person's portrait. In Landscape orientation, the paper is wider than it is tall—like a painting of a landscape. Landscape orientation is the default setting for your PowerPoint slides, and Portrait orientation is the default setting for your notes, handouts, and outline.

Here, then, is how to change your presentation's page setup:

1 Select **File → Page Setup** from the menu.

The Page Setup dialog box appears, as shown in Figure 3-26.

2 Click the **Slides sized for list**.

As you can see in the Slides sized for list, there are several types of slides you can make:

- On-screen Show (the default setting)
- Letter Paper
- Ledger Paper
- A3 Paper
- A4 Paper
- B4 (ISO) Paper
- B5 (ISO) Paper

127

Lesson 3.12
Changing the Page Setup

- 35mm Slides
- Overhead (transparencies)
- Banner
- Custom (use the Width and Height boxes to specify the size of the page)

For this exercise, we'll be creating 35mm slides.

3 Select the 35mm Slides option from the Slides sized for list.

Specifying a different slide size will usually be the only change you'll need to make in the Page Setup dialog box, and it's the only one we'll be making in this exercise.

4 Click OK to close the Page Setup dialog box.

Guess what? You've just put another PowerPoint chapter under your belt. Move on to the next step and then take a look at the chapter review to see how much you've learned.

5 Exit Microsoft PowerPoint without saving any of your changes.

QUICK REFERENCE

TO CHANGE A SLIDE'S ORIENTATION:

1. SELECT FILE → PAGE SETUP FROM THE MENU.
2. IN THE ORIENTATION SECTION, SELECT EITHER THE PORTRAIT OR LANDSCAPE OPTION.

TO CHANGE THE PAPER SIZE:

1. SELECT FILE → PAGE SETUP FROM THE MENU.
2. CLICK THE SLIDE SIZED FOR LIST TO SELECT FROM A LIST OF COMMON PAGE SIZES.

Chapter Three Review

Lesson Summary

Formatting Fonts with the Formatting Toolbar

The quickest and easiest way to format the text in your slides is by using the Formatting toolbar.

To Boldface Text: Click the **B** Bold button on the Formatting toolbar or press Ctrl + B.

To Italicize Text: Click the *I* Italics button on the Formatting toolbar or press Ctrl + I.

To Underline Text: Click the U Underline button on the Formatting toolbar or press Ctrl + U.

To Change Font Size: Select the point size from the Font Size list on the Formatting toolbar.

To Change Font Type: Select the desired font from the Font list on the Formatting toolbar.

Advanced Font Formatting with the Font Dialog Box

To Open the Font Dialog Box: Select Format → Font from the menu.

Using the Format Painter

The Format Painter lets you copy the formatting of text or an object and apply or paste the formatting to another text or object.

To Use the Format Painter: Select the text or object with the formatting options you want to copy, click the Format Painter button on the Standard toolbar, and select the text or object where you want to apply the copied formatting.

Double-click the Format Painter button on the Standard toolbar to apply formatting to several locations. Click the Format Painter button again when you're finished.

Applying a Template's Formatting

To Apply a Template Design to a Presentation: Click the Design button on the Formatting toolbar and click the template you want to apply to the presentation from the task pane.

To Apply a Template Design to a Single Slide: Click the Design button on the Formatting toolbar, move the pointer over the template in the task pane, click the arrow, and select Apply to Selected Slides from the menu.

Using Masters

You can edit, format, or insert something on every slide in your presentation with the Slide Master.

To Edit the Slide Master: Select View → Masters → Slide Master from the menu. Edit and format the Slide Master as needed. Any text, graphics, or formatting you add to the Slide Master will appear on every slide in your presentation. Click the Close Master View button on the Slide Master View toolbar when you're finished.

To Override the Slide Master: Edit and format the slide you want to override.

Choosing a Color Scheme

A Color scheme is a set of eight coordinated colors you can use as the main colors in your presentation.

To Change the Slide Color Scheme: Click the Design button on the Formatting toolbar and click Color Schemes in the task pane. Select a color scheme from the task pane or move the pointer over the template in the task pane, click the arrow, and select a color scheme option from the list.

To Change a Color in a Color Scheme: Click the Design button on the Formatting toolbar and click Edit Color Schemes in the task pane. Select the color you want to change, click the Change Color button, select the color you want to use, and click OK. Click Apply when you've finished making changes to the color scheme.

Changing the Background of Your Slides

To Change the Slide Background: Select Format → Background from the menu and select a color from the drop-down color list. If you want to use a more vibrant background, follow the next steps; otherwise, click Apply or Apply to All.

129

Chapter 3
Chapter Three Review

To Use Fill Effects for the Background: Follow the steps above to open the Background dialog box. Select the Fill Effects option from the drop-down color list, click the Fill Effects tab (Gradient, Texture, Pattern, or Picture), and specify how you want the fill effect to appear.

Working with Bulleted Lists

To Add Bullets to Several Paragraphs: Select the paragraph that you want to bullet and click the Bullet button on the Formatting toolbar.

To Change or Format the Bullet Symbol: Select Format → Bullets and Numbering from the menu, click Customize to use a symbol as the bullet(s) or Picture to use a picture or graphic as the bullet(s). If you select Customize, select the symbol you want to use and click OK. If you select Picture, select the picture you want to use and click OK.

Changing Paragraph Alignment and Line Spacing

To Change Line Spacing: Switch to Normal View and select the paragraphs whose line spacing you want to change. Change the line spacing using one of these methods:

- Select Format → Line Spacing from the menu, adjust the line spacing settings in the dialog box, and click OK.

- Click the Increase Paragraph Spacing button or Decreasing Paragraph Spacing button on the Formatting toolbar.

Adding Headers and Footers

To Insert a Header or Footer: Select View → Header and Footer from the menu. Fill in any of these boxes:

- **Date:** Displays the date and time.
- **Number:** Displays the slide number.
- **Footer:** Displays text that appears on each and every one of your slides.

Click Apply (to apply the header and/or footer to the current slide) or Apply to All (to apply the header and/or footer to the entire presentation.

Working with Tabs and Indents

To Set a Tab Stop Using the Ruler: Click the Tab selector box on the ruler until you see the type of tab you want to use (left, center, right, and decimal). Click on the ruler where you want to set the tab stop.

Changing the Page Setup

To Change a Slide's Orientation: Select File → Page Setup from the menu. In the Orientation section select either the Portrait or Landscape option.

To Change the Paper Size: Click the Slide Sized for list to select from a list of common page sizes.

Quiz

1. Which of the following can you format using buttons on the formatting toolbar? (Select all that apply.)

   A. Font Size
   B. Font Color
   C. Underlining
   D. Your hard drive

2. What is the purpose of the Format Painter?

   A. To paint pretty pictures on your slides
   B. To highlight important text
   C. To copy formatting from one object or piece of text and then apply it elsewhere
   D. To change the background color of your slides.

3. Which of the following Fill Effects can you use for the slide background? (Select all that apply.)

   A. Gradient
   B. Brightness
   C. Picture
   D. Texture

4. Although you can format text with any color, you should try to stick with the color scheme's eight coordinated colors to give your slides a professional, consistent appearance. (True or False?)

5. How can you easily add text or a picture that will appear on each and every one of your slides?

   A. Open the Slide Master by selecting View → Master → Slide Master and add the text or picture.

   B. There is no quick and easy way to add something to every slide in a presentation. You have to go to each slide and add the text or picture.

   C. Click the Add to All Slides button on the Standard toolbar and add the text or picture.

   D. Use the Format All Slides Wizard to add text to a picture.

6. Once you change the appearance of your slides with the Slide Master, you can't change the formatting of specific slides. (True or False?)

Homework

1. Open the Homework 3 presentation, located in your Practice folder or disk, and save it as "Three's Company.

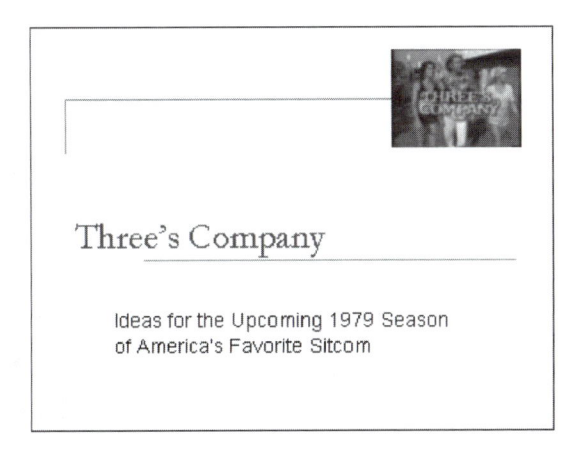

2. Go to Slide 2 and select all of the bulleted items on this slide.

3. Click the Font Size list arrow on the Formatting toolbar and select 28, then click the Font list arrow on the Formatting toolbar and select Arial.

4. With the same text still selected, click the Format Painter button on the Standard toolbar. Go to Slide 3 and apply the copied formatting by selecting all the bulleted items on the slide.

5. Click the Design button on the Formatting toolbar and then click Design Templates. Click the Edge template in the task pane.

6. Add bold and italics formatting to the title font on every slide in the presentation using the Slide Master: select View → Masters → Slide Master from the menu, select the slide title, and click the Bold button and the Italics button on the Formatting toolbar. Click the Normal or Normal View button to leave the Master Normal View.

7. Change the presentation's Color scheme. Select Format → Color Schemes from the Slide Design menu and select a Color scheme you like. Click Apply to All to apply the Color scheme to all the slides in the presentation.

8. Add a header to all your slides that includes the current date and a footer that says "Three's Company." Select View → Header and Footer from the menu to open the Header and Footer dialog box. Make sure the Date and Time box is checked as well as the "Update Automatically" button, check the Footer check box and type "Three's Company" in the Footer text box. Click Apply to All when you're finished.

9. Change the background for the slides. Select Format → Background from the menu and select a color from the background fill list. Click Apply to All to apply the background to all the slides in the presentation.

Extra Credit: Add a two color gradient background to all the slides in your presentation. Hint: Select Format → Background from the menu, select Fill Effects from the background fill list, click the Gradient tab, and create the background.

Chapter 3
Chapter Three Review

Quiz Answers

1. A, B, and C.

2. C. The Format Painter tool copies formatting from one object or piece of text so that you can apply or paste it elsewhere.

3. A, C, and D. Brightness is not one of the four Fill Effects. The correct answer would be Pattern.

4. True. You can format the text on your slides with any color you want, but it's usually best to stick with the eight coordinated colors of the presentation's color scheme.

5. A. The Slide Master is where you want to go if you want to change the appearance of every slide in your presentation.

6. False. Formatting an individual slide overrides the Slide Master for that slide.

CHAPTER 4
DRAWING AND WORKING WITH GRAPHICS

CHAPTER OBJECTIVES:

Drawing on your slides
Adding, arranging, and formatting text boxes
Selecting, resizing, formatting, and deleting objects
Inserting clip art and pictures
Aligning and grouping objects
Drawing AutoShapes
Flipping and rotating objects
Layering objects
Applying shadows and 3-D effects

CHAPTER TASK: ADD DRAWINGS AND PICTURES TO AN EXISTING SLIDE

Prerequisites

- **Windows basics: know how to use menus, toolbars, dialog boxes, and shortcut keystrokes.**
- **Know how to select objects.**
- **Be proficient with the mouse—especially dragging and dropping.**

Get ready to get in touch with your artistic side! Slide shows with pictures, graphics, and visuals are much more compelling and effective at conveying messages than slide shows that contain only boring text. Even if you don't have any artistic ability, PowerPoint makes it easy to add pictures and drawings to your slides, making them look as though you hired a professional graphic design company to create them.

This chapter explains how to use PowerPoint's unique drawing tools to add lines, shapes, and text boxes to your slides, as well as how to format them. You will also learn how to add pictures to your slides from the Microsoft Clip Art Gallery (which includes more than 4,000 clip art pictures!) or from an external file. This chapter will also teach you how to move, resize, align and group, and flip and rotate graphic objects. Let's get started!

LESSON 4.1   Drawing on Your Slides

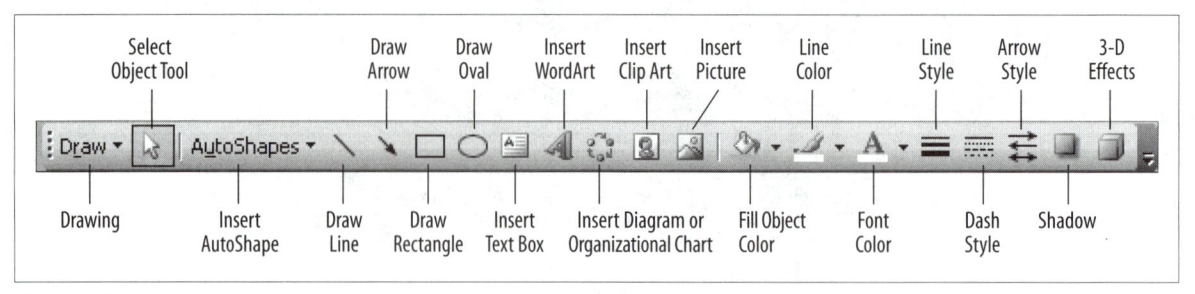

Figure 4-1. The Drawing toolbar.

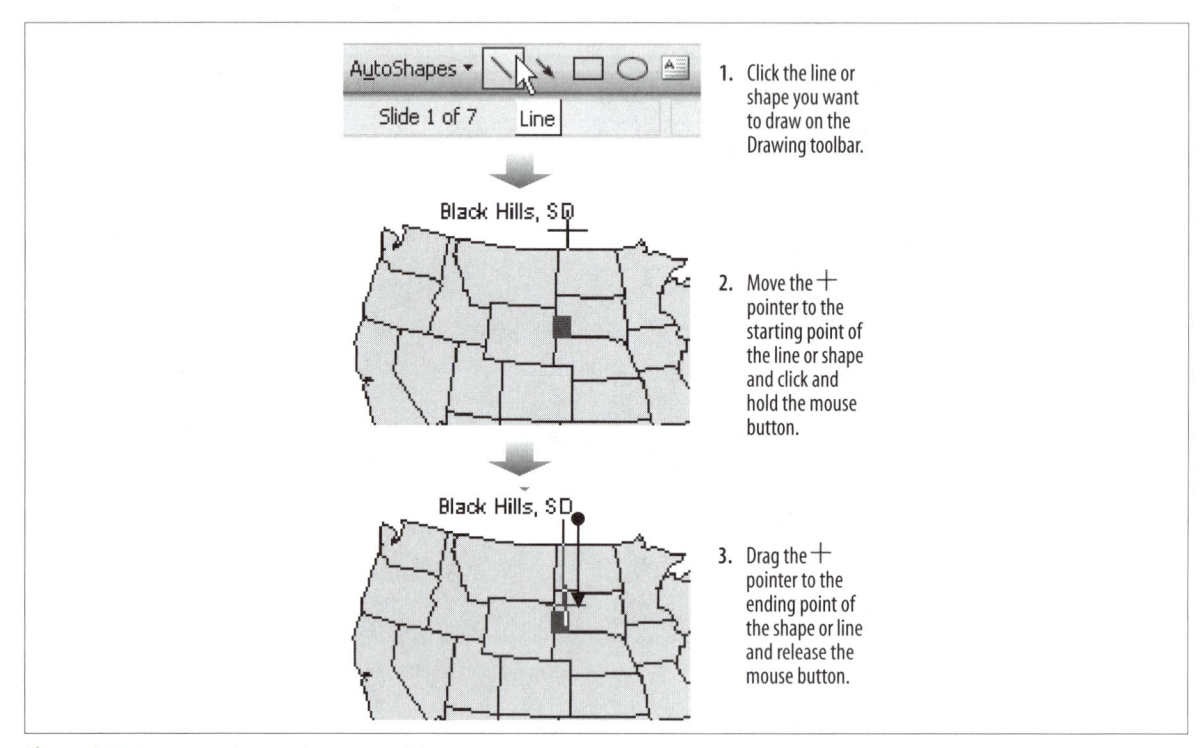

Labels: Select Object Tool, Draw Arrow, Draw Oval, Insert WordArt, Insert Clip Art, Insert Picture, Line Color, Line Style, Arrow Style, 3-D Effects, Drawing, Insert AutoShape, Draw Line, Draw Rectangle, Insert Text Box, Insert Diagram or Organizational Chart, Fill Object Color, Font Color, Dash Style, Shadow

1. Click the line or shape you want to draw on the Drawing toolbar.
2. Move the + pointer to the starting point of the line or shape and click and hold the mouse button.
3. Drag the + pointer to the ending point of the shape or line and release the mouse button.

Figure 4-2. Drawing a line or shape on a slide.

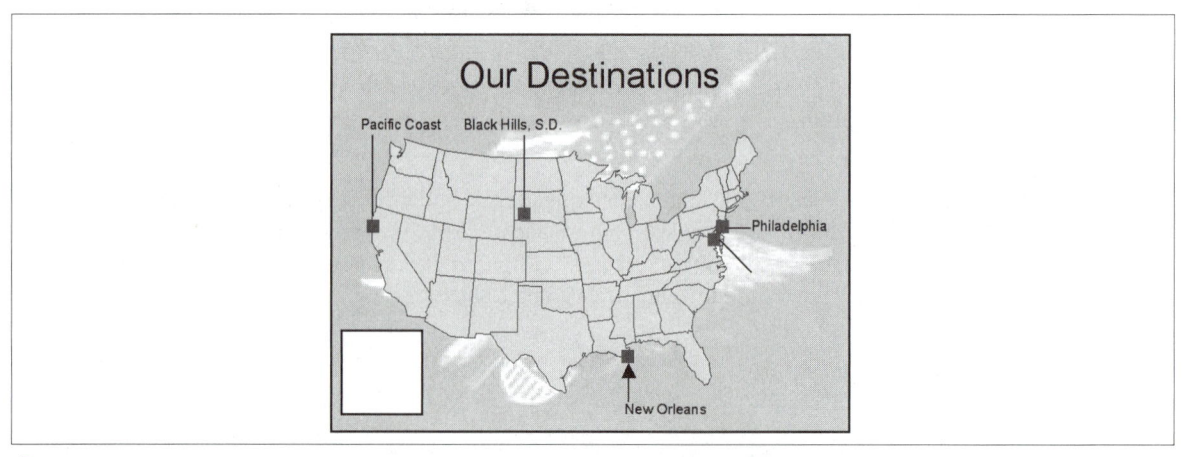

Figure 4-3. The updated slide with lines added from the text labels to their destinations on the map.

134

Chapter 4
Drawing and Working with Graphics

Most of PowerPoint's drawing tools can be found on the Drawing toolbar, located at the bottom of the screen. The Drawing toolbar contains tools for drawing lines, shapes, and arrows, and for formatting graphic objects with different coloring, shadow, and 3-D effects.

1 Start PowerPoint.

2 Open the presentation named Lesson 4A and save it as American History.

First, we have to move to the slide where we want to add our drawings.

3 Press Page Down or use the vertical scroll bar to go to Slide 2.

This slide is supposed to show the destinations of a tour package, but, if you look closely, you'll notice that several things are missing from it. Several of the lines connecting text labels to points on the map have disappeared. Go to the next step and we'll learn how to fix this problem.

4 Click the Line button on the Drawing toolbar.

Line button

The pointer changes to a +, indicating that you can draw the selected shape.

5 Place the + pointer below the Black Hills, S.D. text label. Click and drag the + pointer to the ■ South Dakota marker on the map and release the mouse button, as shown in Figure 4-2.

That's all there is to drawing a line. Try drawing another one.

6 Following the same procedure as Step 4, draw a line between the Philadelphia text label and the ■ Philadelphia marker on the map.

If you can draw a line, you can draw an arrow to point to an item of interest. That's because an arrow is really nothing more than a line with a tiny triangle at one end. Actually, you can format any line and change it into an arrow or vice versa—but we'll cover how to format drawing objects in another lesson. Move on to the next step and let's try drawing an arrow.

7 Click the Arrow button on the Drawing toolbar.

Arrow button

The pointer again changes to a + indicating you can draw an arrow.

8 Using the procedure you just learned, draw a line between the New Orleans text label and the ■ New Orleans marker on the map.

Congratulations! You've just drawn an arrow on your slide.

NOTE *Arrows point at whatever you drag the destination line to—not where you first click. Remembering where to click and where to drag can be a bit confusing, and some people never master it. If your arrow points in the wrong direction, you can always change the format. For more information, see Lesson 4.4.*

Now let's try drawing an oval.

9 Click the Oval button on the Drawing toolbar.

The pointer changes to a +. Drawing shapes is similar to drawing lines—you click on the slide where you want to draw the shape and then drag until the shape reaches the desired size.

10 Click just above and to the left of the northwest corner of California with the + pointer and drag down and to the right until an oval covers the state of California.

To draw a perfect circle, rectangle, straight line, or other shape, hold down the Shift key as you drag.

11 Click the Rectangle button on the Drawing toolbar and hold down the Shift key as you drag a square in the bottom-left corner of the slide, as shown in Figure 4-3.

12 Delete the oval and save your work.

135

Lesson 4.1
Drawing on Your Slides

QUICK REFERENCE

TO DRAW AN OBJECT:

1. CLICK THE OBJECT YOU WANT TO DRAW ON THE DRAWING TOOLBAR (SUCH AS A LINE OR CIRCLE).
2. DRAW YOUR SHAPE BY CLICKING ON THE SLIDE AND DRAGGING UNTIL THE SHAPE REACHES THE DESIRED SIZE.

TO DRAW A PERFECT SQUARE, CIRCLE, OR LINE:

- HOLD DOWN THE SHIFT KEY AS YOU DRAW A SELECTED OBJECT.

Adding, Arranging, and Formatting Text Boxes

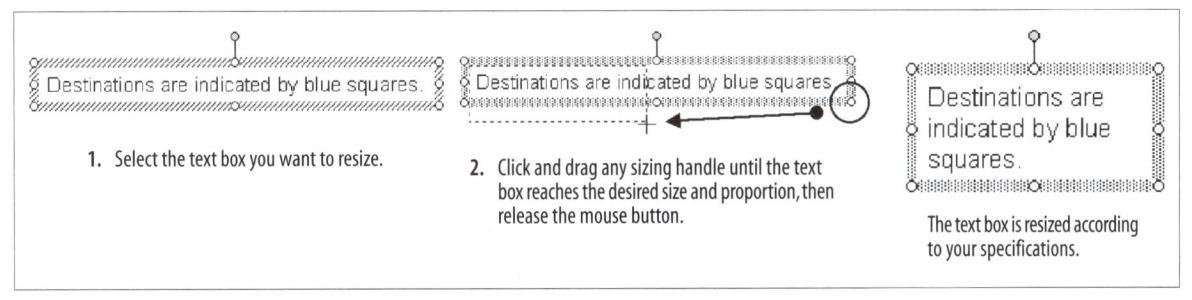

LESSON 4.2

Figure 4-4. Changing the size and proportions of a text box.

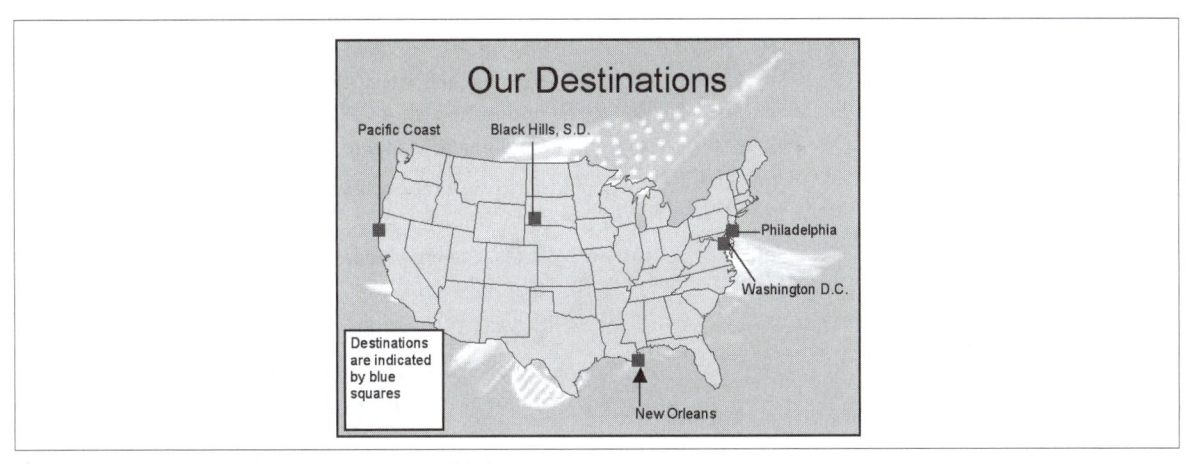

1. Select the text box you want to resize.
2. Click and drag any sizing handle until the text box reaches the desired size and proportion, then release the mouse button.

The text box is resized according to your specifications.

Figure 4-5. The updated slide with text boxes added.

Text boxes are the most important objects that you can add to your slides. Almost every slide you add to your presentation comes with at least one or two text boxes where you can add text. You can also add your own text boxes to your slides by clicking the Text Box button on the Drawing toolbar, clicking where you want the text to appear with the I pointer, and typing your text.

Here are a few more pointers about text boxes:

- Thin dashed lines surround text boxes. You can type in a text box by clicking inside its boundaries.
- You can add or delete text boxes to and from your slides as needed.
- As with any other slide object, you can change the size of a text box by clicking it and dragging its sizing handles.
- You can move text boxes by clicking and dragging them.

1 Click the Text Box button on the Drawing toolbar.

Text Box button

The pointer changes to a ↧, indicating you can click and add text to your slide. First we need to add a "Washington D.C." text label to the slide.

2 Click at the end of the line pointing to Washington D.C., located below the Philadelphia label, with the ↧ pointer.

Before we enter the text for the "Washington D.C." text label, we need to change the font formatting so that it matches the other text labels on the slide.

3 Select Arial from the Font List on the Formatting toolbar.

Font List

137

Lesson 4.2
Adding, Arranging, and Formatting Text Boxes

Any text we type now will appear in the Arial font type. We still need to change the font size.

4 Select 18 from the Font Size List on the Formatting toolbar.

Font Size List

OK, we're ready to enter text in our text box.

5 Type Washington D.C. and click anywhere outside the text box when you have finished typing.

That's all there is to adding a text box to a slide. We changed the font formatting in the text box *before* we entered any text, but you can also change the font formatting in a text box *after* text has been typed. Simply select the text and then format it.

When you add text to a shape, a text box actually holds the text. Here's how…

6 Click the box you added in the previous lesson to select it. Select Edit → Text Object from the menu.

Move on to the next step to format the text box's text.

7 Repeat Steps 3 and 4 to change the text box's font formatting.

Now enter the text.

8 Type Destinations are indicated by blue squares.

Yikes! The text we typed is spilling out of the box! Don't worry—you can easily change the size and proportions of any text box. Here's how:

9 Make sure the box is still selected, and select Format → AutoShape from the menu. Select the Text Box tab and check the Word wrap text in Autoshape option and click OK. Your box should look like the third image in Figure 4-4.

The text wraps to fit inside the AutoShape object.

10 Compare your slide to the one in Figure 4-5 and then save your work.

NOTE *If your box doesn't look like Figure 4-5, check your text alignment (it should be left aligned) and the size of your rectangle.*

QUICK REFERENCE

TO ADD A TEXT BOX TO A SLIDE:

- CLICK THE TEXT BOX BUTTON ON THE DRAWING TOOLBAR, CLICK WHERE YOU WANT TO INSERT THE TEXT WITH THE INSERTION POINT, AND THEN TYPE THE TEXT.

TO RESIZE A TEXT BOX:

1. CLICK THE TEXT BOX TO SELECT IT.
2. DRAG THE TEXT BOX'S SIZING HANDLES TO RESIZE IT.

Selecting, Resizing, Moving, and Deleting Objects

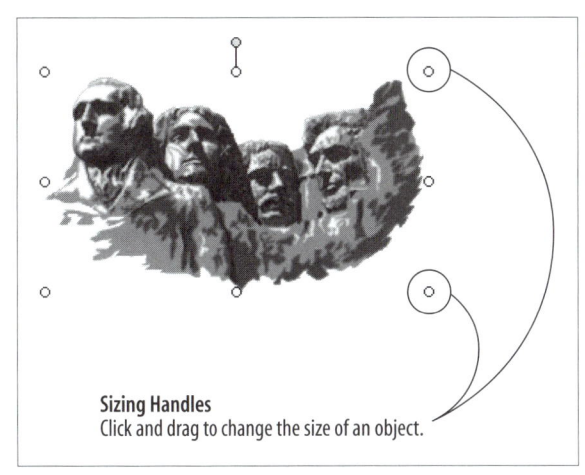

LESSON 4.3

Figure 4-6. Sizing handles appear around the edges of any selected object.

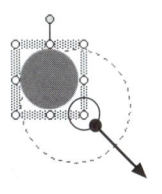

Figure 4-7. The updated slide.

Resize an object by clicking it to select it and then grabbing one of its sizing handles, dragging, and then releasing the mouse button when the object reaches the desired size.

Selecting, resizing, moving, and deleting objects—we've got a lot of ground to cover in this lesson! But before you can edit, format, resize, move, or delete anything on a slide, you have to select the object. Before you select anything, make sure that the pointer is a selection pointer ( ). Ninety-nine percent of the time it will be, but if it isn't, click the Select Objects button on the drawing toolbar.

1 Go to **Slide 3**. Click the **Mt. Rushmore picture** to select it.

When you select an object, sizing handles appear around the edge of the object, as shown in Figure 4-6. You can use these sizing handles to change the size and proportions of the selected object. Move on to the next step to see how we can increase the size of the selected Mt. Rushmore picture.

2 Position the pointer over the **bottom right sizing handle** until it changes to a . Click and hold down the mouse button and **drag down and to the right** until the picture is the same width as the double-arrowed line below, then release the mouse button.

As you drag an object's sizing handle, a dotted outline appears to help you resize it.

You already know that you can select an object by clicking it with the pointer. What you probably *don't* know is that you can also select slide objects by pressing the Tab key. Press Tab once to select the first object on the slide, press Tab again to select the next object, and so on.

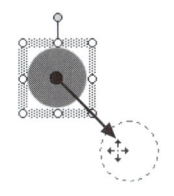

Move an object by clicking it and holding down the mouse button, dragging the object to a new location, and then releasing the mouse button.

3 Press the **Tab** key several times until the bottom, shorter horizontal line is selected.

Sizing handles appear at both ends of the line, indicating it's selected. Here's another sizing trick: holding down the shift key while you drag an object's sizing handles maintains the object's proportions. If you're resizing a line, holding down the Shift key while you resize the line redraws the line in 15-degree increments; 15, 30, 45, 60, 75—great for keeping your lines straight!

4 Hold down the **Shift** key and drag the line's **left sizing handle** to the **left** until the line is the same length as the line above it.

Now that you've resized the line and Mt. Rushmore objects, let's move on to the next task—moving an object. We need to place the sun in a more suitable place on the slide.

139

Lesson 4.3
Selecting, Resizing, Moving, and Deleting Objects

5 Click the sun object to select it.

Sizing handles appear around the sun object indicating it is selected. Here's how to move an object.

6 Click and hold down the mouse button anywhere inside the sun object. Drag the sun object to the right of the scenery picture and between the two horizontal lines, as shown in Figure 4-7, and then release the mouse button.

By simply dragging and dropping with the mouse, you can move any object—shapes, lines, pictures, or text boxes—on a slide.

Sometimes, after moving an object, you'll find you want to move the object just a smidgen. Use the keyboard to move or nudge objects with greater precision.

7 With the sun object still selected, press the ← (left arrow) key.

You can also hold down the Ctrl key while pressing any of the arrow keys to nudge the selected object by a single pixel—the smallest possible increment. See Table 4-1 for more helpful hints.

One final topic in this lesson is how to delete an object. Deleting an object is very, very easy—simply select the object and press the Delete key.

8 Click the green circle to select it, and then delete it by pressing the Delete key.

9 Compare your slide to the one in Figure 4-7 and then save your work.

Table 4-1. Keystroke/Mouse Combinations

Hold Down This Key	While Dragging This	To Do This
Nothing	An object's sizing handles	Resize the object
Shift	An object's sizing handles	Maintain the object's proportions while resizing it
Ctrl	An object's sizing handles	Keep the object centered while resizing it
Nothing	An object	Move the object
Shift	An object	Move the object along a straight horizontal or vertical line
Ctrl	An object	Copy the object

QUICK REFERENCE

TO RESIZE AN OBJECT:
- CLICK THE OBJECT TO SELECT IT, GRAB ONE OF ITS SIZING HANDLES, DRAG AND RELEASE THE MOUSE BUTTON WHEN THE OBJECT REACHES THE DESIRED SIZE.
- HOLD DOWN THE SHIFT KEY WHILE DRAGGING TO MAINTAIN THE OBJECT'S PROPORTIONS WHILE RESIZING IT.

TO MOVE AN OBJECT:
- CLICK THE OBJECT AND HOLD DOWN THE MOUSE BUTTON, DRAG THE OBJECT TO A NEW LOCATION, AND THEN RELEASE THE MOUSE BUTTON TO DROP THE OBJECT.

TO COPY AN OBJECT USING DROP AND DRAG:
- FOLLOW THE SAME PROCEDURES AS MOVING AN OBJECT ONLY HOLD DOWN THE CTRL KEY WHILE YOU DRAG THE OBJECT.

LESSON 4.4 Formatting Objects

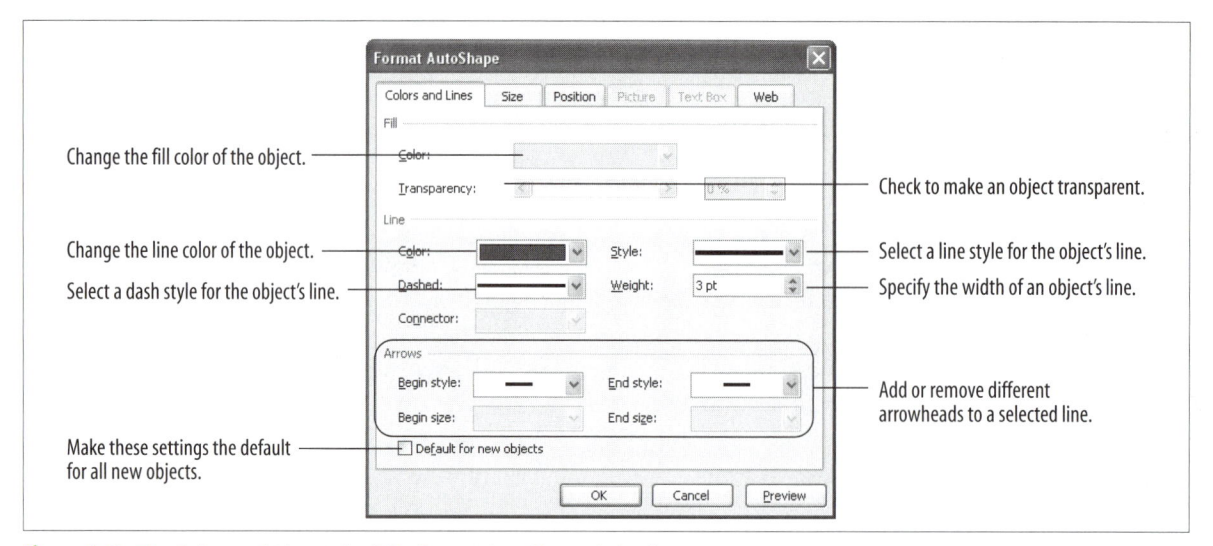

Figure 4-8. The Colors and Lines tab of the Format AutoShape dialog box.

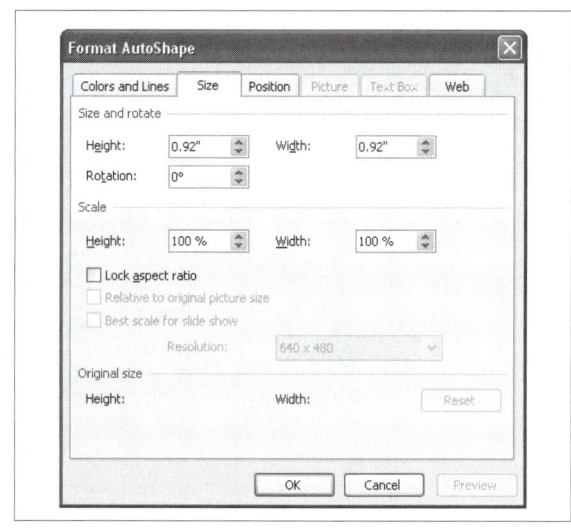

Callouts around the dialog box:
- Change the fill color of the object.
- Change the line color of the object.
- Select a dash style for the object's line.
- Make these settings the default for all new objects.
- Check to make an object transparent.
- Select a line style for the object's line.
- Specify the width of an object's line.
- Add or remove different arrowheads to a selected line.

Figure 4-9. The Size tab of the Format AutoShape dialog box.

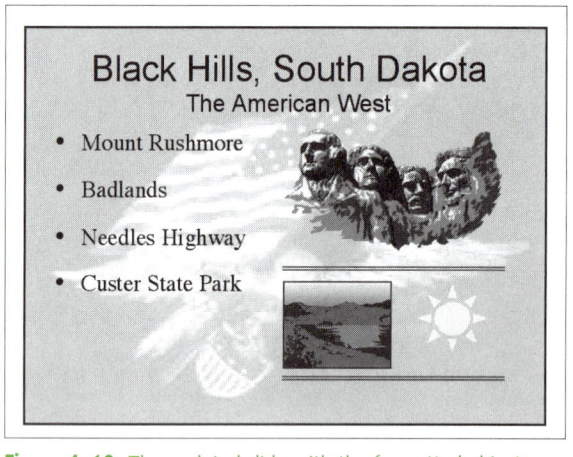

Figure 4-10. The updated slide with the formatted objects.

In this lesson, you'll learn how to format slide objects. Although there are many different types of shapes in PowerPoint, the procedure for formatting each one is pretty much the same. Here it is:

1 If necessary, find and open the **Lesson 4B** presentation and save it as `American History`.

TIP *You can also format any object by right-clicking the object and selecting the Format AutoShape option from the shortcut menu.*

2 On Slide 3, click the **sun object** to select it.

Here's how to change the fill color (the color used to fill the inside) of an object.

3 Click the **Fill Color button arrow** on the Drawing toolbar.

Fill Color button

Other Ways to Change Fill Colors:
- Select **Format → AutoShape** from the menu.

142

Chapter 4
Drawing and Working with Graphics

You can fill an object using:

- **Color palette color:** Fills the background with one of the eight colors from the slide's current color scheme.
- **More colors:** Fills the background with one of the hundreds of rainbow colors from the Color dialog box.
- **Fill Effects:** Fills the background with more dramatic looking effects. There are four types of fill effects: gradient, texture, pattern, and picture.

We want the sun to appear yellow, but since yellow isn't one of the eight colors in the current color scheme, we'll have to select it from the More colors option.

4 Select More Fill colors from the fill list.

NOTE *Although we're assigning an individual color to the sun object, the point of the color scheme is to keep you from doing just that. Try to stick to the color scheme whenever possible. The reason for this is if you change the color scheme later on, the fill colors will also reflect the color change, unless you've assigned them individual colors.*

5 Select a yellow color and click OK.

The sun object is filled with the selected yellow color. You can also change an object's line color—or remove the line that surrounds the object altogether.

6 Click the Line Color button arrow on the Drawing toolbar and select No Line to remove the line.

The black line surrounding the sun disappears. Now let's remove the arrowheads from the top line on the slide.

7 Click the upper double-arrowhead line to select it, then click the Arrow Style button on the Drawing toolbar and select the Arrow Style 1 option (the line without any arrowheads).

Next, let's change the color of the selected line.

8 With the top line still selected, click the Line Color button arrow on the Drawing toolbar and select the blue color.

Line Color button

Other Ways to Change an Object's Line Color:

- Select **F**ormat → Aut**o**Shape from the menu.

We have one more change to make to the selected line—the line style.

9 With the top line still selected, click the Line Style button on the Drawing toolbar and select the 3 pt. double line.

So far, we've been using the mouse and the Drawing toolbar to change the size and format of our slide objects. You can also use the Format AutoShape dialog box to resize and/or format a selected object. The Format AutoShape dialog box isn't quite as quick and convenient as the Drawing toolbar, but it contains more formatting options that you can choose from. Some people actually prefer formatting objects with the Format AutoShape dialog box because it allows them to format and resize objects with a greater degree of precision.

We'll use the Format AutoShape dialog box to format the bottom line on the slide—then you can decide for yourself which method you like better.

10 Click the bottom line to select it and select Format → AutoShape from the menu.

The AutoShape dialog box appears with the Colors and Lines tab selected, as shown in Figure 4-8. You can also open the Format AutoShape dialog box by right-clicking any object and selecting Format AutoShape from the menu.

11 Click the Line Color list arrow and select the blue color, then click the Line Style list arrow and select the 3 pt. double line.

We've finished formatting the bottom line, but let's take a look at one more thing before we close the Format AutoShape dialog box.

143

Lesson 4.4
Formatting Objects

12 Click the Size tab.

The Size tab of the Format AutoShape dialog box appears, as shown in Figure 4-9. Here you can resize an object with greater precision than the mouse. You can enter an exact height and width for the selected object or you can adjust its size, specifying a percentage of the original size. If the Lock aspect ratio check box is selected, the Height and Width settings change in relation to one another.

13 Click OK to close the dialog box and compare your slide to the one in Figure 4-10.

QUICK REFERENCE

TO FILL A SHAPE WITH A COLOR:

- SELECT THE SHAPE, THEN CLICK THE FILL COLOR BUTTON ARROW ON THE DRAWING TOOLBAR AND SELECT THE COLOR YOU WANT.

TO CHANGE LINE COLOR OR REMOVE A LINE:

- SELECT THE SHAPE, THEN CLICK THE LINE COLOR BUTTON ARROW ON THE DRAWING TOOLBAR AND SELECT THE COLOR YOU WANT.

TO CHANGE THE LINE STYLE:

- SELECT THE LINE, THEN CLICK THE LINE STYLE BUTTON ON THE DRAWING TOOLBAR AND SELECT THE LINE STYLE YOU WANT.

TO CHANGE THE DASH STYLE:

- SELECT THE LINE, THEN CLICK THE DASH STYLE BUTTON ON THE DRAWING TOOLBAR AND SELECT THE DASH YOU WANT.

TO ADD OR REMOVE ARROW HEADS:

- SELECT THE LINE, THEN CLICK THE ARROW STYLE BUTTON ON THE DRAWING TOOLBAR AND SELECT THE ARROW STYLE YOU WANT.

TO USE THE FORMAT OBJECT DIALOG BOX:

- SELECT THE OBJECT AND SELECT FORMAT → AUTOSHAPE FROM THE MENU.

Inserting Clip Art

LESSON 4.5

Figure 4-11. The Microsoft Clip Art Gallery.

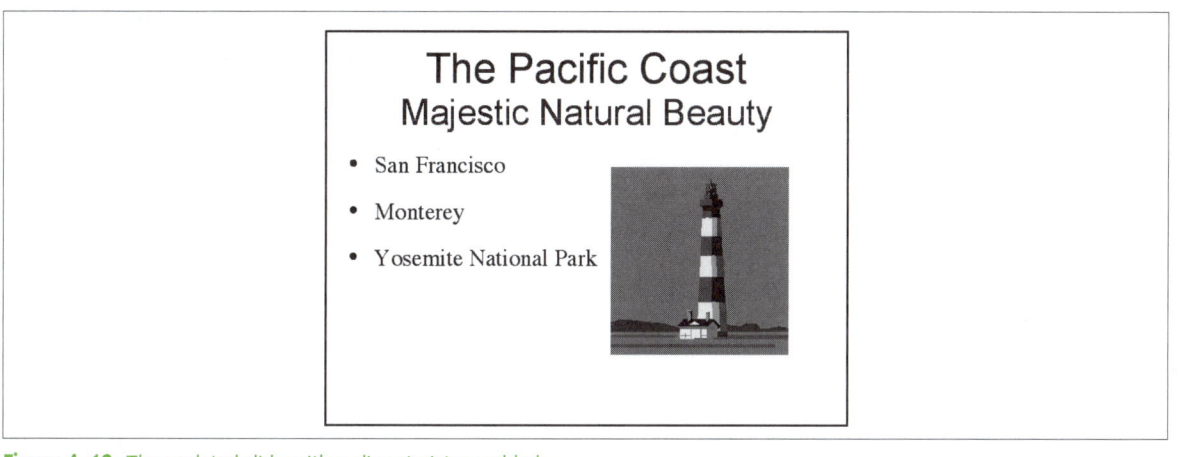

Figure 4-12. The updated slide with a clip art picture added.

Microsoft Office 2003 comes equipped with several thousand graphics you can use to make your presentations more visually attractive. The graphics are called Clip Art, and each image is stored and managed by a program called the Microsoft Clip Art Gallery (as you can see, Microsoft has never been very imaginative when it comes to naming their products). The Clip Art Gallery program categorizes its pictures by topic—such as holidays, business, or sports—making it easier to find a clip art graphic that meets your specific needs.

1 Press **Ctrl** + **End** to move to the end of the presentation.

We want to add a clip art picture to this slide.

2 Select **Insert** → **Picture** → **Clip Art** from the menu.

145

Lesson 4.5
Inserting Clip Art

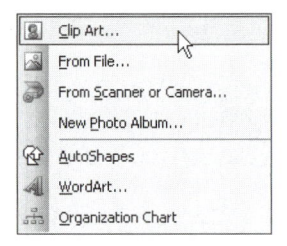

Inserting a Picture from the Clip Art Gallery

The Clip Art task pane appears, as shown in Figure 4-12 (your Clip Art Gallery window may look slightly different, depending on how much Clip Art is installed on your computer). Microsoft Office 2003 comes with a small selection of clip art pictures that you can use in your presentations. The pictures are categorized and indexed by keywords, making it easier to find what type of picture you want to use.

3 Type `lighthouse` in the Search for text box and click the Go button.

PowerPoint searches your hard disk for lighthouse-related clip art.

4 Browse through the clip art pictures until you find a picture of a lighthouse similar to the one shown in Figure 4-12.

Depending on your computer's setup, there may be several pictures of lighthouses or only one. Now that you have found an appropriate graphic you will need to insert it into the slide. Here's how:

5 Click the lighthouse picture shown in Figure 4-12.

The selected graphic is inserted into the slide.

NOTE *Depending on how PowerPoint is installed and configured on your computer system, you may get a "The file is not available..." error message. This means PowerPoint cannot locate the Clip Art pictures. If you are using PowerPoint by yourself, you may need to insert either the Office 2003 or PowerPoint 2003 CD-ROM into your computer.*

6 Close the task pane.

Often the pictures you insert will be either too large or too small. When this happens you will have to resize the picture to a more suitable dimension. You resize a picture just like any other object: by selecting it and dragging it by its sizing handles. You can also adjust the object's size on the Size tab of the Format Picture dialog box.

7 Click the image to select it. Position the pointer over the lower-left sizing handle, until the pointer changes to a ↖, then click and hold the left mouse button. Drag the mouse diagonally down and to the left until the picture is roughly 50% larger, and then release the mouse button.

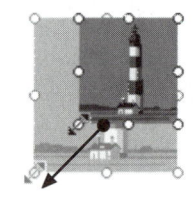

Resize a picture by clicking it to select it, then grab one of its sizing handles and drag. Release the mouse button when the object reaches the desired size.

You probably noticed there were several other options listed in the Insert → Picture menu. Here's what they are and what they do:

Table 4-2. The Insert Picture Menu

Insert	Description
Clip Art	Opens the Clip Gallery where you can select a clip art image to insert.
From File	Inserts a graphic file created in another program.
From Scanner	Scans an image and inserts it at the insertion point.
New Photo Album	Inserts photographs from a file, disk, scanner or camera.
AutoShapes	Inserts a ready-made shape, such as a circle, rectangle, star, arrow, etc.

Chapter 4
Drawing and Working with Graphics

Table 4-2. The Insert Picture Menu (Continued)

Insert	Description
WordArt	Creates spectacular text effects, such as WordArt.
Organization Chart	Inserts a Microsoft Organization Chart object.

QUICK REFERENCE

TO INSERT A CLIP ART GRAPHIC:

1. SELECT INSERT → PICTURE → CLIP ART FROM THE MENU.
2. TYPE THE NAME OF WHAT YOU'RE LOOKING FOR IN THE SEARCH FOR BOX AND PRESS ENTER OR GO.

   OR...

   CLICK A CLIP ART CATEGORY.
3. SCROLL THROUGH THE CLIP ART PICTURES AS NEEDED UNTIL YOU FIND AN APPROPRIATE GRAPHIC.
4. CLICK THE GRAPHIC YOU WANT TO INSERT.
5. CLOSE THE TASK PANE.

LESSON 4.6 **Inserting and Formatting Pictures**

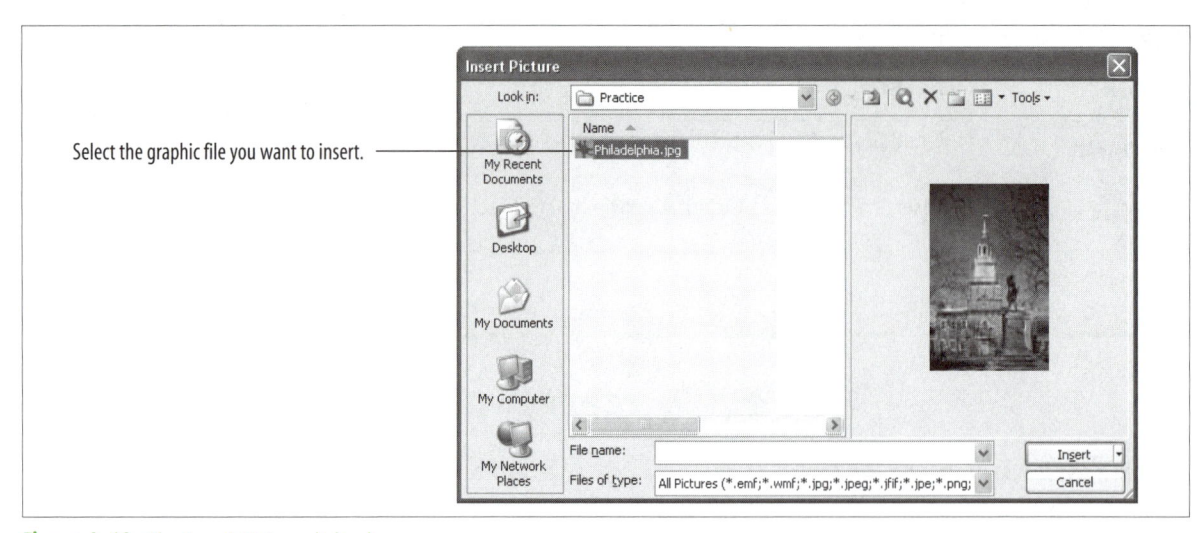

Figure 4-13. The Insert Picture dialog box.

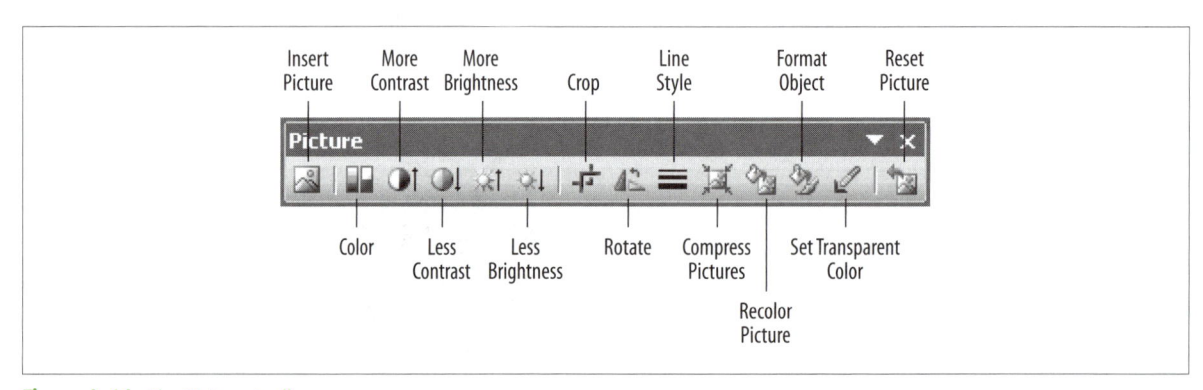

Figure 4-14. The Picture toolbar.

Figure 4-15. The updated slide with an external picture file inserted.

148

Chapter 4
Drawing and Working with Graphics

Click the crop button on the Picture toolbar and then drag picture's sizing handles to crop a picture.

Figure 4-16. How to crop a picture.

If the Microsoft Clip Gallery doesn't have the graphic you're looking for, you can insert graphics created with other programs. There are many other clip art collections available that are much larger than the Microsoft Clip Gallery. Additionally, you can use graphics and pictures created with graphics programs such as Microsoft Paint (which comes with Windows) or Corel Draw. In this lesson, you will learn how to insert a picture into a slide.

1 Go to Slide 4 and select Insert → Picture → From File from the menu.

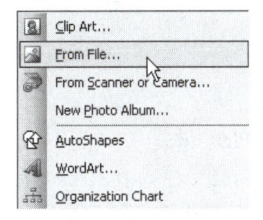

The Insert Picture dialog box appears, as shown in Figure 4-13. Here you need to specify the name and location of the graphic file to be inserted into your slide.

2 If necessary, navigate to your Practice folder or disk.

All the graphic files located in your Practice folder or disk appear in the file window.

3 Select the Philadelphia file.

PowerPoint displays a preview of the graphic in the right side panel of the Insert Picture dialog box.

4 Click the Insert button to insert the Philadelphia picture.

PowerPoint inserts the Philadelphia picture into the current slide.

Sometimes an inserted picture may need some "tweaking"—perhaps it is too dark, too light, or is using the wrong colors. This is where the Picture toolbar comes in. The Picture toolbar is like your very own photo studio and contains a variety of tools for adjusting and formatting any pictures you insert.

The Picture toolbar should appear whenever you select a picture—if it doesn't, move on to the next step; otherwise, skip ahead to Step 6.

5 If the Picture toolbar does not appear, summon it by selecting View → Toolbars → Picture from the menu.

First let's change the colors in the Philadelphia picture.

6 With the Philadelphia picture still selected, click the Color button on the Picture toolbar and select Grayscale.

Color button

PowerPoint changes the color of the Philadelphia picture to grayscale.

NOTE *The Picture toolbar should appear whenever a picture is selected. If the Picture toolbar doesn't appear when you select a picture, you can still display it by selecting View → Toolbars → Picture from the menu.*

Another useful tool on the Picture toolbar is the Crop button. When you crop a picture you trim its horizontal and vertical sides. Cropping is useful if you want to include only a specific portion of a picture, or when a picture contains something you want to cut out, like an ex-boyfriend.

7 Click the Crop button on the Picture toolbar.

Crop button

The pointer changes to indicate that you can crop pictures.

149

Lesson 4.6
Inserting and Formatting Pictures

8 Position the pointer over the right-middle sizing handle then click and hold the left mouse button and drag the mouse to the left about a half-inch, as shown in Figure 4-16.

The area you cropped no longer appears in the picture.

9 Click the Crop button on the Picture toolbar to exit cropping mode, then click the Undo button on the Standard toolbar twice to undo the cropping and gray-scale formatting you applied to the picture.

Table 4-3. Common Graphic File Formats

Format	File Size	Description
BMP	Large	Known as a *bitmap*, this is a graphic format used by many programs.
CGM	Small	Clip art pictures often come in Computer Graphics Metafile format.
GIF	Small	Picture file format commonly used on the Internet.
JPEG	Small	Digital photographs are usually saved as JPEG files. Because of its small size, JPEG files are also commonly used on the Internet.
WMF	Small	Another file format used for clip art pictures.
TIF	Large	A file format used by scanners, fax programs, and some drawing programs.

QUICK REFERENCE

TO INSERT A GRAPHIC CREATED IN ANOTHER PROGRAM:

1. SELECT INSERT → PICTURE → FROM FILE FROM THE MENU.
2. SELECT THE FILE LOCATION AND NAME, AND CLICK OK.

TO CHANGE A PICTURE'S COLOR OPTIONS:

- SELECT THE PICTURE, CLICK THE COLOR BUTTON ON THE PICTURE TOOLBAR, AND SELECT A COLORING OPTION.

TO CROP A PICTURE:

1. SELECT THE PICTURE AND CLICK THE CROP BUTTON ON THE PICTURE TOOLBAR.
2. CLICK AND DRAG THE EDGE OF THE PICTURE UNTIL YOU HAVE TRIMMED APPROPRIATELY.

Aligning and Grouping Objects

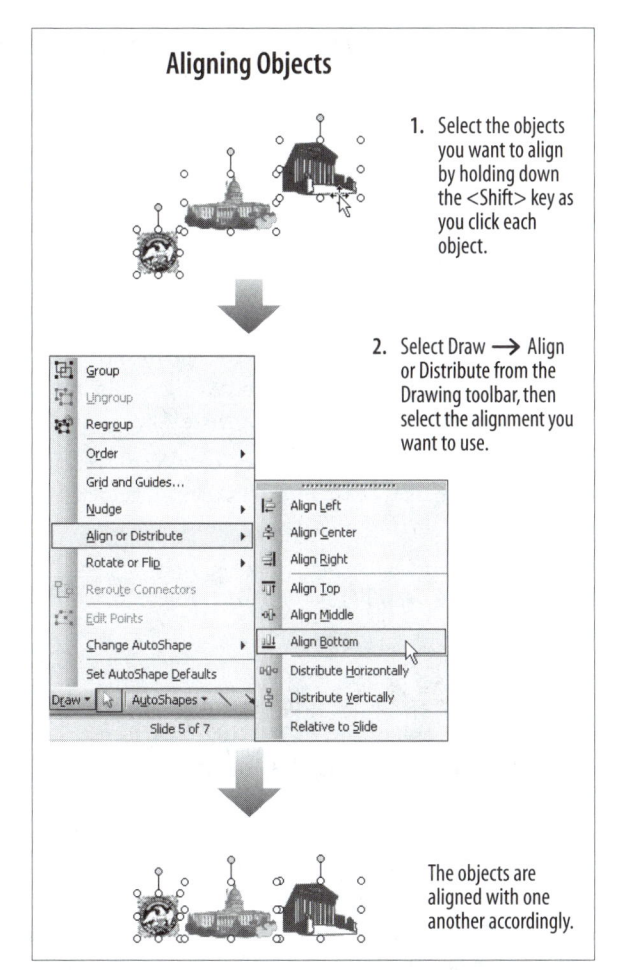

LESSON 4.7

Figure 4-17. The steps for aligning objects with one another.

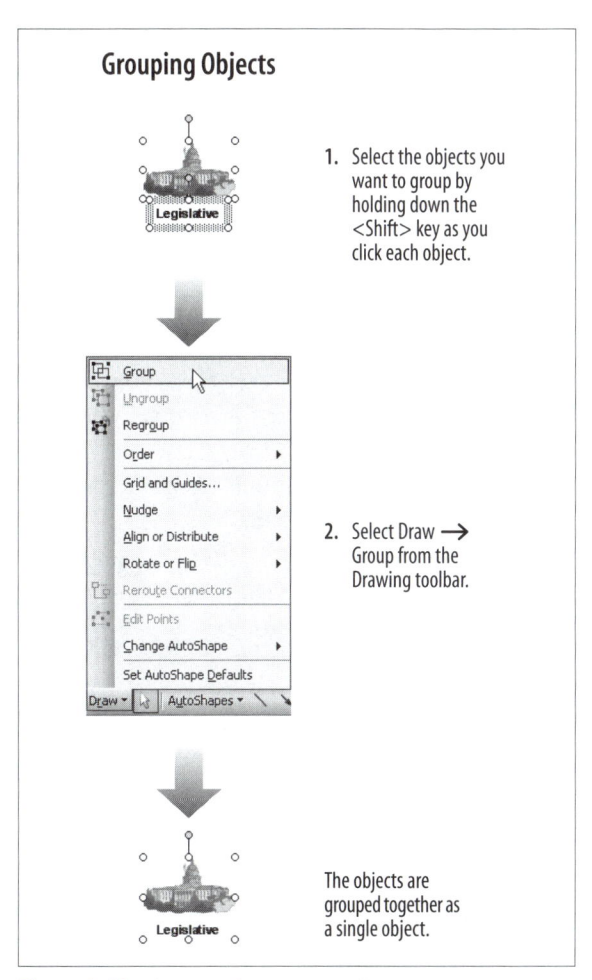

Figure 4-18. The steps for grouping objects.

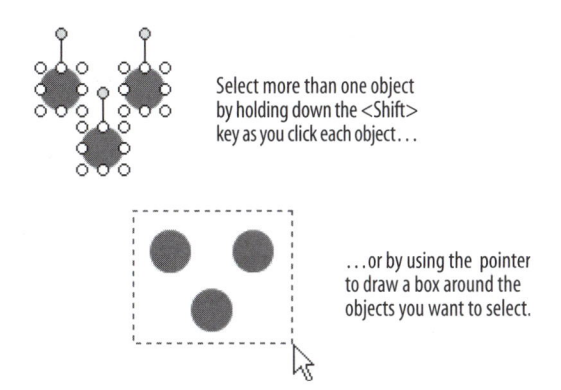

Slides that have objects scattered randomly about them look terrible. The Align command, located under the Draw button on the Drawing toolbar, aligns objects relative to one another. You can align objects so that they are lined up with one another or spaced equally apart from one another. This lesson will give you some practice aligning objects with PowerPoint's alignment commands.

This lesson also explains how to group and ungroup objects. It's often easier to move and work with a single object than it is to work with several smaller objects. A *group* is a collection of objects that PowerPoint treats as though it were a single object. By grouping several objects together, you can move or resize the entire group instead of moving and resizing each object one by one.

151

Lesson 4.7
Aligning and Grouping Objects

1 If necessary, find and open the Lesson 4C presentation and save it as American History. Go to Slide 5.

Someone sure was sloppy when they created this slide—the pictures and text are all over the place! You could manually move the objects and align the objects with one another by using the mouse—but that would require a lot of time, and unless you have eyes like a hawk, it would be difficult to align the objects perfectly. Instead we'll align the objects using PowerPoint's alignment commands.

First you need to select the objects you want to align with one another. There are two ways you can select more than one object:

- Press and hold down the Shift key as you click each object that you want to select.
- Use the arrow pointer to draw a box around the objects that you want to select. Point to a location above and to the left of the objects that you want to select, and click and drag the mouse down and to the right until the box surrounds all the objects. When you release the mouse button, all the objects in the box will be selected. The disadvantage of this method is that it's not as selective as using the Shift + click method.

2 Hold down the Shift key as you select the Executive, Legislative, and Judicial pictures, as shown in Figure 4-17.

Now you can align the selected objects with one another. Here's how:

3 Click the Draw button on the Drawing toolbar and select Align or Distribute → Align Bottom.

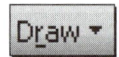

Draw button

The selected objects are aligned with the bottom-most object, the Executive branch picture. Next we need to center align the Judicial text box with the Judicial branch picture.

4 Click the Judicial branch picture to select it (and deselect any other objects), then hold down the Shift key and click the Judicial text box.

Now let's center align the two selected objects.

5 Click the Draw button on the Drawing toolbar and select Align or Distribute → Align Center.

PowerPoint centers the picture and text label.

The procedure for grouping several objects into a single object is very similar to aligning several objects—first you select the objects you want to group, then you select the Group command from the Draw button on the Drawing toolbar.

6 Press Esc to deselect the objects, and then click the Legislative branch picture to select it. Then hold down the Shift key and click the Legislative text box.

Since these two objects should always remain together, it makes sense to group them together and work with a single object instead of two.

7 Click the Draw button on the Drawing toolbar and select Group.

PowerPoint groups the selected picture and text box into a single object. You can break a group back into its original components at any time by selecting the grouped object, clicking the Draw button and selecting Ungroup.

8 Following the procedure you learned in Steps 6 and 7, group the Judicial branch picture and the Judicial text box together and then do the same to the Executive branch picture and the Executive text box.

You can also use the Align and Distribute command to distribute selected objects so there is equal horizontal or vertical distance between all the objects. Move on to the next step to try distributing the selected objects horizontally.

9 Select the Executive, Legislative, and Judicial objects, click the Drawing button on the Drawing toolbar, and select Align or Distribute → Distribute Horizontally.

PowerPoint evenly distributes the selected objects.

Give yourself a pat on the back when you have finished this lesson—probably less than 10 percent of all PowerPoint users know how to align and group the objects on their slides.

Chapter 4
Drawing and Working with Graphics

QUICK REFERENCE

TO SELECT MULTIPLE OBJECTS:

- PRESS AND HOLD DOWN THE **SHIFT** KEY AS YOU CLICK EACH OBJECT THAT YOU WANT TO SELECT.

OR...

- USE THE ARROW POINTER TO DRAW A BOX AROUND THE OBJECTS THAT YOU WANT TO SELECT.

TO ALIGN OBJECTS WITH EACH OTHER:

1. FOLLOW THE ABOVE STEPS TO SELECT THE OBJECTS YOU WANT TO ALIGN.
2. CLICK THE **DRAW BUTTON** ON THE DRAWING TOOLBAR, SELECT **ALIGN OR DISTRIBUTE**, AND SELECT HOW YOU WANT TO ALIGN OR DISTRIBUTE THE SELECTED OBJECTS.

TO GROUP SEVERAL OBJECTS:

1. SELECT THE OBJECTS YOU WANT TO GROUP TOGETHER.
2. CLICK THE **DRAW BUTTON** ON THE DRAWING TOOLBAR AND SELECT **GROUP**.

TO UNGROUP A GROUPED OBJECT:

- SELECT THE GROUPED OBJECT, CLICK THE **DRAW BUTTON** ON THE DRAWING TOOLBAR, AND SELECT **UNGROUP**.

LESSON 4.8 Drawing AutoShapes

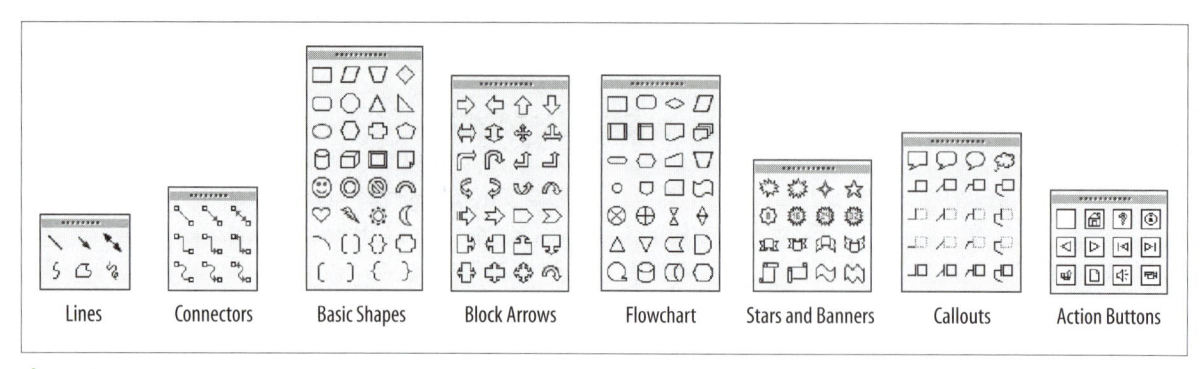

Figure 4-19. Shapes available under the AutoShapes button on the Drawing toolbar.

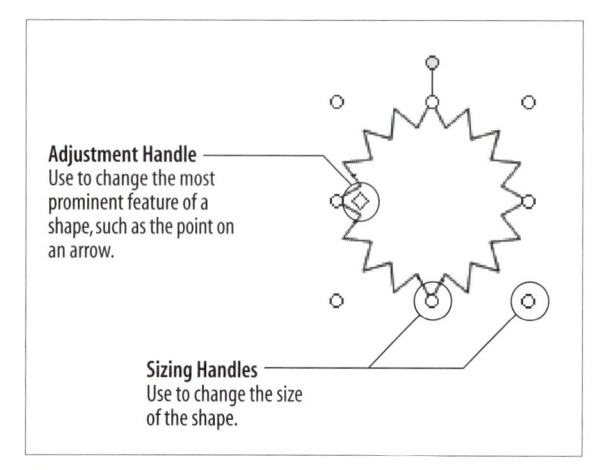

Figure 4-20. Many AutoShapes have an Adjustment handle in addition to sizing handles.

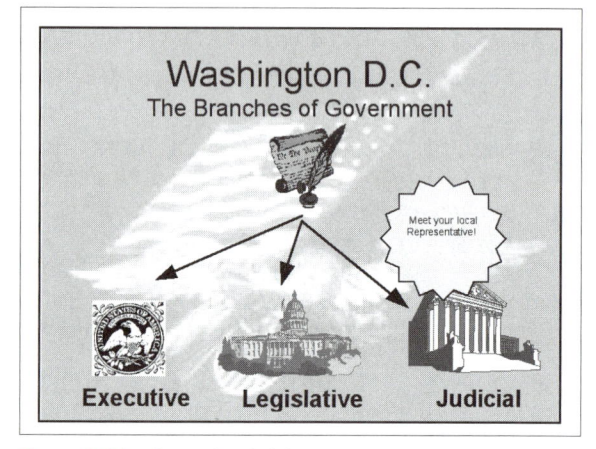

Figure 4-21. The updated slide.

You're not limited to drawing simple rectangles, ovals, and lines with PowerPoint. The AutoShapes button on the Drawing toolbar contains over 100 common shapes and lines, such as arrows, stars, and pentagons. Figure 4-19 shows all the AutoShapes that are available. As you can see from the illustration, the AutoShapes menu is organized into several categories:

- **Lines:** Straight lines, curved lines, scribbly lines, arrows, and free form drawing shapes.
- **Connectors:** Various types of lines used to connect shapes and objects to one another.
- **Basic Shapes:** Squares, rectangles, triangles, circles, pentagons, and more.
- **Block Arrows:** Arrows that point up, down, left, and right.
- **Flowchart:** Basic shapes used to create flowcharts.
- **Stars and Banners:** Shapes that boldly announce something.

- **Callouts:** Text box shapes that point to and describe something.
- **Action Buttons:** Navigation buttons like those found on a VCR, used to jump to another slide or run a macro.

1 Click the AutoShapes button on the Drawing toolbar.

AutoShape button

A menu listing the various AutoShape categories appears. Figure 4-19 lists the AutoShapes that are available under each category.

2 Select the Stars and Banners category and select the 16-Point Star shape.

Chapter 4
Drawing and Working with Graphics

16-Point Star Shape

The pointer changes to a +, indicating you can draw the selected shape. Drawing an AutoShape is no different than drawing an ordinary shape—just click and drag until the shape is the size you want.

3 Place the + pointer just above the judicial building. Click and drag the + pointer down and to the right until the right edge of the shape is about 1 inch from the right edge of the slide, then release the mouse button. Compare the size and position of your AutoShape with the one in Figure 4-21.

If your AutoShape is still selected, you'll notice a yellow diamond ◇ on the left side. This is an *adjustment handle*—some AutoShapes sneak them in along with the object's sizing handles. By grabbing and dragging an adjustment handle, you can adjust the most prominent feature of an AutoShape, such as the point on an arrow or the spikes on a star. Adjustment handles are not used to resize an object—you still need to click and drag one of the object's sizing handles to do that.

4 Click and drag the 16-Point Star's yellow **adjustment handle** (◇) to the left just a bit.

By dragging the star's adjustment handle, you've changed the size of the star's spikes. You can move, resize, and format an AutoShape just like any other shape. Go to the next step and we'll change the color of our star shape.

5 With the 16-Point Star still selected, click the **Fill Color button arrow** on the Drawing toolbar, select **More Fill Colors**, and select a **yellow color**.

Here's another shape trick: you can add text to any shape by right-clicking the shape, selecting Add Text from the shortcut menu, and typing in the text.

6 Right-click the 16-Point Star and select **Add Text** from the shortcut menu.

A blinking insertion point (|) appears in the star, indicating that the shape is ready to accept any text that you type. First, we have to change the font size and type so that it will fit in the AutoShape.

7 Select **Arial** from the **Font List** and **14** from the **Font Size List** on the Formatting toolbar.

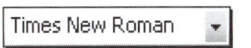

Font List

Any text we type now will appear in Arial 14-point font type. OK, we're ready to enter text in our text box.

Font Size List

8 Type `Meet your local` press **Enter** to add a new line and type `Representative!`

Let's try adding some more AutoShapes to the current slide. The Connectors AutoShape contains lines that connect objects on your slide. Connector lines are great if you want to create a flowchart—and that's what we'll do in the next step.

9 Click the **AutoShapes button** on the Drawing toolbar, select **Connectors**, and select the **Straight Arrow Connector**.

Straight Arrow Connector

Next you need to select the two objects you want to connect.

10 Position the pointer over the **Constitution picture's bottom middle sizing handle** until the pointer changes to a ⊕. Click the bottom sizing handle and then click the **Executive branch object's top middle sizing handle** with the ⊕ pointer.

You've just connected the Constitution object and the Executive branch object. Complete the next step and you've finished the lesson!

11 Following the procedure you learned in **Steps 9 and 10**, connect the **Constitution** with the **Legislative** and **Judicial** objects.

Compare your slide with the one in Figure 4-21 when you've finished.

155

Lesson 4.8
Drawing AutoShapes

QUICK REFERENCE

TO INSERT AN AUTOSHAPE:

1. Click the **AutoShapes** AUTOSHAPES BUTTON on the Drawing toolbar and select the category and AutoShape that you want to insert.
2. Drag the crosshair pointer to draw the AutoShape.

TO RESIZE AN AUTOSHAPE:

- Select the AutoShape and drag its SIZING HANDLES to resize it.

TO ADJUST AN AUTOSHAPE:

- Select the AutoShape and drag its ADJUSTMENT HANDLES (◊) to adjust the most prominent feature of the shape.

TO ADD TEXT TO A SHAPE:

- Right-click the shape, select ADD TEXT from the shortcut menu and type the text.

LESSON 4.9

Flipping and Rotating Objects

1. Select the object you want to rotate.
2. Click and drag the object's rotate handle.

The rotated object.

Figure 4-22. How to rotate an object with the Free Rotate tool.

Enter the amount of degrees you want to rotate the selected object.

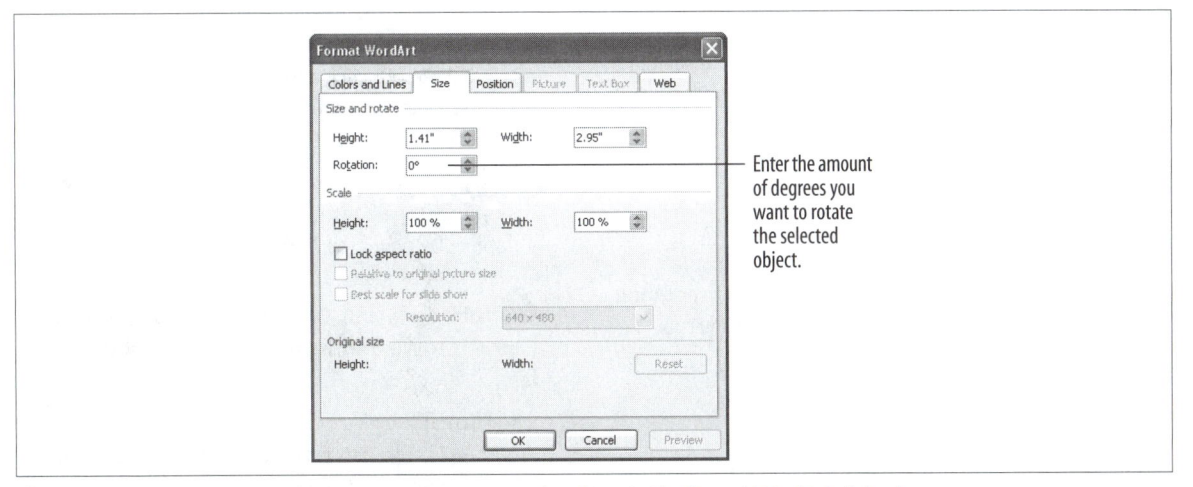

Figure 4-23. Enter how many degrees you want to rotate the object in the Format WordArt dialog box.

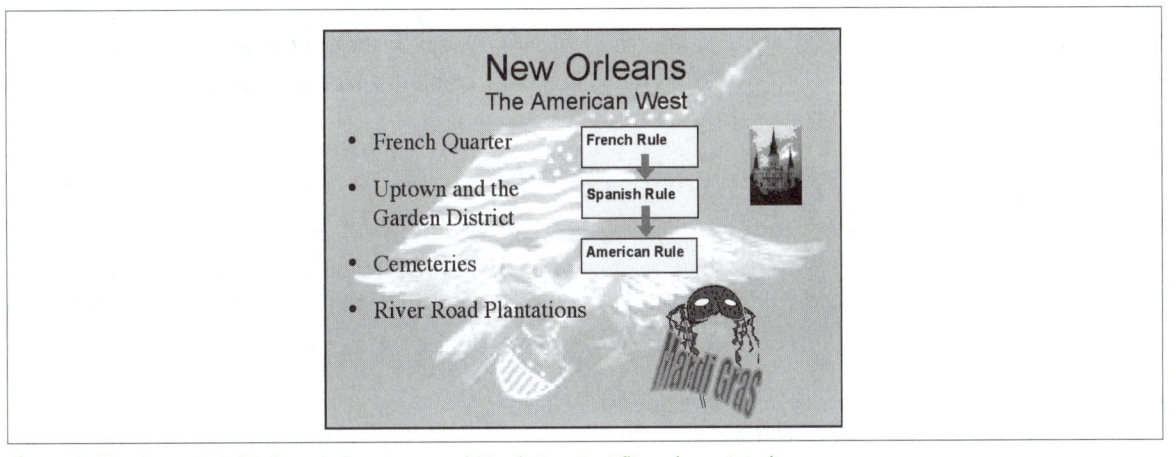

Figure 4-24. The updated slide with the arrows and Mardi Gras text flipped or rotated.

In this lesson, you will learn how to flip and rotate drawing objects on your slides. When you flip an object, you create a mirror image of it. PowerPoint's flip commands allow you to flip an object vertically or horizontally to create a mirror image of the object.

When you rotate an object, you turn it around its center. You can rotate objects in 90° increments, or you can use the *rotate tool* to rotate an object to any angle.

157

Lesson 4.9
Flipping and Rotating Objects

Rotate Right 90°

1 Go to Slide 6.

This slide contains several objects that need to be flipped and rotated. The first object we'll fix is the arrow located between the "French Rule" and "Spanish Rule" boxes, which should be pointing in the opposite direction.

2 Click the upward-pointing arrow object to select it, click the Draw button on the Drawing toolbar, and select Rotate or Flip → Flip Vertical.

Flip Vertical

PowerPoint vertically flips the upward-pointing arrow, changing it to a downward-pointing arrow.

Next, we have the second arrow located between the "Spanish Rule" and "American Rule" boxes.

3 Click the right-pointing arrow to select it, click the Draw button on the Drawing toolbar and select Rotate or Flip → Rotate Right 90°.

Free Rotate option
Other Ways to Rotate an Object:

- Select the object, select **Format→AutoShape** from the menu, click the **Size tab** and enter the amount in degrees you want to rotate the object in the **Rotation box**.

PowerPoint rotates the right-pointing arrow 90 degrees to the right, transforming it into a downward-pointing arrow.

NOTE *The Flip and Rotate commands can sometimes be a little tricky, especially if you're directionally challenged. If you accidentally flip or rotate an object in the wrong direction, simply use the Undo command to return the object to its original state.*

The rotate command has one limitation—it can only rotate objects in 90-degree increments. To rotate objects by other degree intervals you will need to use the object's rotate handle or the Format AutoShape dialog box. Move on to the next step and we'll see how to use the rotate handle.

4 Select the Mardi Gras text object.

A • green rotate handle appears near the top of the Mardi Gras object.

5 Place the pointer over the Mardi Gras object's rotate handle (•), click and hold the mouse button, and drag the object around until it's at a 45° angle, as shown in Figure 4-22, then release the mouse button.

Dragging an object's rotate handle is the fastest and easiest way to rotate an object, but you can also rotate an object by using the Format AutoShape dialog box.

6 With the Mardi Gras object still selected, select Format → WordArt from the menu and click the Size tab.

The Format WordArt dialog box appears, as shown in Figure 4-23. You can rotate a selected object by entering the number of degrees you want to rotate the object in the Rotation box.

7 Type 15 in the Rotation box and click OK.

PowerPoint rotates the Mardi Gras object by 15 degrees.

8 Compare your slide to the one in Figure 4-24 and save your work.

If you're having trouble remembering how each rotate command rotates an object, look at Table 4-4 for visual reference.

Chapter 4
Drawing and Working with Graphics

Table 4-4. Flip and Rotate Commands

Heading		Heading	
	Original Picture		Flip Horizontal
	Rotate Left		Flip Vertical
	Rotate Right		Free Rotate

QUICK REFERENCE

TO ROTATE AN OBJECT BY 90 DEGREES:

- SELECT THE OBJECT, CLICK THE [Draw] DRAW BUTTON ON THE DRAWING TOOLBAR AND SELECT ROTATE OR FLIP, THEN SELECT ROTATE RIGHT 90° OR ROTATE LEFT 90°.

TO FLIP AN OBJECT:

- SELECT THE OBJECT, CLICK THE [Draw] DRAW BUTTON ON THE DRAWING TOOLBAR AND SELECT ROTATE OR FLIP, THEN SELECT FLIP HORIZONTAL OR FLIP VERTICAL.

TO FREE ROTATE AN OBJECT:

- SELECT THE OBJECT AND THEN CLICK AND DRAG THE OBJECT'S ROTATE HANDLE (•) WITH THE POINTER.

OR...

- SELECT THE OBJECT, SELECT FORMAT → WORDART, PICTURE OR AUTOSHAPE (DETERMINED BY WHICH TYPE OF OBJECT YOU HAVE SELECTED) FROM THE MENU, CLICK THE SIZE TAB, AND THEN ENTER THE AMOUNT OF DEGREES YOU WANT TO ROTATE THE OBJECT IN THE ROTATION BOX.

159

LESSON 4.10 Layering Objects

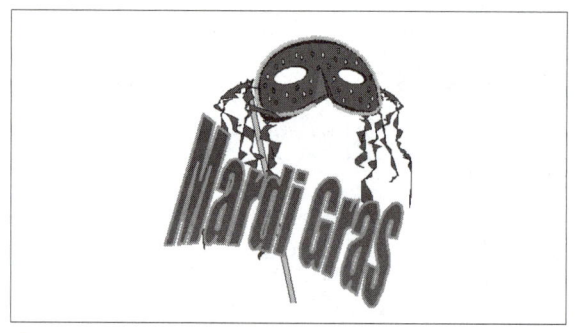

Figure 4-25. Here the Mardi Gras text object appears before the mask.

Figure 4-26. Now the Mardi Gras text object is behind the mask.

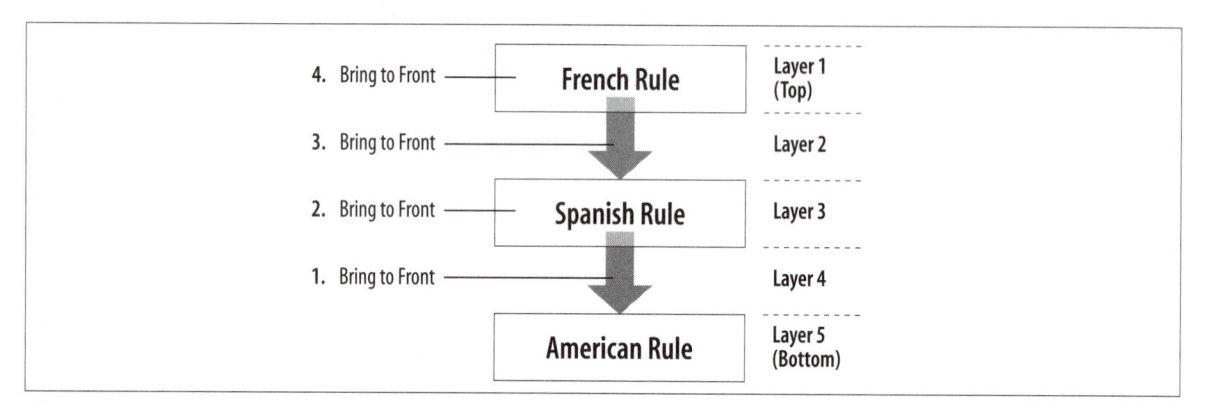

Figure 4-27. The order in which you select and send objects to the front or back is very important.

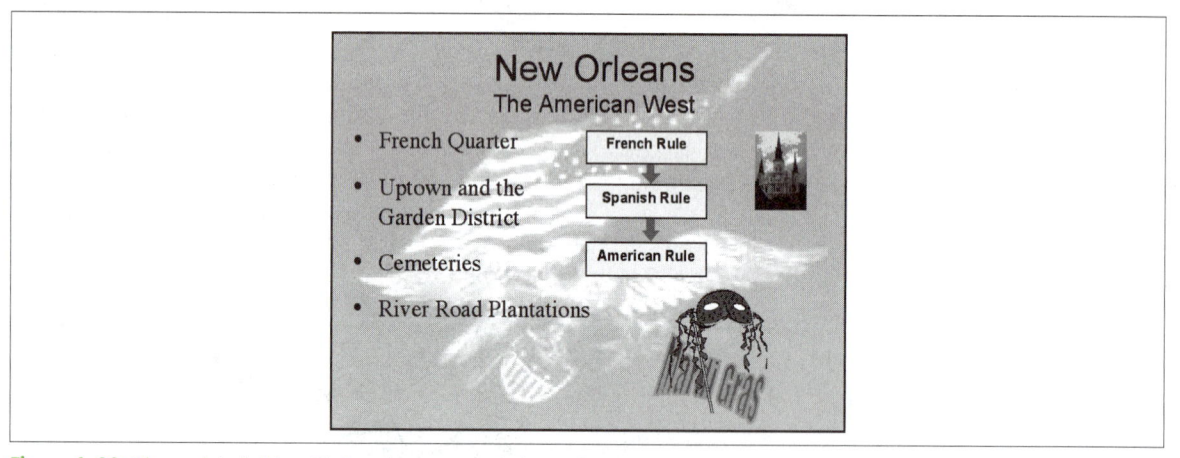

Figure 4-28. The updated slide with the objects properly layered.

Whenever you have more than one object on a slide, it's possible for one or more objects to overlap one another. This presents you with a problem: how can you make sure one object appears in front of, or in back of, another object? PowerPoint (and most other drawing programs) solves this problem by layering objects, like a stack of papers. The first object you draw is on the bottom layer, and the last object you draw is on the top layer. Of course, you can change the order in which objects appear in front or back, and that's the topic of this lesson.

Chapter 4
Drawing and Working with Graphics

There are four layering commands:

- **Bring to Front:** Places the selected object on the very top layer of the slide. All other objects will appear behind the selected object.
- **Send to Back:** Places the selected object on the very bottom layer of the slide. All other objects will appear in front of the selected object.
- **Bring Forward:** Brings the selected object one layer up on the slide.
- **Send Backward:** Sends the selected object one layer down on the slide.

Ready to get some layering practice? Let's get started…

1 If necessary, find and open the Lesson 4D presentation and save it as American History.

2 Make sure you're on Slide 6, then click the Mardi Gras text object to select it.

We want to send the Mardi Gras object to the back layer of the slide so that it appears behind the mask.

3 Click the Draw button on the Drawing toolbar and select Order → Send Backward.

The selected Mardi Gras text object is sent one layer backward so that it appears behind the mask graphic.

When you want to layer several objects in a particular sequence, the order in which you select the object and then send it to the front or back is very important. For example, if you bring object A to the front (or on top), and then bring object B to the front (or on top), object A moves down one layer so that it would appear behind object B.

Confused? Let's try layering the objects in the slide's flowchart so you'll better understand why the order in which you select and layer objects is so important.

4 Select the arrow between Spanish Rule and American Rule, click the Draw button on the Drawing toolbar, and select Order → Bring to Front.

PowerPoint brings the selected arrow to the front layer, in front of both the Spanish Rule and American Rule boxes. We want the arrow to appear in front of the American Rule box, but not in front of the Spanish Rule box. Move on to the next step to bring the Spanish Rule box in front.

5 Select the Spanish Rule object, click the Draw button on the Drawing toolbar and select Order → Bring to Front.

PowerPoint brings the Spanish Rule object to the front layer, in front of the arrow that had previously been on the top layer. Notice that the bottom arrow still appears on top of the American Rule box.

Go to the next step and finish layering the object in the flowchart.

6 Follow the sequence shown in Figure 4-27 (you're on Step 3) and layer the remaining arrow and French Rule box.

When you're finished, your slide should look like the one in Figure 4-28. Had you selected the objects and brought them to the front in any other sequence, the objects wouldn't appear in the correct order.

Lesson 4.10
Layering Objects

QUICK REFERENCE

TO CHANGE THE ORDER IN WHICH OBJECTS APPEAR ON A SLIDE:

1. SELECT THE OBJECT.
2. CLICK THE `Draw` DRAW BUTTON ON THE DRAWING TOOLBAR, SELECT ORDER AND SELECT ONE OF THE FOLLOWING LAYERING COMMANDS:

    BRING TO FRONT: PLACES THE SELECTED OBJECT ON THE VERY TOP LAYER OF THE SLIDE. ALL OTHER OBJECTS WILL APPEAR BEHIND THE SELECTED OBJECT.

    SEND TO BACK: PLACES THE SELECTED OBJECT ON THE VERY BOTTOM LAYER OF THE SLIDE. ALL OTHER OBJECTS WILL APPEAR IN FRONT OF THE SELECTED OBJECT.

    BRING FORWARD: BRINGS THE SELECTED OBJECT ONE LAYER UP ON THE SLIDE.

    SEND BACKWARD: SENDS THE SELECTED OBJECT ONE LAYER DOWN ON THE SLIDE.

- THE ORDER IN WHICH YOU SELECT AND LAYER OBJECTS WILL DETERMINE THE ORDER IN WHICH THEY APPEAR ON THE SLIDE. FOR EXAMPLE, THE LAST OBJECT YOU BRING TO THE FRONT WILL ALWAYS APPEAR ON THE TOP LAYER.

Applying Shadows and 3-D Effects

LESSON 4.11

Figure 4-29. A photograph with and without a shadow effect.

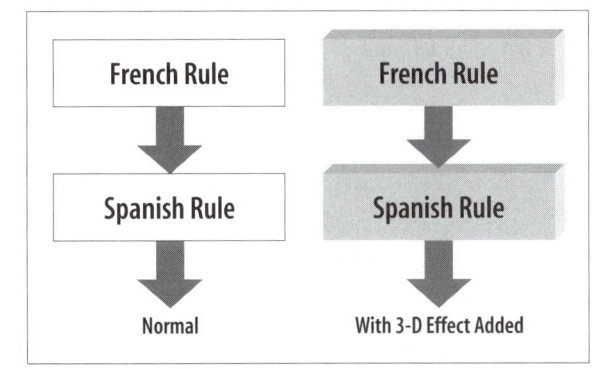

Figure 4-30. Graphic objects with and without 3-D effects.

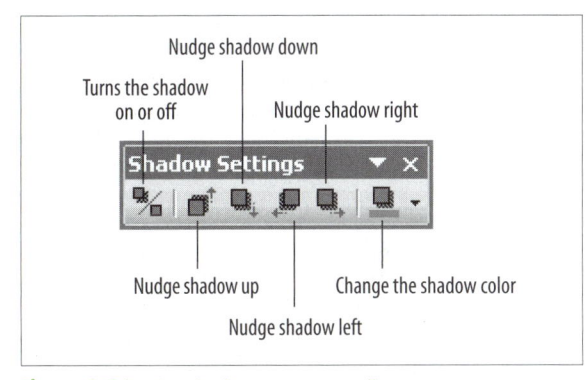

Figure 4-31. The Shadow Settings toolbar.

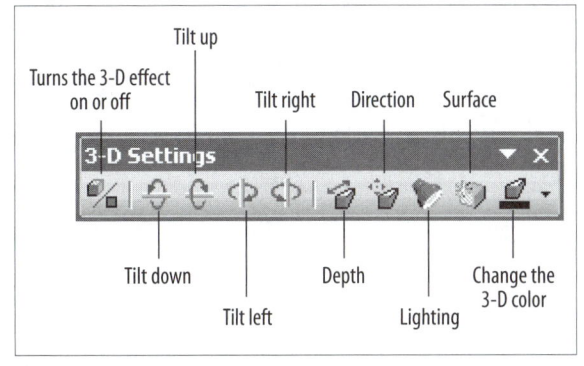

Figure 4-32. The 3-D Settings toolbar.

Figure 4-33. The updated slide with shadow and 3-D effects added to its objects.

Breathe new life into the flat and boring objects on your slides! Adding shadows and 3-D effects to slide objects make them stand out and look exciting. In this lesson we'll learn how to apply both shadows and 3-D effects to slide objects.

Adding a shadow to an object gives it a sense of depth by making it appear as if the object were casting a shadow. Not only can you add a shadow to an object, but you can also change the length of the shadow and where it falls.

The 3-D button on the drawing toolbar turns a lifeless object into a dramatic three-dimensional object without your having to put on a pair of 3-D glasses. As with shadowing, you can change the perspective and depth of any 3-D object.

1 Make sure you're on Slide 6, then click the **photograph** object to select it and click the **Shadow button** on the Drawing toolbar.

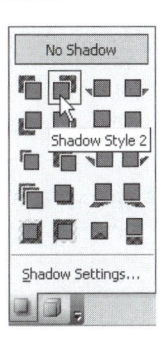

Effects under the Shadow Button

163

Lesson 4.11
Applying Shadows and 3-D Effects

A list of different shadow angles and effects appear above the Shadow button—all you have to do is select the type of shadow you want.

2 Select the Shadow Style 2 option (the second option in the top row) from the shadow list.

If the selected shadow still isn't exactly what you're looking for, you can change the position and color of the shadow. Here's how:

3 With the photograph still selected, click the Shadow button on the Drawing toolbar and select Shadow Settings.

The Shadow Settings toolbar appears, as shown in Figure 4-31. By clicking the Shadow Settings toolbar's buttons, you can adjust the shadow's position and change the shadow's color. Let's try it!

4 Click the Nudge Shadow Left button on the Shadow Settings toolbar twice, then click the Nudge Shadow Down button twice.

Clicking any of the Shadow Settings toolbar's Nudge buttons moves the shadow a smidgen in the specified direction.

5 Close the Shadow Settings toolbar by clicking its Close button.

The 3-D button is probably the coolest button on the Drawing toolbar. It turns ordinary two-dimensional objects into dazzling three-dimensional objects that look as though a professional graphic designer created them.

6 Click the Mardi Gras text object to select it.

It may be a little difficult to click the Mardi Gras object, since the mask graphic covers most of it. Try clicking the far-left side of the Mardi Gras object.

7 Click the 3-D button on the Drawing toolbar.

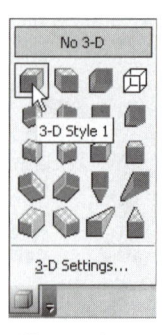

Effects under the 3-D Button

A list of different 3-D effects appears above the 3-D button. Just like the Shadow button, you need to select the 3-D effect you want to apply to your object.

8 Select the 3-D Style 1 option from the 3-D list.

PowerPoint applies the 3-D effect to the Mardi Gras text object, transforming it into a 3-D object. You can fine-tune the appearance of any 3-D object by adjusting its angle, depth, and lighting effects.

9 With the Mardi Gras text object still selected, click the 3-D button on the Drawing toolbar and select 3-D Settings.

The 3-D Settings toolbar appears, as shown in Figure 4-32. The 3-D Settings toolbar contains buttons that adjust the depth and direction of the 3-D object, as well as change the object's color and light effects.

10 Click the Depth button on the 3-D Settings toolbar, select the Custom option, type 24, and press Enter.

The Mardi Gras 3-D object now only extends 24 points instead of 36 points.

11 Close the 3-D Settings toolbar by clicking its Close button.

Move on to the next step to add 3-D effects to the flow chart boxes on the slide.

164

Chapter 4
Drawing and Working with Graphics

12 Following the procedure you learned in Steps 6–8, add the 3-D Style 1 effect to the three text boxes in the flow chart (Spanish, French and American Rule).

Guess what? You've completed the chapter and have become a genuine PowerPoint artist!

13 Save your work and exit the PowerPoint program.

QUICK REFERENCE

TO ADD A SHADOW TO AN OBJECT:
- SELECT THE OBJECT, CLICK THE SHADOW BUTTON ON THE DRAWING TOOLBAR, AND SELECT THE SHADOW EFFECT YOU WANT TO USE.

TO MODIFY A SHADOW:
- SELECT THE OBJECT, CLICK THE SHADOW BUTTON ON THE DRAWING TOOLBAR, SELECT SHADOW SETTINGS, AND MODIFY THE SHADOW BY CLICKING THE APPROPRIATE BUTTON(S) ON THE SHADOW SETTINGS TOOLBAR.

TO ADD A 3-D EFFECT TO AN OBJECT:
- SELECT THE OBJECT, CLICK THE 3-D BUTTON ON THE DRAWING TOOLBAR, AND SELECT THE 3-D EFFECT YOU WANT TO USE.

TO MODIFY A 3-D EFFECT:
- SELECT THE OBJECT, CLICK THE 3-D BUTTON ON THE DRAWING TOOLBAR, SELECT 3-D SETTINGS AND MODIFY THE 3-D OBJECT BY CLICKING THE APPROPRIATE BUTTON(S) ON THE 3-D SETTINGS TOOLBAR.

Chapter Four Review

Lesson Summary

Drawing on Your Slides

To Draw an Object: Click the object you want to draw on the drawing toolbar (such as a line or circle) and draw your shape by clicking on the slide with the + pointer and dragging until the shape reaches the desired size.

To Draw a Perfect Square, Circle, or Line: Hold down the Shift key as you draw a selected object.

Adding, Arranging, and Formatting Text Boxes

To Add a Text Box to a Slide: Click the Text Box button on the Drawing toolbar, click where you want to insert the text box with the insertion point, and then type the text.

To Resize a Text Box: Click the text box to select it, drag the object's sizing handles until the box reaches the desired size, and then release the mouse button.

Selecting, Resizing, Moving, and Deleting Objects

To Resize an Object: Click the object to select it, drag the object's sizing handles until the shape reaches the desired size, then release the mouse button.

To Resize an Object Proportionally: Follow the above procedures, only hold down the Shift key while dragging in order to maintain the object's proportions while resizing it.

To Move an Object: Click the object and hold down the mouse button, drag the object to a new location, and then release the mouse button to drop the object.

To Copy an Object Using Drop and Drag: Follow the above procedure, only hold down the Ctrl key while dragging to copy the object.

Formatting Objects

To Fill a Shape with a Color: Select the shape, then click the Fill Color button arrow on the Drawing toolbar and select the color you want.

To Change Line Color or Remove a Line: Select the shape, then click the Line Color button arrow on the Drawing toolbar and select the color you want.

To Change the Line Style: Select the line, then click the Line Style button on the Drawing toolbar and select the line style you want.

To Change the Dash Style: Select the line, then click the Dash Style button on the Drawing toolbar and select the dash you want.

To Add or Remove Arrow Heads: Select the line, then click the Arrow Style button on the Drawing toolbar and select the arrow style you want.

To Use the Format Object Dialog Box: Select the object and select Format → AutoShape from the menu, or right-click the object you want to format and select Format AutoShape from the shortcut menu.

Inserting ClipArt

To Insert a Clip Art Graphic: Select Insert → Picture → Clip Art from the menu, select a clip art category, then click on the clip art you want to use.

Inserting and Formatting Pictures

To Insert a Graphic Created in Another Program: Select Insert → Picture → From File from the menu, then select the file location and name and click OK.

Use the Picture toolbar to change the brightness and contrast of a selected picture.

Use the Image Control Button on the Picture toolbar to modify a picture's colors, making it appear in black and white, grayscales, or as a watermark.

To Crop a Picture: Click the picture to select it, click the Crop button on the Picture toolbar, and drag one of the picture's edges with the **crop tool**.

Aligning and Grouping Objects

To Select Multiple Objects: Press and hold down the Shift key as you click each object that you want to select, or use the arrow pointer ( ) to draw a box around the objects that you want to select.

Chapter 4
Drawing and Working with Graphics

To Align Objects with Each Other: Follow the above steps to select the objects you want to align, click the `Draw` Draw button on the Drawing toolbar, select Align or Distribute, and select how you want to align or distribute the selected objects.

To Group Several Objects: Select the objects you want to group together, click the `Draw` Draw button on the Drawing toolbar, and select Group.

To Ungroup a Grouped Object: Select the grouped object, click the `Draw` Draw button on the Drawing toolbar, and select Ungroup.

Drawing AutoShapes

To Insert an AutoShape: Click the `AutoShapes` AutoShapes button on the Drawing toolbar and select the category and AutoShape that you want to insert. Drag the crosshair pointer to draw the AutoShape.

To Adjust an AutoShape: Select the AutoShape and drag its adjustment handle (◇) to adjust the most prominent feature of the shape.

To Add Text to a Shape: Right-click the shape, select Add Text from the shortcut menu, and type the text.

Flipping and Rotating Objects

To Rotate an Object by 90 Degrees: Select the object, click the `Draw` Draw button on the Drawing toolbar and select Rotate or Flip, then select Rotate Right 90° or Rotate Left 90°.

To Flip an Object: Select the object, click the Draw button on the Drawing toolbar and select Rotate or Flip, then select Flip Horizontal or Flip Vertical.

To Free Rotate an Object: Select the object and click and drag the object's rotate handle (●) with the pointer. You can also rotate an object by selecting the object, selecting Format → AutoShape from the menu, clicking the Size tab, and entering the amount in degrees you want to rotate the object in the Rotation box.

Layering Objects

To Change the Order in Which Objects Appear on a Slide: Select the object, click the `Draw` Draw button on the Drawing toolbar, select Order, and select one of the following layering commands:

Bring to Front: Places the selected object on the very top layer of the slide. All other objects will appear behind the selected object.

Send to Back: Places the selected object on the very bottom layer of the slide. All other objects will appear in front of the selected object.

Bring Forward: Brings the selected object one layer up on the slide.

Send Backward: Sends the selected object one layer down on the slide.

The order in which you select and layer objects will determine the order in which they appear on the slide. For example, the last object you bring to the front will always appear on the top layer.

Applying Shadows and 3-D Effects

To Add a Shadow to an Object: Select the object, click the Shadow button on the Drawing toolbar, and select the shadow effect you want to use.

To Modify a Shadow: Select the object, click the Shadow button on the Drawing toolbar, select Shadow Settings, and modify the shadow by clicking the appropriate button(s) on the Shadow Settings toolbar.

To Add a 3-D Effect to an Object: Select the object, click the 3-D button on the Drawing toolbar, and select the 3-D effect you want to use.

To Modify a 3-D Effect: Select the object, click the 3-D button on the Drawing toolbar, select 3-D Settings and modify the 3-D object by clicking the appropriate button(s) on the 3-D Settings toolbar.

Chapter 4
Chapter Four Review

Quiz

1. Which of the following statements is NOT true?

   A. Holding down the Shift key while you draw an object creates perfect squares, circles, and straight lines.

   B. The Drawing toolbar contains tools for drawing shapes, lines, arrows and more.

   C. The text in a text box can't be formatted.

   D. You can change the size of a text box by selecting it and dragging its sizing handles.

2. Which of the following are methods to select multiple objects on a slide? (Select all that apply.)

   A. Click the Select Object button on the Standard toolbar, click the objects you want to select, and press Enter when you're finished.

   B. Hold down the Shift key as you select each object.

   C. You can only select one object at a time in PowerPoint.

   D. Click the Arrow button on the Drawing toolbar and drag a rectangle around the objects you want to select.

3. You can format drawing objects by: (Select all that apply.)

   A. Selecting the object and formatting it with the Drawing toolbar.

   B. Selecting the object, selecting Format → AutoShape from the menu, and specifying your formatting options from the Format AutoShape dialog box.

   C. Right-clicking the object, selecting Format AutoShape from the shortcut menu, and specifying your formatting options from the Format AutoShape dialog box.

   D. Selecting the object, pressing Ctrl + F, and specifying your formatting options from the Format AutoShape dialog box.

4. You can change the brightness, contrast, and crop a picture using the buttons on the Drawing toolbar. (True or False?)

5. Block Arrows, Stars and Banners, and Callouts are all examples of:

   A. Different types of children's building blocks.

   B. Clip art categories located in the Microsoft Clip Gallery.

   C. AutoShape categories.

   D. More technical terms that I don't understand.

6. You need to wear special glasses in order to see and appreciate 3-D effects created by the 3-D Effects button on the Drawing toolbar. (True or False?)

7. You are creating a slide about the life of Harvester ants and have inserted several dozen ant pictures into your slide. Now you're having problems moving and keeping track of all of all those pictures. What can you do to make working with these pictures easier?

   A. Delete the ants, insert a picture of an anteater and write a note to your audience explaining what happened.

   B. Group the ants together—select all the ants by holding down the Shift key as you click each ant or by drawing a box around them with the pointer. Once you have selected all the ants, group them together by clicking the Draw button on the Drawing toolbar and selecting Group.

   C. Select Edit → Select Ants from the menu whenever you want to move or work with all the ants at once.

   D. Do a project on something else.

8. Some AutoShapes have a yellow diamond ◇ on them. What is this yellow diamond and what is it used for?

   A. It's a *sizing* handle and is used for making AutoShapes larger or smaller.

   B. It's a *moving* handle—click and drag it to move the AutoShape to a different location on the screen.

   C. It's an *adjustment* handle and is used to change an AutoShape's most prominent feature, such as the point on an arrow or the spikes on a star.

   D. It's the *confusion* handle—it doesn't have any function and is only there to perplex you.

Chapter 4
Drawing and Working with Graphics

Homework

1. Open the Homework 4 presentation and save it as "Paper Games."

2. Go to Slide 2. Click the Oval button on the Drawing toolbar. Position the pointer in the upper-left corner of the middle box, press and hold the Shift key, then drag down and to the right to create a circle that is the same size as the circle below it.

3. Click the Fill Color list arrow on the Drawing toolbar and select No Fill.

4. Go to Slide 3. Select all of the hangman objects (hold down the Shift key as you click each object or click and drag a rectangle around the objects). Click the Draw menu button on the Drawing toolbar and select Group.

5. Select Insert → Picture → Clip Art from the menu. Type "cartoon person" in the search box and click Go, select any of the cartoon characters, and then click Insert.

6. Click the clip art picture to select it, then click and drag any of its sizing handles until the figure is small enough to fit under the gallows.

7. Click and drag the cartoon figure under the gallows.

Quiz Answers

1. C. Of course you can format a text box's text!

2. B and D. Either of these methods will select multiple objects.

3. A, B, and C. You can format drawing objects using any of these methods.

4. False. You will have to summon the Picture toolbar to accomplish these tasks.

5. C. AutoShape categories.

6. False. Of course not! What a silly question!

7. B. Grouping all those ants will make them easier to work with.

8. C. That yellow diamond is the adjustment handle and is used to change an AutoShape's most prominent feature or angle.

CHAPTER 5
WORKING WITH TABLES AND WORDART

CHAPTER OBJECTIVES:

Creating and working with a table
Adjusting column width and row height
Inserting and deleting rows and columns
Adding borders and shading to a table's cells
Inserting a WordArt object
Formatting and editing a WordArt object

CHAPTER TASK: ADD A TABLE AND A WORDART OBJECT TO A SLIDE

Prerequisites

- **Know how to use menus, toolbars, dialog boxes, and shortcut keystrokes.**
- **Move the mouse pointer and navigate between the slides in a presentation.**
- **Open and save a presentation.**

If you want to create a slide that displays lots of information in a neat and organized manner, don't struggle with PowerPoint's limited tab stops and text layout features—insert a table instead. A table neatly arranges text and data in a grid, organized by columns and rows. This chapter explains how to embed a Word table into a PowerPoint slide.

If you're making the switch from PowerPoint 97, you will want to be sure to peruse this chapter, as many of the procedures for working with tables have changed in PowerPoint 2003. PowerPoint 97 required that you had a copy of Microsoft Word 97 installed in order to create and work with tables, while PowerPoint 2003 has all the tools you'll need.

You will also get a chance to use Microsoft's WordArt program in this chapter. WordArt is a program that turns ordinary text into stunning 3-D headlines—great for emphasizing simple messages, such as "Limited Offer!"

LESSON 5.1 Creating a Table

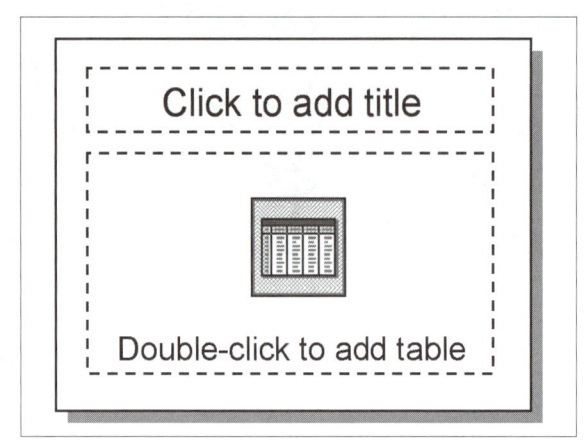

Figure 5-1. The Title and Table layout—click the table placeholder to add a table.

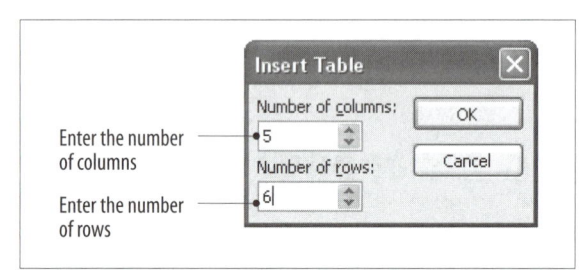

Figure 5-2. The Insert Table dialog box.

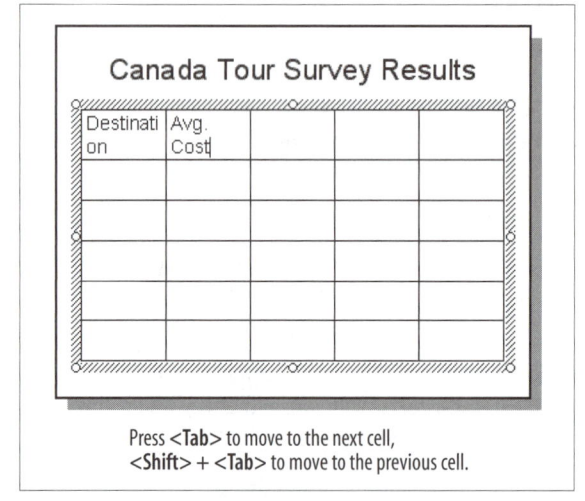

Figure 5-3. Entering information into a table.

Figure 5-4. The completed table.

In this lesson, you will learn how to add a table slide and then enter information into it. To create a table, you must specify how many columns (which run up and down) and rows (which run left to right) you want to appear in your table. Cells are small rectangular-shaped boxes that appear where the rows and columns of a table intersect. The number of columns and rows will determine how many cells will be in the table and how much information your table can contain. If you're not certain how many columns and rows you want in your table, take an educated guess—you can always add or delete columns and rows from a table later.

Cells, Rows, and Columns

1 **Start Microsoft PowerPoint.**

Microsoft PowerPoint will start with a blank presentation. Let's change the layout of this slide.

New Slide button

2 **Select Format → Slide Layout from the menu.**

The Slide Layout task pane appears with different slide types.

3 Scroll down the task pane until you find the Title and Table layout. Select the Title and Table layout and close the task pane.

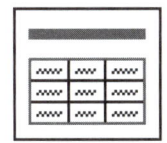

Title and Table layout

A blank table slide appears, as shown in Figure 5-1.

4 Click the Title placeholder and type Canada Tour Survey Results.

We're ready to create the table.

5 Double-click the Table placeholder.

The Insert Table dialog box appears, as shown in Figure 5-2. This is where you tell PowerPoint how many columns and rows you want in your table.

6 In the Number of columns box, type 5, press Tab to move to the Number of rows box, type 6, and click OK.

A blank table appears with six rows and five columns, similar to the one in Figure 5-3. The Tables and Borders toolbar, required for working with tables, also appears.

Move on to the next step and we'll enter some information into the table. Notice a blinking insertion point (|) appears in the first cell in the table—all you have to do is type the text you want to appear in this cell.

You can also insert a table by clicking the **Insert Table button** and dragging how many columns and rows you want.

3 x 4 Table

7 Type Destination, then press Tab to move to the next cell.

Don't worry if your text is too large to fit into the cell—we'll fix that in a minute. Pressing Tab moves the insertion point to the next cell in the row, pressing Shift + Tab moves the insertion point to the previous cell in the row. Finish adding the column headings for our table. Make sure you press Tab after each entry to move to the next cell.

8 Type Avg. Cost, press Tab, type Avg. Tour Length, press Tab, type Projected Bookings, press Tab, and type Projected Income.

Now let's fix the font formatting used in our table. Formatting text in a table isn't much different than formatting text anywhere else on a slide—you simply select the text you want to format and then use the Formatting toolbar to change the font size, type, and color. You use the Table button on the Tables and Borders toolbar to select the information in a table.

9 Click the Table button on the Tables and Borders toolbar and select Select Table from the list.

Table button

The entire table is selected—now you can change the font that is used throughout the table.

10 Click the Font Size list on the Formatting toolbar and select 20.

Finish filling out the table.

11 Click the first cell in the second row (the one directly beneath the "Destination" heading).

12 Type the following text in the table. Press Tab after entering the text in each cell. *Don't press Tab at the end of the last row.*

Ottawa	$1,500	2 weeks	105	$157,000
Nova Scotia	$1,350	1.5 weeks	60	$81,000
Vancouver	$1,600	2 weeks	90	$144,000
Winnipeg	$1,200	1.5 weeks	50	$60,000
Toronto	$1,050	1 week	65	$68,250

When you're finished, your table should look like the one in Figure 5-4.

Lesson 5.1
Creating a Table

13 Click anywhere outside the table when you're finished, and save your presentation with the name Canada Survey.

Congratulations! You've created your first table. Sorry for all the typing you had to do in this lesson, but it gives you an idea of how easy it is to enter and present information in a table. Should you want to edit your table later on, just double-click it.

QUICK REFERENCE

TO INSERT A TABLE SLIDE:

- CLICK THE NEW SLIDE BUTTON ON THE FORMATTING TOOLBAR AND SELECT THE TITLE AND TABLE LAYOUT.

TO INSERT A TABLE ON AN EXISTING SLIDE:

- SELECT INSERT → TABLE FROM THE MENU, SPECIFY THE NUMBER OF ROWS AND COLUMNS YOU WANT, AND CLICK OK.

OR...

- CLICK THE INSERT TABLE BUTTON ON THE STANDARD TOOLBAR AND DRAG THE GRID TO SELECT HOW MANY COLUMNS AND ROWS YOU WANT.

TO MOVE FROM CELL TO CELL IN A TABLE:

- PRESS TAB TO MOVE FORWARD ONE FIELD OR CELL, AND PRESS SHIFT + TAB TO MOVE BACK ONE FIELD OR CELL.

TO DELETE THE CONTENTS OF A CELL:

- SELECT THE CELL(S) AND THEN PRESS THE DELETE KEY.

LESSON 5.2

Working with a Table

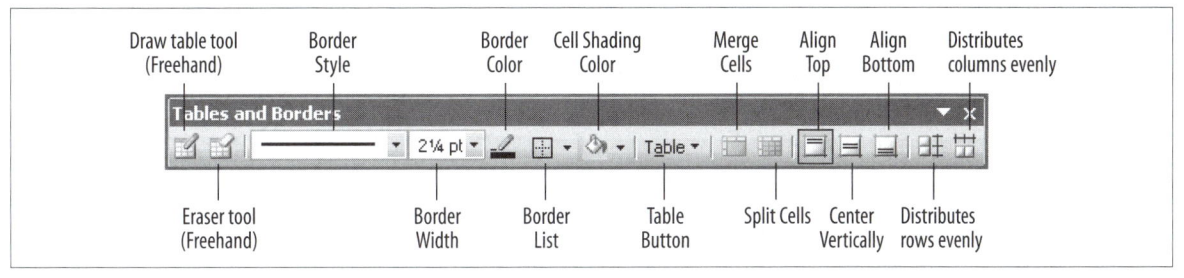

Figure 5-5. The Tables and Borders toolbar.

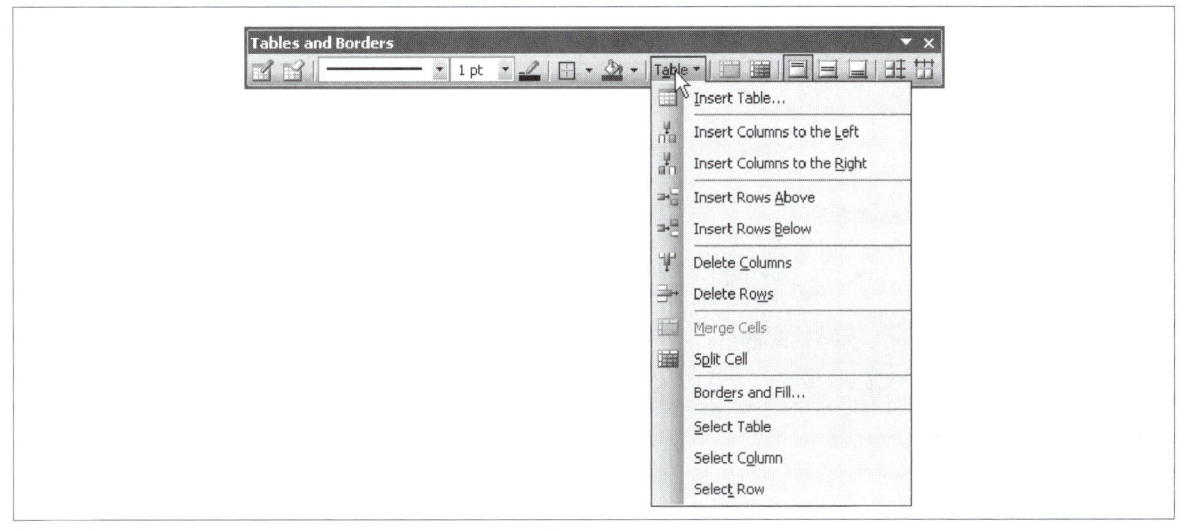

Figure 5-6. The Table menu on the Tables and Borders toolbar.

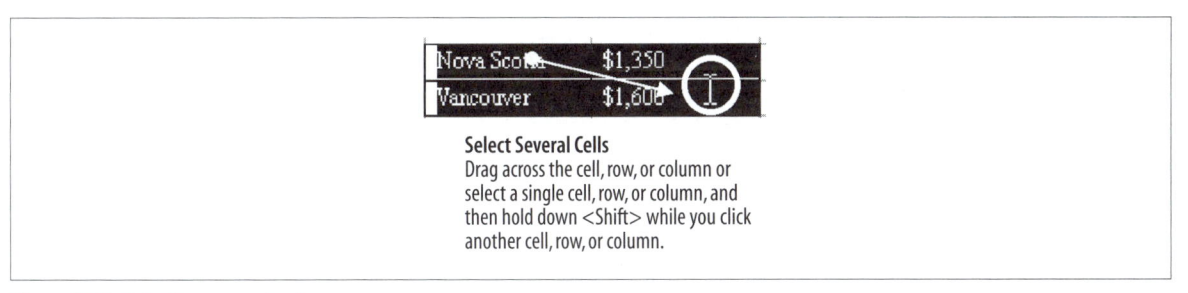

Figure 5-7. Selecting several cells.

This lesson will give you some more practice working with tables—specifically how to select and format a table's columns and rows.

1 Double-click the table to edit it.

The table is now selected, indicating that you can edit it. Here's how to select a row.

2 Place the insertion point anywhere in the table's top row, then select the row by clicking the **Table button** on the Tables and Borders toolbar and selecting **Select Row** from the list.

Table button

175

Lesson 5.2
Working with a Table

You can also select several rows or cells by placing the insertion point in the first cell you want to select and then clicking and dragging the mouse to the last cell, as shown in Figure 5-7.

Now that you have selected the row, you can format its text.

If the Tables and Borders toolbar doesn't automatically appear when you edit a table, click the **Tables and Borders button** on the Standard toolbar

3 With the row still selected, click the Center button and the Bold button on the Formatting toolbar.

Center button

The text in the selected row appears in bold and is centered in each row. Try selecting and formatting a column next.

4 Place the insertion point anywhere in the last column in the table (Projected Income) then select the column by clicking the Table button on the Tables and Borders toolbar and selecting Select Column from the list.

Now that you have selected the column, you can format its contents.

5 Click the Bold button on the Formatting toolbar.

Bold button

The contents of the selected column appear in bold. We don't really want this entire column to appear in bold, so click the undo button on the standard toolbar and then move on to the next step.

6 Select the Ottawa cell by clicking just inside the right side of the cell and dragging the insertion point across the text.

Remember that anything you type replaces the current selection—and the contents of a cell are no exception to this rule.

Undo button

7 Type Montreal and press the Tab key.

Selecting cells, rows, and columns might seem very boring to you, but it's crucial that you get it down if you're going to work with tables. When people have problems doing something with a table, about 90% of the time it's because they didn't properly select the table.

QUICK REFERENCE

TO SELECT A ROW:

- PLACE THE INSERTION POINT ANYWHERE IN THE ROW YOU WANT TO SELECT, CLICK THE Table ▾ TABLE BUTTON ON THE TABLES AND BORDERS TOOLBAR, AND SELECT SELECT ROW FROM THE LIST.

TO SELECT A COLUMN:

- PLACE THE INSERTION POINT ANYWHERE IN THE COLUMN YOU WANT TO SELECT, CLICK THE Table ▾ TABLE BUTTON ON THE TABLES AND BORDERS TOOLBAR, AND SELECT SELECT COLUMN FROM THE LIST.

TO SELECT SEVERAL CELLS:

- DRAG ACROSS THE CELL, ROW, OR COLUMN; OR SELECT A SINGLE CELL, ROW, OR COLUMN, AND THEN HOLD DOWN SHIFT WHILE YOU CLICK ANOTHER CELL, ROW, OR COLUMN.

Adjusting Column Width and Row Height

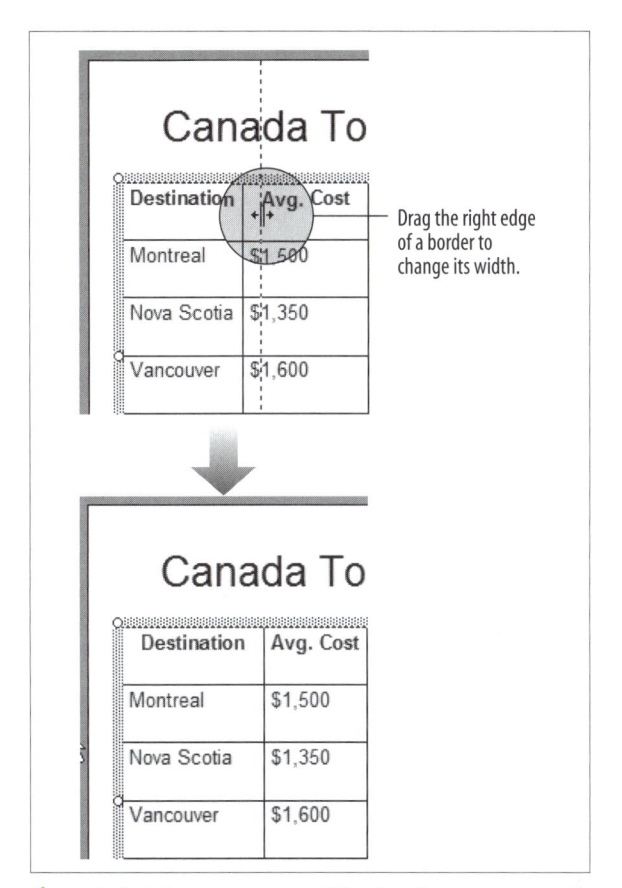

LESSON 5.3

Figure 5-8. Adjusting column width using the mouse.

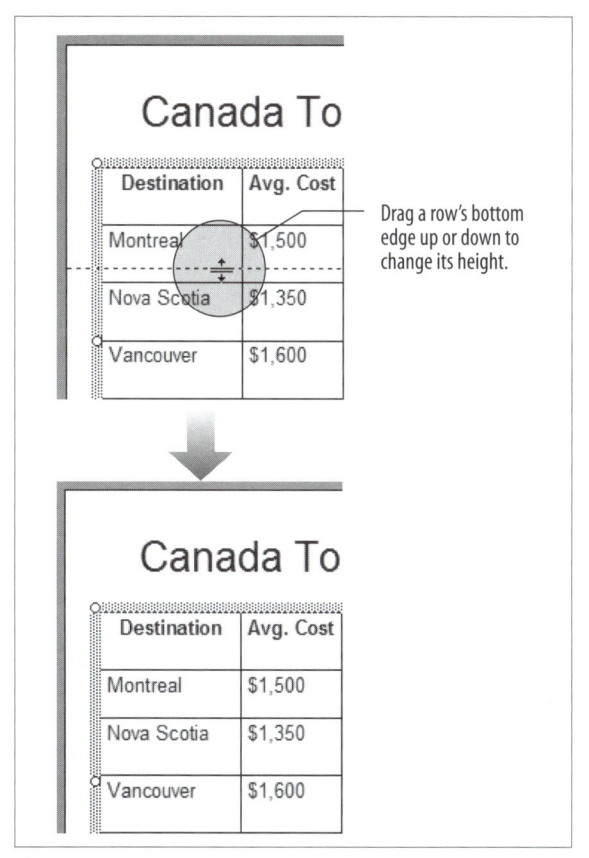

Figure 5-9. Adjusting the height of a row using the mouse.

When you create a table, all of the rows and columns normally appear as the same size. As you enter information in a table, you will quickly discover that some of the columns are not wide enough to properly display the information they contain. This lesson explains how to change the width of a column and the height of a row.

1 If necessary, find and open the Lesson 5A presentation and save it as Canada Survey.

2 Double-click the table object to edit it.

Here's how to adjust the width of a column:

3 Carefully position the pointer over the first column border, after the Destination heading, until it changes to ↔, as shown in Figure 5-8. Click and hold the mouse button, drag the pointer to the right just a smidgen (as shown in Figure 5-8), then release the mouse button.

The width of the "Destination" column is now wide enough to properly display its contents.

Now that you know how to change the width of a column, we'll look at changing the height of a row. Actually, you will seldom need to change a row's height, because unless you specify otherwise, rows automatically expand to the size of the tallest cell in the table—the one that contains the most lines of text. Nevertheless, here's how to manually adjust the height of a row:

4 Position the pointer directly on the bottom border of the first row, until it changes to ↕, then click and hold the mouse button, drag the pointer up just a smidgen, (as shown in Figure 5-9), then release the mouse button.

5 Save your work.

Lesson 5.3
Adjusting Column Width and Row Height

QUICK REFERENCE

TO ADJUST THE WIDTH OF A COLUMN:
- CLICK AND DRAG THE COLUMN'S RIGHT BORDER TO THE LEFT OR RIGHT.

TO ADJUST THE HEIGHT OF A ROW:
- ROWS AUTOMATICALLY EXPAND TO DISPLAY THEIR CONTENTS...

    ...OTHERWISE, YOU CAN MANUALLY RESIZE A ROW BY DRAGGING THE ROW'S BOTTOM BORDER UP OR DOWN.

LESSON 5.4

Inserting and Deleting Rows and Columns

Figure 5-10. Deleting a row.

Figure 5-11. Inserting a new column.

In the previous lesson you learned how to adjust the size of rows and columns. In this lesson, you will learn how to delete entire columns and rows (and any text they contain) and also how to insert new columns and rows into a table.

1 Place the insertion point anywhere in the **Montreal row**.

Here's how to delete the current row:

2 Click the **Table button** on the Tables and Borders toolbar and select **Delete Rows** from the menu.

The Montreal row is deleted. Now try inserting a new row.

Table button

3 Place the insertion point anywhere in the **Nova Scotia row**.

You can insert new rows either above or below the current row.

4 Click the **Table button** on the Tables and Borders toolbar and select **Insert Rows Above** from the menu.

A new row is inserted immediately above the Nova Scotia row.

5 Place the insertion point in the first cell in the new row, type **Quebec**, press **Tab**, then type the following numbers in the cells in the new row: **$2,000 Tab 2.5 weeks Tab 150 Tab $300,000**.

If you're in the last cell of a table, there is another, very easy way to insert rows.

6 Place the insertion point in the very last cell in the bottom right-hand corner of the table.

7 Press the **Tab** key.

PowerPoint adds a new row at the end of the table and moves the insertion point to the first cell in the new row. Normally, pressing the Tab key moves the insertion point to the next cell in a table, but since this is the last cell in the table, PowerPoint assumes you need another row so it automatically adds one.

179

Lesson 5.4
Inserting and Deleting Rows and Columns

8 Click the Undo button on the Standard toolbar to remove the new row from your table.

Now that you have deleted and inserted a row, try deleting and inserting a column.

9 Place the insertion point anywhere in the Avg. Tour Length column, click the Table button on the Tables and Borders toolbar, and select Delete Columns from the menu.

The Avg. Tour Length column is deleted. Now try inserting a column. You can insert new columns either to the right or left or the current column.

10 Place the insertion point anywhere in the Projected Bookings column, click the Table button on the Tables and Borders toolbar, and select Insert Columns to the Left from the menu.

A new column appears to the left of the Projected Bookings column. Go ahead and type some information in this new column:

11 Place the insertion point in the top cell of the new column and type Avg. Days.

12 Press the Down Arrow Key ↓ to move down to the next empty cell in the column.

13 Type 14, press the Down Arrow Key ↓ to move down to the next empty cell in the column, type 10, press ↓, type 15, press ↓, type 12, press ↓, and type 1.5.

14 Save your work.

QUICK REFERENCE

TO DELETE A COLUMN OR ROW:

1. PLACE THE INSERTION POINT ANYWHERE IN THE COLUMN OR ROW YOU WANT TO DELETE.

2. CLICK THE TABLE BUTTON ON THE TABLES AND BORDERS TOOLBAR AND SELECT EITHER DELETE COLUMNS OR DELETE ROWS FROM THE MENU.

TO INSERT A COLUMN OR ROW:

1. PLACE THE INSERTION POINT ANYWHERE IN THE COLUMN OR ROW ABOVE, BELOW, TO THE RIGHT, OR TO THE LEFT OF WHERE YOU WANT THE NEW COLUMN OR ROW TO BE INSERTED.

2. CLICK THE TABLE BUTTON ON THE TABLES AND BORDERS TOOLBAR AND SELECT ONE OF THE FOLLOWING:
INSERT ROW ABOVE
INSERT ROW BELOW
INSERT COLUMN TO THE RIGHT
INSERT COLUMN TO THE LEFT

Adding Borders to a Table

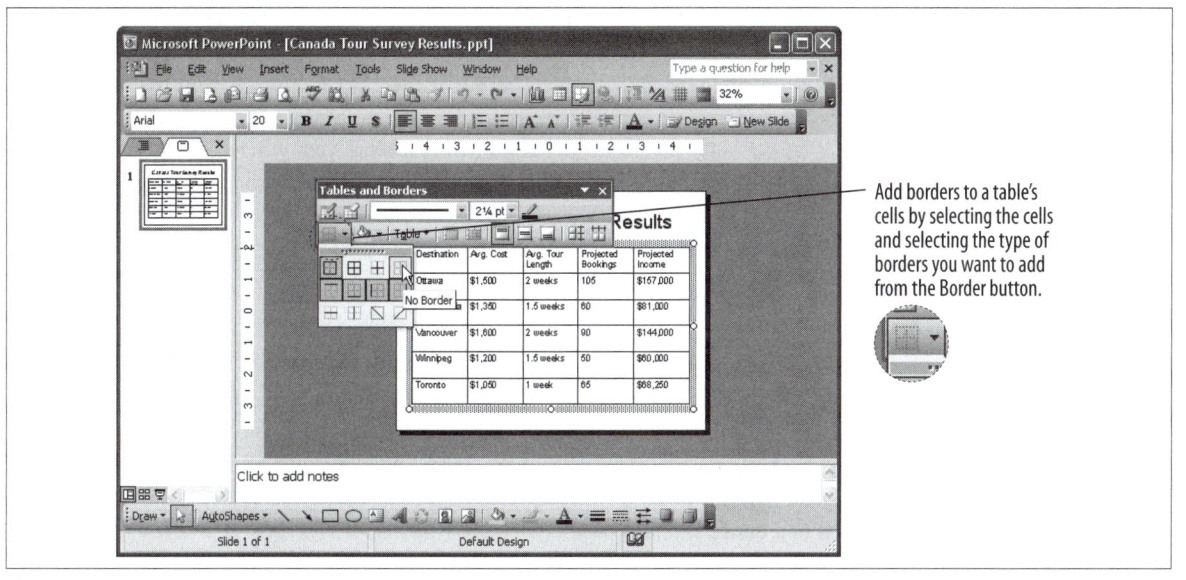

LESSON 5.5

Figure 5-12. Selecting a border from the Border list.

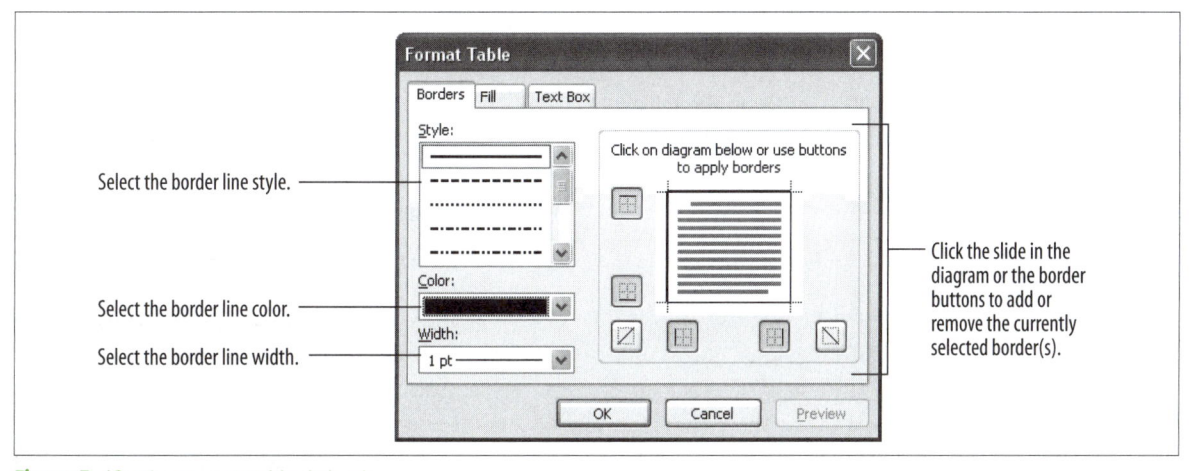

Add borders to a table's cells by selecting the cells and selecting the type of borders you want to add from the Border button.

Figure 5-13. The Format Table dialog box.

Select the border line style.
Select the border line color.
Select the border line width.
Click the slide in the diagram or the border buttons to add or remove the currently selected border(s).

Borders improve the appearance of your tables, giving them a polished, professional look. Borders can also make it easier to read the table's information, especially numbers. This lesson will give you some practice working with borders.

New tables have borders around every cell by default. You will want to remove these gridline borders to start this lesson.

1 Click the table object to edit it.

Next you need to select the entire table so that you can remove its default borders.

2 Click the **Table button** on the Tables and Borders toolbar and select **Select Table** from the menu.

Now that the entire table is selected, you can remove its borders.

3 Click the **Border button arrow** on the Tables or Borders toolbar.

A list appears with several border options.

Border button

181

Lesson 5.5
Adding Borders to a Table

4 Select the No Border option from the Border list.

PowerPoint removes the gridline borders from the selected table. Now that you have removed the default borders, you can add some of your own.

5 Select the table's top row, click the Border button arrow on the Tables or Borders toolbar, and select the Outside Borders option (the first choice).

PowerPoint adds an outside border around the selected cells.

You can also use the Tables and Borders toolbar to change the border's style, width, and color.

6 If it is not already selected, select the top row by placing the insertion point anywhere in the row, clicking the Table button on the Tables and Borders toolbar, and selecting Select Row from the menu.

You want to add a thick, dark border to the bottom of the cells in this row. Here's how to change the border's width.

7 Click the Border Width button arrow on the Tables and Borders toolbar and select 2 1/4π pt. from the list.

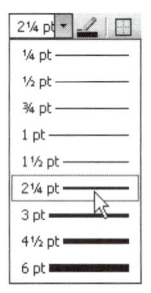

Border Width button

Now that you've selected the border's width (or weight), you can add the border.

8 With the top row still selected, click the Border button arrow on the Tables or Borders toolbar and select the Bottom Border option.

PowerPoint adds a thick border to the bottom of the row.

The Tables and Borders toolbar is by far the fastest and easiest way to add and format borders to your tables, but you can also add and format table borders using a dialog box.

9 Click the Table button on the Tables and Formatting toolbar and select Borders and Fill from the menu.

The Format Table dialog box appears, as shown in Figure 5-13. Here you can find every conceivable option for adding, removing, and configuring your table's borders.

10 Click Cancel to close the Format Table dialog box.

The Format Table dialog box closes. Now we need to make sure we switch the mouse pointer back into an arrow.

11 Click the Select Objects button on the Drawing toolbar, then save your work.

Select Objects button

QUICK REFERENCE

TO ADD A BORDER TO A TABLE:

1. SELECT THE CELL(S) WHERE YOU WANT TO APPLY THE BORDERS.

2. CLICK THE BORDER LIST ARROW ON THE TABLES AND BORDERS TOOLBAR AND SELECT THE BORDER OPTION YOU WANT.

OR...

CLICK THE Table TABLE BUTTON ON THE TABLES AND BORDERS TOOLBAR, SELECT BORDERS AND FILLS FROM THE MENU, SELECT YOUR BORDER OPTIONS, AND CLICK OK.

Adding Shading and Fills

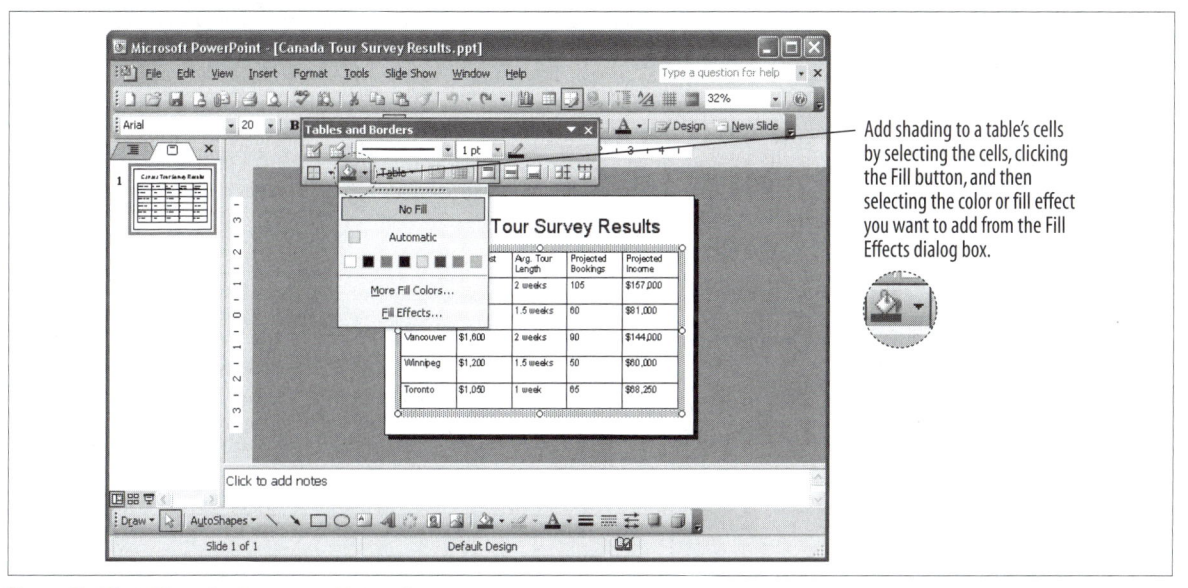

LESSON 5.6

Figure 5-14. Adding shading to a table's cells.

Add shading to a table's cells by selecting the cells, clicking the Fill button, and then selecting the color or fill effect you want to add from the Fill Effects dialog box.

You can also apply shading to selected cells using the Fill tab of the Format Table dialog box.

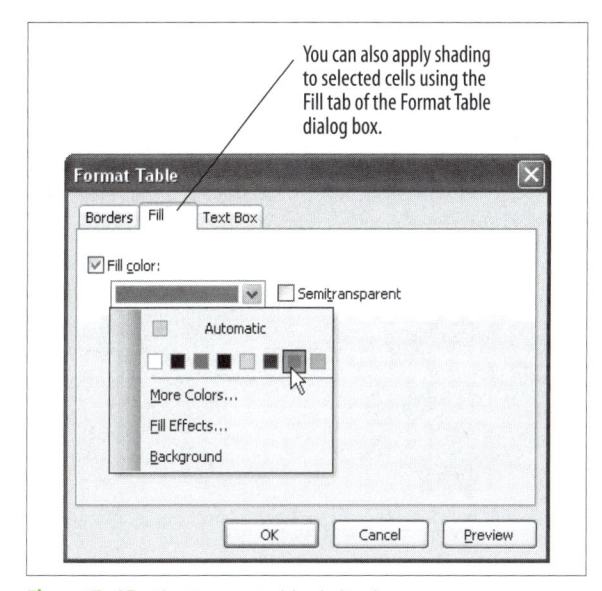

Figure 5-15. The Format Table dialog box.

Fill button

Other Ways to Apply Shading:

- Click the **Table button** on the Tables and Borders toolbar, select **Borders and Fill** from the menu, click the Fill tab, select your fill options and click **OK**.

Adding shading, colors, and patterns to a table is very similar to adding borders. You will be using the Format Table dialog box once again, only this time you'll be using the Fill tab instead of the Borders tab. You can also add shading to your table's cells by using the Fill button on the Tables and Borders toolbar. This lesson will give you some practice adding colors and shading to your table.

1 If necessary, find and open the Lesson 5B presentation and save it as Canada Survey.

2 Select the table's top row.

This is where you want to apply shading.

3 Click the Fill Color button arrow on the Tables and Borders toolbar.

A color palette of colors that coordinate with the current design appears below the Fill button. To select more colors, select More Fill Colors.

4 Select the teal color.

The selected row is shaded with the selected color.

As with adding borders, you can also apply shading to a table using the Format Table dialog box—although you probably won't want to use this method since the Fill Color button has all the same options. Nevertheless, here's how to apply shading using a dialog box:

183

Lesson 5.6
Adding Shading and Fills

5 Click the Table button on the Tables and Borders toolbar, select Borders and Fill from the menu and then click the Fill tab.

The Fill tab of the Format Table dialog box appears, as shown in Figure 5-15. To select a fill option, make sure the Fill color box is checked and then select your fill color from the combo box.

6 Click Cancel to close the dialog box.

The dialog box closes. Now let's add some shading.

7 Make sure the top row is still selected, click the Fill button arrow on the Tables and Borders toolbar, and select the Fill Effects option.

The Gradient tab of the Fill Effects dialog box appears. Now we need to decide what we want our shading to look like.

8 Click Two colors in the Colors section and then click Horizontal in the Shading Styles section.

Preview what your shading is going to look like in the Sample window, located in the lower right-hand corner of the dialog box.

9 Click OK to close the dialog box, then click anywhere outside of the table to deselect it.

The shading is applied to the top row of the table.

QUICK REFERENCE

TO ADD SHADING TO A TABLE:

1. SELECT THE CELLS WHERE YOU WANT TO APPLY THE SHADING.
2. CLICK THE FILL LIST ARROW ON THE TABLES AND BORDERS TOOLBAR AND SELECT THE FILL EFFECTS OPTION.

OR...

- CLICK THE TABLE BUTTON ON THE TABLES AND BORDERS TOOLBAR, SELECT BORDERS AND FILL FROM THE MENU, CLICK THE FILL TAB, SELECT YOUR FILL OPTIONS, AND CLICK OK.

Inserting a WordArt Object

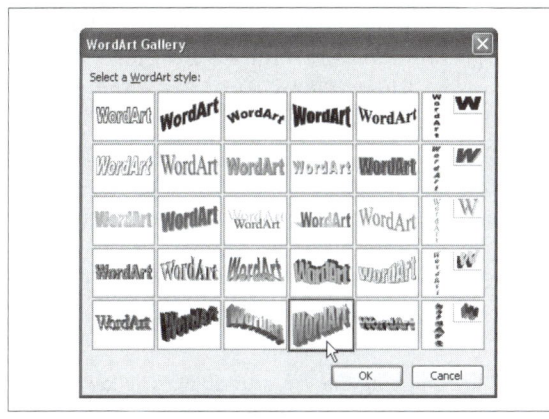

LESSON 5.7

Figure 5-16. The WordArt Gallery dialog box.

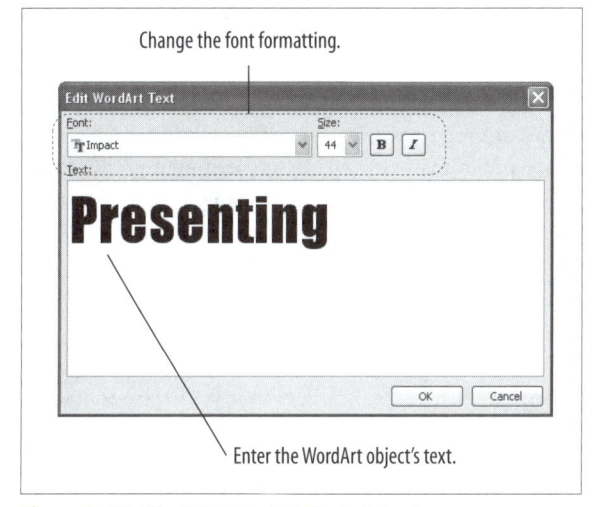

Figure 5-17. The Edit WordArt Text dialog box.

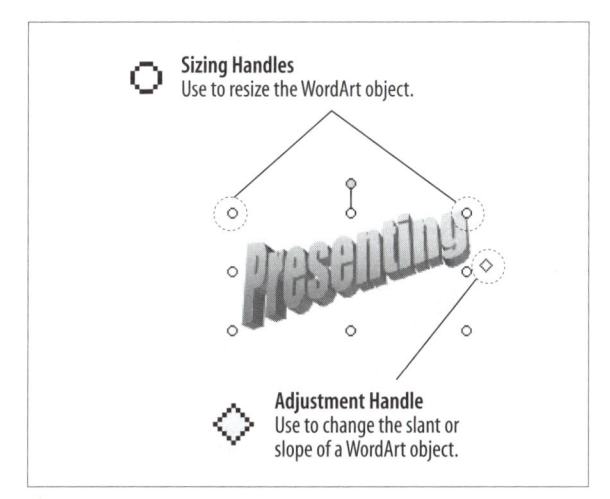

Figure 5-18. An Inserted WordArt object.

Figure 5-19. The updated slide with an inserted WordArt object.

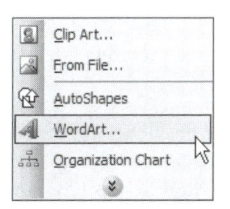

Inserting a WordArt Object

WordArt is definitely one of the coolest "bonus programs" that comes with Microsoft Office. WordArt lets you add dramatic, colorful text effects to your slide, even if you're not an artistic person. In this lesson, you will use WordArt to make a somewhat boring title slide stand out.

1 Open **Lesson 5C** and save it as **Rail Europe**.

Actually this title slide doesn't look too shabby—but it could look even better if we added a WordArt object to it.

2 Select **Insert** → **Picture** → **WordArt** from the menu.

The WordArt Gallery dialog box appears, as shown in Figure 5-16. The WordArt Gallery displays the various formats you can apply to your text.

3 Select the fourth option in the bottom row—the WordArt option—then click **OK**.

185

Lesson 5.7
Inserting a WordArt Object

The Edit WordArt Text dialog box appears, as shown in Figure 5-17. This is where you enter what you want your WordArt to say.

4 Type Presenting.

You can also change the font type and size in the Edit WordArt Text dialog box.

5 Click the Size list arrow, select 44, and then click OK.

The WordArt object is inserted into the slide, and the WordArt toolbar appears. The WordArt toolbar contains buttons that modify a WordArt object and appears whenever a WordArt object is selected. You can move and resize a WordArt object just like any other object; all you have to do is use its sizing handles, as shown in Figure 5-18. Now let's position the WordArt object over the left side of the slide's title.

6 Position the pointer over the WordArt object until the pointer changes to a ✥, then drag the WordArt object just over and to the left of the slide's title, as shown in Figure 5-19.

Next, we want to change the angle that our WordArt slants. If your WordArt is still selected, you'll notice a little yellow diamond ◇ on its right side. This is called an adjustment handle—some WordArt objects sneak them in along with the object's sizing handles. By grabbing and dragging an adjustment handle, you can change the angle at which some WordArt objects slant or loop. Adjustment handles are not used to resize a WordArt object—you still need to click and drag one of the sizing handles to do that.

7 Click and drag the WordArt object's yellow adjustment handle (◇) down a quarter inch.

Compare your slide to the one in Figure 5-19, then…

8 Save your work.

One more important note: WordArt is actually an external program, so you can use it with any of your Microsoft Office programs—perhaps to add a dramatic title to an Excel chart, or even a snazzy headline to a Microsoft Word document.

QUICK REFERENCE

TO INSERT A WORDART OBJECT:

1. SELECT INSERT → PICTURE → WORDART FROM THE MENU.
2. SELECT A TEXT STYLE.
3. TYPE THE TEXT FOR THE WORDART OBJECT, CHANGE THE FONT TYPE AND SIZE IF NECESSARY, AND CLICK OK.

TO MOVE A WORDART OBJECT:

- CLICK THE WORDART OBJECT TO SELECT IT, AND DRAG THE OBJECT TO A NEW LOCATION.

TO RESIZE A WORDART OBJECT:

- CLICK THE WORDART OBJECT TO SELECT IT AND DRAG THE WORDART OBJECT'S SIZING HANDLES UNTIL THE WORDART OBJECT IS THE SIZE YOU WANT.

Formatting a WordArt Object

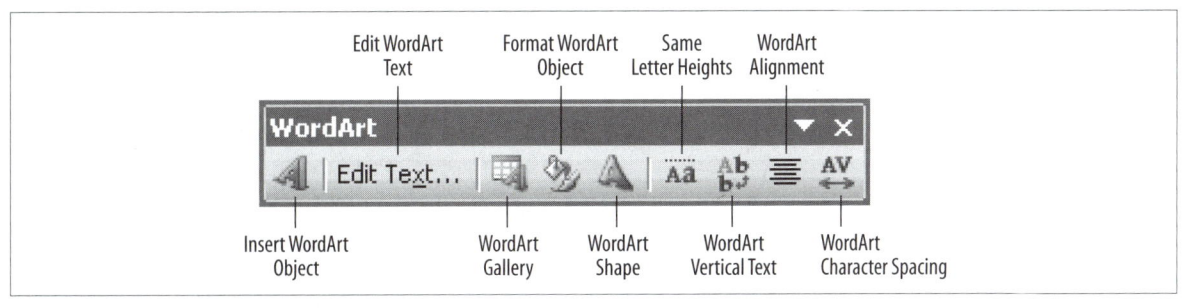

LESSON 5.8

Figure 5-20. The WordArt toolbar.

Labels: Insert WordArt Object, Edit WordArt Text, Format WordArt Object, Same Letter Heights, WordArt Alignment, WordArt Gallery, WordArt Shape, WordArt Vertical Text, WordArt Character Spacing

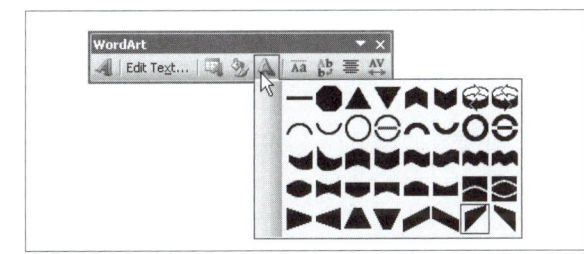

Figure 5-21. Change the shape of a WordArt object by clicking the Shape button and selecting the desired shape.

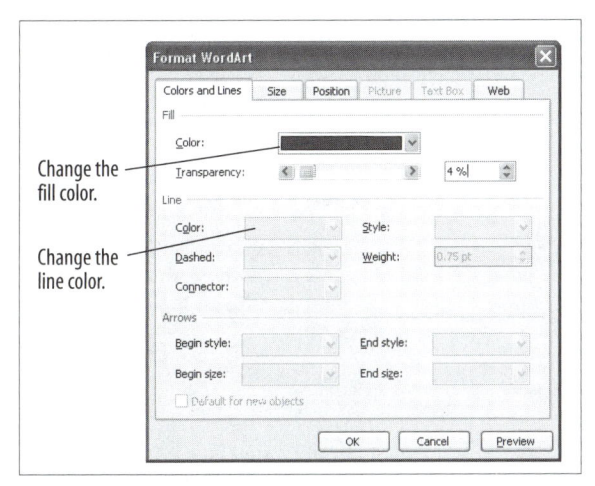

Figure 5-22. The Format WordArt dialog box.

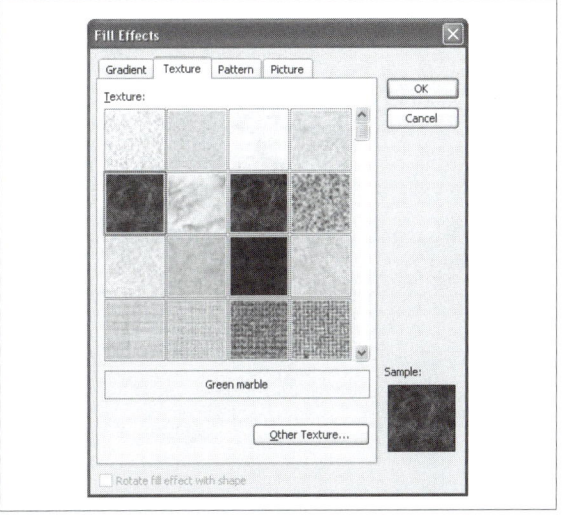

Labels: Change the fill color. Change the line color.

Figure 5-23. The Texture tab of the Fill Effects dialog box.

Figure 5-24. The updated WordArt object.

187

Lesson 5.8
Formatting a WordArt Object

Once you have created a WordArt object, you can change its appearance in many ways. You can change the style or shape of the WordArt object, how much space appears between its letters, or even rotate the WordArt object. What's more, you can format a WordArt object just like any other object, changing its fill and line color, size and shape, and even add a shadow or 3-D effect. In this lesson, you will experiment with several different WordArt formatting options.

1 Click the WordArt object if it's not already selected.

The WordArt toolbar appears, as shown in Figrure 5-20. You can use the WordArt toolbar to modify the selected WordArt object.

2 Click the WordArt Gallery button on the WordArt toolbar.

WordArt Gallery button

The WordArt Gallery dialog box appears where you can select a different style for the selected WordArt object.

3 Select the second option in the third row, the WordArt option, and click OK.

WordArt Character Spacing button

The WordArt object is formatted with the selected style. You can also easily change the shape of the WordArt object.

4 Click the WordArt Shape button on the WordArt toolbar. Then select the Slant Up option, as shown in Figure 5-21.

WordArt Shape button

The WordArt text appears in the selected style.

5 Click the WordArt Character Spacing button on the WordArt toolbar, then select Tight.

The letters in the WordArt object appear closer together. You can also go back and edit the WordArt object's text, even after you've formatted it.

6 Click the Edit Text button on the WordArt toolbar.

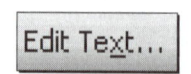

Edit Text button

The Edit WordArt Text dialog box appears. Now you can change the text, font style, or font size.

7 Add a colon (:) to the end of the text and then click OK.

The Edit WordArt Text dialog box closes and the text of the WordArt object is changed. Next let's change the WordArt object's fill color.

8 Click the Format WordArt button on the WordArt toolbar and ensure that the Colors and Lines tab is selected.

Format WordArt button

The Format WordArt dialog box appears, as shown in Figure 5-22. If you have formatted other PowerPoint shapes before, you'll already be familiar with the Format WordArt dialog box.

9 Click the Line Color list and select No Line.

This will remove the line that appears around the WordArt object. We'll finish this lesson by changing the WordArt object's fill color. You can fill WordArt objects with solid colors or you can use the Fill Effect command to create more dramatic effects and fill the WordArt object with a gradient, texture, pattern, or picture.

10 Click the Fill Color list, select Fill Effects and click the Texture tab.

The Texture tab of the Fill Effect dialog box appears, as shown in Figure 5-23.

188

Chapter 5
Working with Tables and WordArt

11 Click the Green marble texture, click OK, and click OK again.

The Format WordArt dialog box closes and the WordArt object is colored with the green marble fill effect.

12 Compare your slide to the one in Figure 5-24, then save your work and exit the PowerPoint program.

QUICK REFERENCE

TO CHANGE THE STYLE OF A WORDART OBJECT:

1. CLICK THE WORDART OBJECT TO SELECT IT AND CLICK THE WORDART GALLERY BUTTON ON THE WORDART TOOLBAR.
2. SELECT A STYLE FROM THE WORDART GALLERY.

TO CHANGE THE SHAPE OF A WORDART OBJECT:

- SELECT THE WORDART OBJECT, CLICK THE WORDART SHAPE BUTTON ON THE WORDART TOOLBAR, AND SELECT A SHAPE.

TO CHANGE THE TEXT SPACING OF A WORDART OBJECT:

- SELECT THE WORDART OBJECT, CLICK THE WORDART CHARACTER SPACING BUTTON ON THE WORDART TOOLBAR, AND SELECT A SPACING OPTION.

TO EDIT A WORDART OBJECT'S TEXT:

- SELECT THE WORDART OBJECT, CLICK THE EDIT TEXT BUTTON ON THE WORDART TOOLBAR, AND EDIT THE TEXT.

Chapter Five Review

Lesson Summary

Creating a Table

To Insert a Table Slide: Click the [New Slide] New Slide button on the Formatting toolbar, select the Title and Table layout, and click OK.

To Insert a Table on an Existing Slide: Select Insert → Table from the menu, specify the number of rows and columns you want, and click OK. Or, click the Insert Table button on the Standard toolbar and drag the grid to select how many columns and rows you want.

To Move from Cell to Cell in a Table: Press Tab to move forward one field or cell, and press Shift + Tab to move back one field or cell.

To Delete the Contents of a Cell: Select the cell(s), and then press the Delete key.

Working with a Table

To Select a Row: Place the insertion point anywhere in the row you want to select, click the [Table ▾] Table button on the Tables and Borders toolbar, and select Select Row from the list.

To Select a Column: Place the insertion point anywhere in the column you want to select, click the [Table ▾] Table button on the Tables and Borders toolbar and select Select Column from the list.

To Select Several Cells: Drag across the cell, row, or column; or select a single cell, row, or column, and then hold down Shift while you click another cell, row, or column.

To Select the Entire Table: Click the [Table ▾] Table button on the Tables and Borders toolbar and select Select Table from the list.

Adjusting Column Width and Row Height

To Adjust the Width of a Column: Click and drag the column's right border to the left or right.

To Adjust the Height of a Row: Rows automatically expand to display their contents. If you want to manually resize the height of a row, however, drag the row's bottom border up or down.

Inserting and Deleting Rows and Columns

To Delete a Column or Row: Place the insertion point anywhere in the column or row you want to delete, click the [Table ▾] Table button on the Tables and Borders toolbar, and select either Delete Columns or Delete Rows from the menu.

To Insert a Column or Row: Place the insertion point anywhere in the column or row above, below, to the left, or to the right of where you want the new column or row to be inserted, click the [Table ▾] Table button on the Tables and Borders toolbar and select one of the following:

- Insert Row Above
- Insert Row Below
- Insert Column to the Right
- Insert Column to the Left.

Adding Borders to a Table

To Add a Border to a Table (Using the Tables and Borders Toolbar): Select the cell(s) where you want to apply the border(s), click the Border list arrow on the Tables and Borders toolbar and select the border option you want.

To Add a Border to a Table (Using the Format Table Dialog Box): Select the cell(s) where you want to apply the border(s), then click the [Table ▾] Table button on the Tables and Borders toolbar, select Borders and Fill from the menu, select your border options and click OK.

Adding Shading and Fills

To Add Shading to a Table (Using the Tables and Borders Toolbar): Select the cell(s) where you want to apply the shading, click the Fill list arrow on the Tables and Borders toolbar, and select the Fill Effects option.

To Add Shading to a Table (Using the Format Table Dialog Box): Select the cell(s) where you want to apply the shading. Click the [Table ▾] Table button on the Tables and Borders toolbar, select Borders and Fills from the menu, click the Fill tab, select your fill options, and click OK.

Chapter 5
Working with Tables and WordArt

Inserting a WordArt Object

To Insert a WordArt Object: Select Insert → Picture → WordArt from the menu, select a text style, type the text for the WordArt object, change the font type and size if necessary, and click OK.

To Move a WordArt Object: Click the WordArt object to select it and then drag the object to a new location.

Formatting a WordArt Object

To Change the Style of a WordArt Object: Click the WordArt object to select it and click the WordArt Gallery button on the WordArt toolbar. Select a style from the WordArt Gallery.

To Change the Shape of a WordArt Object: Select the WordArt Object, click the WordArt Shape button on the WordArt toolbar, and select a shape.

To Change the Text Spacing of a WordArt Object: Select the WordArt Object, click the WordArt Character Spacing button on the WordArt toolbar, and select a spacing option.

To Edit a WordArt Object's Text: Select the WordArt Object, click the Edit Text button on the WordArt toolbar, and edit the text.

Quiz

1. Which keys are best to use when entering information and navigating in a table?

    A. Tab to move to the next cell, Shift + Tab to move to the previous cell.

    B. Enter to move to the next cell, Shift + Enter to move to the previous cell.

    C. → to move to the next cell, Shift + ← to move to the previous cell.

    D. All of the above.

2. Which of the following statements is NOT true?

    A. You can create a slide with a table by clicking the Insert Slide button on the Standard toolbar and selecting the Table layout.

    B. The Tables and Borders toolbar is what you use to work with tables.

    C. A table's fonts are static and cannot be formatted.

    D. PowerPoint 2003 no longer requires Microsoft Word to create and work with tables.

3. Which of the following statements is NOT true?

    A. Double-click a table object to edit it.

    B. To select a row: Place the insertion point in the row, click the Table button on the Tables and Borders toolbar, and select Select Row from the menu.

    C. To select a column: Place the insertion point in the column, click the Table button on the Tables and Borders toolbar, and select Select Column from the menu.

    D. Triple-click a table to select the entire table.

4. You can adjust the width of a column by dragging the column's right border with the mouse. (True or False?)

5. Which of the following is the correct procedure for deleting a column (not just clearing its contents)?

    A. Select the column and press the Delete key.

    B. Select the column and click the Delete Column button on the Formatting toolbar.

    C. Place the insertion point anywhere in the column, click the Table button on the Tables and Borders toolbar, and select Delete Column from the menu.

    D. Select the column and select Table → Delete Column from the menu.

6. You can change the angle at which some WordArt objects slant or loop by dragging their ◇ adjustment handles. (True or False?)

Chapter 5
Chapter Five Review

7. Which of the following statements is NOT True?

    A. WordArt is an independent program and can be used by any Microsoft Office program, such as Word or Excel.

    B. WordArt has its own toolbar that features buttons to change the shape, angle, and color of a WordArt object.

    C. You can change the color or texture of a WordArt object by clicking the Format WordArt object on the WordArt toolbar, clicking the Colors and Lines tab, and selecting a color from the Fill Color list.

    D. You can animate WordArt objects so that they shimmer, spin, dance, or flash on the screen.

Homework

1. Start PowerPoint, select the Blank presentation option, and click OK.

2. Select the Title and Table slide layout from the New Slide task pane and click OK.

3. Double-click the table object.

4. Type 5 in the Number of columns box, type 5 in the number of rows box and click OK.

5. Change the font size used in the table to 20 point. Select the entire table by selecting Table → Select Table from the Tables and Borders toolbar and then 20 from the Font Size list on the Formatting toolbar.

6. Enter the following information into the table:

Quarter	Q1	Q2	Q3	Q4
Flights	15,000	15,000	15,000	15,000
Tours	25,000	25,000	25,000	25,000
Cruises	5,000	5,000	5,000	5,000
Scams	1,500	1,500	1,500	1,500

Remember to use the arrow keys, Tab, and Shift + Tab to move from cell to cell.

7. Change the width of the first column by clicking and dragging the column's right border to the left a half inch.

8. Add borders around every cell in the table. Select the entire table by double-clicking it. Then click the Outside Borders button arrow on the Tables and Borders toolbar and select the ▦ option.

9. Add a WordArt object for the slide title. Select Insert → Picture → WordArt from the menu, select the WordArt option, and click OK.

10. Type "Annual Income" and click OK. Click and drag the WordArt object's sizing handles and resize the WordArt object so that it is about half as long as the slide.

11. Click and drag the WordArt object so that it appears centered and on top of the slide title.

    NOTE *In order to create an empty title bar, you will have to click on it and enter a single space before placing the WordArt.*

Quiz Answers

1. A. Press Tab to move to the next cell, Shift + Tab to move to the previous cell.

2. C. You can format a table's text just like you would any other text.

3. D. Click the Table button on the Tables and Borders toolbar and select Select Table from the menu to select the entire table.

4. True.

5. C. Place the insertion point anywhere in the column, click the Table button on the Tables and Borders toolbar, and select Delete Column from the menu.

6. True.

7. D. The current version of WordArt does not have these features.

CHAPTER 6
WORKING WITH GRAPHS AND ORGANIZATION CHARTS

CHAPTER OBJECTIVES:

Creating a chart and modifying a chart
Selecting a chart type
Creating an organization chart
Modifying and formatting an organization chart

CHAPTER TASK: ADD A CHART AND AN ORGANIZATION CHART TO A SLIDE

Prerequisites

- **Know how to use menus, toolbars, dialog boxes, and shortcut keystrokes.**
- **Move the mouse pointer and navigate between the slides in a presentation.**

"A picture is worth a thousand words." Nowhere is this truer than in PowerPoint. In this chapter, you'll learn how to convey information with two different types of charts: organization charts and "plain vanilla" charts.

One of the best ways to present numbers is with a chart, and the Microsoft Graph program makes adding charts to your slides easy. This chapter explains just about everything you need to know about charts—how to create dynamic-looking charts, how to edit and format charts, and how to work with different types of charts.

If you have ever worked for a large organization, you probably know what an organization chart is. Organization charts show the hierarchy of an organization—who reports to whom, who's on top, who's on the bottom, and so on. Organization charts display employee relations, family genealogies, and other hierarchical relations. You could use PowerPoint's text box and line drawing tools to create an organization chart, but this process would take hours to complete. Instead, use the Microsoft Organization Chart program to add an organization or flow chart to your slide.

LESSON 6.1 Creating a Chart

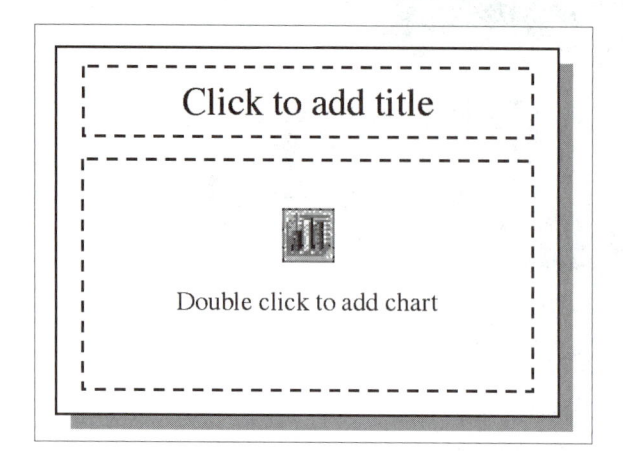

Figure 6-1. A blank chart slide.

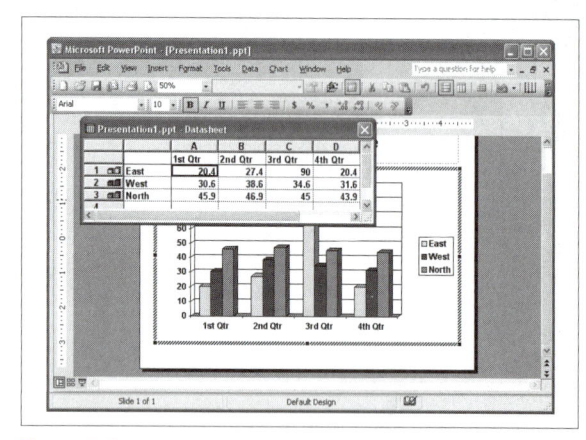

Figure 6-2. The Microsoft Graph program contains sample data for an example chart.

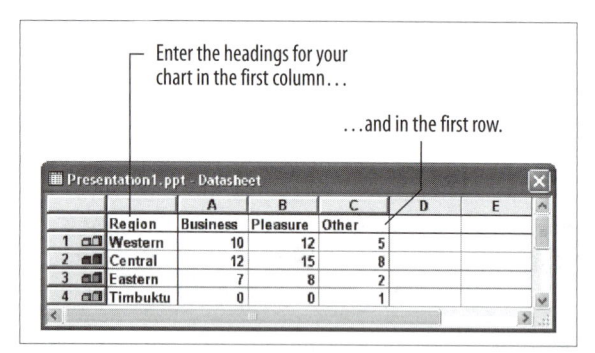

Figure 6-3. Enter what you want the chart to plot in the data sheet.

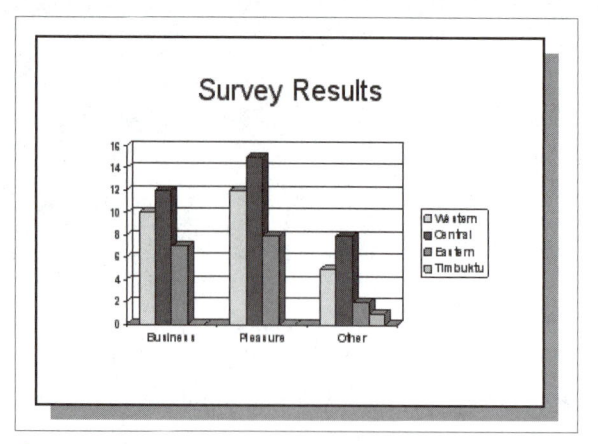

Figure 6-4. The completed chart.

You already know what a chart is—charts illustrate data, relationships, or trends. Like the idiom "a picture is worth a thousand words", charts are often much better at presenting information than hard to read numbers in a table. PowerPoint comes with a great built-in program for creating charts called Microsoft Graph. This lesson introduces charts and explains how to create a chart slide.

1 Start Microsoft PowerPoint.

Microsoft PowerPoint starts with a blank presentation. Here's how to add a chart slide to a presentation…

2 Find and click the Title and Chart layout from the Slide Layout task pane.

Title and Chart layout

A blank chart appears, as shown in Figure 6-1.

3 Close the task pane.

Let's add the slide title before we create the actual chart.

194

Chapter 6
Working with Graphs and Organization Charts

4 Click the Title placeholder and type Survey Results.

Now let's create the chart.

5 Double-click the Chart placeholder to add the chart object.

Cells, Rows, and Columns

The Microsoft Graph program window appears and creates a sample chart from make-believe data. To create a chart, you have to replace the sample data in the data table with your own information. The datasheet is made up of columns and rows and works like a simple spreadsheet program. There are several ways that you can enter information and move between the cells in the datasheet:

- Use the mouse to click the cell that you want to select or edit with the ✣ pointer.
- Use the arrow keys to move the active cell.
- Press Enter to move down.
- Press the Tab key to move to the next cell or to the right, or press Shift + Tab to move to the previous cell or to the left.

6 Click the D button to select the entire D column. Then press Delete.

The data in the D column vanishes. Now let's enter data into the cells.

7 Click the first cell in the data table, type Region and press Enter.

Pressing Enter confirms the cell entry and moves down one cell. Finish entering the column labels.

8 Type Western, press Enter, type Central, press Enter, type Eastern, press Enter, type Timbuktu, and press Enter.

Notice that anything you type replaces the cell's previous contents.

9 Complete the data table by entering the following information:

Region	Business	Pleasure	Other
Western	10	12	5
Central	12	15	8
Eastern	7	8	2
Timbuktu	0	0	1

Remember to use the arrow keys, the Enter key, and the Tab/Shift+Tab keys to confirm your cell entries and move around the data table.

10 Click anywhere outside the Microsoft Graph window when you're finished entering the information in the data table.

The Microsoft Graph window closes and a chart based on the information you entered in the data table appears in the slide. Your inserted chart will rarely be the right size, so you'll have to do some resizing. Like any other object, you resize a chart by clicking it and then clicking and dragging one of its eight sizing handles until the chart reaches the desired size.

11 Save the presentation with the file name Chart.

Super! You've created your first chart. The next several lessons explain how to modify a chart and work with different types of charts.

Lesson 6.1
Creating a Chart

QUICK REFERENCE

TO INSERT A CHART SLIDE:

1. CLICK THE [New Slide] **NEW SLIDE BUTTON** ON THE FORMATTING TOOLBAR, THEN FIND AND CLICK THE **TITLE AND CHART LAYOUT** FROM THE TASK PANE.
2. DOUBLE-CLICK THE CHART PLACEHOLDER TO OPEN MICROSOFT GRAPH.
3. ENTER YOUR OWN DATA INTO THE DATASHEET.

TO MOVE AROUND IN THE DATASHEET:

- USE THE MOUSE TO CLICK THE CELL THAT YOU WANT TO SELECT OR EDIT WITH THE ✛ POINTER.
- USE THE ARROW KEYS TO MOVE THE ACTIVE CELL.
- PRESS **ENTER** TO MOVE DOWN.
- PRESS THE **TAB** KEY TO MOVE TO THE NEXT CELL OR TO THE RIGHT; PRESS **SHIFT** + **TAB** TO MOVE TO THE PREVIOUS CELL OR TO THE LEFT.

Modifying a Chart

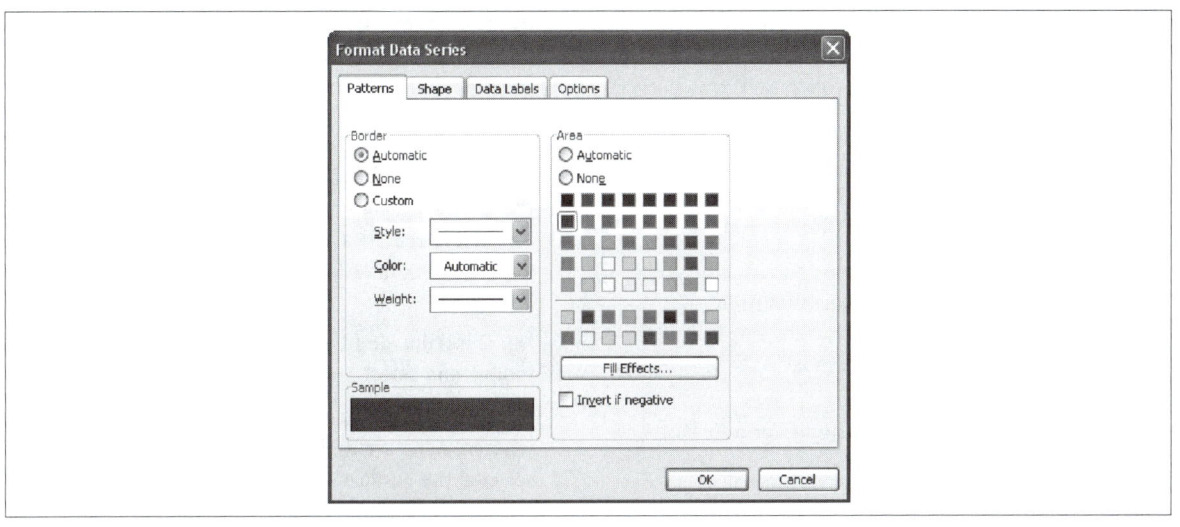

LESSON 6.2

Figure 6-5. The Patterns tab of the Format Data Series dialog box.

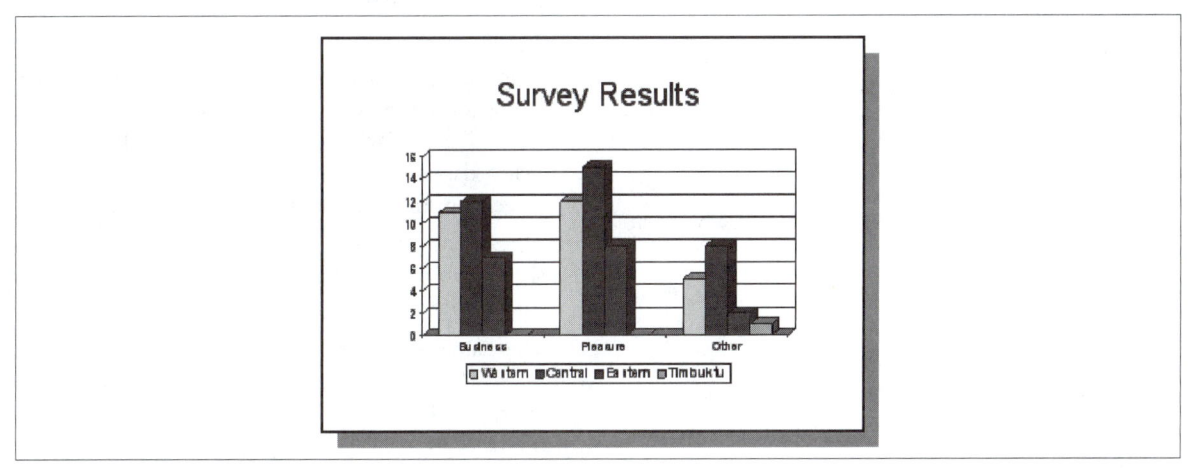

Figure 6-6. The modified chart.

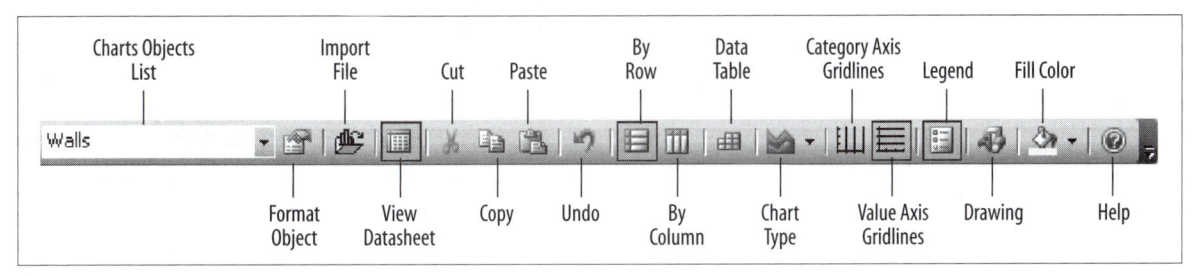

Figure 6-7. Part of the Graph toolbar.

197

Lesson 6.2
Modifying a Chart

Here's an important fact: you can select, format, and edit every object in a chart. For example, you can change the style, size, and color of any of the fonts used in a chart or the background color of the chart. After you've completed this lesson, you'll be a pro at formatting anything and everything in a chart. Some items that can be formatted and edited in a chart include:

- Chart Title
- Any Data Series
- Chart's Gridlines
- Chart Legend
- Chart Background Area
- Chart Plot Area
- Data Tables
- Category Axis

TIP *Double-click a chart to modify or edit it.*

There are two methods you can use to select a chart object:

- **Click the object you want to select.** This is the fastest, most straightforward method to select an object.
- **Select the object from the Chart Object list on the Chart toolbar.** This method is useful when you're not sure what to click on the chart (for example, what would you click to select the chart's plot area?).

1 If the datasheet window is not already open, double-click the chart.

The first thing we want to do is change one of the numbers in the chart.

2 Click the cell that contains the value 10 (where the Business column and Western row intersect), type 11, and press Enter.

The chart is updated and plots the new value. Next let's try formatting the chart. Before you can format the chart, you need to select it.

Format Object button

Other Ways to Format an Object:
- Double-click the object.
- Right-click the object and select **F**ormat Object from the shortcut menu.
- Click the object to select it and select **F**ormat **S**elected Object from the menu

3 Click the chart to select it.

NOTE *Make sure you select the chart itself and not simply the text box containing the chart.*

Sizing handles appear around the selected chart.

The first object you want to format on the chart is the Pleasure data series. Of course, you must first select the Pleasure Data series before you can format it. You can select the Pleasure Data series from the Chart Object list on the Chart toolbar.

4 Click the Chart Objects list arrow on the Chart toolbar and select Series "Eastern" from the list.

Selection boxes appear on the three columns of the Eastern data series in the chart. Now that you've selected the Eastern series, you can format it.

5 Click the Format Data Series button on the Chart toolbar and click the Patterns tab if necessary.

The Format Data Series dialog box appears, as shown in Figure 6-5. You are presented with a variety of different formatting options that you can apply to the selected series. We'll take a closer look at how to format a data series in an upcoming lesson—for now, just change the color of the data series.

6 Click a dark red color from the color palette in the Area section and click OK.

The dialog box closes and the color of the Eastern data series changes to dark red. Next, try formatting the chart's legend so you can place it in a better location on the chart.

7 Double-click the chart's legend to format it and select the Placement tab.

The Format Legend dialog box appears.

8 Select the Bottom option and click OK.

The dialog box closes and the legend appears at the bottom of the chart.

The last thing to format in this lesson is the chart's title.

9 Double-click the Category Axis (the horizontal line at the bottom of the chart where the labels "Business," "Pleasure," and "Other" appear) to format it, and click the Font tab.

Chapter 6
Working with Graphs and Organization Charts

The Format Axis dialog box appears. Change the font of the chart's category axis labels as follows:

10 Select **Arial** from the Font list, select **16** from the Size list, and click **OK**.

The dialog box closes and the category axis is formatted with the font options you selected.

11 Compare your chart to the one in Figure 6-6 and save your work.

There are so many different types of chart objects, each with its own individual formatting options, that it would take days to go through all of them. Instead, this lesson has given you a general guideline to follow to select and format any type of chart object you encounter.

QUICK REFERENCE

TO SELECT A CHART OBJECT:

- CLICK THE [Walls] **CHART OBJECTS LIST ARROW** ON THE CHART TOOLBAR AND SELECT THE OBJECT.

OR...

- CLICK THE OBJECT.

TO FORMAT A CHART OBJECT:

1. DOUBLE-CLICK THE OBJECT.

   OR...

   SELECT THE OBJECT AND CLICK THE **FORMAT OBJECT BUTTON** ON THE CHART TOOLBAR.

   OR...

   RIGHT-CLICK THE OBJECT AND SELECT **FORMAT OBJECT** FROM THE SHORTCUT MENU.

   OR...

   SELECT THE OBJECT AND SELECT **FORMAT → FORMAT OBJECT** FROM THE MENU.

2. CLICK THE TAB THAT CONTAINS THE ITEMS YOU WANT TO FORMAT, AND SPECIFY YOUR FORMATTING OPTIONS.

199

LESSON 6.3　Selecting a Chart Type

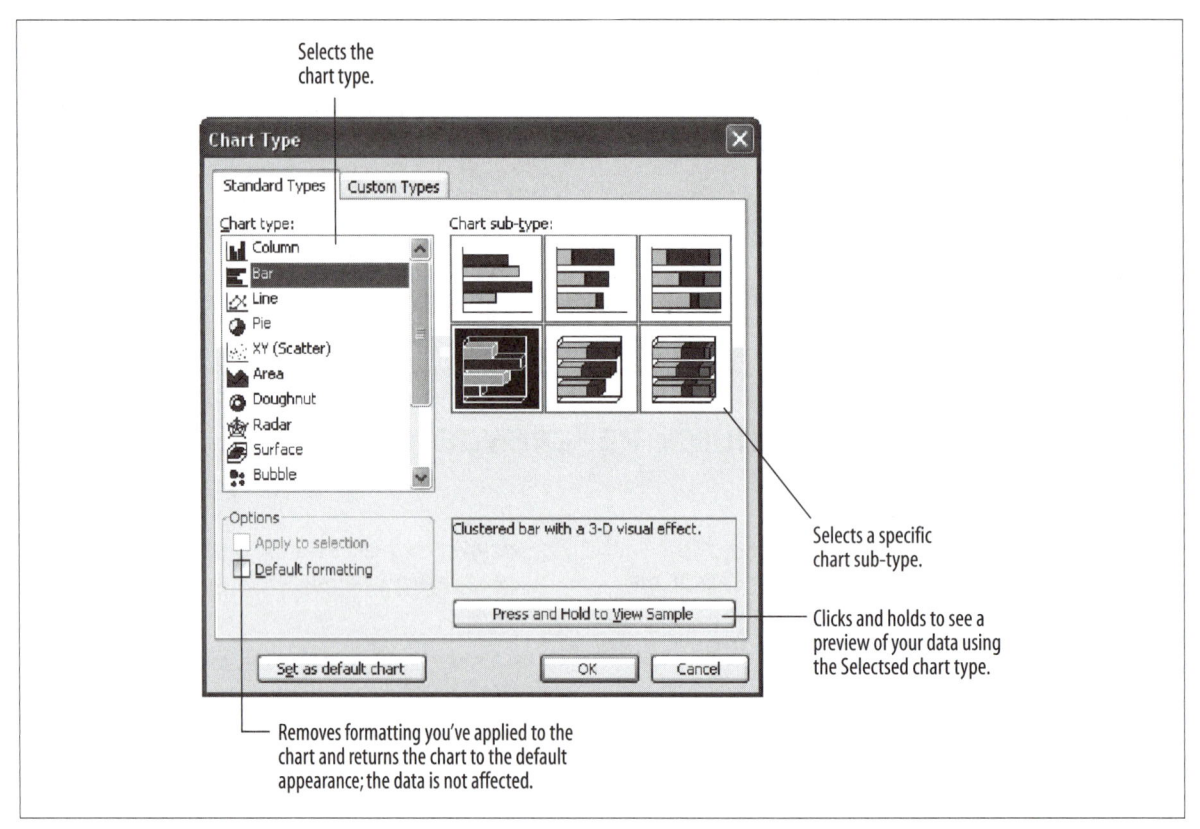

Figure 6-8. The Chart Type dialog box.

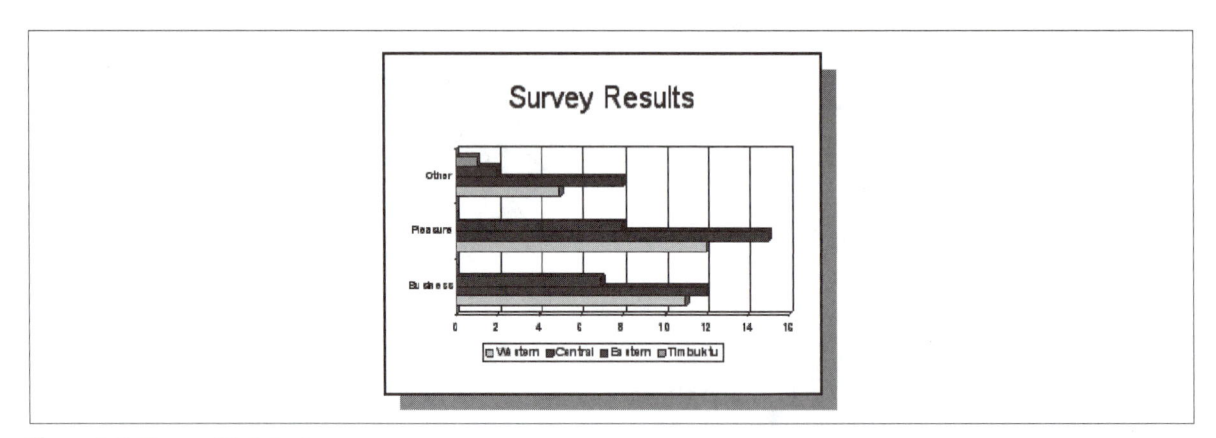

Annotations on figure:
- Selects the chart type.
- Selects a specific chart sub-type.
- Clicks and holds to see a preview of your data using the Selectsed chart type.
- Removes formatting you've applied to the chart and returns the chart to the default appearance; the data is not affected.

Figure 6-9. The modified chart.

Just as some lures are better than others for catching certain types of fish, there are different types of charts that are better than others for presenting different types of information. So far, you have been working on a column chart, which is great for comparing values for different items, but not so great for illustrating trends or relationships. In this lesson, you will learn how and when to use different types of charts available in Microsoft Graph.

Chart Type list

200

Chapter 6
Working with Graphs and Organization Charts

1 If necessary, find and open Lesson 6A and save it as Chart.

2 If the datasheet window is not already open, double-click the chart.

3 Select Chart → Chart Type from the menu.

Selecting a Chart Type

The Chart Type dialog box appears. Here, you can specify the type of chart or graph you want to use to display your data. Note that some charts are better than others at displaying certain types of information (see Table 6-1). Let's change our chart from a column chart to a 3-D bar chart.

4 In the Chart type list, click Bar. In the Chart sub-type section, click the Clustered bar with a 3-D effect option, as shown in Figure 6-8, and click OK.

The Chart Type dialog box closes and the column chart is changed to a bar chart, which doesn't display the data as well. You can quickly change chart types by clicking the Chart Type button on the Graph toolbar.

5 If you haven't already done so, save this presentation as Chart, and then close the Lesson.

Because Microsoft Graph offers so many different types of charts and graphs, you should have a general idea which charts are best suited for your needs. Table 6-1 shows some of the more commonly used charts and graphs and gives an explanation on how and when they are used.

Table 6-1. Types of Charts and Graphs

Chart or Graph Type	Description
Column	Column charts are used when you want to compare different values vertically side-by-side. Each value is represented in the chart by a vertical bar. If there are several values in an item, each value is represented by a different color.
Bar	Bar charts are just like column charts, except they display information in horizontal bars rather than in vertical columns.
Line	Line charts are used to illustrate trends. Each value is plotted as a point on the chart and is connected to other values by a line. Multiple items are plotted using different lines.
Pie	Pie charts are useful for showing values as a percentage of a whole. The values for each item are represented by different colors.
XY (Scatter)	Scatter charts are used to plot clusters of values using single points. Multiple items can be plotted by using different colored points or different point symbols.

Lesson 6.3
Selecting a Chart Type

Table 6-1. Types of Charts and Graphs (Continued)

Chart or Graph Type	Description
Area	Area charts are the same as line charts, except the area beneath the lines is filled with color.

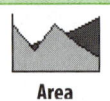

QUICK REFERENCE

TO CHANGE THE CHART TYPE:
- SELECT CHART → CHART TYPE FROM THE MENU.

OR...
- CLICK THE CHART TYPE LIST ARROW ON THE GRAPH TOOLBAR.

Creating an Organization Chart

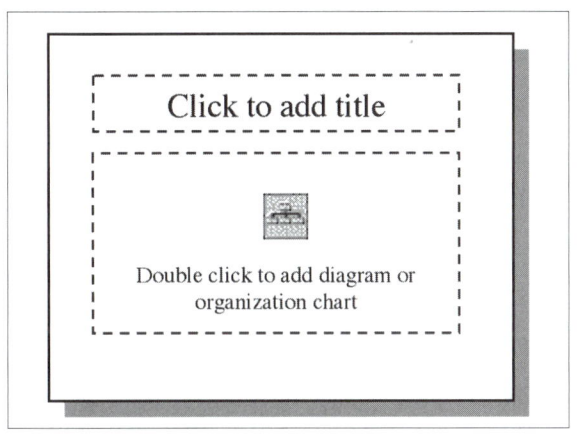

LESSON 6.4

Figure 6-10. A blank organization chart slide.

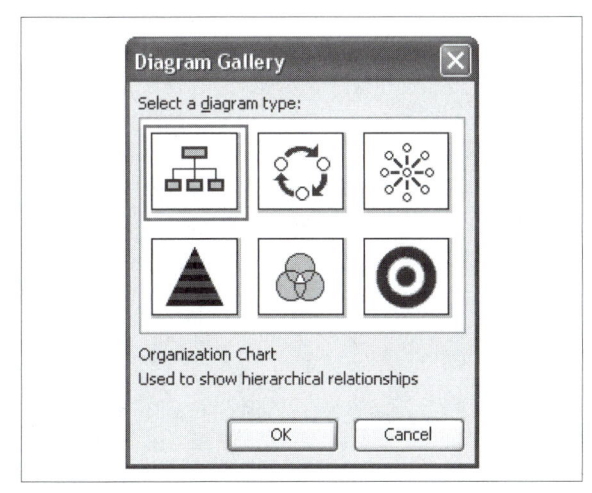

Figure 6-11. The Diagram Gallery dialog box.

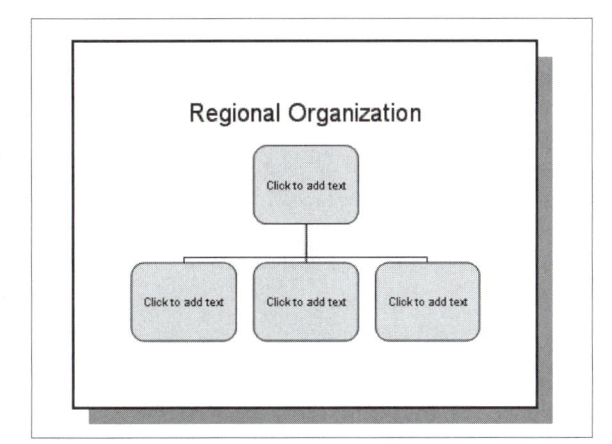

Figure 6-12. The Microsoft Organization Chart program window.

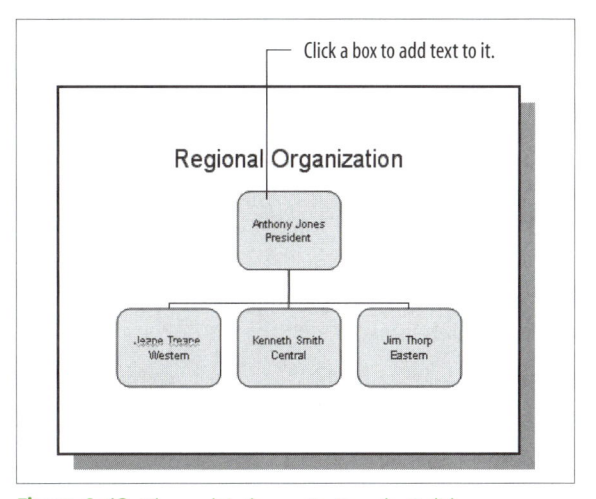

Figure 6-13. The updated organization chart slide.

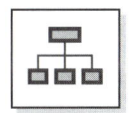

Title and Diagram or Organization Chart Layout

The easiest way to begin an organization chart is to select an organization chart slide from the Slide Layout pane when you first start, or to insert a new slide.

1 Click the **New Slide button** on the Formatting toolbar, and select the **Title and Diagram or Organization Chart** layout from the Slide Layout task pane.

A blank Diagram or Organization Chart slide appears, as shown in Figure 6-10.

2 Click the **Title placeholder** and type Regional Organization.

We're ready to add the actual organization chart.

3 Double-click the **Organization Chart placeholder**.

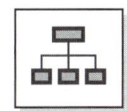

Organization Chart Type

203

Lesson 6.4
Creating an Organization Chart

The Diagram Gallery dialog box appears. There are six different types of diagrams you can choose from—see Table 6-2 for more information about each of these diagrams. We want to add an Organization chart.

4 Make sure the Organization Chart type is selected and click OK.

The Microsoft Organization Chart window appears, as shown in Figure 6-12. Microsoft Organization Chart is actually an external program with its own toolbar, and you can use it in any Microsoft Office program.

As you can see, you have been provided with a sample organization chart to help you get started. The top box, called a manager box, represents the highest level of the organization chart, and the three lower boxes represent the subordinates. The top box is already selected, ready for you to enter your information.

5 Click the top box, type Anthony Jones, press Enter, and type President.

The text box resizes itself to fit the text you just typed. That's all there is to entering text into an organization chart. Let's start on the next box.

6 Click the left subordinate box, type Jeane Treane, press Enter, and type Western.

This organization chart stuff isn't really that difficult, is it? Just two more steps and we'll be finished entering text into our basic organization chart.

7 Click the middle subordinate box, type Kenneth Smith, press Enter, and type Central, then click and type Jim Thorp in the right subordinate box, press Enter, and type Eastern.

If North Shore Travel was only a small, four-person show, we'd be finished with our organization chart. We'll add some more boxes to the organization chart in the next lesson.

8 Compare your slide with the one in Figure 6-13, and then save your presentation as Org Chart.

Let's move on to modifying organization charts, which is the main topic of the next lesson.

Table 6-2. Diagram Types

Diagram Type	Name	Description
	Organization Chart	Used to show hierarchical relations
	Cycle Diagram	Used to show a continuous cycle or process
	Radial Diagram	Used to show relationships of a core element
	Pyramid Diagram	Used to show foundation-based relationships
	Venn Diagram	Used to show areas of overlap between elements
	Target Diagram	Used to show steps towards a goal

Chapter 6
Working with Graphs and Organization Charts

QUICK REFERENCE

TO INSERT AN ORGANIZATION CHART SLIDE:

1. CLICK THE **NEW SLIDE BUTTON** ON THE FORMATTING TOOLBAR AND SELECT THE **TITLE AND DIAGRAM OR ORGANIZATION CHART LAYOUT** FROM THE TASK PANE.

2. DOUBLE-CLICK THE ORGANIZATION CHART PLACEHOLDER.

3. REPLACE THE INFORMATION IN THE SAMPLE ORGANIZATION CHART WITH YOUR OWN INFORMATION.

TO CHANGE THE TEXT IN A BOX:

- CLICK THE BOX AND REPLACE ITS TEXT. PRESS **ENTER** TO ADD A NEW LINE. CLICK OUTSIDE THE BOX WHEN YOU'RE FINISHED.

LESSON 6.5

Modifying Your Organization Chart

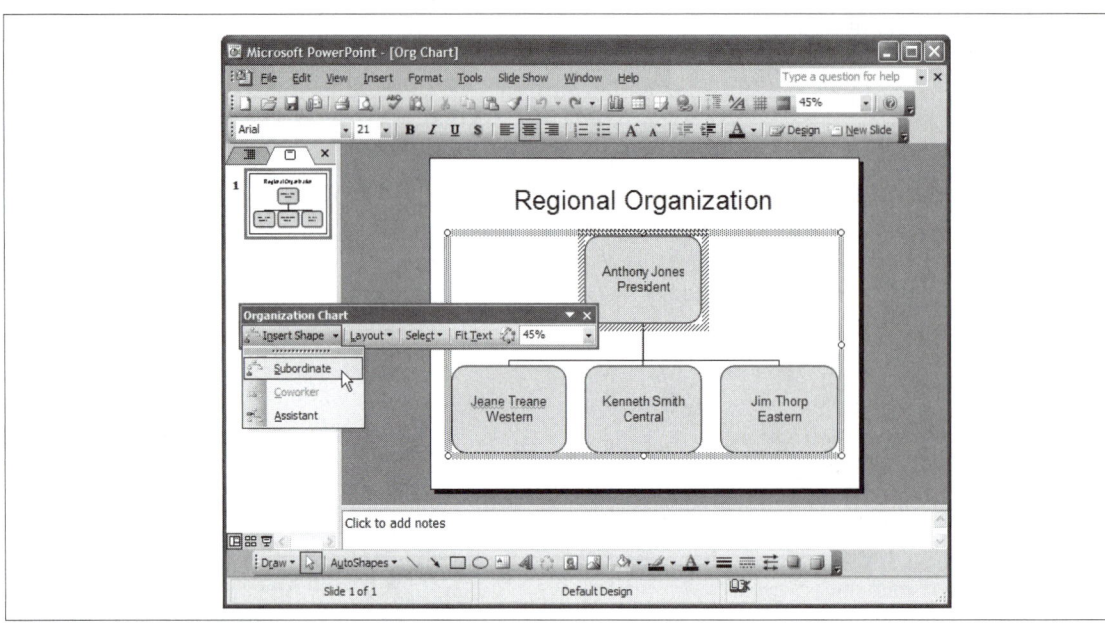

Figure 6-14. Insert a new box using the Organization Chart toolbar.

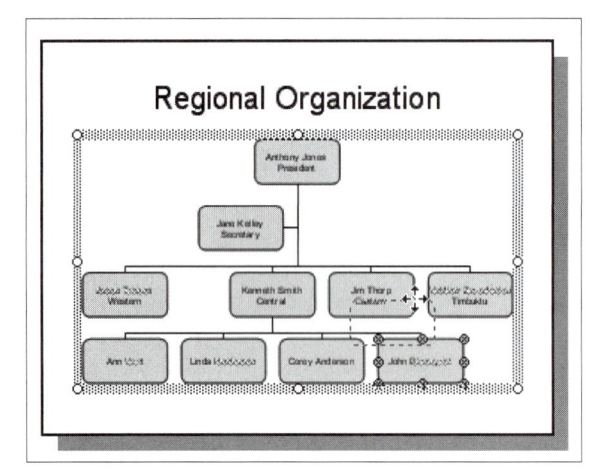

Figure 6-15. Move a box to a different position in an organization chart by dragging and dropping.

Organization charts are not limited to the four sample boxes that are provided when you begin a new organization chart. This lesson explains how to add new boxes to your organization chart and how to move boxes in an organization chart from one position to another.

1 Click the Anthony Jones box to select it.

Let's expand North Shore Travel's operation by adding another subordinate under Anthony Jones. Click the Insert Shape Button whenever you want to add another box to an organization chart. By default, the Insert Shape Button will insert a subordinate.

2 Click the ▾ Insert Shape button arrow on the Organization Chart toolbar.

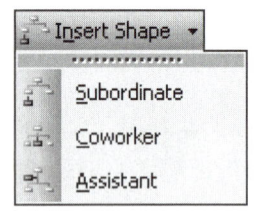

Insert Shape button

The Insert Shape list lets you select the type of shape you want to add.

3 Select Subordinate from the Insert Shape list, as shown in Figure 6-14.

A new subordinate box appears beneath the President's, along with the other three regions. Move on to the next step and add the text for this new subordinate box.

206

Chapter 6
Working with Graphs and Organization Charts

4 Click on the newly inserted subordinate box, type Vladimir Zavodoskoi, press Enter, and type Timbuktu.

Move on to the next step and we'll add several subordinates to the Central region.

5 Select the Kenneth Smith box, click the Insert Shape button on the Organization Chart toolbar, and type Ann Vant in the new box. Click anywhere outside the box when you're finished.

Ann Vant appears in a subordinate box under Kenneth Smith.

6 Repeat the procedure you learned in Step 5 and add three more subordinate boxes under Kenneth Smith: Linda Haefeman, Corey Anderson, and John Blumquist.

You can also add other types of boxes to your organization charts, such as a box that represents an assistant or secretary.

7 Click the President box. Now click the ▾ Insert Shape button arrow and select the Assistant option from the list.

A new assistant box appears beneath the President's box.

8 Click on the newly inserted Assistant box, type Jane Kelley, and press Enter, type Secretary, and click anywhere outside the box when you're finished.

You can rearrange an organization chart by dragging and dropping, for example, if a person moves to another position.

9 Click on the edge of the John Blumquist box and drag it over the Jim Thorp box, as shown in Figure 6-15. Release the mouse button when the box outline is directly above the Jim Thorp box.

The John Blumquist box appears under the Jim Thorp box.

Table 6-3. Organization Chart Levels

Shape	Description
Subordinate	Creates a box that reports to a manager box. The box will be placed at the level below the selected box.
Coworker	Creates a box on the same level of the selected box for co-workers in the same group.
Assistant	Creates a subordinate box that provides assistance or advice to its manager.

Lesson 6.5
Modifying Your Organization Chart

QUICK REFERENCE

TO ADD A BOX TO AN ORGANIZATION CHART:

1. ON THE ORGANIZATION CHART, CLICK THE BOX THAT CORRESPONDS TO WHERE YOU WANT TO ADD THE NEW BOX.
2. CLICK THE **INSERT SHAPE BUTTON ARROW** AND SELECT THE TYPE OF SHAPE YOU WANT TO ADD.
3. ENTER THE TEXT TO THE NEWLY ADDED BOX AND CLICK OUTSIDE THE BOX WHEN YOU'RE FINISHED.

TO MOVE A BOX:

1. CLICK THE BOX YOU WANT TO MOVE.
2. DRAG THE BOX TO ITS NEW POSITION AND RELEASE THE MOUSE BUTTON.

TO DELETE A BOX:

- CLICK THE BOX TO SELECT IT AND PRESS THE **DELETE** KEY.

LESSON 6.6
Formatting Your Organization Chart

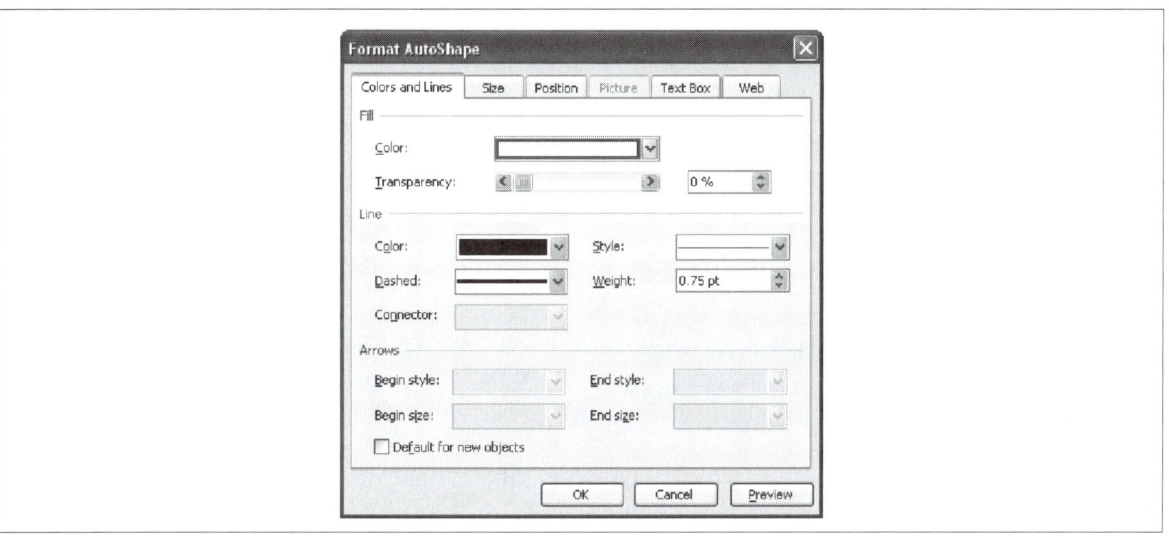

Figure 6-16. The Format AutoShape dialog box.

Insert Shape
Adds a shape below the selected shape in an organization chart.

Select
Use to select multiple objects in the organization chart.

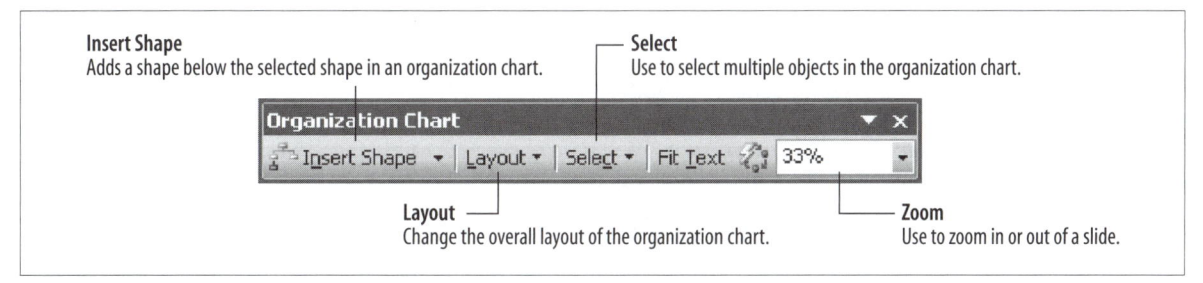

Layout
Change the overall layout of the organization chart.

Zoom
Use to zoom in or out of a slide.

Figure 6-17. The Organization Chart toolbar.

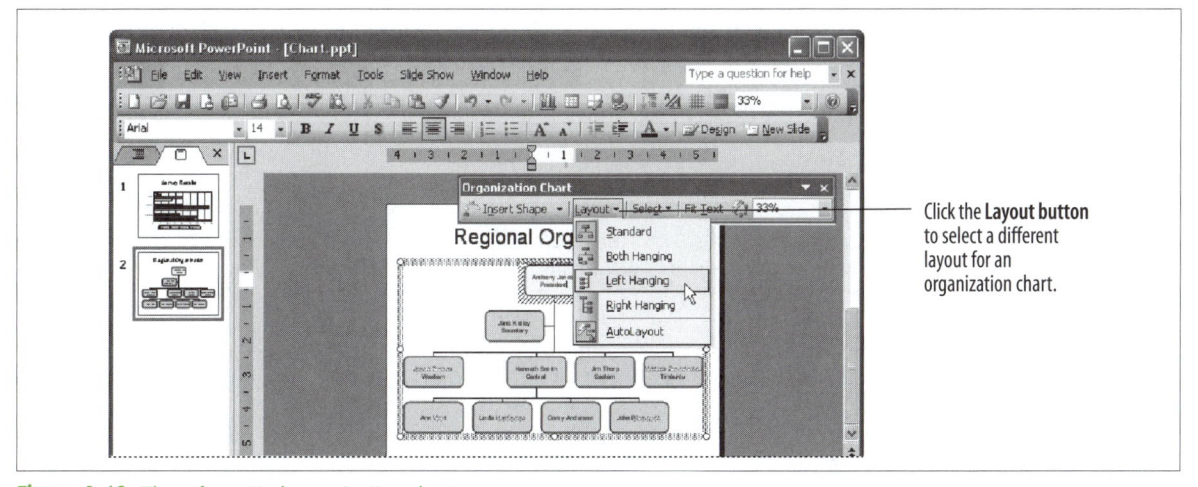

Click the **Layout button** to select a different layout for an organization chart.

Figure 6-18. The reformatted organization chart.

Lesson 6.6
Formatting Your Organization Chart

When first created, organization charts are rather plain and ordinary—and sometimes this is for the best, since organization charts should be easy to read and understand. Occasionally, however, you will want to spice up your organization charts by formatting them with cool colors, shapes, and font types. Just like any other object in PowerPoint, you can add shadow effects, format text, and change the color and line type in your organization chart. In this lesson you will learn how to do just that.

For reasons unbeknownst to everyone except the developers at Microsoft, PowerPoint 2003 has much *fewer* formatting options for organization charts than previous versions. So, if you're a pro when it comes to working with organization charts in PowerPoint 97 or 2000 and were thinking about skipping over this lesson, think again. You're going to need this lesson just as much as the novices do!

1 If necessary, find and open the Lesson 6B presentation and save it as Org Chart.

The bluish-gray color of the boxes in the organization chart is a little dull. Let's try changing the color of the president's box to something a little brighter.

2 Right-click the Anthony Jones box and select Format AutoShape from the shortcut menu.

The Format AutoShape dialog box appears.

If you have used PowerPoint's drawing tools before, you should already be familiar with this dialog box. The Format AutoShape dialog box contains options to change the various colors used in any object.

3 Click the Color list arrow and select a yellow color in the Fill section.

Move on to the next step to close the Format AutoShape dialog box.

4 Click OK.

The Format AutoShape dialog box closes and PowerPoint formats the president's box with the selected color.

You can also change the layout of an organization chart—for example, you can place all the subordinate shapes to the left or right of the superior shape instead of below it. Here's how to change the layout of an organization chart…

5 Click the Layout button arrow on the Organization Chart toolbar.

Layout button

A list of organization chart layouts appears. Table 6-4 describes each of the available layouts.

6 Select Left Hanging from the Layout list.

The organization chart is reformatted with the left hanging layout.

7 Close Microsoft PowerPoint without saving any of your changes.

Table 6-4. Layout Options

Layout	Description
Standard	Arranges the subordinate shapes horizontally below the superior (manager) shape that is selected.
Both Hanging	Places all subordinate shapes equally to the left and right of the selected superior shape connector.
Left Hanging	Places all subordinate shapes to the left of the selected superior shape connector.
Right Hanging	Places all subordinate shapes to the right of the selected superior shape connector.

Chapter 6
Working with Graphs and Organization Charts

QUICK REFERENCE

TO SELECT AN ORGANIZATION CHART'S BOXES:

- CLICK THE BOX YOU WANT TO SELECT.
- TO SELECT MORE THAN ONE BOX, HOLD DOWN THE **SHIFT** KEY AS YOU CLICK EACH BOX.
- CLICK THE **SELECT BUTTON** FROM THE ORGANIZATION CHART TOOLBAR TO SELECT ONLY CERTAIN POSITIONS IN AN ORGANIZATION CHART OR TO SELECT THE ENTIRE ORGANIZATION CHART.

TO FORMAT THE BOXES IN AN ORGANIZATION CHART:

- RIGHT-CLICK THE BOX AND SELECT **FORMAT AUTOSHAPE** FROM THE SHORTCUT MENU.

TO CHANGE THE LAYOUT OF AN ORGANIZATION CHART:

- CLICK THE **LAYOUT BUTTON** FROM THE ORGANIZATION CHART TOOLBAR AND SELECT THE DESIRED LAYOUT.

Chapter Six Review

Lesson Summary

Creating a Chart

To Insert a Chart Slide: Click the New Slide button on the Formatting toolbar, then find and click the Title and Chart layout in the task pane. Double-click the chart placeholder to open Microsoft Graph and replace the sample information in the datasheet with your own information.

To Move Around in the Datasheet:

- Use the mouse to click the cell that you want to select or edit with the ✛ pointer.
- Use the arrow keys to move the active cell.
- Press Enter to move down.
- Press the Tab key to move to the next cell or to the right; press Shift + Tab to move to the previous cell or to the left.

Modifying a Chart

To Select a Chart Object: Click the Chart Objects list arrow on the Chart toolbar and select the object or simply click the object if you can find it.

To Format a Chart Object: Use any of these methods:

- Double-click the object.
- Select the object and click the Format Object button on the Chart toolbar.
- Right-click the object and select Format Object from the shortcut menu.
- Select the object and select Format → Format Object from the menu, then click the tab that contains the items you want to format, and specify the formatting options.

Selecting a Chart Type

To Change the Chart Type: Select Chart → Chart Type from the menu.

Creating an Organization Chart

To Insert an Organization Chart Slide: Click the New Slide button on the Formatting toolbar and click the Title and Diagram or Organization Chart layout in the task pane. Double-click the organization chart placeholder. Replace the information in the sample organization chart with your own information.

To Change the Text in a Box: Click the box and replace its text. Press Enter to add a new line. Click outside the box when you're finished.

Modifying Your Organization Chart

To Add a Box to an Organization Chart: On the organization chart, click the box that corresponds to where you want to add the new box. Click the Insert Shape → Insert Shape button arrow and select the type of shape you want to add. Enter the text to the newly added box and click outside the box when you're finished.

To Move a Box: Click the box you want to move, drag the box to its new location, and release the mouse button.

To Delete a Box: Click the box to select it and press the Delete key.

Formatting Your Organization Chart

To Select an Organization Chart Box: Click the box you want to select.

To Select Several Organization Chart Boxes: To select more than one box, hold down the Shift key as you click each box.

To Select Certain Positions in an Organization Chart: Click the Select → Select button from the Organization Chart toolbar to select only certain positions in an organization chart or to select the entire organization chart.

To Format the Boxes in an Organization Chart: Right-click the box and select Format AutoShape from the shortcut menu.

To Change the Layout of an Organization Chart: Click the Layout button from the Organization Chart toolbar and select the desired layout.

Chapter 6
Working with Graphs and Organization Charts

Quiz

1. You can edit or format a chart object using any of the following methods, except…

   A. Double-clicking the object.
   B. Right-clicking the object and selecting Format Object from the shortcut menu.
   C. Selecting the object and clicking the Format Object button on the Chart toolbar.
   D. Clicking the Chart Objects list arrow on the Chart toolbar and selecting the object.

2. The datasheet for a new chart contains sample information that you replace with new information that you want the chart to plot. (True or False?)

3. You want to track the progress of the stock market on a daily basis. Which type of chart should you use?

   A. Line chart
   B. Column chart
   C. Row chart
   D. Pie chart

4. What kind of information would you most likely place in an organization chart?

   A. A military unit's chain of command.
   B. The number of hamburgers a restaurant sold during the past month.
   C. The cash flow of five regional offices, broken down by month.
   D. The number of students that fail or pass their first driver's test.

5. Which of the following statements is NOT true? (Trick Question!)

   A. Organization charts are actually created in a separate program.
   B. In an organization chart, the Assistant box and the Subordinate box are two different names for the same type of organization chart box.
   C. An assistant box appears *directly* below the selected box.
   D. New organization charts have sample boxes with sample text that you can replace with your own information.

Homework

1. Start PowerPoint, select the Blank presentation option, and click OK.

2. Select the Title and Chart slide layout from the task pane.

3. Double-click the chart object.

4. Enter the following information into the datasheet table:

	Qtr 1	Qtr 2	Qtr 3	Qtr 4
Vancouver	42,000	28,000	38,000	35,000
Prince Edward Island	20,000	9,000	14,000	14,000
Nova Scotia	49,000	38,000	54,000	45,000
Montreal	65,000	45,000	63,000	5,000

5. Change the font of the chart legend to Arial 12 pt. Click the legend to select it, select Arial from the Font list on the Formatting toolbar, and 12 from the Font Size list on the Formatting toolbar.

6. Change the chart type to a 3-D Bar chart. Click the Chart Type list arrow and select the option.

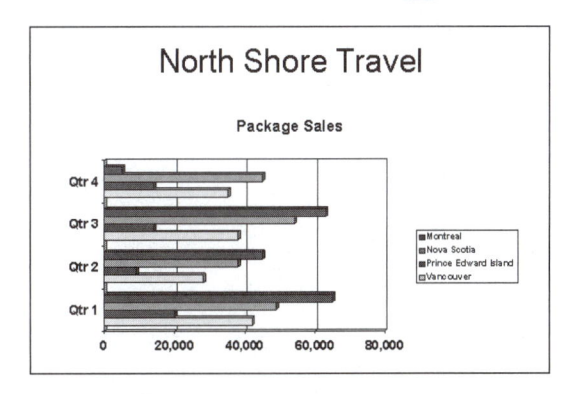

Chapter 6
Chapter Six Review

7. Give the chart the title "Package Sales". Select Chart → Chart Options from the menu, type "Package Sales" in the Chart title box, and click OK.

8. In the title bar, type North Shore Travel.

9. Change the color of the Montreal color series to dark red. Double-click any of the Montreal bars, select a dark red color, and click OK.

10. Click anywhere outside the chart.

11. Click the New Slide button on the Standard toolbar and select the Title and Diagram or Organization Chart slide layout.

12. Double-click the organization chart object, make sure "Organization Chart" is selected, and click OK.

13. Create the following organization chart:

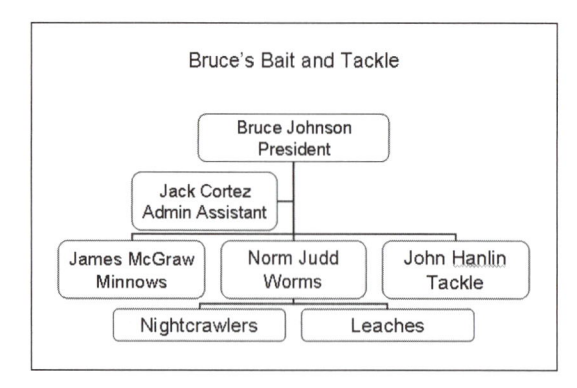

```
                Bruce's Bait and Tackle

                    Bruce Johnson
                       President
                           |
                    Jack Cortez
                    Admin Assistant
        _____|_____
        |                  |                   |
   James McGraw        Norm Judd          John Hanlin
     Minnows            Worms               Tackle
                   _____|_____
                   |               |
              Nightcrawlers      Leaches
```

Remember: Click inside the boxes and replace their sample text. To add a box, click the box that corresponds to where you want to add your new box, then select the type of box you want to add from the Insert Shape menu on the Organization Chart toolbar.

14. Select the entire organization chart by clicking on the boxes while pressing the Shift key. Right click on any of the boxes and select Format AutoShape from the shortcut menu. Select a white color from the Fill menu, and click OK.

15. Click the Organization Chart window's close button.

Quiz Answers

1. D. This is not a method for formatting a chart object (This question was really difficult—sorry!)

2. True.

3. A. Line charts are great at illustrating trends or illustrating changes that occur over time.

4. A.

5. C. Assistant boxes *do* appear beneath their supervisor's box, but they are offset to the left or right and therefore don't appear *directly* beneath the supervisor's box.

CHAPTER 7
DELIVERING YOUR PRESENTATION

CHAPTER OBJECTIVES:

Delivering a presentation on a computer
Using slide transitions
Animating text and objects
Rehearsing slide show timings
Creating a presentation that runs by itself
Creating a custom show
Using the package for CD feature to play a presentation on another computer

CHAPTER TASK: DELIVER A SLIDE SHOW USING TRANSITIONS AND ANIMATION

Prerequisites

- Know how to use menus, toolbars, dialog boxes, and shortcut keystrokes.
- Move the mouse pointer and navigate between the slides in a presentation.

It's show time! This chapter explains what PowerPoint is all about: giving an interesting presentation.

If you plan to run a slide show on your computer, you will learn how to add exciting transition effects to your slides, changing how PowerPoint advances from one slide to the next. You will also learn how to animate the text and objects on your slides. For example, you could make each paragraph in your slides appear successively, one at a time.

If you plan to run a slide show on another computer, you will also learn how to use the Package for CD feature to take your presentation on the road.

LESSON 7.1

Delivering a Presentation on a Computer

Figure 7-1. In Slide Show View, each slide fills the entire screen.

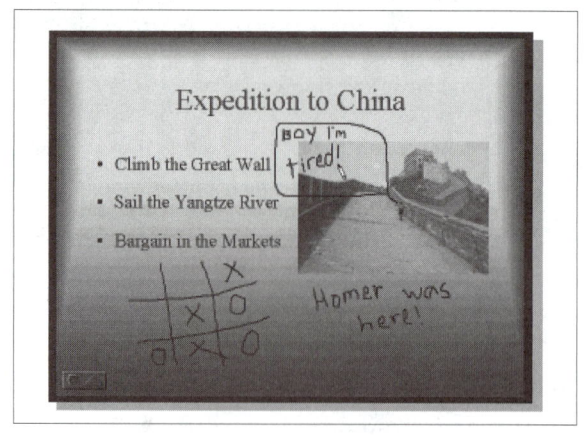

Figure 7-2. The pen tool.

You can deliver a PowerPoint presentation in several ways: by giving everyone paper handouts of your presentation, by creating overheads or 35mm slides and then displaying them with an overhead projector, or by running the presentation on a computer. Running a presentation on a computer is the preferred method because it gives you the most control over the presentation and allows you to use multimedia, animation, and other nifty effects. You can even use a mouse pen to doodle on your slides just like sports announcers do when they illustrate football plays.

Even if you've already figured out how to display a presentation as an onscreen slide show, you'll still want to review this lesson to learn some cool tricks and keyboard/mouse shortcuts that you probably didn't know before.

1 Start Microsoft PowerPoint, open the Lesson 7A presentation, and save it as 2003 Tours.

Once you've started PowerPoint and saved the "Lesson 7A" presentation file as "2003 Tours," move on to the next step to display the slide show on your computer.

2 Start the onscreen slide show by clicking the Slide Show button on the horizontal scroll bar.

Slide Show button

Other Ways to Switch to Slide Show View:
- Select **View → Slide Show** from the menu.
  Or...
- Press **<F5>**.

The first slide in the presentation fills the entire screen, as shown in Figure 7-1. In Slide Show View, you display your presentation as an electronic slide show. Advancing through the slides in your presentation is so easy that you probably don't even need any instructions.

3 Advance to the next slide using any of the methods listed in Table 7-1.

One neat feature in Slide Show View is an electronic pen that lets you doodle on your slides. Here's how to use the pen:

4 Press **Ctrl** + **P** to activate the pen tool.

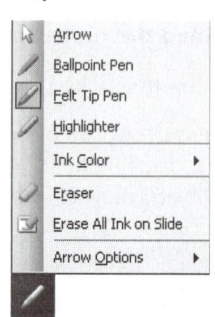

Click the **Pen Tool menu button** to display a list of pen tool options.

The mouse pointer changes to a ✏, which you can use to add notes, doodles, or diagrams to your slides. There is also a new Highlighter tool in PowerPoint 2003.

5 Use the ✏ tool to draw some doodles on the current slide.

If you want to erase your doodles, press E.

Chapter 7
Delivering Your Presentation

NOTE *Notes are not permanent and are deleted the moment you stop your slide show. If you want to add permanent notes to a slide, switch to Notes Page View and add the notes.*

6 Press the E key to erase your doodles.

Finished drawing? To change the pen back into the familiar arrow, simply press Ctrl + A or Esc.

7 Press Ctrl + A to switch the pen pointer back into an arrow.

If you move the mouse pointer during a slide show presentation, several small, unobtrusive boxes appear in the lower left corner of the screen. That's the Slide Show toolbar. Click the Slide Show menu button to display a list of commands.

8 Click the Slide Show menu button, located in the lower-left corner of the screen.

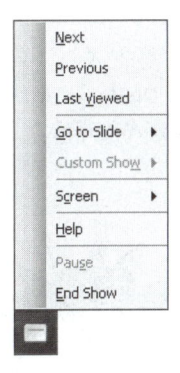

Click the **Slide Show menu button** to display a list of slide show commands.

A list of slide show commands appears. You can also right-click anywhere on a slide during an on-screen presentation to display the same menu.

9 Click on the slide to close the menu. Press Esc to close the slide show menu without selecting any commands.

That's all there really is to running a slide show on your computer. Let's go to the next step and finish the show.

10 Use any of the methods shown in Table 7-1 to advance through the slides, one at a time, until you're finished with the slide show.

That sure was easy, wasn't it? Should you want to quit a presentation prematurely, simply press the Esc key to exit Slide Show View and return to the previous view. The following table lists the most common shortcuts you can use during a slide show.

Table 7-1. Slide Show Keystrokes

To Do This...	...Do This
Advance to the next slide	Press Enter, press Spacebar, press →, press ↓, press Page Down, or click the left mouse button
Go back to the previous slide	Press ↑, ←, or Page Up
Go to slide number	Enter the slide number and press Enter
Toggle between the presentation and a black screen	Press B
Toggle between the presentation and a white screen	Press W
Show/hide pointer	Press A or =

217

Lesson 7.1
Delivering a Presentation on a Computer

Table 7-1. Slide Show Keystrokes (Continued)

To Do This…	…Do This
Change arrow to an annotation pen	Press Ctrl + P
Change annotation pen to an arrow	Press Ctrl + A or Esc
Erase on-screen annotations	Press E
End slide show	Press Esc

QUICK REFERENCE

TO DISPLAY A SLIDE SHOW:

- CLICK THE SLIDE SHOW BUTTON ON THE HORIZONTAL SCROLL BAR NEAR THE BOTTOM OF THE SCREEN.

OR…

- SELECT VIEW → SLIDE SHOW FROM THE MENU.

TO ADVANCE TO THE NEXT SLIDE:

- CLICK THE LEFT MOUSE BUTTON OR PRESS THE ENTER, SPACEBAR, →, ↓, OR PAGE DOWN KEYS.

TO STOP A SLIDE SHOW:

- PRESS ESC.

TO DOODLE ON THE CURRENT SLIDE WITH THE PEN:

- PRESS CTRL + P AND DRAW ON THE SCREEN WITH THE PEN TOOL. PRESS CTRL + A TO SWITCH BACK TO THE ARROW POINTER.

TO ERASE YOUR DOODLES:

- PRESS E.

TO DISPLAY A LIST OF SLIDE SHOW COMMANDS:

- RIGHT-CLICK ANYWHERE ON THE SLIDE OR CLICK THE SLIDE SHOW MENU BUTTON.

LESSON 7.2

Using Slide Transitions

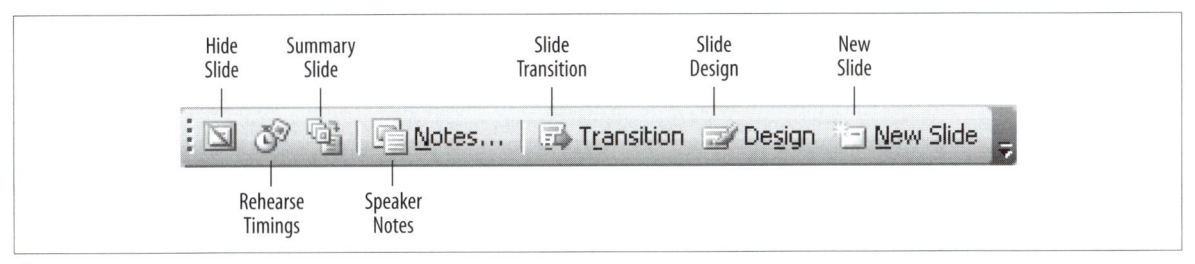

Figure 7-3. The Slide Sorter toolbar.

Figure 7-4. A transition is how PowerPoint gets from one slide to the next during an on-screen slide show.

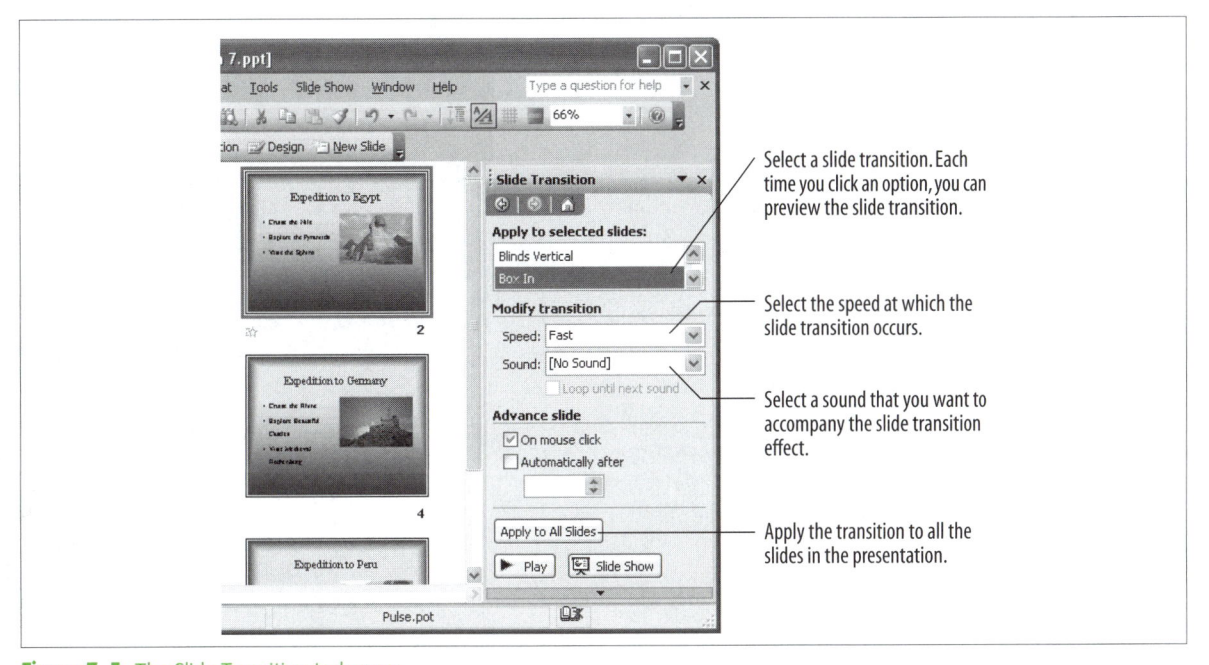

Figure 7-5. The Slide Transition task pane.

A transition is how PowerPoint advances from one slide to the next during an on-screen slide show. PowerPoint transitions from slide to slide by having the new slide instantly replace the old, just like an older 35mm slide projector. PowerPoint's slide transition feature lets you make transitions more interesting by providing you with more than 40 different special effects you can use to move between slides. For example, you can have one slide slowly dissolve and be replaced by the next slide.

Slide transitions can only be set up in Slide Sorter View, so let's start there.

Slide Sorter View button

1 Click the Slide Sorter View button in the Slides pane.

219

Lesson 7.2
Using Slide Transitions

Once you're in Slide Sorter View, you can add transition effects to your slides. First, select the slide(s) you want to transition to.

2 Click Slide 2 to select it.

Let's add a transition effect to the selected slide.

3 Click the Slide Transition button on the Slide Sorter toolbar.

Slide Transition button

Other Ways to Add Slide Transitions:

- Select Sli**d**e Show → Slide **T**ransition from the menu.

The Slide Transition task pane appears, as shown in Figure 7-5. The Slide Transition task pane gives you choices for your slide transition effects. For example, you can select the speed of the slide transition and add optional sound effects.

4 Select the Box In effect from the Slide Transition task pane.

A lightning-quick preview of the slide transition appears when you select it from the list, giving you an idea of what the transition looks like. Notice the small icon that appears at the bottom of Slide 2, indicating that the slide has a transition effect.

You can add transition effects to several slides at once by selecting each slide that you want to add the effect to. To select several slides, hold down the Ctrl or Shift key while you click each slide.

5 Hold down the Shift key as you click Slides 3 through 6.

Now we want to apply the same slide transition effect to the recently selected slides.

6 Select the Box In option from Slide Transition task pane.

You can also change the speed of the slide transition, although Fast is almost always the best choice (unless you're trying to kill time).

Next, let's select a sound to accompany the transition. PowerPoint has several common sounds to choose from.

7 Click the Sound list arrow and select Camera.

Voila! We're finished adding transition effects to the selected slide. Now let's see how our presentation looks when it's delivered on-screen.

NOTE *If the camera sound is not available on your computer, you may have to download it.*

8 Click on Slide 1 to select it and then click the Slide Show button on the horizontal scroll bar.

The first slide appears on your screen in Slide Show View.

9 Step through several of the slides in the presentation by clicking the mouse button. Press Esc to exit the on-screen presentation when you're finished.

Transition effects are cool, but try not to use too many different types of effects in the same presentation, or they may distract your viewers rather than intrigue them.

QUICK REFERENCE

TO ADD A SLIDE TRANSITION:

1. SWITCH TO SLIDE SORTER VIEW.

2. CLICK THE SLIDE WHERE YOU WANT TO ADD A TRANSITION. TO SELECT MULTIPLE SLIDES, HOLD DOWN THE SHIFT KEY AS YOU CLICK EACH SLIDE.

3. CLICK THE Transition SLIDE TRANSITION BUTTON ON THE SLIDE SORTER TOOLBAR.

4. SELECT A TRANSITION FROM THE TRANSITION LIST IN THE SLIDE TRANSITION TASK PANE.

5. (OPTIONAL) SELECT A TRANSITION SPEED, SOUND, AND HOW YOU WANT TO ADVANCE THE SLIDE.

Using an Animation Scheme

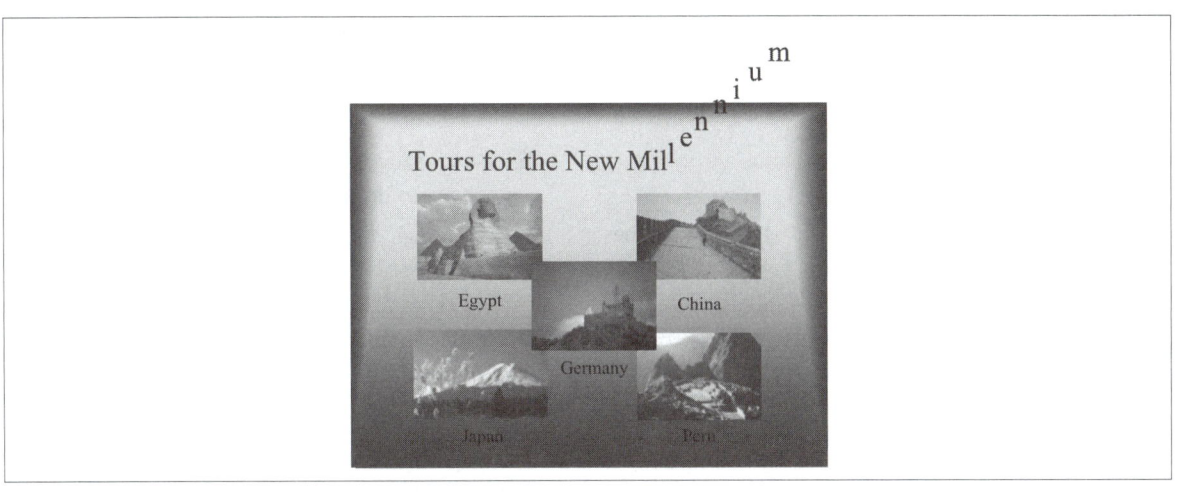

LESSON 7.3

Figure 7-6. An animation scheme.

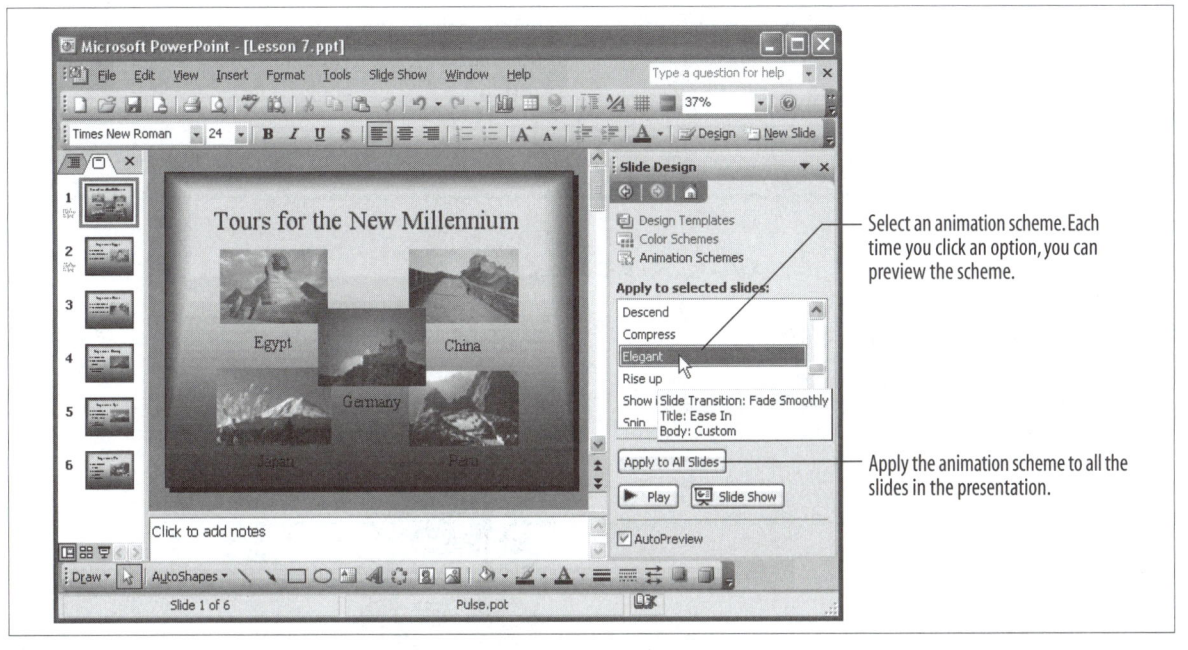

Figure 7-7. Select an animation scheme from the PowerPoint 2003 task pane.

Another way you can make your presentations more interesting is by using one of PowerPoint 2003's new animation schemes. An animation scheme adds a preset visual effect to the text on a slide. Ranging from subtle to exciting, each scheme usually includes an effect for the slide title and an effect that is applied to the bullets or paragraphs in a slide.

In this lesson you'll get some practice adding animation to the text and objects on your slides. Normal View is the best place to work with animation, so we'll start by going there.

Normal View button

Lesson 7.3
Using an Animation Scheme

1 If you're still in Slide Sorter View, select Slide 1 and then click the Normal View button on the horizontal scroll bar.

Here's how to add an animation scheme to a selected slide…

2 Select Slide Show → Animation Schemes from the menu.

The Animation Scheme task pane appears. The Animation Scheme task pane contains several categories of preset animation effects that you can use. For example, the *Bounce* scheme, listed in the *Exciting* category, makes the selected slide fly in from the left side of the screen and the title bounce in shortly thereafter.

3 Scroll down and select the Elegant effect, listed in the Moderate category of the Animation Scheme task pane.

PowerPoint applies the Elegant animation scheme to the current slide and displays a quick preview of the selected scheme.

4 Go to Slide 2 and apply the animation effect of your choice to the slide.

That's enough animation schemes for this presentation. Let's see how they look.

5 Switch to Slide Show View and step through the presentation by clicking the mouse button. Press Esc once you've seen all the animation schemes you added.

Animation schemes are definitely one of the coolest features in PowerPoint, and it can be tempting to add a bunch of different schemes to the same presentation. Remember that animations are supposed to call attention to the main points of your slide, not distract the viewers' attention.

QUICK REFERENCE

TO ADD AN ANIMATION SCHEME:

1. SWITCH TO NORMAL VIEW AND GO TO THE SLIDE WHERE YOU WANT TO ADD THE ANIMATION SCHEME.

2. SELECT SLIDE SHOW → ANIMATION SCHEME FROM THE MENU.

3. SELECT THE DESIRED ANIMATION SCHEME FROM THE TASK PANE.

LESSON 7.4

Using Custom Animations

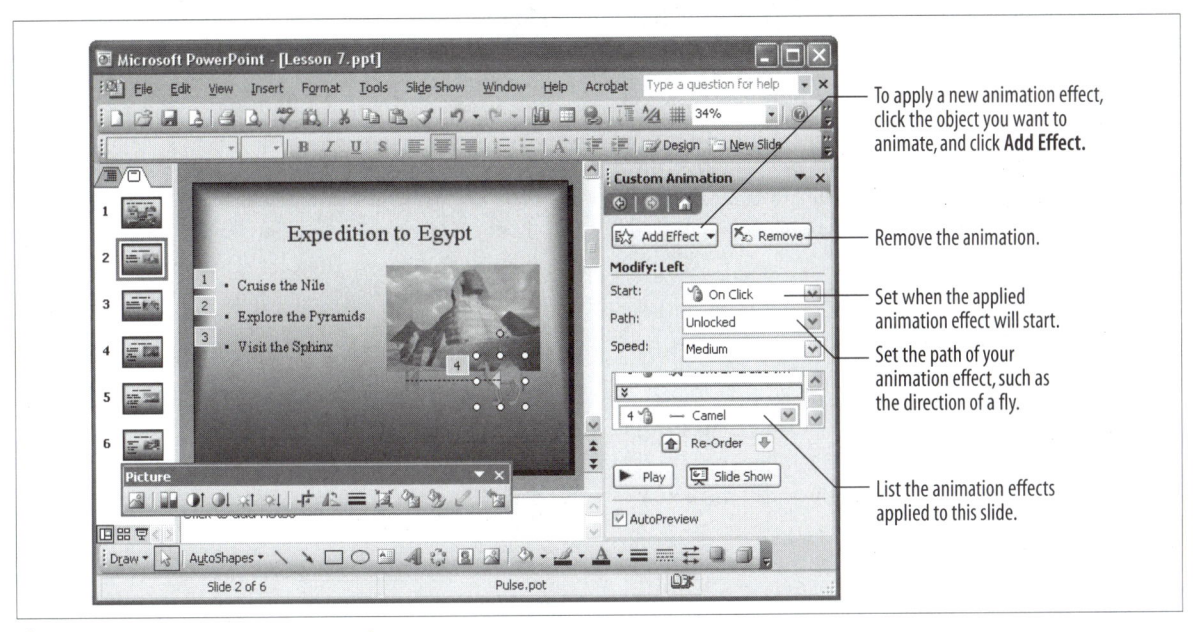

Figure 7-8. The Custom Animation task pane

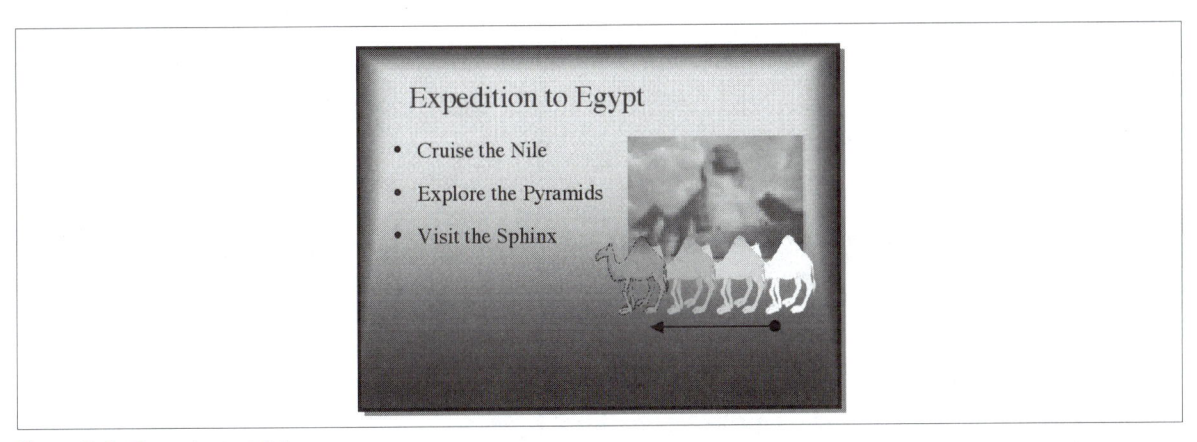

Figure 7-9. The animated slide

In the previous lesson, you learned how to add animation effects to your slides' text and objects the fast and easy way—with Animation Schemes. In this lesson you'll learn how to add animation effects the hard way, with the Custom Animation task pane. While the Custom Animation task pane isn't as easy to use as Animation Schemes, it lets you select from over 60 animation effects, and gives you more flexibility and control when applying them. In fact, once you learn how to animate the text and objects on your slides with the Custom Animation task pane, you may never want to use Animation Schemes ever again.

1 If you have been skipping around lessons, find and open the Lesson 7B presentation and save it as 2003 Tours.

Before we add an animation, let's start with a clean slide that doesn't already have animations on it.

2 With the Animation Schemes task pane open, go to Slide 2 and select No Animation from the Animation Schemes task pane.

Now that our slide has been cleared of previously applied effects, let's start by adding animation to the bulleted list on this slide.

223

Lesson 7.4
Using Custom Animations

3 Click the bulleted list. Select Slide Show → Custom Animation from the menu.

The Custom Animation task pane appears, as shown in Figure 7-8.

4 Click the Add Effect button in the task pane and select Entrance → Blinds from the menu.

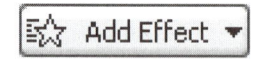

Add Effect button

PowerPoint applies the Blinds effect to the bulleted list and displays a preview of how the bullets will appear on the slide. Notice that the numbers 1, 2, 3, and so on have appeared on the slide. These numbers indicate the order in which each elements on the slide will appear.

Let's add something fun to this slide—a camel cartoon. First we need to insert the camel graphic file into the current slide...

5 Select Insert → Picture → From File from the menu.

The Insert Picture dialog box appears. Here you need to specify the name and location of the graphic file to be inserted into your slide.

6 Navigate to your Practice folder.

All the graphic files in the disk or folder appear in the file window.

7 Select the Camel file and click Insert.

PowerPoint inserts the camel graphic into the current slide. We don't need to resize the camel graphic since it's already the correct size, but we do have to move the camel to a better location on the slide.

8 Drag the camel to the bottom right of the Sphinx picture, as shown in Figure 7-8.

Now let's animate the camel object. We want to animate the camel so that it appears to be walking in from the right of the slide.

9 With the Camel picture still selected, click the Add Effect button in the task pane and select Motion Paths → Left from the menu.

Let's see how our new animation looks.

10 Switch to Slide Show View and step through the presentation by clicking the mouse button to activate the animation. Press Esc once you've seen all the animation schemes you added.

NOTE By default, custom animations start on a click. So when you view the animation in Slide Show View, you must click to step through each animation individually. For example, the camel will not move until your fourth click in Slide 2. You can adjust an animation effect's starting point in the Custom Animation task pane by clicking on the Start list arrow and selecting an option from the list.

Move on to the next step...

11 Close the task pane.

QUICK REFERENCE

TO ADD CUSTOM ANIMATION TO A SLIDE OBJECT:

1. IN NORMAL VIEW, GO TO THE SLIDE WHERE YOU WANT TO ADD THE ANIMATION.

2. SELECT THE OBJECT YOU WANT TO ANIMATE.

3. SELECT SLIDE SHOW → CUSTOM ANIMATION FROM THE MENU.

   OR...

   RIGHT-CLICK THE OBJECT AND SELECT CUSTOM ANIMATION FROM THE SHORTCUT MENU.

4. CLICK THE [Add Effect] ADD EFFECT BUTTON IN THE TASK PANE AND SELECT THE DESIRED ANIMATION.

5. (OPTIONAL) SPECIFY THE SPEED AND PARAMETERS OF THE ANIMATION.

Rehearsing Slide Show Timings

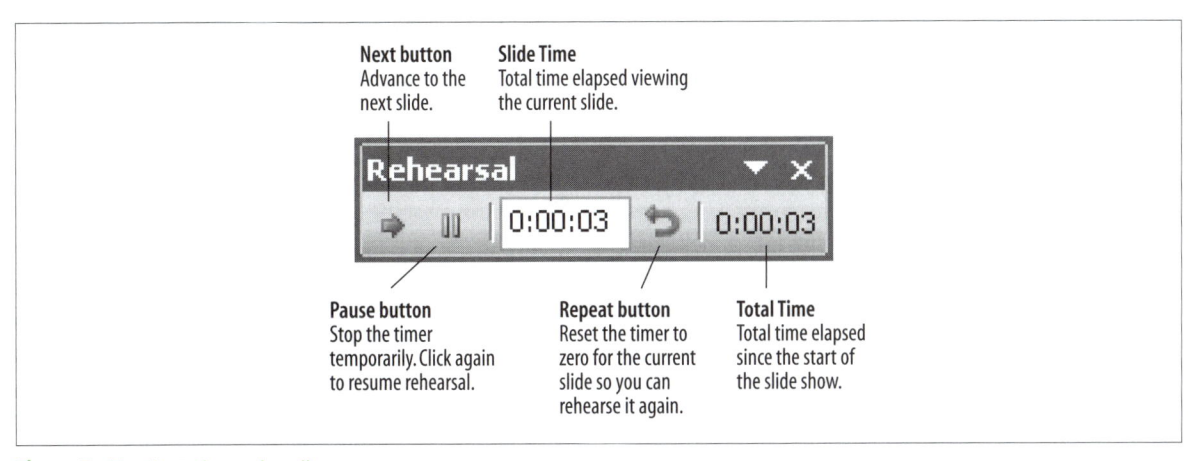

LESSON 7.5

Figure 7-10. The Rehearsal toolbar.

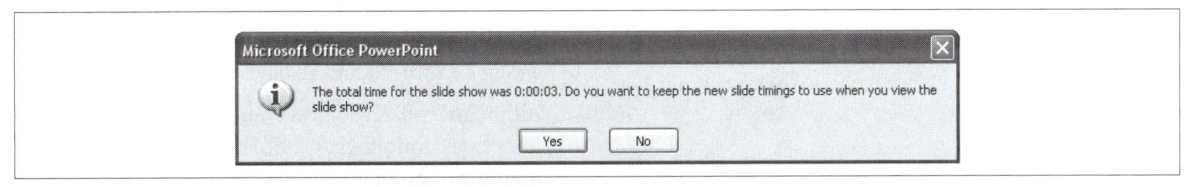

- **Next button** — Advance to the next slide.
- **Slide Time** — Total time elapsed viewing the current slide.
- **Pause button** — Stop the timer temporarily. Click again to resume rehearsal.
- **Repeat button** — Reset the timer to zero for the current slide so you can rehearse it again.
- **Total Time** — Total time elapsed since the start of the slide show.

Figure 7-11. PowerPoint asks if you want to save the slide show timings.

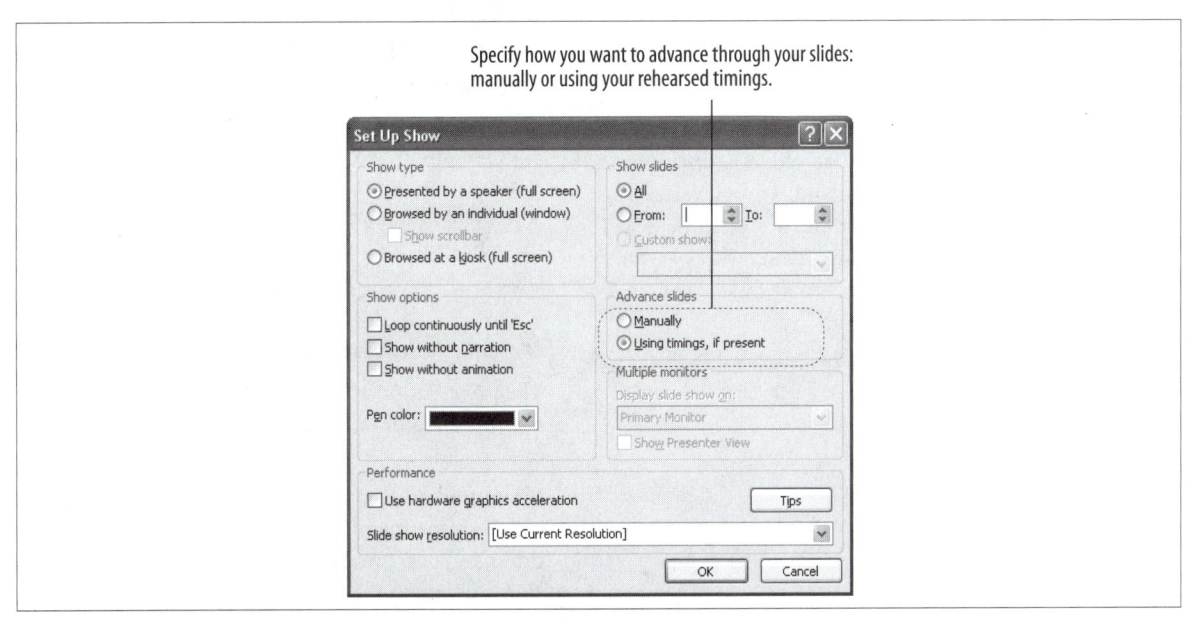

Figure 7-12. The Set Up Show dialog box.

Specify how you want to advance through your slides: manually or using your rehearsed timings.

225

Lesson 7.5
Rehearsing Slide Show Timings

Rehearse Timings button

Other Ways to Rehearse Timings:

- Click the **Rehearse Timings button** on the Slide Sorter toolbar

When you run your presentation, you want to make sure each slide is displayed for an adequate amount of time. You don't want your audience to think you're long-winded, do you? A slide that is displayed for too long will quickly lose audience interest, and a slide that moves too fast will not give your audience enough time to read its contents. PowerPoint's Rehearse Timings feature lets you rehearse your presentation so that you can be sure you're moving at an accurate pace. You can even set slides to advance automatically, based on your rehearsal timings. The only thing the Rehearse Timings feature won't do for you is critique your performance—you'll still need a human being to do that.

1 Select **Slide Show → Rehearse Timings** from the menu.

You immediately switch to Slide Show View, and the Rehearsal dialog box appears in the upper-left corner of the screen, as shown in Figure 7-10.

You can see the seconds in the Rehearsal toolbar ticking away. No slide transitions or object animations will occur without your command. Unless you're a speed-reader, it's likely that some wasted time has been recorded in the slide timings! Don't worry—you can easily reset the time on the current slide.

2 Click the **Repeat button** on the Rehearsal toolbar.

Repeat button

The time resets to zero and the text animation effect on the first slide begins.

If you ever feel that you have made a mistake on the timing for a specific slide, click the Repeat button to start over.

3 Click the **Next button** on the Rehearsal toolbar to advance to the next slide.

The second slide in the presentation appears.

Notice that the Slide Time box, which records the elapsed time for the current slide, resets to zero. However, the total elapsed time in the right side of the toolbar, which records the elapsed time for the entire presentation, keeps on ticking.

Slide timings appear in the lower-left corner of each slide in Slide Sorter view.

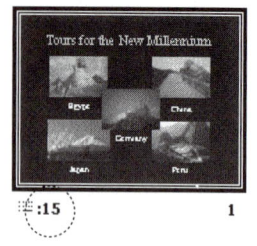

4 Advance through the slide's animations, allowing **1 or 2 seconds** between each animation. When you've finished displaying all the animation effects, wait another **3 seconds** and advance to the next slide.

Although you have to advance through them, you may have noticed that animation effects do not get their own timing in the slide.

5 Continue through the rest of the slides in the presentation, being careful to display each slide for at least **5 seconds**.

When you finish the presentation, a dialog box appears, asking if you want to save the slide timings, as shown in Figure 7-11. If you save the timings, the slides will automatically advance using the results of the rehearsal timing the next time you run the slide show.

6 Click **Yes** to save the timings.

The presentation appears in Slide Sorter View. Notice that the slide timings appear in the lower-left corner of each slide.

If you find all of this automation too restrictive, you can always turn off the timings and manually step through your presentation's animations and slides. Here's how:

7 Select **Slide Show → Set Up Show** from the menu.

The Set Up Show dialog box appears, as shown in Figure 7-12.

Chapter 7
Delivering Your Presentation

To rehearse how long it takes you to present information compared to the rehearsal timings you set, click on the slide you want to rehearse with and press the Play button at the bottom of the Custom Animation menu. The menu plays one slide at a time for the amount of time you specified in your rehearsal.

8 Select the **Manually** option under Advance Slides and click **OK**.

The dialog box closes. You will now have to manually advance through the animations and slides in your slide show.

9 Advance through the animations and slides in your presentation.

QUICK REFERENCE

TO ADD/REHEARSE SLIDE TIMINGS:

1. SELECT **SLIDE SHOW** → **REHEARSE TIMINGS** FROM THE MENU.

2. DISPLAY THE SLIDE UNTIL YOU ARE READY TO MOVE ON TO THE NEXT ONE. THEN ADVANCE TO THE NEXT SLIDE. POWERPOINT WILL RECORD HOW MUCH TIME IS SPENT ON EACH SLIDE.

   IF YOU MAKE A MISTAKE ON THE TIMING OF A SLIDE, CLICK THE **REPEAT BUTTON** TO RESTART THE TIMING ON THE SLIDE.

3. WHEN YOU'VE FINISHED THE PRESENTATION, CLICK **YES** TO SAVE YOUR TIMINGS.

   TO RUN YOUR SLIDE SHOW MANUALLY INSTEAD OF USING THE TIMINGS, SELECT **SLIDE SHOW** → **SET UP SHOW** FROM THE MENU, SELECT **MANUALLY**, AND CLICK **OK**.

227

LESSON 7.6 Creating a Presentation that Runs by Itself

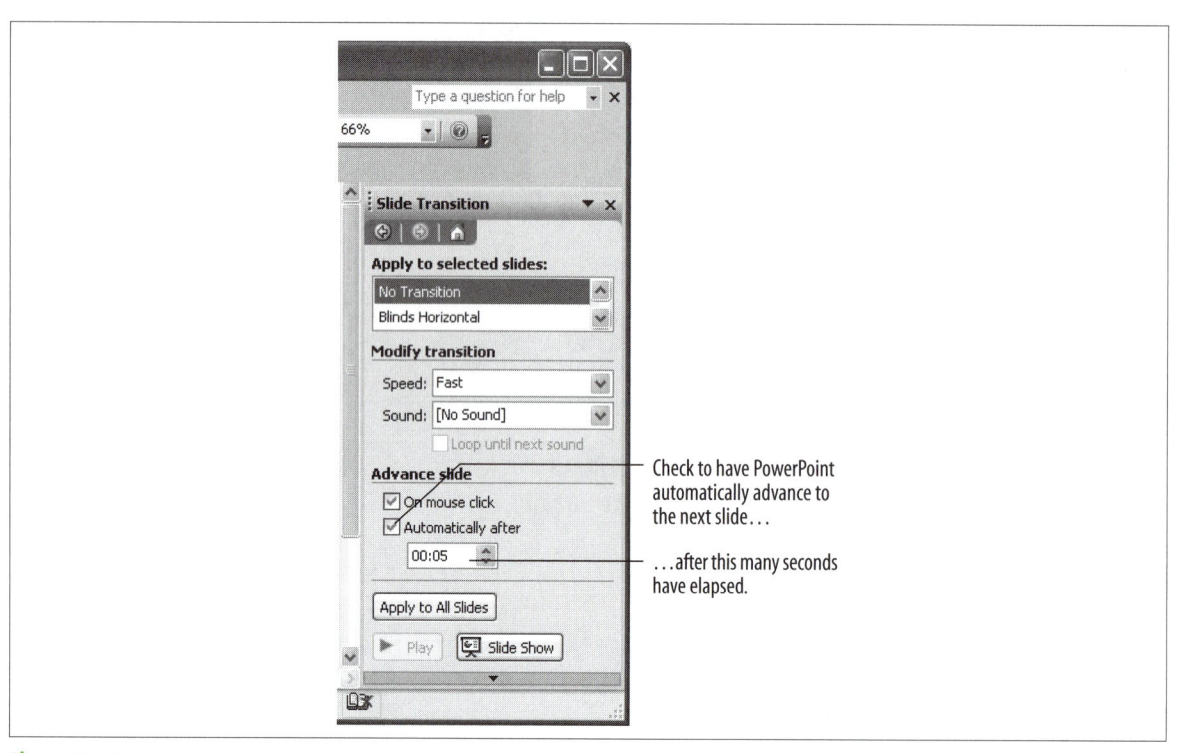

Figure 7-13. Set up a presentation to run automatically in the Slide Transition task pane.

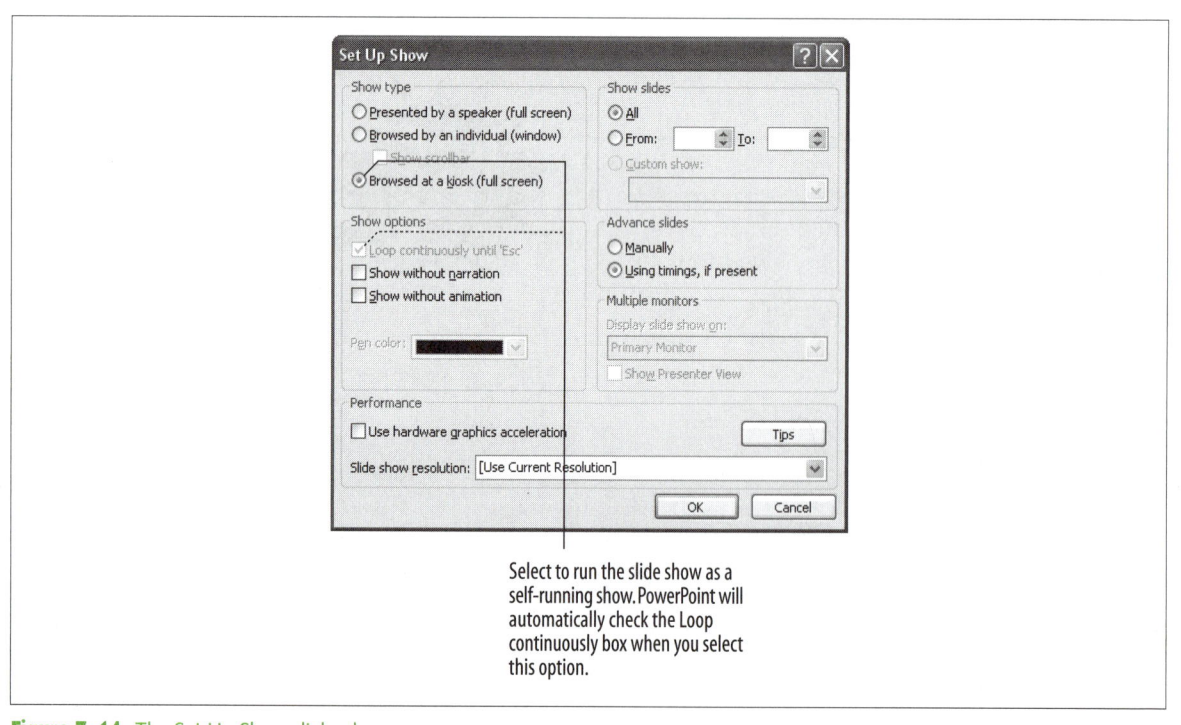

Figure 7-14. The Set Up Show dialog box.

Chapter 7
Delivering Your Presentation

This lesson explains how to create a presentation that runs without assistance. For example, you might want to set up a presentation to run unattended in a booth at a trade show or on a community access cable channel. Except for using the mouse to click certain items, you can make most controls unavailable so users can't make changes to the presentation. A self-running presentation restarts when it's finished, or if it has been idle for over five minutes.

When you design a self-running presentation, you'll want to keep the setting and purpose of the presentation in mind. Will your presentation be in a booth or display window? Do you want viewers to interact with your presentation (if it contains hyperlinks), or do you want to prevent them from tampering with it? Is your presentation self-explanatory, or do you need to add voice narration to it?

Several options you will want to consider when creating a self-running slide show include:

- **Automatic or manual timings:** You can set a slide show to run by itself with automatic timings, or you can set it so that users can move through the show at their own pace using the mouse. Mouse clicks are ignored unless they're on objects that have hyperlinks. See Lesson 7.5 for more information.
- **Hyperlinks:** You can set up hyperlinks to move through the slide show, or to jump to other slides and programs. See Chapter 9 for more information.
- **Voice narration:** You can add recorded narration that plays with your slide show. See Chapter 8 for more information.

Setting up a presentation to run by itself is incredibly easy.

1 Select **View** → **Slide Sorter** from the menu.

You may recall from an earlier lesson that this is the best view for working with slide transitions.

First, you need to set the slides transitions so that they automatically advance.

2 Click the **Slide Transition button** on the Slide Sorter toolbar.

Slide Transition button

Other Ways to Add Slide Transitions:

- Select **Slide Show** → **Slide Transition** from the menu.

The Slide Transition task pane appears, as shown in Figure 7-13. This is where you tell PowerPoint to automatically advance to the next slide(s) after a specified number of seconds have passed.

3 Ensure that the **Automatically after** box in the task pane is checked, and type 5 in the **time** box.

PowerPoint will now automatically advance through the selected slides in your presentation in five-second intervals.

4 Click **Apply to All Slides**.

PowerPoint applies the settings to all the slides in the presentation.

5 Select **Slide Show** → **Set Up Show** from the menu.

The Set Up Show dialog box appears, as shown in Figure 7-14. The Show type section is what's important here. There are three options you can choose from:

- **Presented by a speaker:** This is the typical full-screen slide show. You can advance the slides and animations manually, or you can set automatic timings using the Rehearse Timings command.
- **Browsed by an individual:** Runs the slide show in a standard window, with custom menus and commands that make it easy for an individual reader to browse your presentation.
- **Browsed at a kiosk:** Delivers the slide show as a self-running show that loops continuously, or restarts, at the end of the presentation. The audience can click hyperlinks and action buttons but cannot modify the presentation.

Pressing the Esc key will stop any of these slide shows.

Lesson 7.6
Creating a Presentation that Runs by Itself

6 Select both the Browsed at a kiosk and the Using timings, if present options from the dialog box. Click OK.

Let's try our presentation with the new automatic slide transitions.

7 Switch to Slide Show View.

Sit back and watch as PowerPoint automatically advances through the slides in the presentation. Move on to the next step when you've seen enough.

8 Press Esc to cancel the presentation and return to the previous view.

Select the "On mouse click" check box, and clear the "Automatically after" check box in the task pane if you want the next slide to appear only when you click the mouse.

9 Close the Slide Transition task pane and save your work.

QUICK REFERENCE

TO CREATE A PRESENTATION THAT RUNS BY ITSELF:

1. SWITCH TO SLIDE SORTER VIEW.
2. SELECT ALL THE SLIDES IN THE PRESENTATION BY PRESSING CTRL + A OR BY SELECTING EDIT → SELECT ALL FROM THE MENU.
3. CLICK THE Transition SLIDE TRANSITION BUTTON ON THE SLIDE SORTER TOOLBAR OR SELECT SLIDE SHOW → SLIDE TRANSITION FROM THE MENU.
4. CHECK THE AUTOMATICALLY AFTER BOX, SPECIFY HOW LONG YOU WANT TO DISPLAY EACH SLIDE IN THE SECONDS BOX, AND CLICK APPLY TO ALL SLIDES.
5. SELECT SLIDE SHOW → SET UP SHOW FROM THE MENU.
6. SELECT THE BROWSED AT A KIOSK OPTION, MAKE SURE THE USING TIMINGS, IF PRESENT BUTTON IS SELECTED, AND CLICK OK.
7. SWITCH TO SLIDE SHOW VIEW TO START THE AUTOMATED SLIDE SHOW.

Creating a Custom Show

LESSON 7.7

Click to create a new custom show.

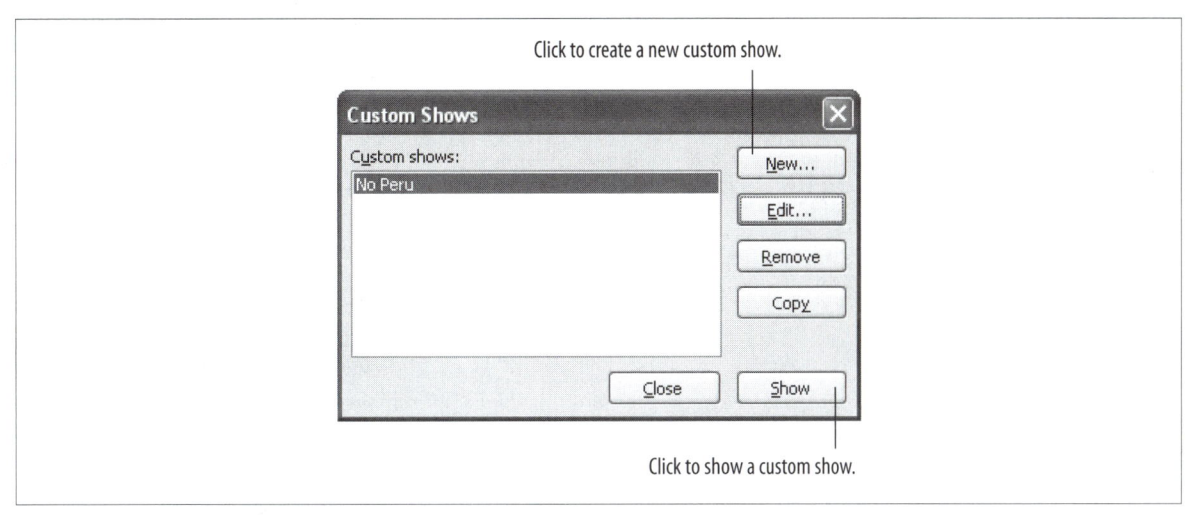

Click to show a custom show.

Figure 7-15. The Custom Shows dialog box

Select the slide you want to appear in the custom show…

…and click Add.

These slides will appear in the custom show.

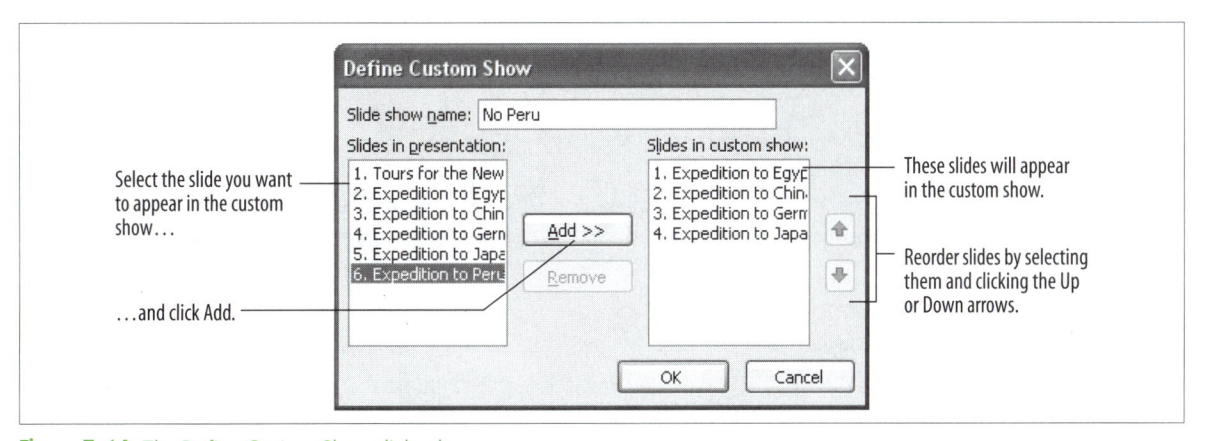

Reorder slides by selecting them and clicking the Up or Down arrows.

Figure 7-16. The Define Custom Show dialog box

When you create a presentation, you may need to customize it for a different audience. For example, if you were the owner of a children's summer camp, you could create a slide show for the kids that only displays slides about how fun the camp is, and another slide show for the parents that only displays slides explaining the benefits of two weeks without children. Instead of having to create and work with several presentation files, Power-Point 2003 has a Custom Shows feature that lets you create several similar slide shows within a single presentation file.

1 Select **Slide Show** → **Custom Shows** from the menu.

The Custom Shows dialog box appears, as shown in Figure 7-15.

2 Click the **New button**.

The Define Custom Show dialog box appears, as shown in Figure 7-16. First, you need to give your custom show a name.

3 Type No Peru in the **Slide show name** box.

Next, add the slides you want to appear in the custom slide show.

4 Click the **Expedition to Egypt** slide from the Slides in presentation box, and click **Add**.

The Expedition to Egypt slide appears in the Slides in custom show list to the right.

231

Lesson 7.7
Creating a Custom Show

5 Following the procedure described in **Step 4**, add the **Expedition to China**, **Expedition to Germany**, and **Expedition to Japan** slides to the custom show.

If you add a slide to a custom show by mistake, you can remove it by clicking the slide in the Slides in custom show list and then clicking the Remove button.

You've finished creating your custom show, so you can move on to the next step and close the Define Custom Show dialog box.

6 Click **OK**.

The Custom Shows dialog box reappears.

7 Select the **No Peru** show in the Custom Show box and click **Show**.

PowerPoint displays the selected custom show in Slide Show View. By now you're probably getting tired of seeing the same slides again and again, so you can quit the slide show as soon as you want.

8 Press **Esc** to cancel the slide show and save your work.

You can add or delete slides from a custom show after it has been created by selecting Slide Show → Custom Shows from the menu, selecting the custom show you want to edit, and clicking the Edit button. Then go ahead and add and/or remove the slides from the custom show.

You can also delete a custom show entirely by selecting Slide Show → Custom Shows from the menu, selecting it, and then clicking the Remove button.

QUICK REFERENCE

TO CREATE A CUSTOM SHOW:

1. SELECT **SLIDE SHOW** → **CUSTOM SHOWS** FROM THE MENU.
2. CLICK THE **NEW** BUTTON AND ENTER A NAME FOR THE CUSTOM SHOW IN THE **SLIDE SHOW NAME** BOX.
3. SELECT THE SLIDE YOU WANT TO ADD TO THE CUSTOM SHOW FROM THE **SLIDES IN PRESENTATION** BOX, AND CLICK **ADD**. REPEAT UNTIL YOU'VE SELECTED ALL THE SLIDES THAT YOU WANT TO INCLUDE.
4. CLICK **OK**, THEN **CLOSE** WHEN YOU'RE FINISHED.

TO SHOW A CUSTOM SHOW:

- SELECT **SLIDE SHOW** → **CUSTOM SHOWS** FROM THE MENU, SELECT THE CUSTOM SHOW, AND CLICK **SHOW**.

TO EDIT A CUSTOM SHOW:

- SELECT **SLIDE SHOW** → **CUSTOM SHOWS** FROM THE MENU, SELECT THE CUSTOM SHOW, CLICK **EDIT**, AND THEN ADD, REMOVE, OR REORDER THE SLIDES IN THE CUSTOM SHOW.

TO DELETE A CUSTOM SHOW:

- SELECT **SLIDE SHOW** → **CUSTOM SHOWS** FROM THE MENU, SELECT THE CUSTOM SHOW AND CLICK **REMOVE**.

Packaging and Copying a Presentation to CD

LESSON 7.8

Figure 7-17. The Package for CD dialog box.

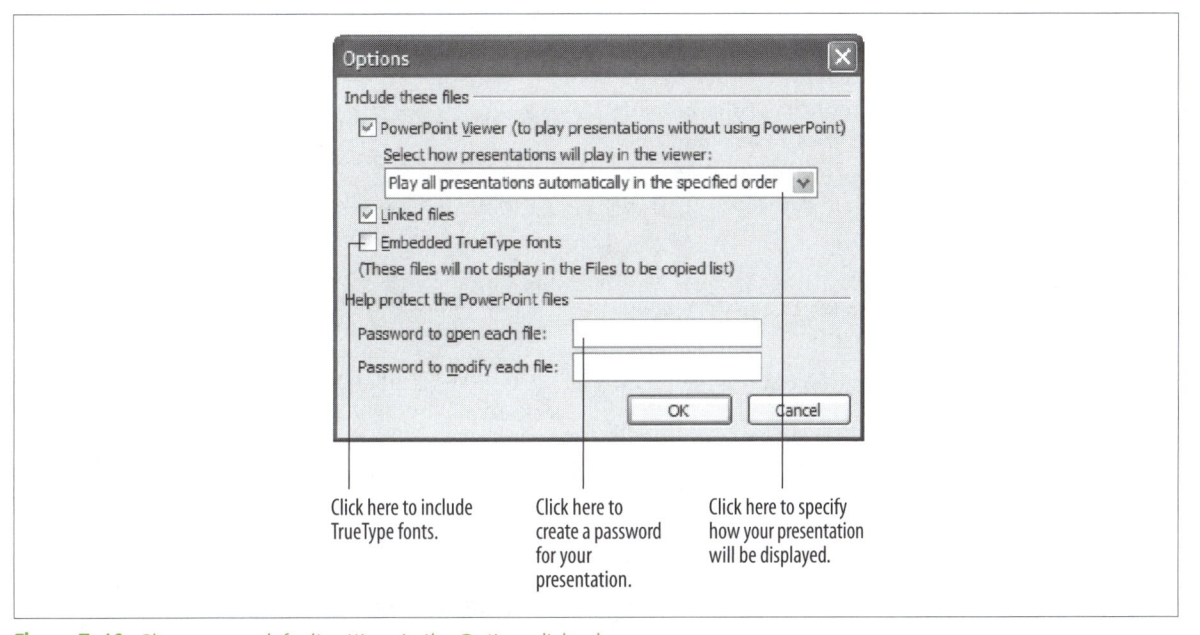

Figure 7-18. Change your default settings in the Options dialog box.

Figure 7-19. The Copy to Folder dialog box.

Lesson 7.8
Packaging and Copying a Presentation to CD

What if you want to run a presentation on a computer that doesn't have PowerPoint installed? The problem is easily solved with PowerPoint's Package for CD feature. The Package for CD feature packs the presentation's files and fonts with the PowerPoint Viewer, so that those without the PowerPoint program can still view your presentation. If you have CD burning hardware, the Package for CD feature can copy presentations to a blank recordable CD (CD-R) or a blank rewritable CD (CD-RW).

You can also use the Package for CD feature to copy the presentation to a folder on your computer, a network location, or—if you do not include the viewer—a floppy disk, instead of directly to CD. This lesson explains how you can use PowerPoint's Package for CD feature to take your show on the road.

NOTE *The Microsoft PowerPoint Viewer program must be installed on your computer in order to use it with the Package for CD feature. If PowerPoint can't find the Viewer when it tries to package your presentation, you'll have to install it from the Microsoft Office CD-ROM, or download it from Microsoft Office Online.*

1 If necessary, find and open the Lesson 7C presentation and save it as 2003 Tours.

Once the presentation is open, you can run the Package for CD feature.

2 Select File → Package for CD from the menu.

The Package for CD dialog box appears, as shown in Figure 7-17.

3 Type 2003 Tours in the Name the CD box.

Choose a name that you can easily recognize so that you don't confuse yourself.

4 Click Options to check out your presentation's default settings.

The Options dialog box appears, as shown in Figure 7-18.

5 Make sure the PowerPoint Viewer, Linked files, and Embedded TrueType fonts boxes are checked and click OK.

The Options dialog box closes and you're back to the Package for CD dialog box.

NOTE *You don't have to include the PowerPoint Viewer if the recipient of your packaged presentation already has PowerPoint or the PowerPoint Viewer program installed. Adding the Viewer to your packaged presentation takes up a lot of file space, so don't include it if you don't have to.*

6 Click the Copy to Folder button, type C:\ in the text box, and click OK.

This will package and save the presentation to a folder in your C: hard drive named "2003 Tours."

7 Click the Close button in the Package for CD dialog box.

The Package for CD dialog box closes, and you're ready to take your presentation on the road! Since we'll be using the PowerPoint Viewer program instead of the actual PowerPoint program in the next lesson, you can move on to the next step and exit Microsoft PowerPoint.

8 Exit Microsoft PowerPoint.

Now that you know how to use the Package for CD feature to copy a PowerPoint slide show to a folder, turn the page and we'll learn how to run the packaged slide show using the PowerPoint Viewer program.

Chapter 7
Delivering Your Presentation

QUICK REFERENCE

TO PACKAGE A PRESENTATION TO A FOLDER:

1. OPEN THE PRESENTATION YOU WANT TO COPY.
2. SELECT **FILE** → **PACKAGE FOR CD** FROM THE MENU.
3. CLICK THE **COPY TO FOLDER** BUTTON AND SPECIFY WHERE TO SAVE THE PRESENTATION.

TO PACKAGE A PRESENTATION TO CD:

1. OPEN THE PRESENTATION YOU WANT TO COPY.
2. SELECT **FILE** → **PACKAGE FOR CD** FROM THE MENU.
3. CLICK THE **COPY TO CD** BUTTON AND INSERT A BLANK CD WHEN PROMPTED.

LESSON 7.9
Viewing a Packaged Presentation

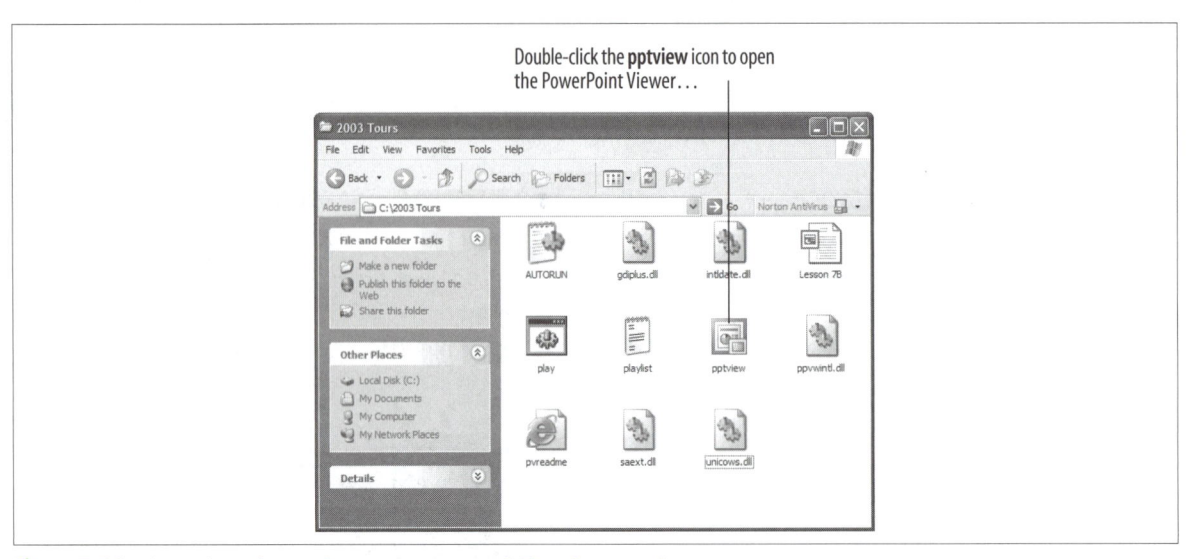

Figure 7-20. The Package for CD feature copies several files when it packages a presentation.

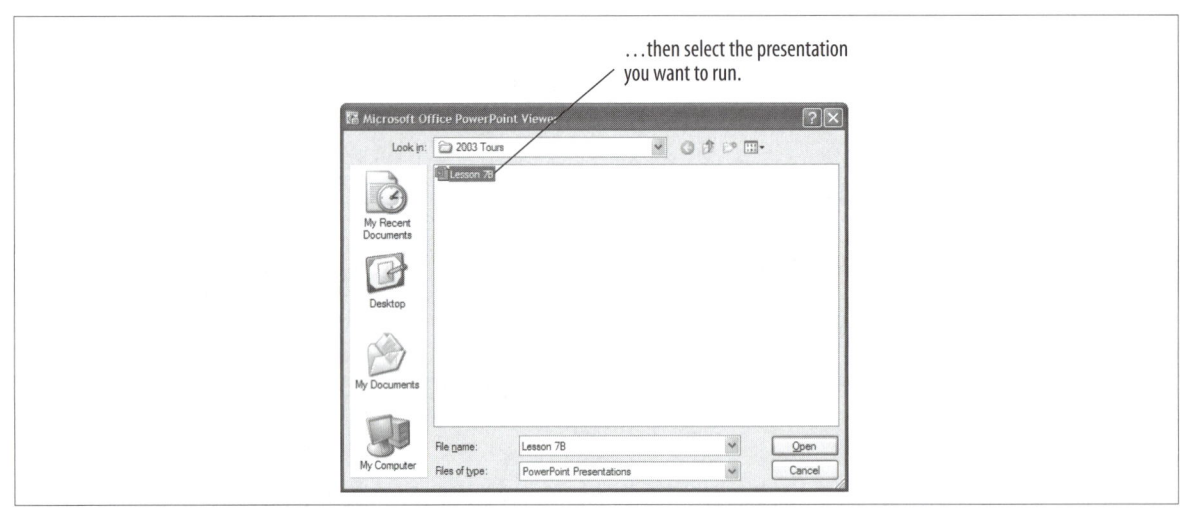

Figure 7-21. Select the presentation you want to run in the Microsoft PowerPoint Viewer.

Once you've copied your presentation to a folder or CD, you can run it using the PowerPoint Viewer program. Loading and running a packed presentation on another computer can be a little tricky the first time you try it, so we'll walk through the entire process in this lesson. PowerPoint Viewer is free to distribute, so you don't need to worry about purchasing another license.

First, we need to find the packaged presentation. There are several ways to find and run a packaged PowerPoint presentation:

- Find the packaged presentation's using My Computer or Windows Explorer. When you've opened the appropriate drive and/or folder, simply double-click the pptview icon and select the presentation.

- Click the Windows Start button and select Run. Type the drive name and folder name of the program you want to run, "2003 Tours." For example, if you had saved a presentation to the C: hard drive, you would type "c:\2003 Tours."

Although both methods work equally well, we'll be using the first method in this lesson.

Chapter 7
Delivering Your Presentation

TIP *If the presentation is packaged on a CD, the presentation may automatically open in the Power-Point Viewer when you insert the CD.*

1 Open **My Computer**.

My Computer

Depending on how your operating system is set up, you will find the My Computer icon on your desktop or under the Start button.

The My Computer window appears, displaying the contents of your computer.

2 Double-click **(C:) Local Disk**.

If you copied your packaged presentation to CD, you would double-click the CD-RW (D:) drive instead.

3 Find and double-click the **2003 Tours** folder.

Several files will appear in the folder where you saved your presentation, as shown in Figure 7-20. One of these files is the PowerPoint Viewer program.

4 Find and double-click the **pptview** program file.

pptview

The Microsoft PowerPoint Viewer program window appears, as shown in Figure 7-21. You're ready to run the packed presentation—all you have to do now is select the presentation you want to view.

5 Select the **2003 Tours** file and click **Open** to run the selected presentation in the Microsoft PowerPoint Viewer program.

Voila! The presentation appears in all its glory, even though you're not actually using PowerPoint to display it.

6 Step through the presentation. Press **Esc** when you've seen enough, then exit the Microsoft Power-Point Viewer program.

Congratulations! You've just learned how to unpack a presentation and run it using the Microsoft PowerPoint Viewer program. Of course, if the computer you want to run a presentation on has the full PowerPoint program, there's no sense in using the PowerPoint Viewer program.

QUICK REFERENCE

TTO RUN A PACKED PRESENTATION:

1. BROWSE TO THE DISK DRIVE AND/OR FOLDER WHERE THE PACKED PRESENTATION IS SAVED USING MY COMPUTER OR WINDOWS EXPLORER.

   OR...

   CLICK THE WINDOWS **START BUTTON**, SELECT **RUN**, CLICK THE **BROWSE** BUTTON, AND BROWSE TO THE DISK DRIVE AND/OR FOLDER WHERE THE PACKED PRESENTATION IS SAVED.

2. FIND AND DOUBLE-CLICK THE FILE FOLDER.

TO USE THE MICROSOFT POWERPOINT VIEWER:

1. BROWSE TO THE DRIVE AND FOLDER WHERE YOU INSTALLED THE PRESENTATION, AND FIND AND DOUBLE-CLICK THE **PPTVIEW** PROGRAM FILE.

2. SELECT THE PRESENTATION YOU WANT TO VIEW AND CLICK **OPEN**.

TO RUN A PACKED PRESENTATION COPIED TO CD:

- SIMPLY INSERT THE CD INTO THE DISC DRIVE.

Chapter Seven Review

Lesson Summary

Delivering a Presentation on a Computer

To Display a Slide Show on a Computer: Click the Slide Show button on the horizontal scroll bar or select View → Slide Show from the menu.

To Advance to the Next Slide: Click the left mouse button or press the Enter, Spacebar, →, ↓, or Page Down keys.

To Stop a Slide Show: Press Esc.

To Doodle on the Current Slide with the Pen: Press Ctrl + P and draw on the screen with the pen tool. Press Ctrl + A to switch back to the arrow pointer.

To Erase Your Doodles: Press E.

To Display a List of Slide Show Commands: Right-click anywhere on the slide or click the Slide Show Menu button.

Using Slide Transitions

A transition is how PowerPoint advances from one slide to the next during an on-screen slide show. You can choose from over 40 different special effects to move between slides.

To Add Slide Transitions Using the Slide Sorter Toolbar: Switch to Slide Sorter View. Click the slide where you want to add a transition. To select multiple slides hold down the Shift key as you click each slide. Click the Slide Transition button on the Slide Sorter toolbar and select a transition from the Transition list in the Slide Transition task pane. (Optional) Select a transition speed, sound, and how you want to advance the slide.

Using an Animation Scheme

An animation scheme adds a preset visual effect to the text on a slide. Ranging from subtle to exciting, each scheme usually includes an effect for the slide title and an effect that is applied to the bullets or paragraphs.

To Add an Animation Scheme: Switch to Normal View and go to the slide where you want to add the animation scheme. Select Slide Show → Animation Scheme from the menu and then select the desired animation scheme from the task pane.

Using Custom Animations

To Add Custom Animation to an Existing Slide Object: Switch to Normal View and go to the slide where you want to add the animation. Select the object you want to animate and select Slide Show → Custom Animation from the menu or right-click the object and select Custom Animation from the shortcut menu. Click the Add Effect button in the task pane and select the desired animation. (Optional) Specify the speed and parameters of the animation.

Rehearsing Slide Show Timings

Slide Show Timings let you practice how long each slide is displayed on-screen during a presentation. These timings can be saved and used later to create an automated slide show.

To Add/Rehearse Slide Timings: Select Slide Show → Rehearse Timings from the menu. Display each slide for whatever duration you want, then advance to the next slide. PowerPoint will record how long each slide is presented. If you make a mistake on the timing, click the Repeat button and try again. When you've finished the last slide, click Yes to accept your timings.

To run your slide show manually instead of using the timings, select Slide Show → Set Up Show from the menu, select Manually, and click OK.

Creating a Presentation that Runs by Itself

To Create a Presentation that Runs by Itself: Switch to Slide Sorter View and select all the slides in the presentation by pressing Ctrl + A or by selecting Edit → Select All from the menu. Click the Slide Transition button on the Slide Sorter toolbar or select Slide Show → Slide Transition from the menu, check the Automatically after box, specify how long you want to display each slide in the seconds box, and then click Apply to All Slides. Select Slide Show → Set Up Show from the menu, select the Browsed at a kiosk option, make sure the Using timings, if present button is selected under Advance slides, and click OK.

Switch to Slide Show View to play the automated slide show. Press Esc to stop playing the presentation.

238

Creating a Custom Show

PowerPoint's Custom Show feature allows you to save several different slide shows within a single presentation file.

To Create a Custom Show: Select Slide Show → Custom Shows from the menu, click the New button, and enter a name for the custom show in the Slide Show name box. Select the slide you want to add to the custom show from the Slides in presentation box, and click Add. Repeat until you've selected all the slides that you want to include. Click OK and then Close when you're finished.

To Run a Custom Show: Select Slide Show → Custom Shows from the menu, select the custom show, and click Show.

To Edit a Custom Show: Select Slide Show → Custom Shows from the menu, select the custom show, click Edit, and then add, remove, or reorder the slides in the custom show.

To Delete a Custom Show: Select Slide Show → Custom Shows from the menu, select the custom show, and click Remove.

Using the Package for CD Feature

The Package for CD feature packages a presentation to a folder or CD so that you can run the presentation on other computers—even if they don't have PowerPoint installed.

To Package a Presentation to a Folder: Open the presentation you want to copy and select File → Package for CD from the menu. Click the Copy to Folder button and specify where to save the presentation.

To Package a Presentation to CD: Open the presentation you want to copy and select File → Package for CD from the menu. Click the Copy to CD button and insert a blank CD when prompted.

Viewing a Packaged Presentation

To Run a Packed Presentation: Use either of these methods:

- Browse to the disk drive and/or folder where the packed presentation is saved using My Computer or Windows Explorer.
- Click the Windows Start button, select Run, click the Browse button, and browse to the disk drive and/or folder where the packed presentation is saved. After using either method, double-click the file folder.

To Use the Microsoft PowerPoint Viewer: Browse to the drive and folder where you installed the presentation and find and double-click the pptview program file, select the presentation you want to view, and click Open.

To Run a Packed Presentation Copied to CD: Simply insert the CD into the CD drive.

Quiz

1. For six monthly payments of just $49, you can purchase additional software for PowerPoint that enables you to doodle on your slides during a presentation. (True or False?)

2. Slide Show view displays your presentation as an electronic slide show on your computer. (True or False?)

3. Which PowerPoint view works best for adding slide transitions?

    A. Normal View
    B. Slide Show View
    C. Slide Sorter View
    D. Notes View

4. Which of the following statements most accurately describes animation as it is used in PowerPoint presentations?

    A. You can animate and program the Office Assistant to give your presentation for you.
    B. You can add several animated characters to your slides that will amuse everyone with their clowning around.
    C. You can animate text and objects so that they appear on your slides by using one of more than 50 different special effects.
    D. You can animate a slide show so that it can run by itself.

Chapter 7
Chapter Seven Review

5. Which of the following statements about rehearsing slide timings is NOT true?

    A. Rehearsing slide timings helps you ensure that each slide is displayed for an appropriate amount of time.

    B. You can record slide timings in Slide Show view. Simply advance to the next slide after each slide has been displayed for the desired duration.

    C. You can manually change slide timings by selecting Slide Show → Timings from the menu and editing the timings in the Slide Timings task pane.

    D. After you've added slide timings, you can save them and later use them to automate the slideshow.

6. You have a presentation that needs to be shown to two different audiences. One audience will see all the slides in the presentation; the other audience only needs to see 75% of the slides. You will need to create two separate presentation files in order to accomplish this. (True or False?)

7. Computers need to have Microsoft PowerPoint installed in order to display slide shows saved by the Package for CD feature. (True or False?)

Homework

1. Open Lesson 8A and save it as "Czech Republic."

2. Switch to Slide Show View by clicking the Slide Show View button on the horizontal scroll bar, located at the bottom of the screen.

3. Press Page Down to advance through the slide show until you reach Slide 3. Press Ctrl + P to activate the electronic pen and draw a smiley face on the slide.

Interesting Facts about Prague

- Prague is the only major European city that wasn't damaged during World War II.
- Prague's famous astrological clock was built in 1140.
- Prague was invaded by the U.S.S.R in 1968.

Click to hear the clock

4. Press E to erase your doodles, then press Esc to stop the slide show.

5. Add a slide transition effect to your presentation. Switch to Slide Sorter View by clicking the Slide Sorter View button on the horizontal scroll bar. Select Slide 1, click the Transition button on the Formatting toolbar, and select Blinds Horizontal from the task pane.

6. Go to Slide 2.

7. Select Animation Schemes from the Slide Show menu to display the Animation Schemes task pane.

8. Animate the text on Slide 2. Click anywhere in the bulleted list and select the desired animation effect from the task pane.

9. Set the timing of your electronic slide show. Select Slide Show → Rehearse Timings from the menu. Display each slide for approximately five seconds. Click Yes to keep the slide timings.

10. Configure the slide show to run automatically. Select Slide Show → Set Up Show from the menu, check the Loop continuously until "Esc" box, and click OK.

Chapter 7
Delivering Your Presentation

Quiz Answers

1. False. PowerPoint already has the ability to doodle on your slides—just press Ctrl + P.

2. True.

3. C. Slide Sorter View is the easiest place to add and work with slide transitions.

4. C.

5. C.

6. False. You can create two custom slide shows—one that includes every slide in the presentation for one audience and another custom show that excludes some of the slides for the other audience.

7. False. The Package for CD feature gives you the option of including the PowerPoint Viewer program, which can display your presentations on computers that don't have PowerPoint installed.

CHAPTER 8
WORKING WITH MULTIMEDIA

CHAPTER OBJECTIVES:

Inserting sound files into your presentation
Adding voice narration to your slides
Inserting a movie clip
Automating the multimedia in your presentation

CHAPTER TASK: ADD MUSIC, SOUNDS, AND A MOVIE CLIP TO A SLIDE

Prerequisites

- Know how to use menus, toolbars, dialog boxes, and shortcut keystrokes.
- Move the mouse pointer and navigate between the slides in a presentation.

Multimedia is a combination of movie, audio, animation, and graphics. Adding multimedia to your slide shows is a great way to make them more interesting and entertaining. In this chapter you will learn how to create slides that contain not only text and pictures, but also sounds and even movie clips.

To use all of the available multimedia features, your PC must be multimedia-ready, which means it needs CD-ROM, a sound card, speakers, and, if you want to record anything, a microphone. If you plan on using movie clips, you will also need a fast computer.

LESSON 8.1 Inserting Sounds

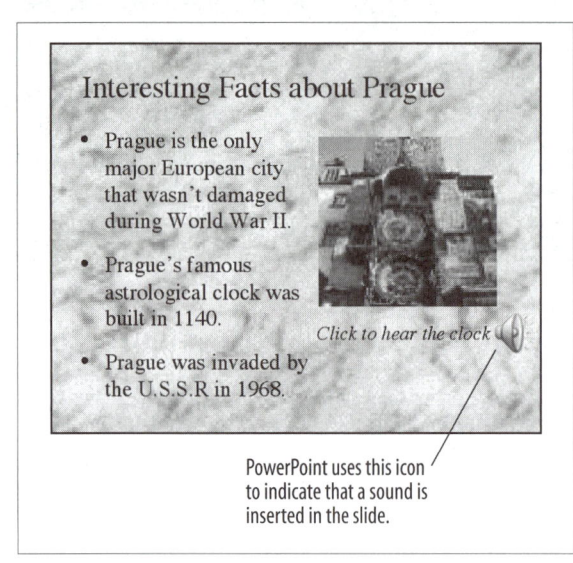

Figure 8-1. A slide with a sound.

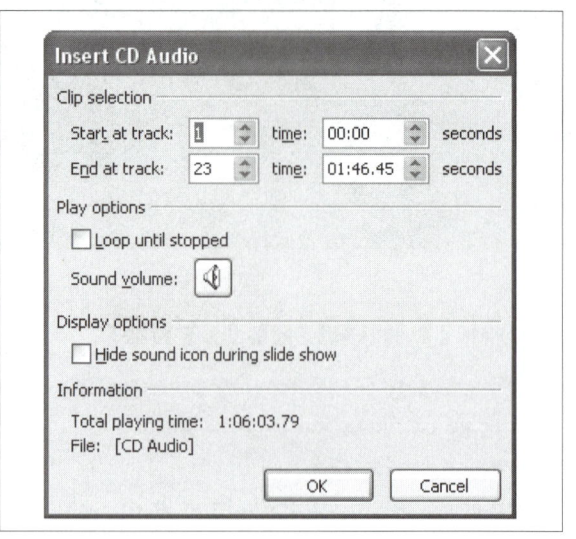

Figure 8-2. The Insert CD Audio dialog box.

TIP *Make sure you have permission to use the audio files you insert in your presentation.*

Since most computers today come with a sound card and speakers, adding music and sound effects to a presentation is a great way to liven things up. PowerPoint comes with a small library of sound files—such as drums rolling, phones ringing, and roosters crowing—that you can incorporate into your presentations. If you can't find the sound you're looking for, you can also insert sounds from external files. There are millions of sound files available on the Internet, if you know where to look. You can even insert songs from your favorite audio CDs into your slides.

There are many types of sound files you can use in your presentations. Refer to Table 8-1 for a list and description of the types of audio files that are compatible with PowerPoint.

Let's get started!

1 Open Lesson 8A, save it as Prague, and then go to Slide 3.

Let's spruce up this slide by adding some classical music from a MIDI file.

2 Make sure you are in Normal View and select Insert → Movies and Sounds → Sound from File from the menu.

Movies and Sounds menu

The Insert Sound dialog box appears. Now all you have to do is find the sound file you want to insert.

3 Navigate to your Practice folder, select the Nocturne 19 file and click OK. Click Automatically in the dialog box that appears.

PowerPoint adds the "Nocturne 19" MIDI sound to the current slide, as indicated by the 🔊 icon. When this slide appears in the slide show, this sound file will automatically play.

Let's hear your computer play Chopin's Nocturne No. 19.

4 Double-click the 🔊 sound icon to start the music. Click the sound icon again to stop the music.

244

Chapter 8
Working with Multimedia

It's easy to remove sounds from your slides—here's how:

5 Delete the Nocturne 19 sound by clicking the 🔊 icon and pressing the Delete key.

Finally, you can also add songs from your favorite audio CDs to your slides.

6 Insert the audio CD that contains the song or track you want to play into your computer's CD-ROM drive.

This audio CD will need to be in your computer's CD-ROM drive each time you want to present the slide show.

7 Select Insert → Movies and Sounds → Play CD Audio Track from the menu.

The Insert CD Audio dialog box appears, as shown in Figure 8-2.

8 Select the Starting and Ending time and track in the appropriate boxes and click OK.

You'll need the CD song list in order to provide PowerPoint with the track(s) that you want to play.

Table 8-1. PowerPoint Compatible Audio Files

File Type	Description
AIFF	Similar to the WAV file format, this file type is common with Mac users. The file is often very large because it is not compressed.
AU	This file type is older and is rarely used.
MIDI	MIDI (pronounced "Mid-ee") files are like sheet music for your computer's sound card. The files are very small, and the quality and sound can vary quite a bit between computers.
MP3	This is probably the most popular audio file type as MP3 players and online music stores increase in popularity. This file is compressed, so it is much smaller than a WAV file.
WAV	This raw audio file is popular, but is not compressed so file types that are much smaller in size are overshadowing it.
WMA	This file is similar to the MP3 in that it is compressed, but it is still larger and is not as compatible with different players.

Lesson 8.1
Inserting Sounds

QUICK REFERENCE

TO INSERT A SOUND FROM THE MICROSOFT CLIP GALLERY:

- SELECT INSERT → MOVIES AND SOUNDS → SOUND FROM CLIP ORGANIZER FROM THE MENU AND THEN DOUBLE-CLICK THE SOUND IN THE TASK PANE.

TO INSERT A SOUND FROM AN EXTERNAL FILE:

1. SELECT INSERT → MOVIES AND SOUNDS → SOUND FROM FILE FROM THE MENU.
2. BROWSE TO THE DRIVE AND FOLDER WHERE THE SOUND FILE IS LOCATED, SELECT THE SOUND FILE, AND CLICK OK.

TO PLAY A SOUND FILE:

- IN NORMAL VIEW: DOUBLE-CLICK THE 🔊 ICON.
- IN SLIDE SHOW VIEW: SINGLE-CLICK THE 🔊 ICON.

TO DELETE A SOUND FILE:

- CLICK THE SOUND FILE'S 🔊 ICON TO SELECT IT AND PRESS THE DELETE KEY.

TO ADD A TRACK FROM AN AUDIO CD:

1. INSERT THE AUDIO CD INTO YOUR COMPUTER'S CD-ROM DRIVE.
2. SELECT INSERT → MOVIES AND SOUNDS → PLAY CD AUDIO TRACK FROM THE MENU.
3. SPECIFY THE STARTING AND ENDING TRACK IN THE APPROPRIATE BOXES AND CLICK OK.

LESSON 8.2

Adding Voice Narration to Your Slides

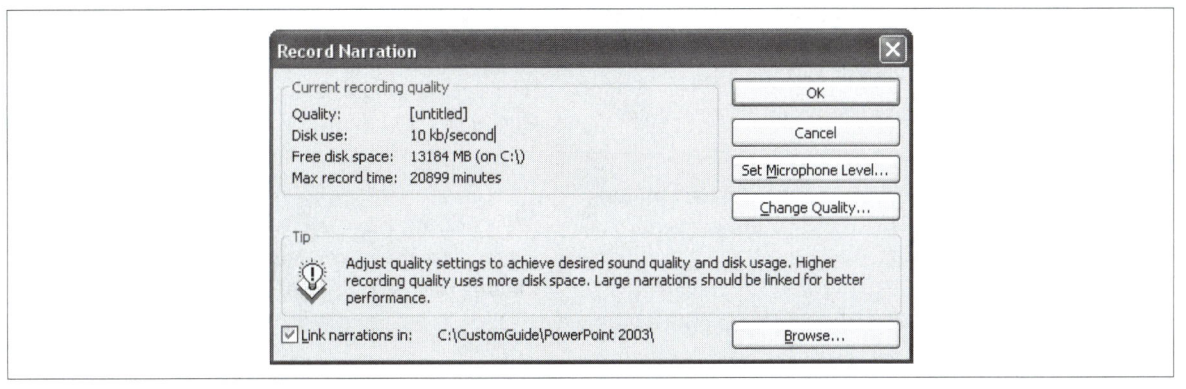

Figure 8-3. The Record Narration dialog box.

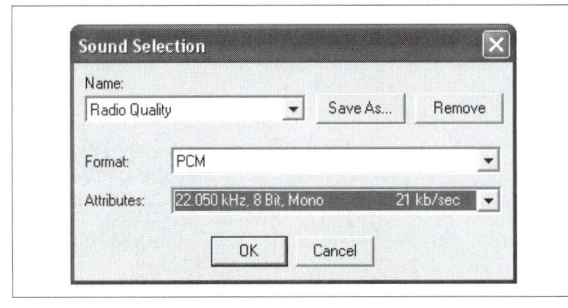

Figure 8-4. The Sound Selection dialog box.

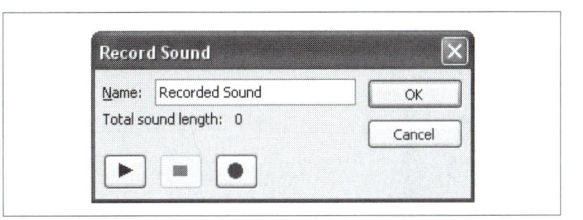

Figure 8-5. The Record Sound dialog box.

TIP *You must have a microphone installed on your computer to record narration.*

Even if you're creating a self-running presentation, you can make sure your audience hears what you have to say by using PowerPoint's Record Narration feature. This feature lets you record your voice to narrate your slide (provided your computer has a microphone).

In this lesson, you'll learn how to record comments for your slides using the Record Narration feature.

1 Select **Slide Show** → **Record Narration** from the menu.

The Record Narration dialog box appears, as shown in Figure 8-3.

2 Click the **Change Quality button**.

The Sound Selection dialog box appears, as shown in Figure 8-4. Here, you can adjust the quality of your recording. You have three choices:

- **CD Quality:** This is the highest recording quality, but it also takes up a lot of storage space. Don't use this setting unless you're planning on singing an opera to narrate your slide show.
- **Radio Quality:** This is a good balance between sound quality and the amount disk space consumed. Radio Quality is the default setting.
- **Telephone Quality:** This is the lowest recording quality setting—the benefit of this setting is that it doesn't require as much storage space as the other settings.

If you're an audio enthusiast, you can also select your own recording quality settings from the Attributes list.

3 Click the **Name** list arrow and select **Telephone Quality** from the list. Click **OK**.

This will allow you to record your voice narration without using much disk space.

Lesson 8.2
Adding Voice Narration to Your Slides

NOTE *No matter which recording quality setting you select, all digital recordings take up a lot of memory. Don't be surprised if the file size of your presentation is several times larger after you add voice narration to it.*

Move on to the next step to record your narration to the slide show. Remember that your computer needs a microphone in order to record your voice.

4 Click OK to start recording the narration. Step through the slide show and add your own voice comments about each slide (be creative).

When you finish stepping through the slide show, PowerPoint asks if you want to save the slide timings (how much time you spent on each slide) in addition to the voice recording. If you're making a self-running slide show, you'll almost always want to answer yes so that the slide show is synchronized with your comments.

5 Click Save to save the slide timings.

PowerPoint displays the presentation in Slide Sorter View. Notice that the slide timings appear to the bottom-left of each slide. If you look hard, you may also be able to see the tiny 🔊 sound icon in the lower-right corner of the slide.

Move on to the next step and see what your updated slide show looks and sounds like.

6 Switch to Slide Show View and watch the narrated slide show.

Deleting a voice narration from an individual slide is no different from deleting any other sound file.

7 Switch to Normal View, go to Slide 1, select the 🔊 sound icon, and press the Delete key.

You've deleted the voice narration for the current slide—the narration on the other slides in the presentation is not affected.

You can also record a sound or command on a single slide. Again, you'll need a microphone to do this.

8 Select Insert → Movies and Sounds → Record Sound from the menu.

The Record Sound dialog box appears, as shown in Figure 8-5. To record a sound, click the ⏺ record button.

9 Click the ⏺ record button and say something clever into the microphone, then stop recording by clicking the ⏹ stop button.

Name your sound.

10 Type My Witty Comment in the Name box and click OK.

The Record Sound dialog box closes and your recorded sound file appears as a 🔊 sound icon on the slide.

Of course you can record other sounds besides your voice with the sound recorder. For example, you could try to get your dog to bark in order to create a sound effect for a slide show on dog shows, or record a baby crying for a slide show about parenting.

Chapter 8
Working with Multimedia

QUICK REFERENCE

YOUR COMPUTER WILL NEED A MICROPHONE TO RECORD SOUNDS.

TO ADD VOICE NARRATION TO A PRESENTATION:

1. SELECT **SLIDE SHOW** → **RECORD NARRATION** FROM THE MENU.
2. (OPTIONAL) CLICK THE **CHANGE QUALITY** BUTTON AND SPECIFY THE RECORDING QUALITY (HIGHER QUALITY = BIGGER FILES). CLICK **OK** WHEN YOU'RE FINISHED.
3. SPECIFY IF YOU WANT TO SAVE THE SLIDE TIMINGS WITH THE NARRATION (USUALLY YOU WILL WANT TO ANSWER **YES**), AND IF YOU WANT TO WATCH THE NARRATED PRESENTATION.

TO RECORD AND INSERT A SOUND ON A SLIDE:

1. SELECT **INSERT** → **MOVIES AND SOUNDS** → **RECORD SOUND** FROM THE MENU.
2. CLICK THE **RECORD BUTTON**, RECORD THE SOUND, AND CLICK THE **STOP BUTTON** WHEN YOU'RE FINISHED.
3. ENTER A NAME FOR YOUR SOUND AND CLICK **OK**.

TO DELETE A SLIDE'S NARRATION:

- SELECT THE **SOUND ICON** IN THE LOWER RIGHT CORNER OF THE SLIDE AND PRESS THE **DELETE** KEY.

LESSON 8.3 Inserting a Movie Clip

Figure 8-6. The updated slide.

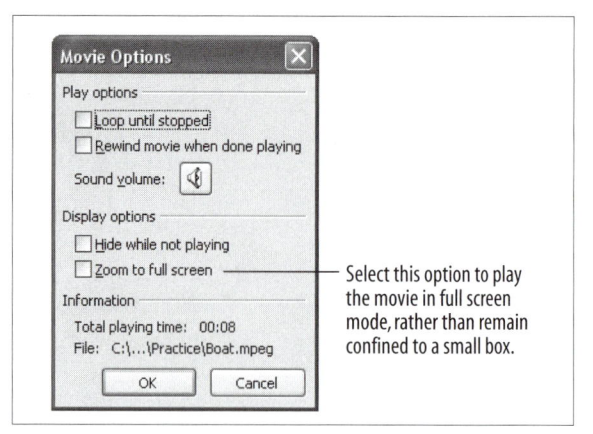

Figure 8-7. The Movie Options dialog box.

One spectacular object you can add to a slide is a movie clip. Adding a movie clip to a slide is similar to adding a sound clip. Since movies are seen *and* heard, you will need to give them ample room on the slide, just like you would if you inserted a picture. Also, movie clips require lots of memory. Movie file sizes are almost always much larger than 1 MB, which is why most people don't use them in their presentations.

Movie clips come in several file formats, including:

- **Animated GIF:** Animated GIF files are short animations that can make your presentations more active and interesting. Many of the annoying advertisements you see all too often on the Internet are animated GIFs.
- **QuickTime:** QuickTime is an older but still very popular movie file format that doesn't require any special hardware to play. QuickTime movies have either a MOV or QT file extension.
- **AVI:** AVI (windows video file) movie files are smaller than QuickTime movies, and many of the movie clips found in the Microsoft Clip Organizer use this file format.
- **MPEG:** MPEG is a compressed movie file format that has much smaller file sizes than either QuickTime or AVI. The only problem with MPEG files is that you may need special decompression software or hardware to play them.

The Microsoft Clip Organizer comes with quite a few GIF and AVI movie files you can use in your slides, or you can also insert external movie files. After you have embedded a movie, you can change its size on your screen, automate when it plays, and/or have it play once or continuously. In this lesson you will learn how to work with a movie object.

1 Make sure you're in Normal View and go to Slide 1.

Here's how to insert a movie file.

2 Select Insert → Movies and Sounds → Movie from File from the menu.

The Insert Movie dialog box appears.

Now all you have to do is rummage around until you find the movie file you want to insert.

3 Navigate to your Practice folder, select the Boat file, and click OK.

Another dialog box appears, asking if you want the movie to start automatically when the slide appears, or when clicked.

4 Click Automatically.

PowerPoint adds the "Boat" movie to the current slide, as shown in Figure 8-6. When your presentation runs, this movie will play automatically. Go ahead and double-click the movie if you want to view it.

5 Double-click the movie picture.

PowerPoint plays the movie clip.

Just like any other slide object, you can format, resize, and delete a movie. Since the movie obscures our slide title, we need to move it.

Chapter 8
Working with Multimedia

6 Drag the movie object to the right of the slide title, as shown in Figure 8-6.

You can also specify if you want to play the movie over and over again in a continuous loop, or just once, by right-clicking the movie object, selecting Edit Movie Object from the shortcut menu, and selecting your options. If this file happened to be an animated GIF file instead of an MPEG file, we would not be able to change its options.

7 Switch to Slide Show View to see the movie in the presentation.

The movie automatically begins to play when the slide appears in the slide show.

Notice that the movie is relatively small and difficult to see in the slide. You can play the movie in full screen mode to get the full effect.

8 Press Esc to quit the slide show. Right-click the movie object. Select Edit Movie Object from the shortcut menu.

The Movie Options dialog box appears.

9 Select the Zoom to full screen checkbox. Click OK.

Now instead of being confined to a small box, the movie will play in the full screen when shown.

Let's try it.

10 Switch to Slide Show View to see the movie in the presentation.

The movie expands to the full screen when shown from the presentation.

If you choose this option, it's probably better to run the movie when clicked, rather than automatically. Otherwise there may not be time to see the rest of the slide.

QUICK REFERENCE

TO INSERT A MOVIE FILE:

1. SELECT INSERT → MOVIES AND SOUNDS → MOVIE FROM FILE FROM THE MENU.
2. BROWSE TO THE DRIVE AND FOLDER WHERE THE MOVIE FILE IS LOCATED, SELECT THE MOVIE FILE, AND CLICK OK.

TO PLAY A MOVIE CLIP CONTINUOUSLY (LOOPING):

- RIGHT-CLICK THE MOVIE OBJECT, SELECT EDIT MOVIE OBJECT FROM THE SHORTCUT MENU, SELECT THE LOOP UNTIL STOPPED OPTION, AND CLICK OK.

TO PLAY A MOVIE CLIP IN FULL SCREEN MODE:

- RIGHT-CLICK THE MOVIE OBJECT, SELECT EDIT MOVIE OBJECT FROM THE SHORTCUT MENU, SELECT THE ZOOM TO FULL SCREEN OPTION, AND CLICK OK.

LESSON 8.4

Automating the Multimedia in Your Presentation

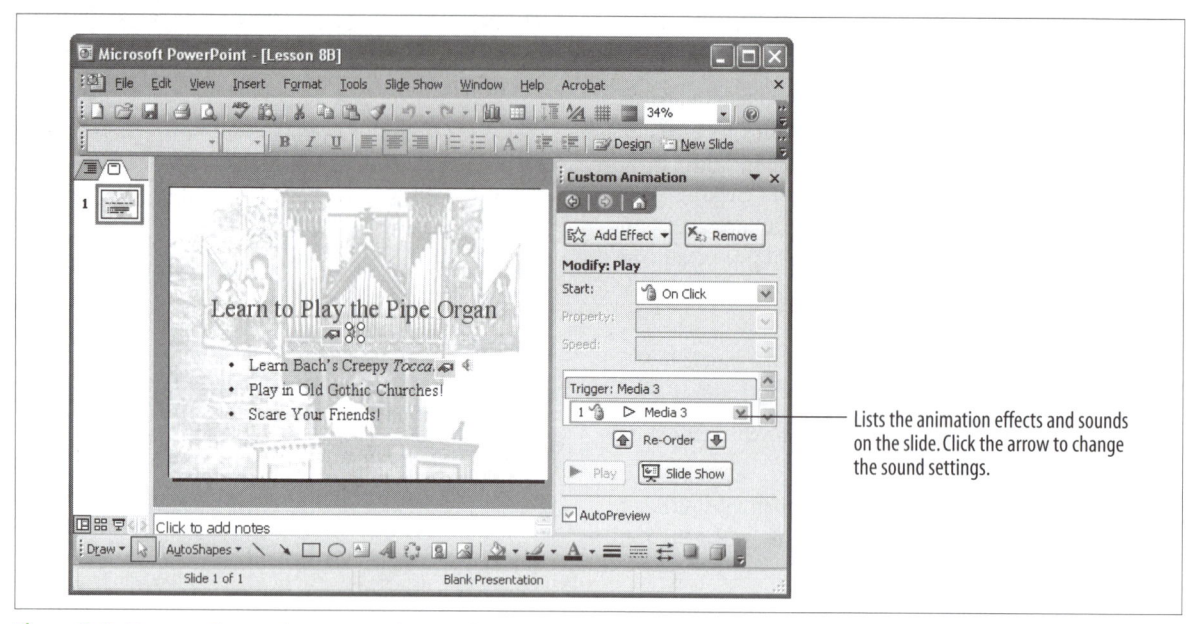

Figure 8-8. You can change the settings of a sound or movie in the Custom Animation task pane.

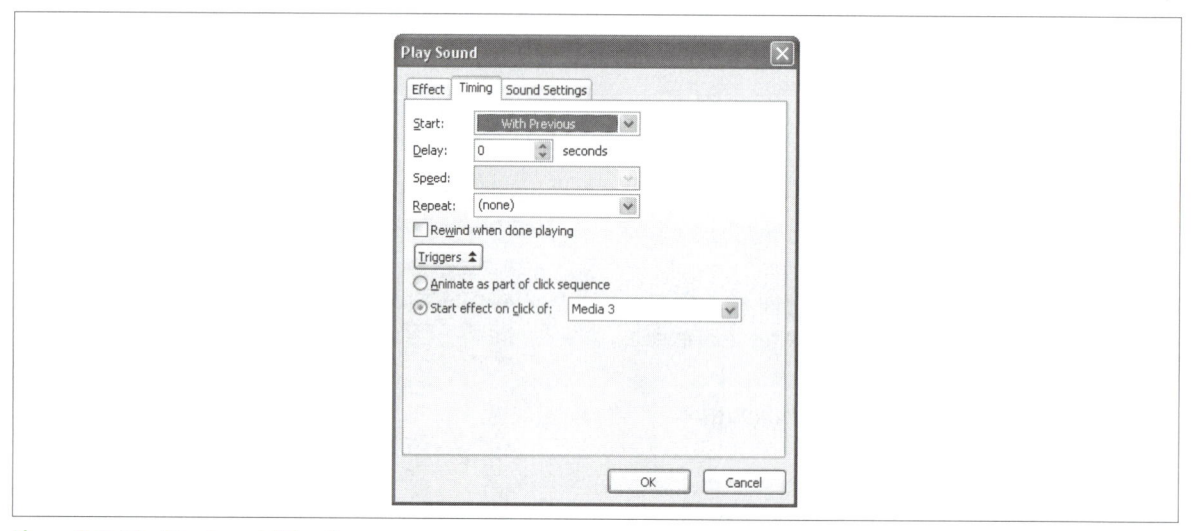

Lists the animation effects and sounds on the slide. Click the arrow to change the sound settings.

Figure 8-9. The Play Sound dialog box.

When you insert a movie or sound, PowerPoint asks if you want it to play automatically or only when clicked. In this lesson you will learn how to change this after the sound or file has been inserted. You will also learn how to arrange the playing order of media files if there are multiple files on the slide.

1 Open **Lesson 8B**.

This presentation contains two sounds. As is, you have to click the 🔊 sound icon in order to play each sound, but we want the sounds to play automatically.

2 Double-click the 🔊 **sound icon** in the middle of the slide.

Dong! It's the sound of a bell. Move on to the next step and change the settings so that the bell sound plays when the slide appears in the slide show.

252

Chapter 8
Working with Multimedia

3 Click the sound icon in the middle of the slide to select it, then select Slide Show → Custom Animation from the menu.

The Custom Animation task pane appears, as shown in Figure 8-8. Since you have selected the icon in the middle of the slide, the option named Media 3 in the task pane should be selected as well. The sound object, which PowerPoint refers to as Media 3, appears first in the list of animation order. Here's how to specify when and how a sound plays…

4 Click the Media 3 list arrow and select Start With Previous from the list.

This will trigger the bell sound to start with the previous event—and we will specify that previous event in the next step.

5 Click the Media 3 arrow and select Timing from the list.

The Play Sound dialog box appears, as shown in Figure 8-9. In this dialog box, you can control the sequence and timings of when an event occurs, such as whether a sound is triggered by clicking the mouse or the order in which a sound occurs. There are two options for triggering when a sound or event occurs:

- **Animate as part of click sequence:** The animation is triggered as part of the click sequence displayed in the animation list.
- **Start effect on click of:** The animation is triggered when you click an object that you select from the drop-down list.

Instead of triggering the bell sound by clicking it, we will tell PowerPoint to play the sound as part of a click sequence.

NOTE *If at this point you're thinking to yourself, "This sound trigger stuff is much more difficult than it should be," you're not alone. Sound animation was, quite frankly, much easier to work with in previous versions of PowerPoint. For reasons unknown, Microsoft decided to needlessly complicate the procedure in PowerPoint 2003. Hopefully they will make things more user-friendly in the next version of PowerPoint.*

6 Select the Animate as part of click sequence option.

This will play the bell sound immediately when the slide appears on the screen.

7 Click OK to close the Play Sound dialog box.

The bell sound on the slide will now play automatically when the slide appears.

You may have noticed that there is a second media object on the slide. Let's change its settings so it plays after the bell sound.

8 Click the Bach's *Toccata* sound icon to select it.

This media object is named Media 4 in the Custom Animations task pane.

9 Click the Media 4 list arrow and select Start After Previous.

Now make sure the sound will play as part of the same sequence as the previous effect.

10 Click the Media 4 arrow and select Timing. Select the Animate as part of click sequence option and click OK.

Let's see if the new settings work.

11 Switch to Slide Show view by clicking the Slide Show button on the horizontal toolbar.

The bell sound plays as soon as the slide appears, and the *Toccata* plays after it.

12 Exit Microsoft PowerPoint without saving your work.

Lesson 8.4
Automating the Multimedia in Your Presentation

QUICK REFERENCE

TO PLAY A SOUND OR MOVIE CLIP AUTOMATICALLY:

1. SELECT THE SOUND OR MOVIE FILE YOU WANT TO AUTOMATE AND SELECT **SLIDE SHOW → CUSTOM ANIMATION** FROM THE MENU.

   OR...

   RIGHT-CLICK THE OBJECT YOU WANT TO ANIMATE AND SELECT **CUSTOM ANIMATION** FROM THE SHORTCUT MENU.

2. CLICK THE SLIDE OBJECT'S **LIST ARROW** AND SPECIFY WHEN YOU WANT THE OBJECT TO START.

TO CHANGE MEDIA TIMING:

1. CLICK THE DESIRED SOUND'S **LIST ARROW** AND SELECT **TIMINGS** FROM THE LIST.

2. SPECIFY THE DESIRED SOUND/EVENT TRIGGER OPTION AND CLICK **OK**.

Chapter Eight Review

Lesson Summary

Inserting Sound Files into Your Presentation

To Insert a Sound from the Microsoft Clip Gallery: Select Insert → Movies and Sounds → Sound from Clip Organizer from the menu and then double-click the selected sound from the task pane.

To Insert a Sound from an External File: Select Insert → Movies and Sounds → Sound from File from the menu, browse to the drive and folder where the sound file is located, select the sound file, and click OK.

To Play a Sound File: Double-click the 🔊 icon if you're in Normal View. If you're in Slide Show View, single-click the 🔊 icon.

To Delete a Sound File: Click the sound file's 🔊 icon to select it and press the Delete key.

To Add a Track from an Audio CD: Insert the audio CD into your computer's CD-ROM drive, select Insert → Movies and Sounds → Play CD Audio Track from the menu, specify the starting and ending track in the appropriate boxes, and click OK.

Adding Voice Narration to Your Slides

To Add Voice Narration to a Presentation: Select Slide Show → Record Narration from the menu. Click OK and record your narration as you advance through the slides.

You can change the recording quality from the Record Narration dialog box by clicking the Change Quality button and specifying the recording quality (higher quality = bigger files). Click OK when you're finished.

To Delete a Slide's Narration: Select the sound file 🔊 icon in the lower right corner of the slide and press the Delete key.

Inserting a Movie Clip

To Insert a Movie File: Select Insert → Movies and Sounds → Movie from File from the menu. Browse to the drive and folder where the movie file is located, select the movie file, and click OK.

To Play a Movie Clip: Double-click the movie clip object if you're in Normal View. If you're in Slide Show View, single-click the movie clip object.

To Play a Movie Clip Continuously (Looping): Right-click the movie object, select Edit Movie Object from the shortcut menu, select the Loop until stopped option, and click OK.

Automating the Multimedia in Your Presentation

Inserted movies and sounds don't automatically play when you display the slide unless you specify otherwise.

To Play a Sound or Movie File Automatically: Select the sound or movie file you want to automate and select Slide Show → Custom Animation from the menu, or right-click the object you want to animate and select Custom Animation from the shortcut menu. Click the desired sound's ▼ arrow and select Timings from the list. Click the ▼ Start arrow and specify when you want the sound to start. Click OK when you're finished with your specifications.

Quiz

1. How can you insert a movie into a PowerPoint slide?

   A. You need a movie camera and a USB cable.
   B. You need to buy Microsoft Movie Maker.
   C. Click the Insert Movie button on the Standard toolbar.
   D. Select Insert → Movies and Sounds → Movie from File from the menu.

2. Which of the following are types of sound files? (Select all that apply.)

   A. AVI files
   B. WAV files
   C. MIDI files
   D. LOG files

255

Chapter 8
Chapter Eight Review

3. Your computer needs a microphone to use which of the following PowerPoint commands:

    A. Insert → Movies and Sounds → Record Sound

    B. Insert → Recording

    C. Insert → Movies and Sounds → Narration

    D. Slide Show → Record Narration

Homework

1. Open the Homework 3 presentation located in your Practice folder or disk and save it as "Television Show."

2. Insert a WAV file into a slide. Make sure that you are on Slide 1 and select Insert → Movies and Sounds → Sound from File from the menu. Navigate to your Practice folder or disk, select the "Three's Company" file, and click OK.

3. Click Automatically in the dialog box that appears. This will ensure that the sound plays automatically when the slide is displayed.

4. Double-click the 🔊 icon to hear the crazy theme song.

5. Switch to Slide Show View and run the slide show with the automated music.

Quiz Answers

1. D.

2. B and C. These are both types of sound files.

3. A and D. You will need a microphone if you are recording any kind of sound or voice narration to your slides.

CHAPTER 9
WORKING WITH OTHER PROGRAMS AND THE INTERNET

CHAPTER OBJECTIVES:

Inserting a presentation into a Microsoft Word document
Embedding a Microsoft Excel worksheet into a slide
Modifying an embedded object
Importing and exporting an outline
Using hyperlinks and action buttons
Saving a presentation as a web page

CHAPTER TASK: EXCHANGE INFORMATION BETWEEN PROGRAMS

Prerequisites

- **Know how to use menus, toolbars, dialog boxes, and shortcut keystrokes.**
- **Move the mouse pointer and navigate between the slides in a presentation.**
- **Know how to browse through drives and folders on your computer.**
- **A basic understanding of Microsoft Word and Microsoft Excel.**

One of the great benefits of working with Windows is that you can share information between different programs, and no other program in Microsoft Office uses information from other programs more than PowerPoint does. Have you ever created a slide that contains a chart, table, or organizational chart? If so, then you've already used PowerPoint with another program—even if you weren't aware of it. In this chapter you will learn how to insert a PowerPoint presentation into a Microsoft Word document, and how to insert Microsoft Excel worksheets and charts into your slides. You'll also learn the subtle differences between embedding and linking files into other programs.

The other main topics this chapter covers are how to add hyperlinks to your slides and how to save your PowerPoint presentations as Web pages, which can then be published on the Internet and viewed by millions of people. Whew! We have a lot of ground to cover. Turn the page and we'll get started.

LESSON 9.1   Inserting a Slide into a Microsoft Word Document

Figure 9-1. The Create New tab of the Object dialog box.

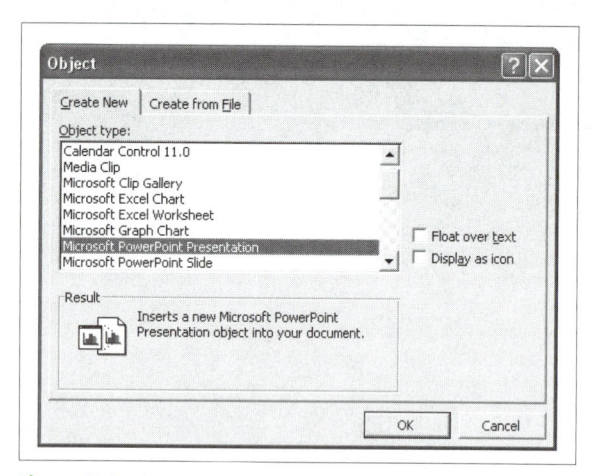

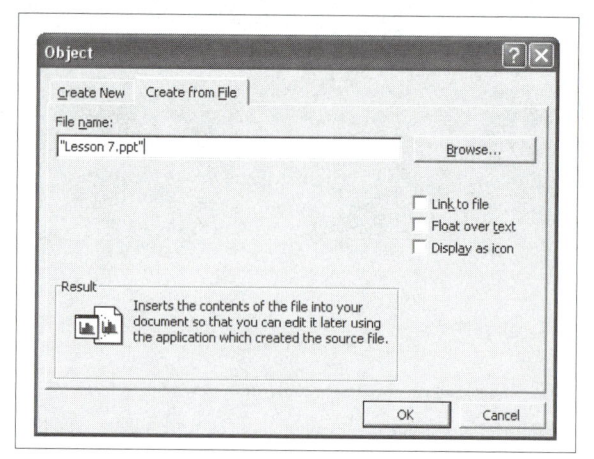

Figure 9-2. The Create from File tab of the Object dialog box.

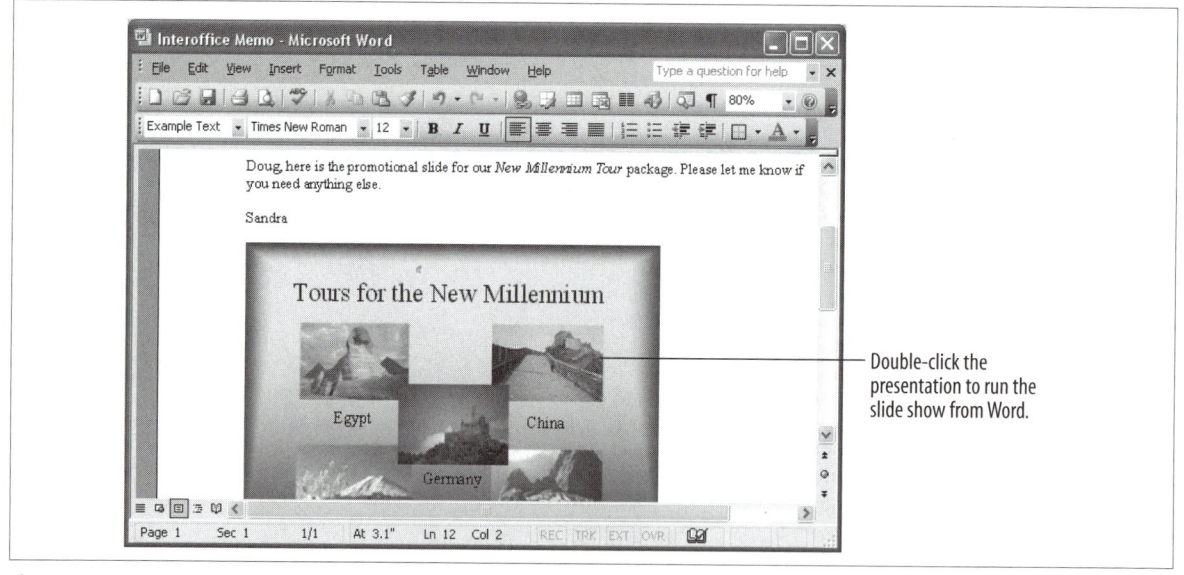

Figure 9-3. A Microsoft PowerPoint presentation inserted in a Word document.

If you work with Microsoft PowerPoint, you probably use Microsoft Word as well. Since Word is part of the Microsoft Office 2003 Suite, it makes sense that people use PowerPoint together with Word more than any other program. In this lesson, you will learn how to embed a PowerPoint presentation into a Word document.

1 Start the Microsoft Office Word 2003 program.

2 Navigate to your Practice folder or disk and open the document named Interoffice Memo.

The procedure for opening a file in Word is identical to opening a file in PowerPoint. Click the Open button on the Standard toolbar or select File → Open from the menu. The Interoffice Memo document appears in Word's main document window.

3 Move the insertion point to the end of the document by pressing the down arrow key ↓, or by clicking the end of the document with the mouse.

This is where you want to insert your presentation.

258

Chapter 9
Working with Other Programs and the Internet

4 Select **Insert → Object** from the menu.

The Object dialog box appears with the Create New tab in front, as shown in Figure 9-1. You can create and insert new objects with the Create New tab, or you can insert an existing file with the Create from File tab. In this exercise you'll be inserting an existing PowerPoint presentation.

5 Click the **Create from File** tab.

The Create from File tab appears in front, as shown in Figure 9-2. You need to specify the name and location of the file you want to insert into the document.

6 Click the **Browse button**.

The Browse dialog box appears, allowing you to find and locate the file you want to insert into your document.

7 If necessary, navigate to your PowerPoint Practice folder.

The file list box is updated to show all the files on the Practice folder.

8 Select the **Lesson 7A** file.

Notice that the icon for the Lesson 7A file indicates that it is a Microsoft PowerPoint file.

9 Click **Insert**.

The Browse dialog box closes and you return to the Create from File tab of the Object dialog box. Notice that the "Lesson 7A" file name and location appear in the File name box.

There are several other options on this page you should know about:

- **Link to file:** Inserted objects are normally *embedded*, or saved, inside the files they are inserted in. If you check the *Link to file* option, the object will still be inserted in the file, but Word will only create a link to the original file instead of saving a copy of it inside the file. You should use the Link to file when you want to ensure that any changes made in the original file are updated and reflected in the file it is inserted in.

- **Display as icon:** Inserted objects are normally viewable directly from the Word document window. Checking the Display as icon box option causes the inserted objects to appear only as an icon. You must double-click the object in order to view it.

10 Click **OK**.

Word accesses the PowerPoint presentation file and then inserts it into the document at the insertion point.

NOTE Double-click the presentation to run the PowerPoint slide show from Word.

11 Compare your document with the one in Figure 9-3, then exit Microsoft Word without saving your changes.

> ### QUICK REFERENCE
>
> **TO INSERT A PRESENTATION INTO A WORD DOCUMENT:**
>
> 1. OPEN THE MICROSOFT WORD DOCUMENT AND PLACE THE INSERTION POINT WHERE YOU WANT THE PRESENTATION INSERTED.
>
> 2. SELECT **INSERT → OBJECT** FROM THE MENU.
>
> 3. CLICK THE **CREATE FROM FILE** TAB TO USE AN EXISTING PRESENTATION FILE, OR CLICK THE **CREATE NEW** TAB TO CREATE A NEW PRESENTATION.
>
> 4. SELECT THE POWERPOINT PRESENTATION FILE YOU WANT TO INSERT (IF YOU SELECTED CREATE FROM FILE) AND CLICK **INSERT**, OR CREATE THE PRESENTATION FROM SCRATCH (IF YOU SELECTED CREATE NEW). CLICK **OK**.

LESSON 9.2 — Embedding a Microsoft Excel Worksheet into a Slide

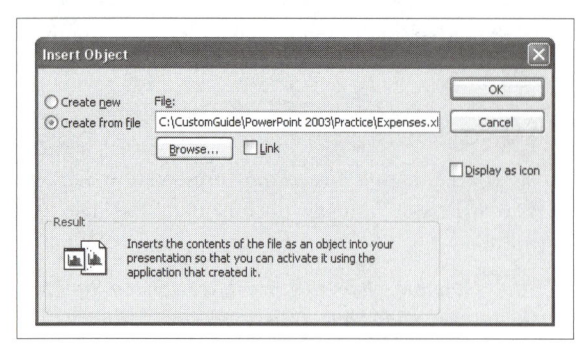

Figure 9-4. The Insert Object dialog box with the Create from file button selected.

Figure 9-5. A Microsoft Excel worksheet inserted in a slide.

Chances are you've already embedded an object or file created in another program into a PowerPoint slide. Organizational charts, tables, and WordArt objects are all examples of embedded objects. PowerPoint makes it easy to insert these and other objects and files created in a different program into your slides.

Microsoft Excel is a spreadsheet program that can calculate numbers and information, create charts and graphs, and perform many other useful functions. Since Excel is part of the Microsoft Office 2003 suite, it is very useful to use with PowerPoint presentations. It is especially helpful when working with presentations made for financial purposes. In this lesson, you will learn how to embed an Excel worksheet into a PowerPoint presentation.

1 Start Microsoft PowerPoint, select File → New from the menu and select Blank presentation from the task pane.

Microsoft PowerPoint starts with a blank presentation.

2 Select the Title Only layout from the Slide Layout task pane.

Title Only layout

Now you're ready to insert the Excel object.

3 Select Insert → Object from the menu.

The Insert Object dialog box appears, as shown in Figure 9-4. You have to select one of the following:

- **Create new:** Inserts a new object on the current slide. Click the type of object you want to create in the Object type list, then create the object.
- **Create from file:** Inserts an object from an existing file into the current slide. Type the object's file name in the File box or click Browse to locate the file.

4 Click the Create from file option.

The Insert Object dialog box updates so that it includes a text box where you can specify the name and location of the file you want to insert, as shown in Figure 9-4. If you don't know the name or location of the file, you can also look for it by clicking the Browse button.

5 Click the Browse button.

The Browse dialog box appears, allowing you to find and locate the file you want to insert into your slide.

6 If necessary, navigate to your Practice folder.

The file list box is updated to show all the files in the Practice folder.

7 Select the Expenses file and click Insert.

Move on to the next step to insert the "Expenses" Excel worksheet into the current slide.

Chapter 9
Working with Other Programs and the Internet

8 Click OK.

The Insert Object dialog box closes and PowerPoint inserts the "Expenses" Excel worksheet into the current slide.

9 Click the title placeholder and type Trade Show Expenses.

10 Save your work as Expenses.

QUICK REFERENCE

TO INSERT AN EMBEDDED OBJECT INTO A SLIDE:

1. MAKE SURE THE SLIDE YOU WANT TO EMBED THE WORKSHEET IN USES THE TITLE ONLY LAYOUT.
2. SELECT INSERT → OBJECT FROM THE MENU.
3. FOLLOW EITHER OF THE FOLLOWING STEPS TO CREATE A NEW OBJECT OR TO INSERT AN EXISTING FILE.

TO INSERT AN EMBEDDED OBJECT (CREATE NEW):

- FOLLOW THE STEPS TO INSERT A SLIDE OBJECT, SELECT THE CREATE NEW OPTION, SELECT THE OBJECT TYPE YOU WANT TO CREATE, AND CLICK OK.

TO INSERT AN EMBEDDED OBJECT (CREATE FROM FILE):

- FOLLOW THE STEPS TO INSERT A SLIDE OBJECT, SELECT THE CREATE FROM FILE OPTION, CLICK BROWSE, BROWSE TO AND SELECT THE FILE YOU WANT TO INSERT, AND CLICK INSERT. CLICK OK.

LESSON 9.3

Modifying an Embedded Object

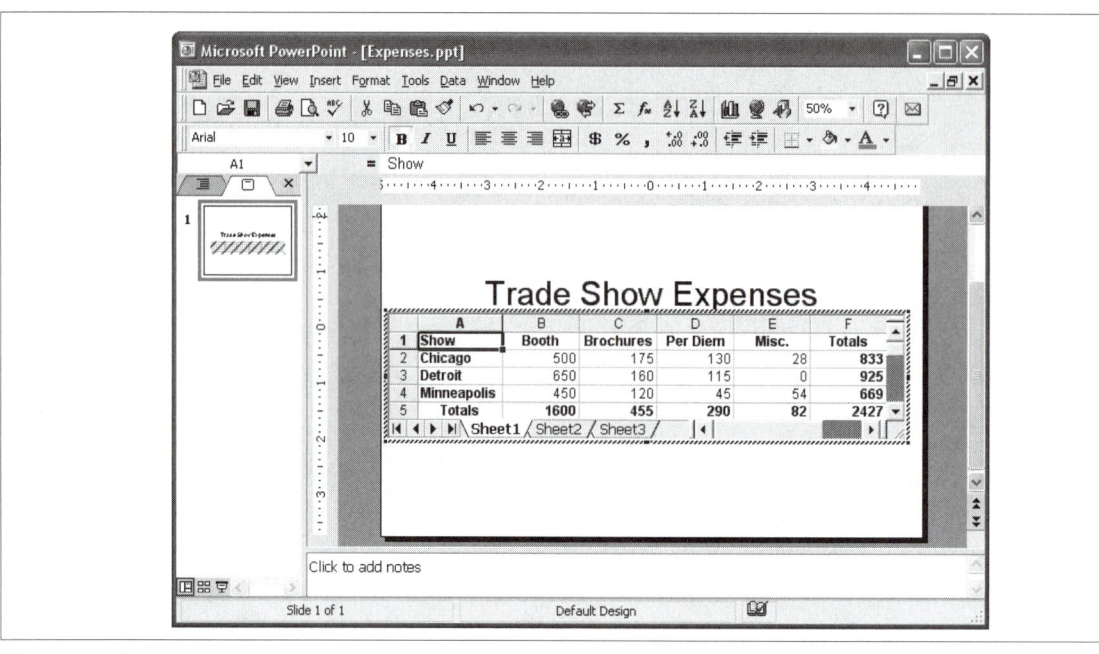

Figure 9-6. Modifying an Excel Worksheet object.

Figure 9-7. The modified worksheet.

Excel Row headings

TIP *Double-click an embedded object to edit or modify it.*

After you insert an Excel worksheet, you can make changes to the worksheet simply by double-clicking it. Double-clicking any embedded or linked object in PowerPoint opens the source program that the object was created in (in the case of this lesson, Microsoft Excel). If the program in which the object was created isn't installed on your computer, you can still view and print the object in PowerPoint; you just can't make changes to it.

1 Double-click the inserted **worksheet** object on the slide.

The Excel program opens inside of PowerPoint, as shown in Figure 9-6. Notice that Excel menus and toolbars replace the PowerPoint toolbars and menus. Now you can make changes to the worksheet object.

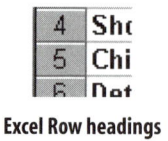

2 Select the cell **B2** (the one containing the 500 Chicago Booth expense).

With the cell selected, you can replace the cell's data simply by typing.

3 Type **515**, then press **Tab**.

The number 515 replaces the number 500 and Excel moves to the next cell.

4 Select the entire Detroit row by clicking the gray **row 3 heading**.

The entire row is selected. Move on to the next step to insert a new row.

5 Select **Insert** → **Rows** from the menu.

A new row is inserted immediately above the Detroit row. Now enter the data for the new row.

262

6 Select the first cell in the new row, type `Milwaukee`, and press Tab to move to the next cell.

7 Type the following information, pressing Tab after making each entry: `470` Tab `135` Tab `110` Tab `25` Tab.

Now that you have entered the data for this row, you can calculate its total.

8 Click the Excel AutoSum button on the Standard toolbar.

Excel AutoSum button

Excel makes an educated guess as to which cells you want to total, and selects them with a line of marching ants. In your case, Excel guesses correctly, so you can confirm the cell selection.

9 Press Enter to accept the formula.

Excel calculates the row total and moves to the next cell. Notice that after you inserted a new row, the bottom total row is no longer displayed. Resize the Excel worksheet object so that the entire worksheet is displayed.

10 Position the pointer over the lower-right sizing handle until the pointer changes to a ↘, then click and hold the left mouse button and drag the mouse diagonally down and to the left until you can see the bottom row of the worksheet. Release the mouse button.

The entire worksheet object should now be visible in the presentation window.

11 Click anywhere outside the worksheet object to stop modifying it and return to PowerPoint.

The standard PowerPoint menu and toolbars replace the Excel menu and toolbars. Compare your presentation to the one in Figure 9-7.

12 Your chart may be too small to be adequately viewed. If necessary, resize and move the chart to make it more viewable.

13 Save your work.

It can be confusing knowing all the differences between linked and embedded objects. Table 9-1 compares both of these methods for inserting information created with other programs into PowerPoint presentations.

Table 9-1. Embedded vs. Linked Objects

Object	Description
Embedded	An embedded object is actually saved within the PowerPoint presentation. PowerPoint presentation files with embedded objects are larger than files with linked objects. The advantage of using embedded objects is that because the objects are actually saved inside the PowerPoint presentation, you don't have to worry about any linked files becoming erased or lost.
Linked	A linked object is not saved in the PowerPoint presentation. Instead, a link contains information on where to find the source data file. The advantage of using linked objects is if the source file is changed, the linked object in the PowerPoint presentation is automatically updated to reflect the changes.

Lesson 9.3
Modifying an Embedded Object

QUICK REFERENCE

TO MODIFY AN OBJECT:
- DOUBLE-CLICK THE OBJECT.

EMBEDDED VS. LINKED OBJECTS:
- EMBEDDED: EMBEDDED OBJECTS ARE ACTUALLY SAVED WITHIN THE POWERPOINT PRESENTATION. THE ADVANTAGE OF EMBEDDED OBJECTS IS THAT YOU DON'T HAVE TO WORRY ABOUT ANY LINKED FILES BECOMING ERASED OR LOST.
- LINKED: LINKED OBJECTS ARE NOT SAVED WITHIN A PRESENTATION BUT ARE LINKED TO AN EXTERNAL FILE. IF THE LINKED FILE IS CHANGED, THE PRESENTATION IS UPDATED TO REFLECT THE CHANGES.

Inserting a Linked Excel Chart

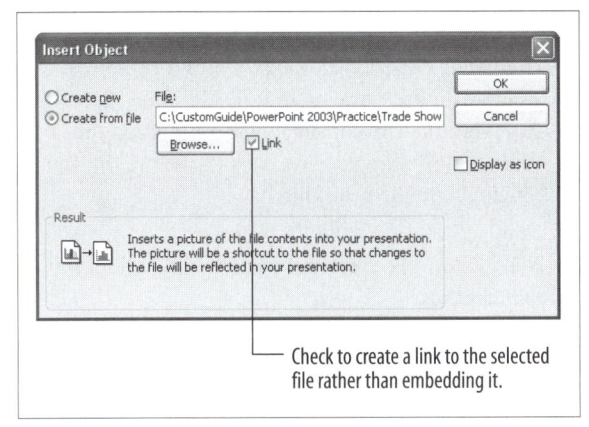

LESSON 9.4

Figure 9-8. You can insert a linked Microsoft Excel chart object.

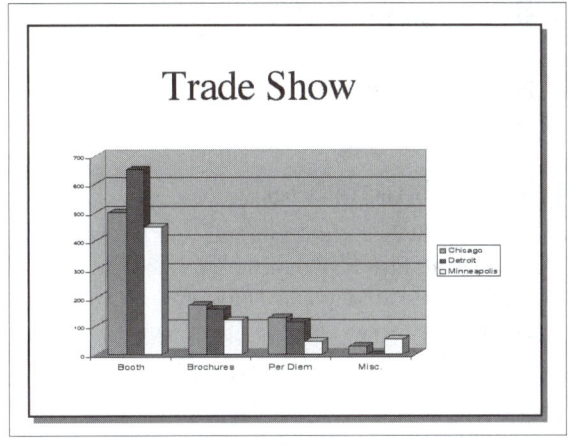

Check to create a link to the selected file rather than embedding it.

Figure 9-9. A linked Excel chart.

So far you have been inserting and working with an embedded Excel worksheet. This lesson mixes things up a bit. You will still be inserting information created in Excel, but this time you will be inserting a *linked* Excel chart. Remember that when you insert an *embedded* object, you are actually storing and saving the object inside the file. A *linked* file is not stored and saved in a PowerPoint presentation, but is connected to it. So if you make changes to the linked source file, it will be automatically updated in the PowerPoint presentation.

1 Click the **New Slide button** on the Formatting toolbar to add a new slide to the current presentation.

New Slide button

Other Ways to Add a Slide:
- Select **Insert** → **New Slide** from the menu.

Again, you'll want to insert a Title Only slide here.

2 Click the **Title Only** slide layout in the task pane.

Title Only layout

PowerPoint adds a blank object slide to your presentation.

3 Click the **title placeholder** and type **Trade Show Expenses**.

Now insert the embedded object.

4 Select **Insert** → **Object** from the menu.

The Insert Object dialog box appears. You have to select one of the following two choices:

- **Create new:** Inserts a new object on the current slide. Click the type of object you want to create in the Object type list, then create the object.
- **Create from file:** Inserts an object from an existing file on the current slide. Type the object's file name in the File box, or click Browse to locate the file.

Since the chart you want to insert already exists in a file, you need to select the Create from file option.

5 Select the **Create from file** option.

The Insert Object dialog box updates so that it includes a text box where you can specify the name and location of the linked file you want to insert, as shown in Figure 9-8.

6 Click the **Browse button**.

The Browse dialog box appears, allowing you to find and locate the file you want to insert into your slide.

7 Navigate to your Practice folder.

The file list box is updated to show all the files in the Practice folder or disk.

265

Lesson 9.4
Inserting a Linked Excel Chart

8 Select the Trade Show Chart file and click OK.

Normally, PowerPoint embeds any files you insert into a slide—here's how to create a link to the inserted file instead.

9 Click the Link check box.

Checking the Link check box only inserts a link to the specified file instead of inserting an embedded copy of the file. You should use the Link option if you want to display any changes made to the original file in the slide.

10 Click OK.

The Insert Object dialog box closes and PowerPoint inserts a linked copy of the "Trade Show Expenses" chart into the current slide. If you modified the chart object, your changes would be saved in the linked "Trade Show Expenses" file.

11 Close the presentation without saving any of your changes.

QUICK REFERENCE

TO INSERT A LINKED OBJECT FILE:

1. CLICK THE NEW SLIDE BUTTON ON THE FORMATTING TOOLBAR AND SELECT THE TITLE ONLY LAYOUT FROM THE TASK PANE.

2. SELECT INSERT → OBJECT FROM THE MENU.

3. SELECT THE CREATE FROM FILE OPTION, CLICK BROWSE, SELECT THE FILE YOU WANT TO INSERT, AND CLICK OK.

4. CHECK THE LINK BOX AND CLICK OK.

Importing and Exporting an Outline

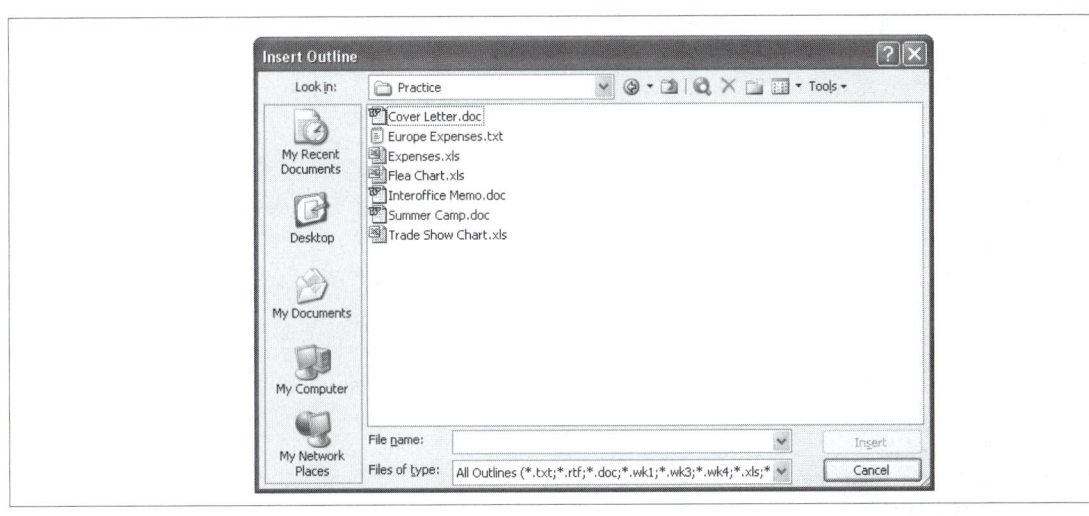

LESSON 9.5

Figure 9-10. The Insert Outline dialog box.

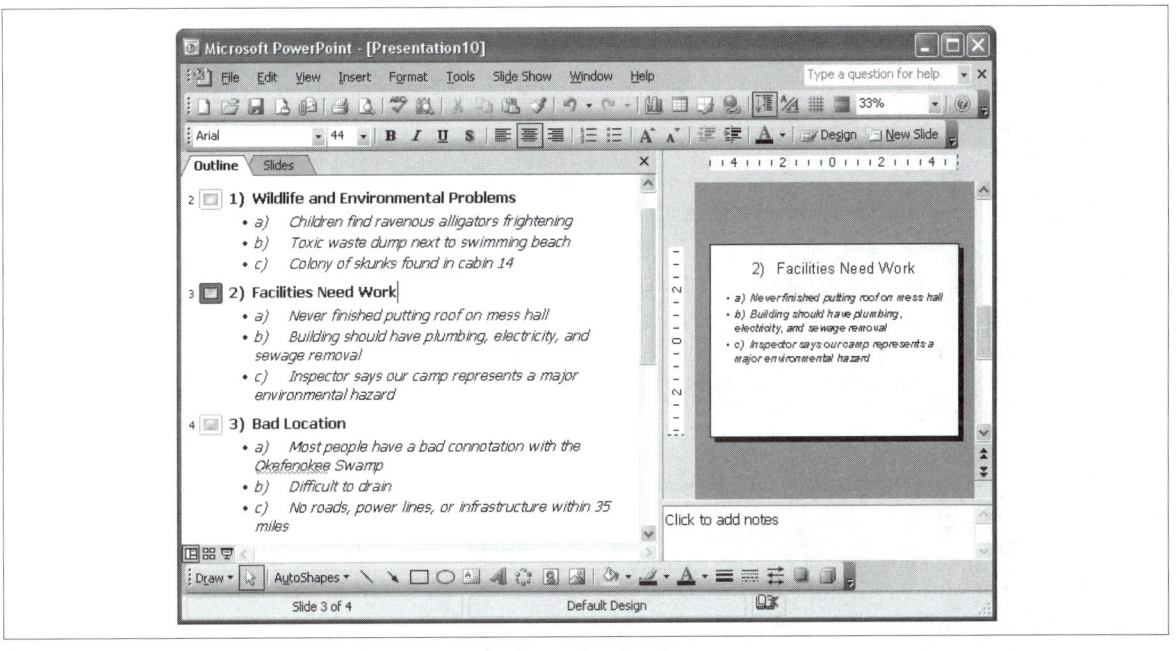

Figure 9-11. PowerPoint creates slides from the Microsoft Word outline document.

People from different countries speak different languages. Likewise, computer programs save their files in different formats. One of the most useful ways PowerPoint uses different file formats is to import outlines. PowerPoint can import outlines created in these file formats:

- **Microsoft Word for Windows:** If you've created an outline using Microsoft Word's outline feature, you can convert the document into a PowerPoint presentation. PowerPoint will convert each Level 1 heading into a new slide and any lower-level headings into bulleted lists. Paragraphs without heading styles are ignored.

- **Rich Text Format (RTF):** Just about every word processing program can read and write in Rich Text Format. To import a document created by another word processor, save the document as a Rich Text File (RTF). If the word processor doesn't use heading styles, PowerPoint will look at how the paragraphs are indented and guess at the outline structure.

Lesson 9.5
Importing and Exporting an Outline

- **Text Files:** Also known as ASCII files, text files don't contain any formatting or fancy features—just plain-old text. Since text files don't support heading styles, PowerPoint will look at how the paragraphs are indented and guess at the outline structure.

In this lesson, you'll learn how to import an outline created in Microsoft Word and then how to save a PowerPoint outline in Rich Text Format (RTF) file—a file format that is recognized by almost every word processing program.

First we need to create a presentation where we can insert the slides.

1 Create a new presentation by clicking the **New button** on the Standard toolbar and selecting the **Title Only** layout from the task pane.

Give the presentation a title.

Title Only layout

2 Click the **title placeholder** and type **What's Wrong with Our Summer Camp**.

Normally you would move to the slide that you want your new slides to follow, but since this is a new presentation, we only have one slide and thus don't have to move anywhere. Here's how to insert slides from a Microsoft Word outline:

3 Select **Insert** → **Slides from Outline** from the menu.

The Insert Outline dialog box appears, as shown in Figure 9-10. You need to select the file that contains the outline you want to copy.

4 If necessary, navigate to your Practice folder.

The file list box is updated to show all the files in your Practice folder.

5 Select the **Summer Camp** file and click **Insert**.

PowerPoint creates slides from the "Summer Camp" outline, as shown in Figure 9-11.

NOTE *If this feature is not installed in PowerPoint, you will need to have your Microsoft Office CD handy at this time. PowerPoint will let you know if this feature is not installed.*

Keep your expectations low when you import a document. PowerPoint will do its best at guessing the outline structure, but it often gets confused and makes some mistakes, in which case you'll have to do some editing.

Now that you've imported an outline from a document into your presentation, let's reserve it and save the presentation's outline in a Rich Text Format (RTF) file so that it can be opened in Microsoft Word or any other word processing program.

6 Select **File** → **Save As** from the menu.

The Save As dialog box appears. You need to tell PowerPoint that you want to save the file in Rich Text Format instead of as a standard PowerPoint presentation.

7 Click the **Save as type** list arrow and select **Outline/RTF (*.rtf)**.

All that's left is giving your Rich Text Format file a name.

8 Type **Camp Outline** in the **File name** box and click **Save**. Now close the presentation.

From here, you can open the outline file in your word processor—just make sure you're looking for RTF files when you try to find the outline file.

Chapter 9
Working with Other Programs and the Internet

QUICK REFERENCE

TO IMPORT NEW SLIDES FROM A MICROSOFT WORD OR RTF OUTLINE:

1. GO TO THE SLIDE WHERE YOU WANT THE NEW SLIDES TO BE INSERTED.
2. SELECT **INSERT → SLIDES FROM OUTLINE** FROM THE MENU.
3. BROWSE TO AND SELECT THE MICROSOFT WORD OR RTF FILE THAT CONTAINS THE OUTLINE YOU WANT TO USE, THEN CLICK **INSERT**.
4. EDIT THE NEW SLIDES AS NEEDED.

TO SAVE A PRESENTATION'S OUTLINE IN A RICH TEXT FORMAT (RTF) FILE:

1. OPEN THE PRESENTATION YOU WANT TO EXPORT.
2. SELECT **FILE → SAVE AS** FROM THE MENU.
3. SELECT **OUTLINE/RTF** FROM THE SAVE AS TYPE BOX.
4. ENTER A FILE NAME AND CLICK **SAVE**.

LESSON 9.6

Using Hyperlinks

Insert a link to an existing file or web page.

Insert a link to a different part of the same presentation.

Create a new presentation and insert a link to it.

Insert a link to an email address.

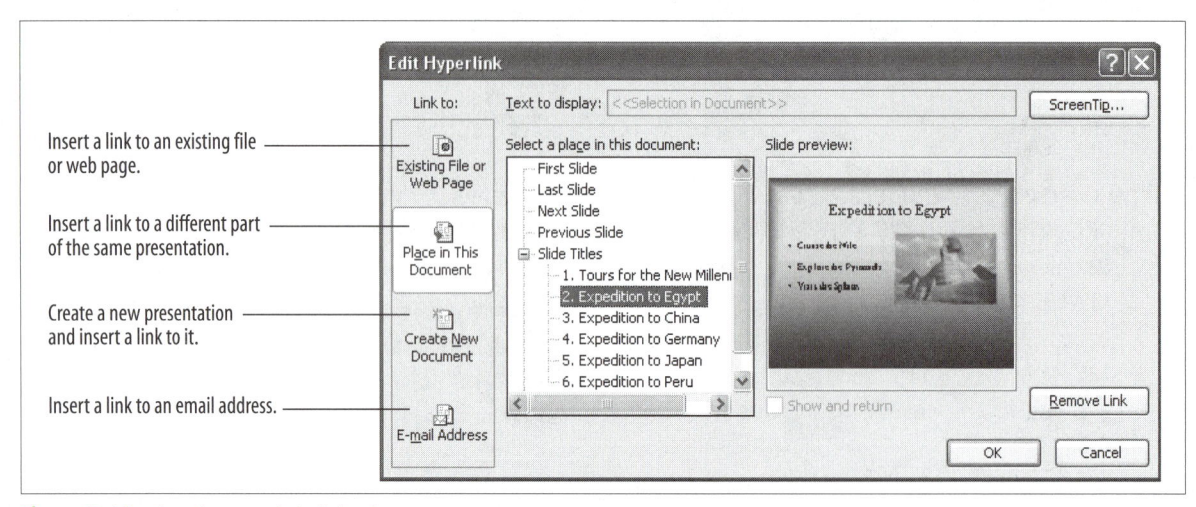

Figure 9-12. The Edit Hyperlink dialog box.

Figure 9-13. A Hyperlink appears as underlined blue text.

In this lesson, you will learn about how to use hyperlinks in PowerPoint. A hyperlink is an area of text or graphic image that will take you somewhere else by clicking it. A hyperlink is usually indicated by colored and underlined text. If you have used the World Wide Web, you've used hyperlinks numerous times to move between different web pages.

Clicking a hyperlink can take you to:

- A different slide in the same PowerPoint presentation
- A different PowerPoint presentation file
- A file created in a different program, such as Microsoft Excel
- A web site on the Internet
- An email address

Hyperlinks are especially useful because they can take you to a different slide in your presentation. For example, suppose you have a slide that contains pictures of several different tour destinations. You could make each of the pictures a hyperlink that would take you to that picture's specific slide in the presentation.

1 Open **Lesson 7A** and save it as `Web Site`.

2 Go to **Slide 1**.

The title slide of this presentation contains pictures of five different tours. Instead of having to step through the presentation to find a particular destination, you can add a hyperlink to each of the pictures that, when clicked, would take to you that slide.

3 Click the **picture of the Sphinx** to select it and click the **Insert Hyperlink button** on the Standard toolbar.

Insert Hyperlink button

Other Ways to Insert a Hyperlink:

- Select **Insert → Hyperlink** from the menu.

The Edit Hyperlink dialog box appears, as shown in Figure 9-12. Here you can specify a web address or name and location of a file you want to add as a hyperlink. If you know the location and name of the file or web address, you can type it directly in the dialog box. Otherwise, you can use the Browse buttons to

Chapter 9
Working with Other Programs and the Internet

locate the file. There are four different browse buttons in the Insert Hyperlink dialog box that let you browse for three different types of Hyperlink destinations.

4 Click the Place in This Document button, then click the Slide Titles plus sign (+), to expand the slides.

A list of the different slides in the presentation appears under Slide Titles, as shown in Figure 9-12.

5 Select 2. Expedition to Egypt and click OK.

You return to Normal View and your picture of the Sphinx now has a hyperlink to the slide that we selected.

6 Switch to Slide Show View and click the picture of the Sphinx.

Poof! The hyperlink whisks you to the Egypt slide.

7 Press Esc to stop the slide show and go back to Slide 1.

You can also create a hyperlink to another file.

8 Select the Germany text and click the Insert Hyperlink button on the Standard toolbar.

The Insert Hyperlink dialog box appears. Use the Existing File or Web Page button when you want the hyperlink to take you to another file or web site on the Internet.

9 Click the Existing File or Web Page button.

A list of files that you can use as the destination for your hyperlink appears in the dialog box.

10 Under the Look in section, navigate to your Practice folder or disk, find and select the Lesson 8* A presentation file, and click OK.

Notice the "Germany" text appears white and underlined, signifying that it's a hyperlink. If you wish, you can run the slide show again and you will see how clicking on the new hyperlink will take you to another file. (By the way, Prague isn't in Germany but in the Czech Republic—this is a lesson on PowerPoint, not geography!)

Removing a hyperlink is simple.

11 Select the Germany text and click the Insert Hyperlink button on the Standard toolbar.

The Edit Hyperlink dialog box appears.

12 Click the Remove link button.

The Edit Hyperlink dialog box closes and the hyperlink is removed.

13 Follow the procedure described in Steps 3–5 and add a hyperlink that goes to the corresponding slide to each picture on the first slide.

QUICK REFERENCE

TO INSERT A HYPERLINK:

1. SELECT THE TEXT OR OBJECT YOU WANT TO USE FOR THE HYPERLINK AND CLICK THE INSERT HYPERLINK BUTTON ON THE STANDARD TOOLBAR.

   OR...

   SELECT THE TEXT OR OBJECT YOU WANT TO USE FOR THE HYPERLINK AND SELECT INSERT → HYPERLINK FROM THE MENU.

2. EITHER SELECT A FILE YOU WANT (USE THE BROWSE BUTTON TO HELP YOU LOCATE THE FILE) OR TYPE A WEB ADDRESS FOR THE HYPERLINK'S DESTINATION AND CLICK OK.

TO EDIT OR REMOVE A HYPERLINK:

- CLICK THE TEXT OR OBJECT THAT CONTAINS THE HYPERLINK, CLICK THE INSERT HYPERLINK BUTTON ON THE STANDARD TOOLBAR AND EDIT THE HYPERLINK'S DESTINATION, OR CLICK THE REMOVE LINK BUTTON TO REMOVE THE HYPERLINK.

LESSON 9.7 Using Action Buttons

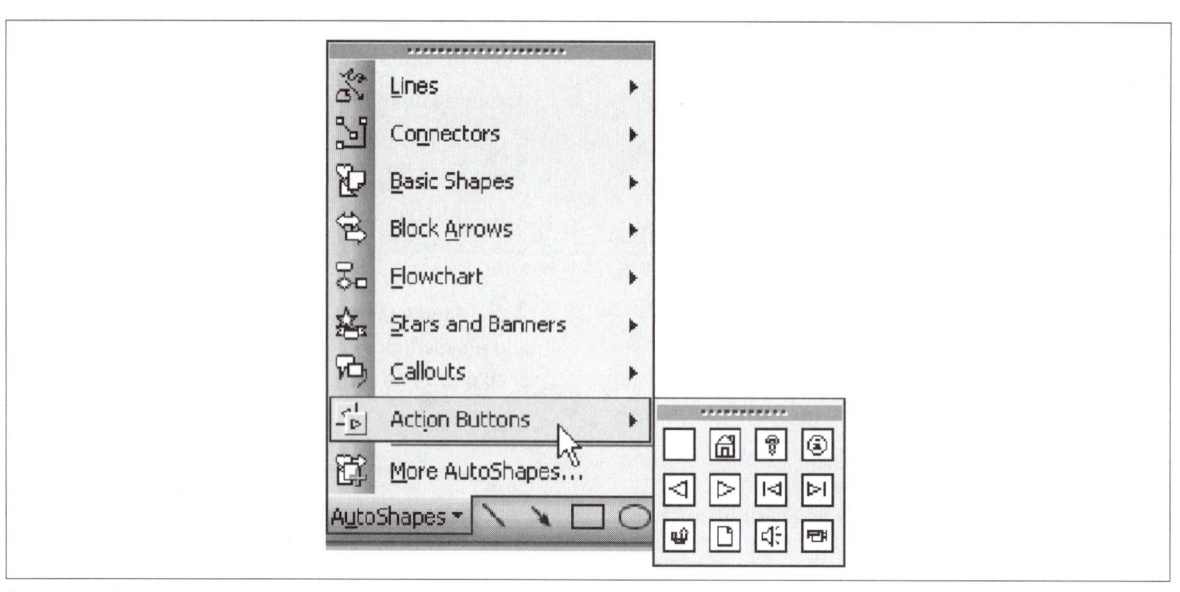

Figure 9-14. Inserting an action button.

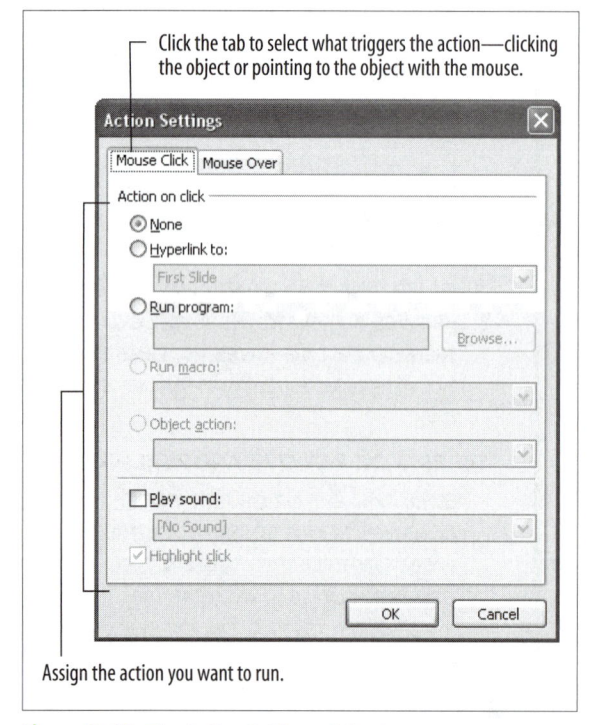

Click the tab to select what triggers the action—clicking the object or pointing to the object with the mouse.

Assign the action you want to run.

Figure 9-15. The Action Settings dialog box.

Action button—clicking this Home button brings you to the first slide in the presentation.

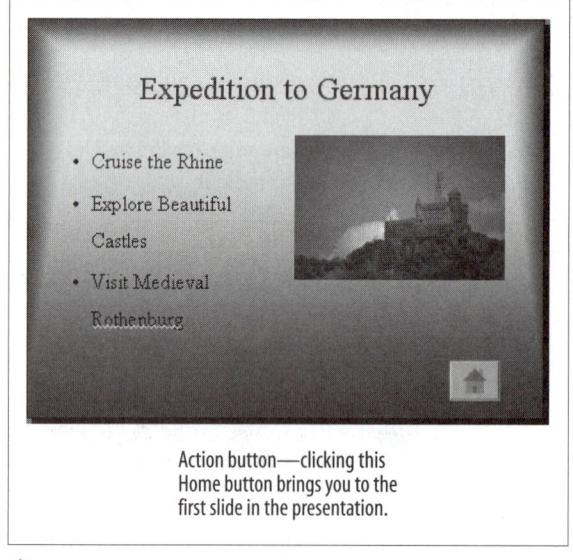

Figure 9-16. A Home button added to a slide.

TIP *You can assign actions to any slide object—simply right-click the object and select* Action Settings *from the shortcut menu.*

Similar to hyperlinks, Action buttons perform a designated action when you click them with the mouse. Action buttons can do any of the following:

- **Go to a Hyperlink:** Jumps to a different slide from the same presentation, a slide from a different presentation, a file created in another program, or a web page

272

Chapter 9
Working with Other Programs and the Internet

on the Internet to appear. This is the most common action.

- **Run a program:** Runs the program you enter in the Run program box. For example, you could create an action button that runs Microsoft Word.
- **Run a macro:** Runs a macro—a series of PowerPoint commands and instructions that are grouped together and executed as a single command. Macros are used to automate repetitive tasks and are covered more in detail in the Advanced Topics chapter.
- **Play a sound:** Plays the sound you select from the play list box. Working with sounds is explained in the Working with Multimedia chapter.

Actually, you don't even have to click an action button—you can simply specify that the action automatically occur whenever you place the mouse pointer over the button. PowerPoint provides several built-in action buttons, as shown in Table 9-2. Plus, you can make any object on your slide, such as a picture, into an action button.

1 Switch to Normal view and click Slide 4.

If you want to add action buttons to multiple slides, you must do so individually on each slide.

2 Click the AutoShapes button on the Drawing toolbar and select Action Buttons.

AutoShapes button

Table 9-2 describes the function of each of the buttons in the Action Button category.

3 Select the Action Button: Home option from the Action Buttons category.

The pointer changes to a +, indicating that you can draw the selected Action button. Drawing an Action button is no different than drawing an ordinary shape—just click and drag until the shape is the size you want.

Home Action button

4 Place the + pointer in the lower right corner of the slide. Click and drag the + pointer to create a half-inch square button, similar to the one shown in Figure 9-16.

As soon as you draw the button, the Action Settings dialog box appears, as shown in Figure 9-15. Since you selected a predefined button, PowerPoint fills in the action to perform (hyperlink to the first slide in the presentation) for you. If you wanted, you could create a custom action by selecting and specifying the action you want to run. Notice the Action Settings dialog box has two tabs—Mouse Click and Mouse Over. These tabs let you specify what triggers the action or causes it to run as follows:

- **Mouse Click:** Runs the action when you click the object (default setting).
- **Mouse Over:** Runs the action when you point at the object with the mouse.

You don't need to change the action settings for the Home action button, so move on to the next step.

5 Click OK.

NOTE *Before testing action buttons, go to Format → Background and make sure the "Omit background graphics from master" box is unchecked.*

6 Switch to Slide Show View, go to Slide 4 and click the Home button. Save your work and close the presentation when you're finished.

Table 9-2. Action Buttons

Button	Description
Custom	There is no preset action assigned to this button.
Home	Moves to the first slide in the presentation

273

Lesson 9.7
Using Action Buttons

Table 9-2. Action Buttons (Continued)

Button	Description
Help	There is no preset action assigned to this button.
Information	There is no preset action assigned to this button.
Back or Previous	Moves to the previous slide in the presentation
Forward or Next	Moves to the next slide in the presentation
Beginning	Moves to the first slide in the presentation
End	Moves to the last slide in the presentation
Return	Displays the most recently viewed slide
Document	There is no preset action assigned to this button.
Sound	There is no preset action assigned to this button.
Movie	There is no preset action assigned to this button.

QUICK REFERENCE

TO ADD AN ACTION BUTTON:

1. SWITCH TO NORMAL VIEW AND GO TO THE SLIDE WHERE YOU WANT TO ADD THE ACTION BUTTON.
2. FROM THE DRAWING TOOLBAR CLICK THE AUTOSHAPES BUTTON → ACTION BUTTONS AND SELECT THE ACTION BUTTON YOU WANT TO ADD (SEE TABLE 9-2).
3. DRAW THE BUTTON BY CLICKING ON THE SLIDE AND DRAGGING UNTIL THE BUTTON REACHES THE DESIRED SIZE.
4. IN THE ACTION SETTINGS DIALOG BOX THAT APPEARS, ASSIGN AN ACTION TO THE BUTTON IF YOU WANT SOMETHING DIFFERENT THAN THE PRESET ACTION, AND CLICK OK.

TO ASSIGN AN ACTION TO AN EXISTING SLIDE OBJECT:

- RIGHT-CLICK THE OBJECT, SELECT ACTION SETTINGS FROM THE SHORTCUT MENU, ASSIGN AN ACTION TO THE OBJECT IN THE ACTION SETTINGS DIALOG BOX, AND THEN CLICK OK.

LESSON 9.8

Saving a Presentation as a Web Page

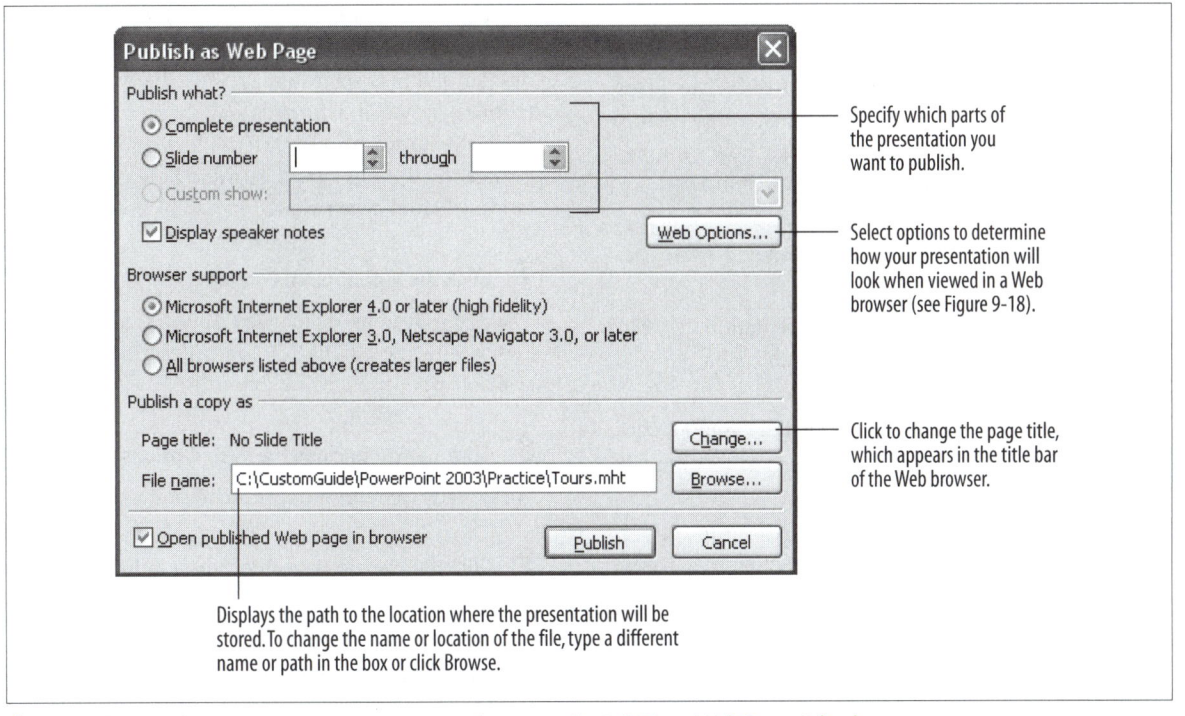

Figure 9-17. Specify how you want to save your web page in the Publish as Web Page dialog box.

Callouts in Figure 9-17:
- Specify which parts of the presentation you want to publish.
- Select options to determine how your presentation will look when viewed in a Web browser (see Figure 9-18).
- Click to change the page title, which appears in the title bar of the Web browser.
- Displays the path to the location where the presentation will be stored. To change the name or location of the file, type a different name or path in the box or click Browse.

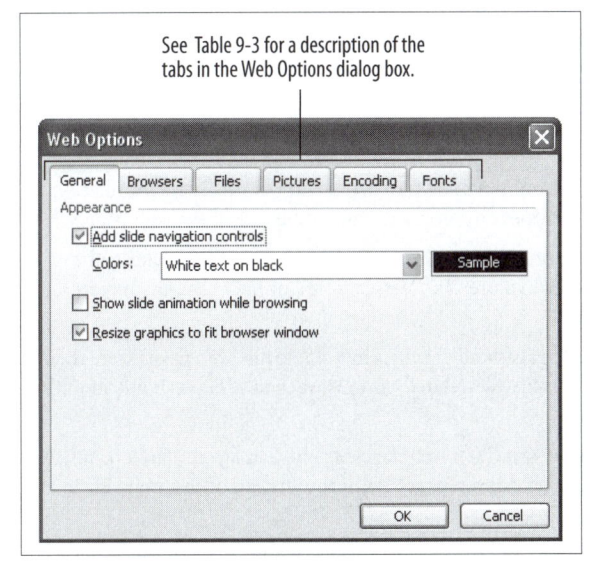

Figure 9-18. Specify how your presentation will look when viewed in a web browser.

See Table 9-3 for a description of the tabs in the Web Options dialog box.

The Internet has instigated some of the biggest changes in how most organizations and computers work, so it's no surprise that the biggest changes and improvements in recent versions of PowerPoint have to do with how it works with the Internet. This lesson explains how you can save a PowerPoint presentation as a web page so that it can be viewed on the Internet.

TIP *You may lose some formatting when you save a presentation for the Web.*

1 Open the **Lesson 7A** presentation.

Here's how to save a PowerPoint presentation as a web page…

2 Select **File** → **Save as Web Page** from the menu.

The Save As dialog box appears. You can also specify what should appear in your presentation and how it will look in a web browser.

TIP *By default, PowerPoint 2003 saves presentations in MHTML format (single file web page). This format encapsulates all the elements of the page into one file, instead of storing the different files together in one folder, making it easier to share and upload. However, this format may not be viewable in all types of browsers, and email applications with high security levels may not accept an MHTML file.*

275

Lesson 9.8
Saving a Presentation as a Web Page

3 Click the **Publish button**.

The Publish as Web Page dialog box appears, as shown in Figure 9-17. The Publish as Web Page dialog box lets you specify which parts of the presentation you want to publish, as well as stipulate how your presentation will look when viewed in a web browser.

4 Click the **Open published Web page in browser** check box.

This will display the finished presentation in your computer's web browser after you publish it.

5 Click the **Browse button**, navigate to your Practice folder or disk if necessary, and type **Tours** in the **File Name box**, and click **OK**.

You should also specify the web page title, which appears in the title bar of the web browser. Here's how…

6 Click the **Change button**, type **North Shore Tours**, and click **OK**.

Currently, there are two major web browsing programs on the market: Microsoft Internet Explorer and Netscape Navigator. Microsoft's monopolistic practices have given it roughly 90 percent of the market, but you still may want to make sure that your presentation is saved in a format that those few Netscape Navigator users can view. Here's how to view and/or change the options that determine how your presentation will look when viewed in a web browser.

7 Click the **Web Options button**.

The Web Options dialog box appears, as shown in Figure 9-18. See Table 9-3 for a description of the available options.

8 Click **Cancel** to close the Web Options dialog box.

We're ready to publish our presentation as a web page!

9 Click **Publish** to save the presentation as a web page.

PowerPoint saves the presentation as a web page and displays it on your computer's web browser. We'll learn how to browse through this presentation in the next lesson.

Table 9-3. Tabs in the Web Options Dialog Box

Tab	Description
General	Set general options, such as whether the web page should include slide navigation controls and animation effects, or if graphics should be resized so that they appear in proportion with the rest of the web page.
Browsers	Specify the web browser and whose features you want to support in the web page. Frankly speaking, the default browser option should be Microsoft Internet Explorer 4.0, Netscape 4.0, or later (shame on you, Microsoft!).
Files	Unlike PowerPoint presentations that store multiple pages and graphics in a single file, web pages store their information in several files. The Files tab lets you specify file-related options, such as if PowerPoint should save supporting files in a separate folder, etc.
Pictures	Specify the screen size that you want for the monitor on which web pages will be displayed. The screen size that you specify can affect the size and layout of images on web pages. As of the writing of this manual, 50% of all computers have a screen size of 800 x 600.
Encoding	If you're using foreign characters, select the language code that you want to use when you save the web page.
Fonts	If you're using foreign characters, specify the character set that is used to encode the file.

Chapter 9
Working with Other Programs and the Internet

QUICK REFERENCE

TO SAVE A PRESENTATION AS A WEB PAGE:

1. Select **File** → **Save as Web Page** from the menu.
2. Specify a file name and click **Save**.

   Or...

   (Optional) Click the **Web Options Button** to specify additional options for your web page.

3. Click **Publish** to save the presentation as a web page.

LESSON 9.9 Viewing a Web-Based Presentation

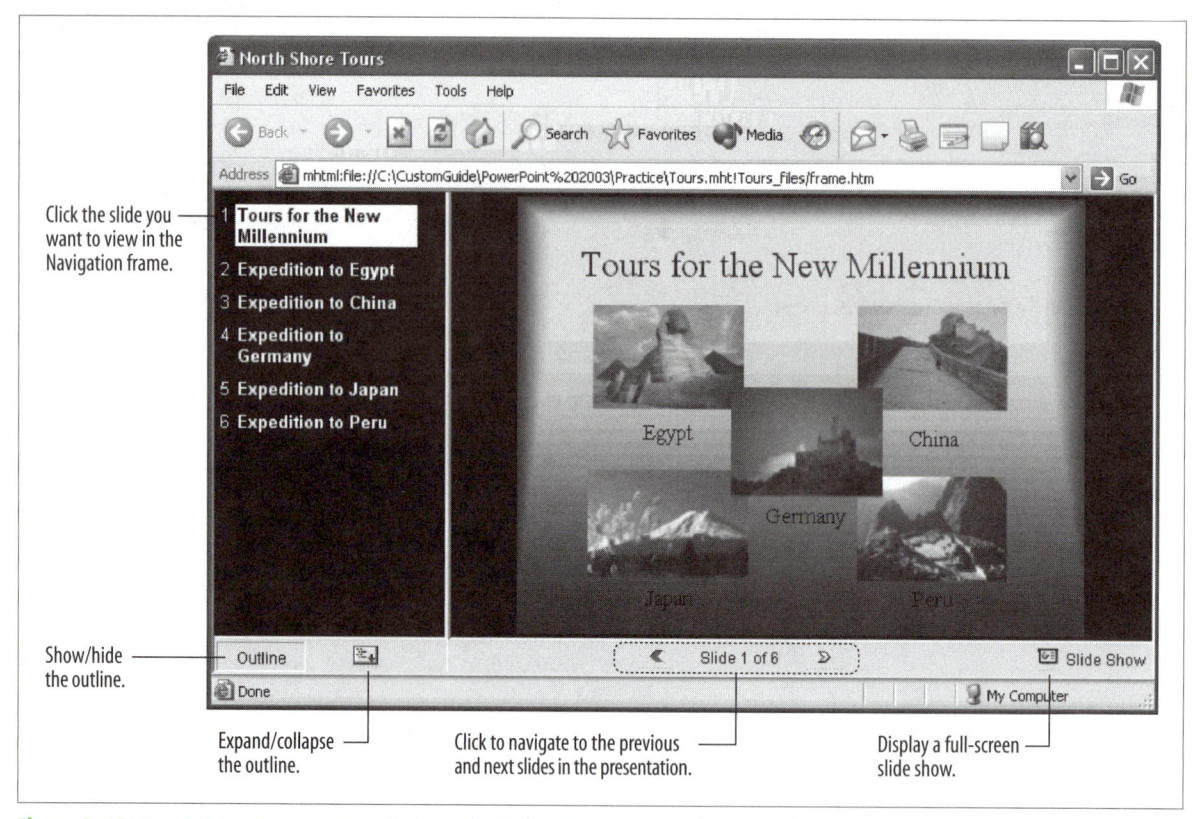

Figure 9-19. A web-based presentation displayed in Microsoft's Internet Explorer web browser.

- Click the slide you want to view in the Navigation frame.
- Show/hide the outline.
- Expand/collapse the outline.
- Click to navigate to the previous and next slides in the presentation.
- Display a full-screen slide show.

Once you have published a PowerPoint presentation as a web page you should preview it in your computer's web browser to make sure everything looks okay. Presentations have a tendency to look different in a web browser than they do in PowerPoint, and viewing a presentation in a web browser ensures that the web page looks the way you want it to.

In this lesson, you will learn how to view and navigate through a web-based PowerPoint presentation.

1 Ensure that your web browser program is open and displays the Tours presentation you created in the previous lesson.

Your web browser should display the Tours presentation, as shown in Figure 9-19. Notice that the web-based presentation has several built-in controls that you can use to navigate through the slide show.

2 Click the ▷ Next Slide button near the bottom of the window.

The slide show advances to the next slide in the presentation.

The left frame of your web browser displays an outline of the PowerPoint presentation, and you can use the Outline pane to navigate through the presentation—simply click the slide you want to go to.

3 Click 5 Expedition to Japan in the Outline pane.

Your web browser displays Slide 5 in the presentation. You can also display a slide show in full-screen mode on a web browser. Here's how:

4 Click the ▯ button on the Web browser.

The web browser displays the PowerPoint presentation in full-screen mode—just as if you were viewing a presentation on PowerPoint in Slide Show View!

5 Click the mouse button to advance through several slides in the presentation. Press Esc when you're ready to leave the presentation.

278

Chapter 9
Working with Other Programs and the Internet

That's all there is to viewing a web-based PowerPoint presentation in a web browser!

6 **Close your computer's web browser and Microsoft PowerPoint without saving any of your changes.**

Now that you have created a web-based presentation, the big question you probably have is how to get it onto the Internet. Unfortunately, that's a question that isn't very easy to answer. First, you will need to have some storage space on a web server where you can upload your web files. Second, you will need a program (called FTP programs) to upload these files with. Third, and most important, you will need to give one of your computer geek friends or co-workers a call and have them help you upload your web-based presentation onto the Internet.

QUICK REFERENCE

TO PREVIEW A POWERPOINT PRESENTATION AS A WEB PAGE:

- SELECT FILE → WEB PAGE PREVIEW FROM THE MENU.

TO NAVIGATE THROUGH A WEB-BASED PRESENTATION:

- CLICK THE PREVIOUS SLIDE AND NEXT SLIDE BUTTONS AT THE BOTTOM OF THE SLIDE SHOW.

OR...

- CLICK THE SLIDE YOU WANT TO VIEW IN THE OUTLINE PANE.

TO DISPLAY A WEB-BASED PRESENTATION IN FULL-SCREEN MODE:

- CLICK THE SLIDE SHOW BUTTON AT THE BOTTOM OF THE WINDOW.

Chapter Nine Review

Lesson Summary

Inserting a Slide into a Microsoft Word Document

To Insert a Presentation into a Word Document: Open the Microsoft Word document in which you want the presentation inserted. Place the insertion point where you want the presentation to be inserted. Select Insert → Object from the menu. Click the Create from File tab to use an existing presentation file or click the Create New tab to create a new presentation. Specify the PowerPoint presentation file you want to insert (if you selected Create from File) and click Insert, or create the presentation from scratch (if you selected Create New). Click OK.

Embedding a Microsoft Excel Worksheet into a Slide

To Insert an Embedded Object (Create New): Select Insert → Object from the menu, select the Create new option, select the object type you want to create, and click OK.

To Insert an Embedded Object (Create from File): Select Insert → Object from the menu, select the Create from file option, click Browse, browse to and select the file you want to insert, and click OK.

Modifying an Embedded Object

To Modify an Object: Double-click the object. Click anywhere outside the object when you've finished.

Embedded objects are actually saved within the PowerPoint presentation. The advantage of embedded objects is that you don't have to worry about any linked files becoming erased or lost.

Linked objects are not saved within a presentation but are linked to an external file. If the linked file is changed, the presentation is updated to reflect the changes.

Inserting a Linked Excel Chart

To Insert a Linked Object File: Click the New Slide button on the Standard toolbar and select the Title Only layout from the task pane. Select Insert → Object from the menu. Select the Create from file option, click Browse, browse to and select the file you want to insert, and click OK. Check the Link box and click OK.

Importing and Exporting an Outline

PowerPoint can create slides from outlines saved in Microsoft Word documents, Rich Text Format (RTF) files, or text files. You can also export a presentation's outline to Rich Text Format (RTF) files.

To Import New Slides from a Microsoft Word or RTF Outline: Go to the slide where you want the new slides to be inserted, switch to Outline View and select Insert → Slides from Outline from the menu, browse to and select the Microsoft Word or RTF file that contains the outline you want to use, then click Insert. You will probably have to edit the new slides.

To Save a Presentation's Outline in a Rich Text Format (RTF) File: Open the presentation you want to export and select File → Save As from the menu. Select Outline/RTF (*.rtf) from the Save as type box, enter a file name, and click OK.

Using Hyperlinks

A hyperlink is a link that points to a file, a specific location in a file, or a web page on the Internet or on an intranet.

To Insert a Hyperlink: Select the text or object you want to use for the hyperlink and either click the Insert Hyperlink button on the Standard toolbar or select Insert → Hyperlink from the menu. Either select the file you want (use the browse button to help you locate the file) or type a web address for the hyperlink's destination and click OK.

To Edit or Remove a Hyperlink: Click the text or object that contains the hyperlink, click the Insert Hyperlink button on the Standard toolbar and edit the hyperlink's destination. Click the Remove link button to remove the hyperlink.

To Edit a Hyperlink: Right-click the hyperlink and select Edit Hyperlink from the shortcut menu.

Using Action Buttons

Action buttons perform a designated action when you click them with the mouse. Action buttons can:

Chapter 9
Working with Other Programs and the Internet

- Go to a hyperlink
- Run a program
- Run a macro
- Play a sound

To Add an Action Button: Switch to Normal View and go to the slide where you want to add the action button. From the Drawing toolbar, click the AutoShapes button → Action Buttons and select the Action button you want to add. Draw the button by clicking on the slide and dragging until the button reaches the desired size. In the Action Settings dialog box that appears, assign an action to the button if you want something different than the preset action, and click OK.

To Assign an Action to an Existing Slide Object: Right-click the object, select Action Settings from the shortcut menu, assign an action to the object in the Action Settings dialog box, and then click OK.

Saving a Presentation as a Web Page

To Save a Presentation as a Web Page: Select File → Save as Web Page from the menu. Specify a file name and click Save or (optional) click the Web Options button to specify additional options for your web page. When you're finished, click Publish to save the presentation as a web page.

Viewing a Web-Based Presentation

To Preview any PowerPoint Presentation as a Web Page: Select File → Web Page Preview from the menu.

To Navigate through a Web-Based Presentation: Click the ◁ ▷ Navigation buttons at the bottom of the slide show or click the slide you want to view in the outline frame.

To Display a Web-Based Presentation in Full-Screen Mode: Click the Slide Show button at the bottom of the slide show.

Quiz

1. What is the difference between an embedded and linked object?

    A. An embedded object is saved within the file; a linked object is a hyperlink to another file.

    B. An embedded object is saved within the file; a linked object is not saved in the file—instead, a connection to the file is inserted.

    C. An embedded object can be inserted on the same page as other text or information; a linked file must be placed on its own separate page.

    D. An embedded object is saved in a separate file; a linked object is saved with the file it was inserted into.

2. Double-click an embedded or linked object to modify it. (True or False?)

3. Which of the following statements is NOT true?

    A. When you insert an object, you can either insert an existing file or you can create a new file.

    B. Clicking the Link check box inserts a link to the file instead of embedding the file.

    C. You can create slides from a Microsoft Word Outline or Rich Text Format file.

    D. You can export your PowerPoint presentations as outlines by selecting File → Export As Outline from the menu.

4. Which of the following statements is NOT true?

    A. To save a PowerPoint presentation as a web page, select File → Save as Web Page from the menu.

    B. Inserting a Hyperlink in a presentation is the same as inserting a linked file.

    C. PowerPoint saves web pages in a single file that includes all the presentation's slides and graphics.

    D. Action buttons perform a designated action when clicked or pointed at.

5. Which of the following are actions you can assign to an action button or slide object? (Select all that apply.)

    A. Jump to a hyperlink

    B. Run a macro

    C. Run a program

    D. Play a sound

281

Chapter 9
Chapter Nine Review

Homework

1. Open the Homework 2 presentation and save it as "Fleas."

2. Press Ctrl + End to go to the last slide in the presentation. Click the New Slide button on the Standard toolbar, select the Title Only layout, and click OK.

3. Type "Summer Attendance" in the slide title placeholder.

4. Select Insert → Object.

5. Select the Create from file option, click Browse, and navigate to your Practice folder or disk. Find and select the "Flea Chart" file, click Insert, and click OK.

6. Add a hyperlink to your presentation. Go to Slide 2. Select the word "Location" and click the Insert Hyperlink button on the Standard toolbar. Select the third slide and click OK.

Quiz Answers

1. B. An embedded object is saved within a file. A linked object is not actually saved within a file but points to the inserted file.

2. True. Double-clicking an object lets you modify it.

3. D. You CAN export your presentations as outlines—this just isn't the command to do it.

4. B. An inserted, linked file actually appears in the presentation. A Hyperlink merely lets you jump to a file.

5. A, B, C, and D. Action buttons can perform all of these actions.

CHAPTER 10
ADVANCED TOPICS

CHAPTER OBJECTIVES:

Adding, positioning, and removing toolbars
Customizing toolbars
Adding comments to a slide
Customizing PowerPoint's default options
Viewing file properties and finding a file
Recording a macro
Playing, editing, and deleting a macro

CHAPTER TASK: LEARN HOW TO CUSTOMIZE MICROSOFT POWERPOINT

Prerequisites

- **Know how to use menus, toolbars, dialog boxes, and shortcut keystrokes.**
- **Move the mouse pointer and navigate between the slides in a presentation.**

You can customize PowerPoint in a variety of ways to meet your own individual needs. This chapter explains how you can tailor PowerPoint to work the way you do. You are already familiar with toolbars and how they make it easy to access frequently used commands. In this chapter, you will have the opportunity to create your very own toolbar which features the commands that you use the most.

You'll also learn how to add electronic Post-it® notes to yourself or to other users, and how to search for and find a presentation file—even if you have forgotten its name!

The last topic covered in this chapter is macros. A macro helps you perform routine tasks by automating them. Instead of manually performing a series of time-consuming, repetitive actions in PowerPoint, you can record a single macro that does the entire task for you in one simple step.

LESSON 10.1 Hiding, Displaying, and Moving Toolbars

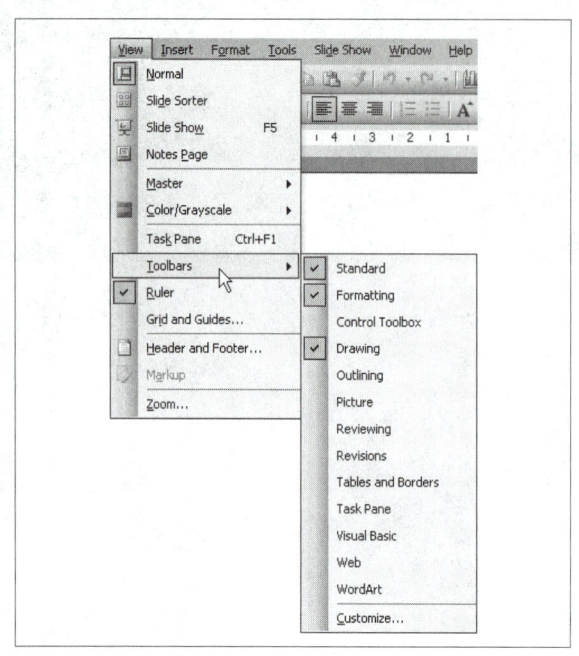

Figure 10-1. Selecting a toolbar to view.

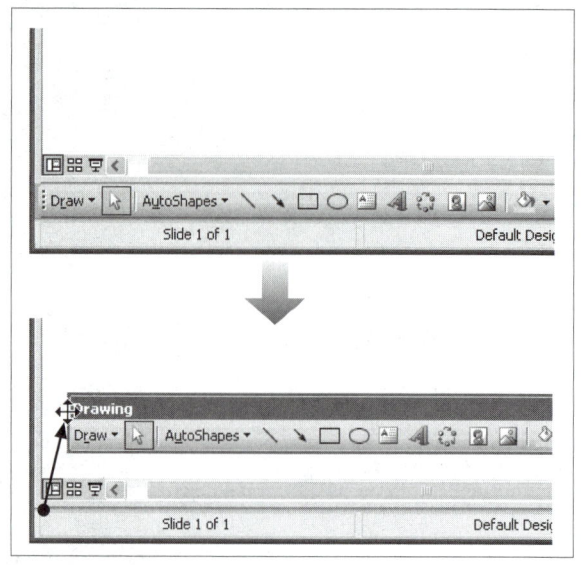

Figure 10-2. Moving a toolbar.

When you first start PowerPoint, three toolbars—Standard, Formatting, and Drawing—appear by default. As you advance with PowerPoint, you may want to display other toolbars, such as the Reviewing toolbar or the Web toolbar, to help you accomplish your tasks. Soon your screen is covered with more buttons than NASA's mission control room. This lesson explains how to remove all that clutter by moving PowerPoint's toolbars to different positions on the screen, or by removing them altogether.

1 Make sure you have the PowerPoint program running and select View → Toolbars from the menu.

A list of available toolbars appears, as shown in Figure 10-1. Notice that check marks appear next to the Standard and Formatting toolbars—this indicates that the toolbars are already selected and appear on the PowerPoint screen.

2 Select Formatting from the toolbar menu.

The Formatting toolbar disappears. You can hide a toolbar if you don't need to use any of its commands, or if you need to make more room available on the screen to view a presentation.

3 Select View → Toolbars → Formatting from the menu.

The Formatting toolbar reappears. Another way to add and remove toolbars is to right-click anywhere on a toolbar or menu.

4 Right-click either the Standard toolbar or the Formatting toolbar.

A shortcut menu appears with the names of available toolbars.

5 Click Web from the shortcut menu.

The Web toolbar appears. You can view as many toolbars as you want; however, the more toolbars you display, the less of the slide pane you will be able to see.

6 Right-click any toolbar and select Web from the shortcut menu.

The Web toolbar disappears.

Although most toolbars are anchored to the top or bottom of the PowerPoint screen, you can easily move them to a new location.

284

Chapter 10
Advanced Topics

Move handle

7 Move the pointer to the move handle, , at the far left side of the Drawing toolbar. Click and drag the toolbar to the middle of the screen, then release the mouse button.

The Drawing toolbar is removed from the bottom of the screen and floats in the middle of the slide pane.

Notice that a title bar appears above the Drawing toolbar. You can move a floating toolbar by clicking its title bar and dragging it to a new position. If you drag a floating toolbar to the edge of the program window, it becomes a docked toolbar.

8 Click the Drawing toolbar's title bar and drag the toolbar down until it becomes docked at the bottom of the PowerPoint screen.

The Drawing toolbar is reattached to the bottom of the screen.

QUICK REFERENCE

TO VIEW OR HIDE A TOOLBAR:

- SELECT VIEW → TOOLBARS FROM THE MENU AND SELECT THE TOOLBAR YOU WANT TO DISPLAY OR HIDE.

OR...

- RIGHT-CLICK ANY TOOLBAR OR MENU AND SELECT THE TOOLBAR YOU WANT TO DISPLAY OR HIDE FROM THE SHORTCUT MENU.

TO MOVE A TOOLBAR TO A NEW LOCATION ONSCREEN:

- DRAG THE TOOLBAR BY ITS MOVE HANDLE (IF THE TOOLBAR IS DOCKED) OR TITLE BAR (IF THE TOOLBAR IS FLOATING) TO THE DESIRED LOCATION.

LESSON 10.2 Customizing PowerPoint's Toolbars

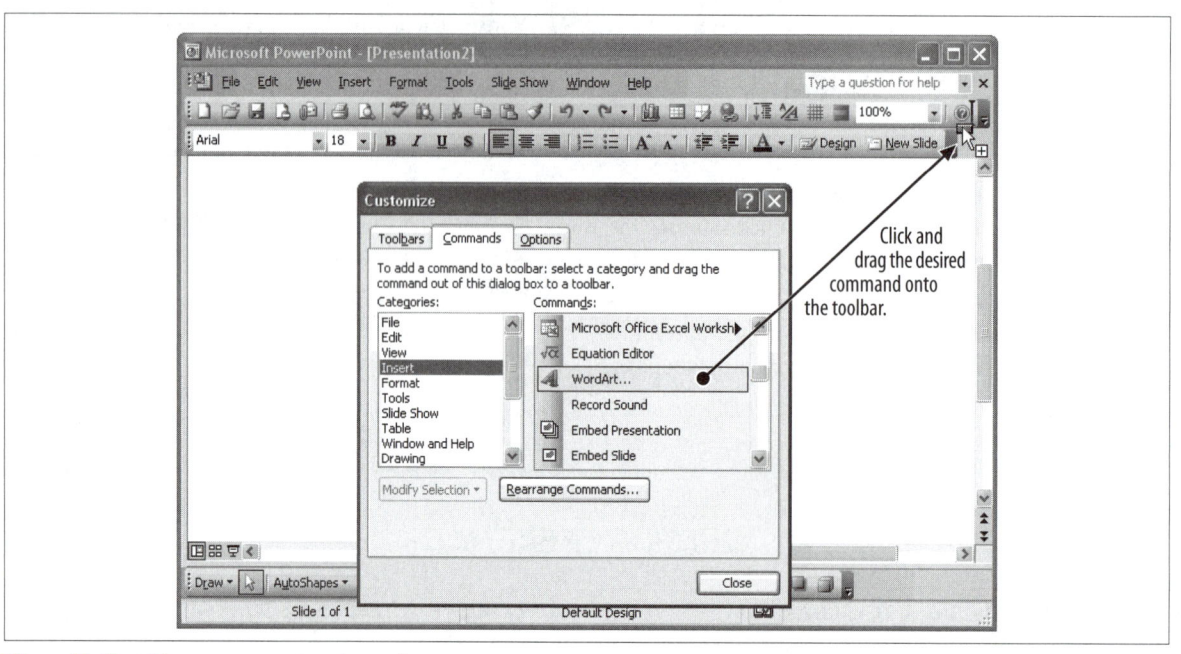

Figure 10-3. Adding a command to the toolbar.

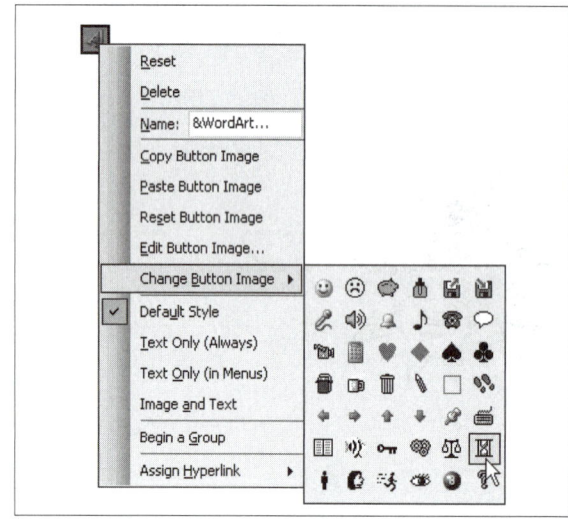

Figure 10-4. Right-click any toolbar button to change the button's text and/or image.

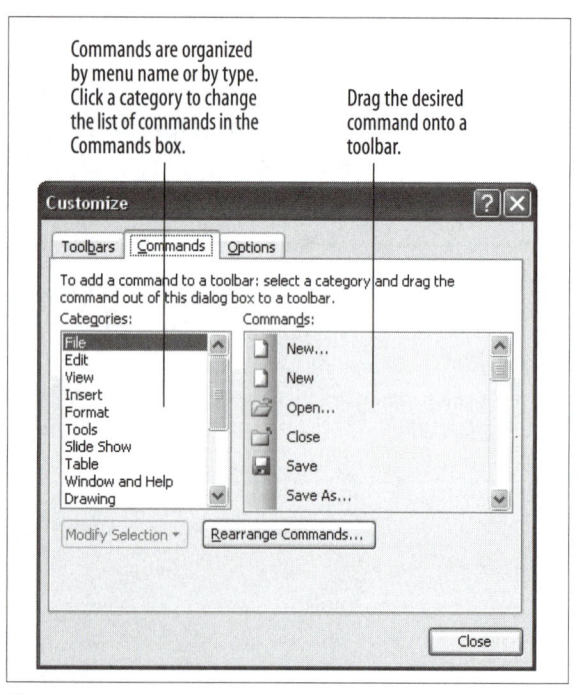

Figure 10-5. The Customize dialog box.

Chapter 10
Advanced Topics

The purpose of PowerPoint's toolbars is to provide buttons for the commands you use most frequently. If PowerPoint's built-in toolbars don't contain enough of your frequently used commands, you can modify PowerPoint's toolbars by adding or deleting their buttons. And if that still isn't enough, you can even create your own custom toolbar.

In this lesson, you will learn how to modify PowerPoint's toolbars.

1 Select View → Toolbars → Customize from the menu.

The Customize dialog box appears, as shown in Figure 10-3. Here you can select the toolbars you want to view or create a new custom toolbar.

2 Click the Commands tab.

The Commands tab appears in front of the Customize dialog box, as shown in Figure 10-5. Here, select the buttons and commands you want to appear on your toolbar. The commands are organized by categories just like PowerPoint's menus.

3 In the Categories list, scroll to and click the Insert category.

Notice that the Commands list is updated to display all of the available commands in the "Insert" category.

4 In the Commands list, scroll to the WordArt button and drag it to the end of the Standard toolbar, as shown in Figure 10-3.

The WordArt button appears on the Standard toolbar.

It's easy to change the image or text that appears on any toolbar button.

5 Right-click the WordArt button on the toolbar and select Change Button Image → ✕ as shown in Figure 10-4.

You're finished modifying the toolbar!

6 Click Close to close the Customize dialog box.

Notice the ✕ icon appears on the new WordArt button on the Standard toolbar. When you no longer need a toolbar button, you can remove it. Here's how:

7 Select View → Toolbars → Customize from the menu.

The Customize dialog box appears. To remove a button, simply drag it off the toolbar.

8 Click and drag the ✕ WordArt button off the toolbar.

Move on to the next step and close the Customize dialog box.

9 Click Close to close the Customize dialog box.

Adding your frequently used commands to the toolbar is one of the most effective ways you can make Microsoft PowerPoint more enjoyable and faster to use.

287

Lesson 10.2
Customizing PowerPoint's Toolbars

QUICK REFERENCE

TO ADD A BUTTON TO A TOOLBAR:

1. SELECT VIEW → TOOLBARS → CUSTOMIZE FROM THE MENU.

   OR...

   RIGHT-CLICK ANY TOOLBAR AND SELECT CUSTOMIZE FROM THE SHORTCUT MENU.

2. CLICK THE COMMANDS TAB.

3. SELECT THE COMMAND CATEGORY FROM THE CATEGORIES LIST, FIND THE DESIRED COMMAND IN THE COMMANDS LIST, AND DRAG THE COMMAND ONTO THE TOOLBAR.

TO CHANGE A BUTTON'S TEXT OR IMAGE:

1. SELECT VIEW → TOOLBARS → CUSTOMIZE FROM THE MENU.

   OR...

   RIGHT-CLICK ANY TOOLBAR AND SELECT CUSTOMIZE FROM THE SHORTCUT MENU.

2. RIGHT-CLICK THE BUTTON AND MODIFY THE TEXT AND/OR IMAGE USING THE SHORTCUT MENU OPTIONS.

Sending Faxes

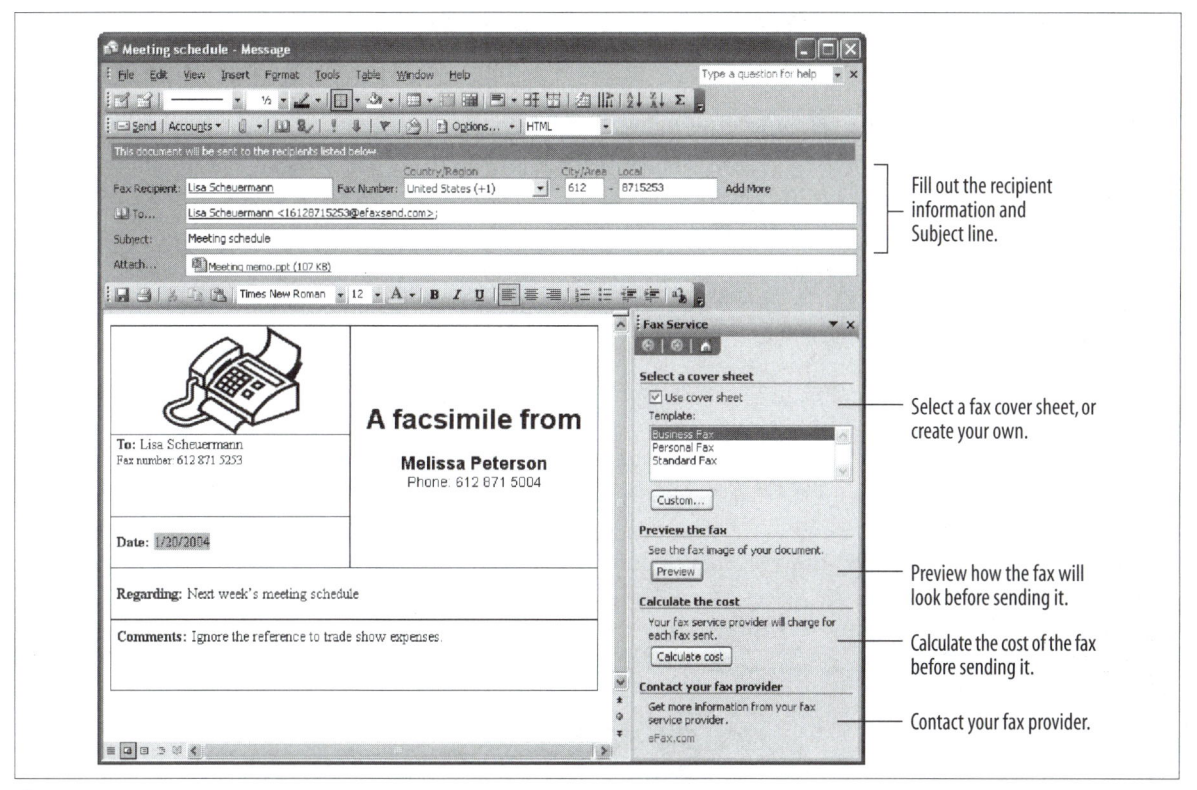

LESSON 10.3

Figure 10-6. The fax message window.

Callouts on the figure:
- Fill out the recipient information and Subject line.
- Select a fax cover sheet, or create your own.
- Preview how the fax will look before sending it.
- Calculate the cost of the fax before sending it.
- Contact your fax provider.

TIP *You must sign up with a fax service provider to use the fax service.*

A new feature in PowerPoint 2003 is the ability to send faxes right from the program. Instead of scanning paper copies into a fax machine, presentation files are sent to the fax service provider in an email. When the fax message is received, the fax service sends the presentation through the telephone wires to the fax machine.

If none of that made sense, all you really need to know is that the new fax feature saves time and a lot of paper, and it is incredibly easy to use.

NOTE *You must have Outlook and Word installed to use the fax service, and Outlook must be open to send your fax. If Outlook is not open and you click Send, the fax will be stored in your Outbox until the next time you open Outlook.*

1 Open the file you want to fax.

If you don't have the file open you can always attach it, just as you would attach a file to an email message.

2 Select **File → Send to → Recipient using Internet Fax Service** from the menu.

An email message window opens, as shown in Figure 10-6.

NOTE *If you do not have a fax service provider installed on your computer, you will be prompted to sign up with a provider over the Internet. It's very easy to sign up; just follow the instructions to choose a provider and sign up for the fax service. Many providers offer a free 30-day trial in case you're trying to decide whether or not you want this service.*

Complete the information in the fax message window.

3 Enter the recipient's name and fax number at the top of the window.

You can send the same fax to multiple recipients by clicking the Add More button at the end of the row.

4 Type the fax subject in the **Subject** line.

289

Lesson 10.3
Sending Faxes

Once you have entered the fax message information, fill out the cover letter.

5 Select the Business Fax cover sheet template in the Fax Service task pane.

The template appears. Replace the template text with information that applies to the fax being sent.

NOTE *The information you include on your cover sheet may require some extra thought if you are sending the fax to multiple recipients.*

Once you've completed the cover letter, check out other options in the Fax Service task pane.

6 Click the Preview button in the Fax Service task pane.

The FaxImage window appears with a preview of the pages in the fax.

You can also get an estimate of how much the fax is going to cost you from your fax service provider.

7 Click the Calculate Cost button in the task pane.

A browser window opens with an estimate of what your provider will charge you for sending the fax.

8 Close the browser window.

Once you're satisfied with how your fax is going to look, you're ready to send it.

9 Click the Send button in the fax message window.

The fax email is sent, and the recipient will receive the fax in no time.

You should also receive an email from your provider, telling you whether the fax was successful.

QUICK REFERENCE

TO USE THE FAX SERVICE:

- YOU MUST BE SIGNED UP WITH A FAX SERVICE PROVIDER.

AND...

- YOU MUST HAVE WORD AND OUTLOOK 2003 INSTALLED ON YOUR COMPUTER.

TO SEND A FAX:

1. OPEN THE DOCUMENT YOU WANT TO FAX.
2. SELECT FILE → SEND TO → RECIPIENT USING INTERNET FAX SERVICE FROM THE MENU.
3. ENTER THE FAX INFORMATION: RECIPIENT NAME, FAX NUMBER, AND A SUBJECT.
4. CHOOSE THE COVER SHEET YOU WANT TO USE IN THE FAX SERVICE TASK PANE AND FILL IT OUT.
5. CLICK THE SEND BUTTON.

TO PREVIEW THE FAX:

- CLICK THE PREVIEW BUTTON IN THE FAX SERVICE TASK PANE.

TO CALCULATE COST OF FAX:

- CLICK THE CALCULATE COST BUTTON IN THE FAX SERVICE TASK PANE.

TO FAX MULTIPLE FILES:

- CLICK THE ATTACH BUTTON IN THE FAX MESSAGE WINDOW AND ATTACH EACH FILE YOU WANT TO FAX.

Adding Comments to a Slide

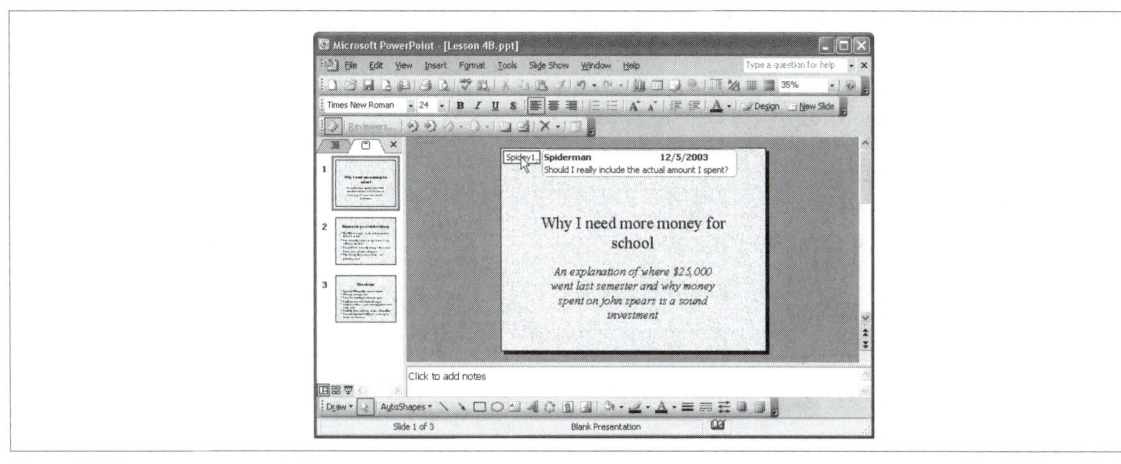

LESSON 10.4

Figure 10-7. A comment on a slide.

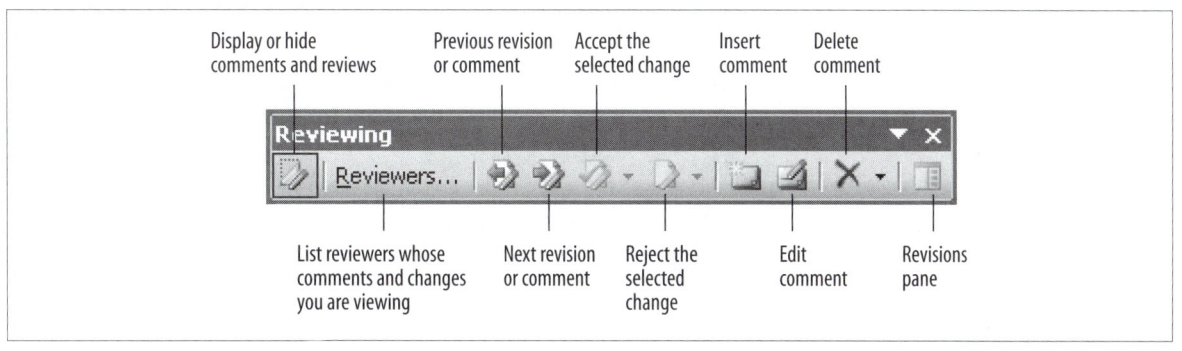

Figure 10-8. The Reviewing toolbar.

This lesson explains how to add comments to a slide. Adding a comment to a slide is like sticking a Post-it® note to it. You can use PowerPoint's comments feature to add suggestions, notes, or reminders to your slide. Your slide comments are almost impossible to miss—they appear just like a Post-it® note right on top of your slide. Comments can also easily be hidden, should you need to show your presentation.

1 Open the **Lesson 4E** presentation file and make sure you're on **Slide 1**.

Move on to the next step and add a comment to the current slide.

2 Select **Insert → Comment** from the menu.

PowerPoint inserts a yellow Post-It® note in the upper-left corner of the current slide, as shown in Figure 10-7. Also notice that a new toolbar, the Reviewing toolbar, makes its debut on the PowerPoint screen, as shown in Figure 10-8. Now all you have to do is type your notes in the Post-it® note. Notice the user name at the beginning of the comment—this is so that other users can see who added the comment.

NOTE *You can change the user name by selecting Tools → Options from the menu, clicking the General tab and entering a new user name in the User name box.*

Let's add the notes for this comment.

3 Type **Should I really include the actual amount I spent?** in the comment box.

If your boss suddenly announces that he or she wants you to present your unfinished slide show in five minutes, you can quickly hide any added comments.

291

Lesson 10.4
Adding Comments to a Slide

4 Click the Show/Hide Markup button on the Reviewing toolbar to hide your comments completely.

Show/Hide Markup button

Other Ways to Show or Hide Comments:
- Select **View** → **Markup** from the menu

Where did that little Post-it® run off to? Move on to the next step to find out.

5 Click the Show/Hide Markup button again to make your comment reappear.

When you click anywhere outside the comment box, the Post-it® shrinks to a small box in the upper left-hand corner of the slide. To see the text you just entered, simply click on the box.

Comments are easy to delete when you no longer need them. The next step explains how to delete a comment.

6 Select the comment by clicking it, then press the Delete key.

Poof! The comment disappears from the screen. If only the Reviewing toolbar would do the same thing, since you probably won't need it anymore…

7 Remove the Reviewing toolbar by right-clicking any toolbar, and selecting Reviewing from the shortcut menu.

QUICK REFERENCE

TO ADD A COMMENT TO A SLIDE:
- SELECT INSERT → COMMENT FROM THE MENU AND TYPE THE NOTE.

TO SHOW OR HIDE SLIDE COMMENTS:
- CLICK THE MARKUP BUTTON ON THE REVIEWING TOOLBAR.

OR…
- SELECT VIEW → MARKUP FROM THE MENU.

TO DELETE A COMMENT:
- CLICK THE COMMENT TO SELECT IT, THEN PRESS THE DELETE KEY.

LESSON 10.5

Customizing PowerPoint's Default Options

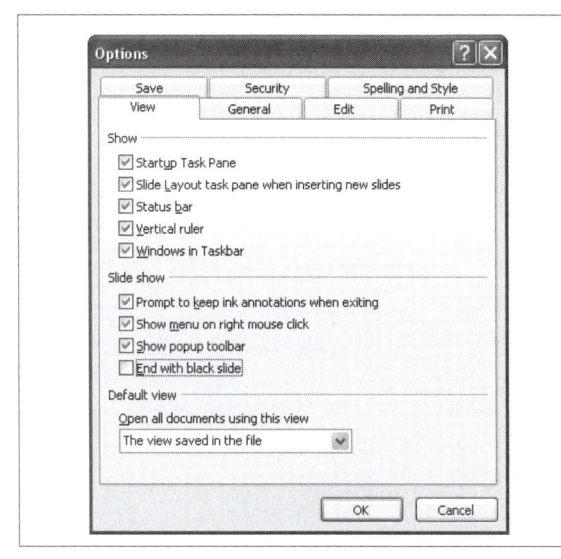

Figure 10-9. The View tab of the Options dialog box.

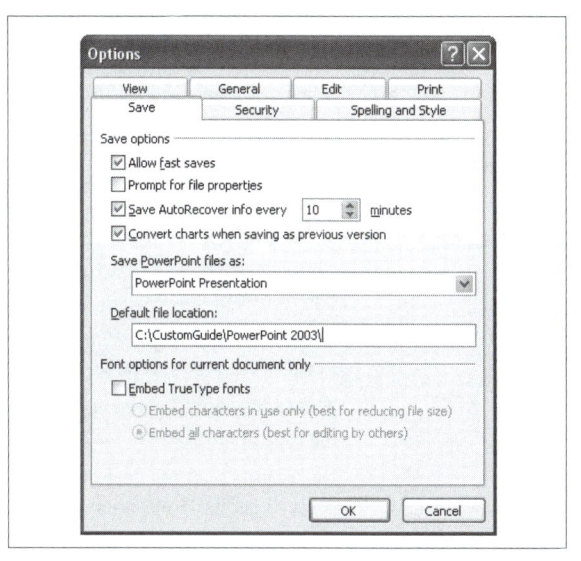

Figure 10-11. The Save tab of the Options dialog box.

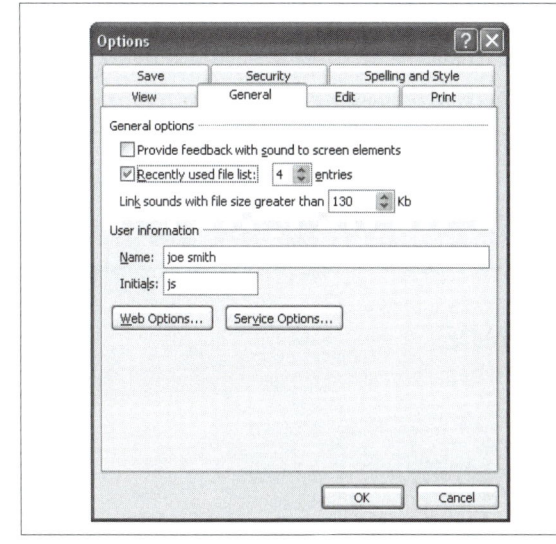

Figure 10-10. The General tab of the Options dialog box.

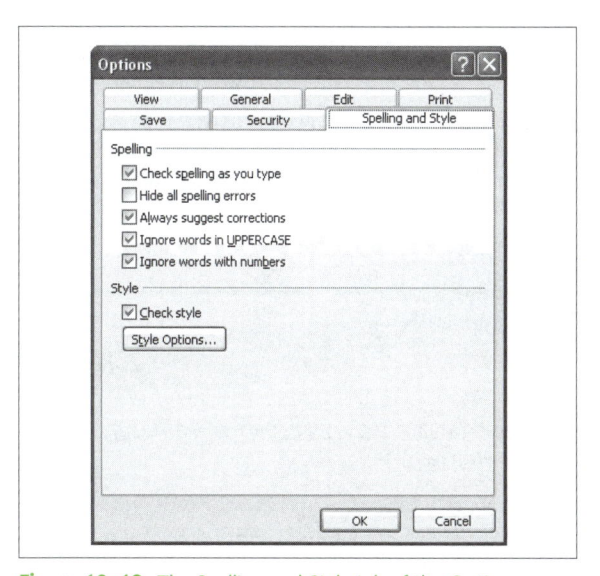

Figure 10-12. The Spelling and Style tab of the Options dialog box.

Microsoft spent a lot of time and research when it decided what the default settings for PowerPoint should be. However, you may find that the default settings don't always fit your own needs. For example, you might want to change the default folder where PowerPoint saves your presentations from C:\My Documents to a drive and folder on the network.

This lesson isn't so much an exercise, but rather a reference on how to customize PowerPoint by changing its default settings.

1 Select **Tools → Options** from the menu.

The Options dialog box appears.

293

Lesson 10.5
Customizing PowerPoint's Default Options

2 Refer to Table 10-1 and click each of the tabs shown in the table to familiarize yourself with the Options dialog box. Click OK when you're finished.

Table 10-1. Tabs in the Options Dialog Box

Tab	Description
View	Controls whether the startup task pane, slide layout task pane, status bar, and vertical ruler are displayed. You can also change several slide show viewing preferences.
General	Allows you to change the user name, how many recently used files should appear in the File menu, as well as change several web options.
Edit	Allows you to change PowerPoint's editing features, such as showing paste option buttons and the maximum number of undos saved.
Print	Determines printing defaults such as printing TrueType fonts, background printing, and whether to print slides, handout, notes, etc.
Save	Allows you to change the default file format that PowerPoint saves its presentations in, to specify whether PowerPoint should automatically save your presentations, and if PowerPoint should automatically prompt you for file properties when you save a file.
Security	Allows you to password protect your presentations. For example, you could specify that a user must enter a password to either open or modify a presentation.
Spelling and Style	Allows you to enable or disable on-the-fly spell checking, or to ignore words in uppercase or words with numbers. You can also set style options that ensure consistent use of punctuation, capitalization, spelling, and visual clarity of text, bulleted lists, and other items in your presentation.

QUICK REFERENCE

TO CHANGE POWERPOINT'S DEFAULT OPTIONS:

- SELECT TOOLS → OPTIONS FROM THE MENU, CLICK THE APPROPRIATE TABS, AND MAKE THE NECESSARY CHANGES.

LESSON 10.6

File Properties and Finding a File

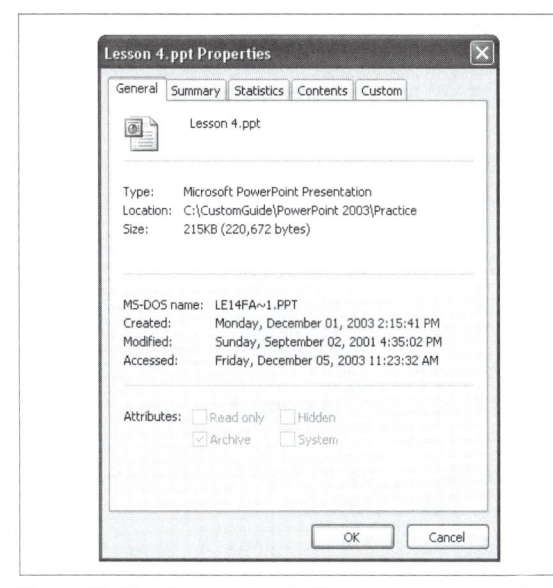

Figure 10-13. The General tab of the Properties dialog box.

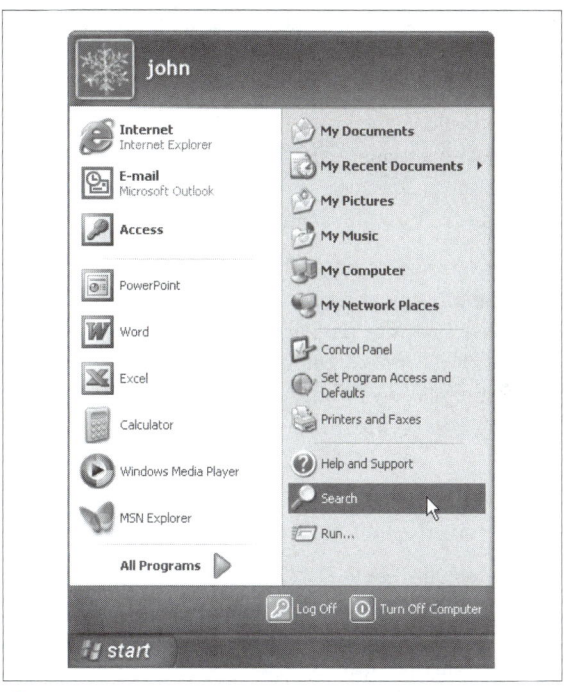

Figure 10-14. The Windows Search command.

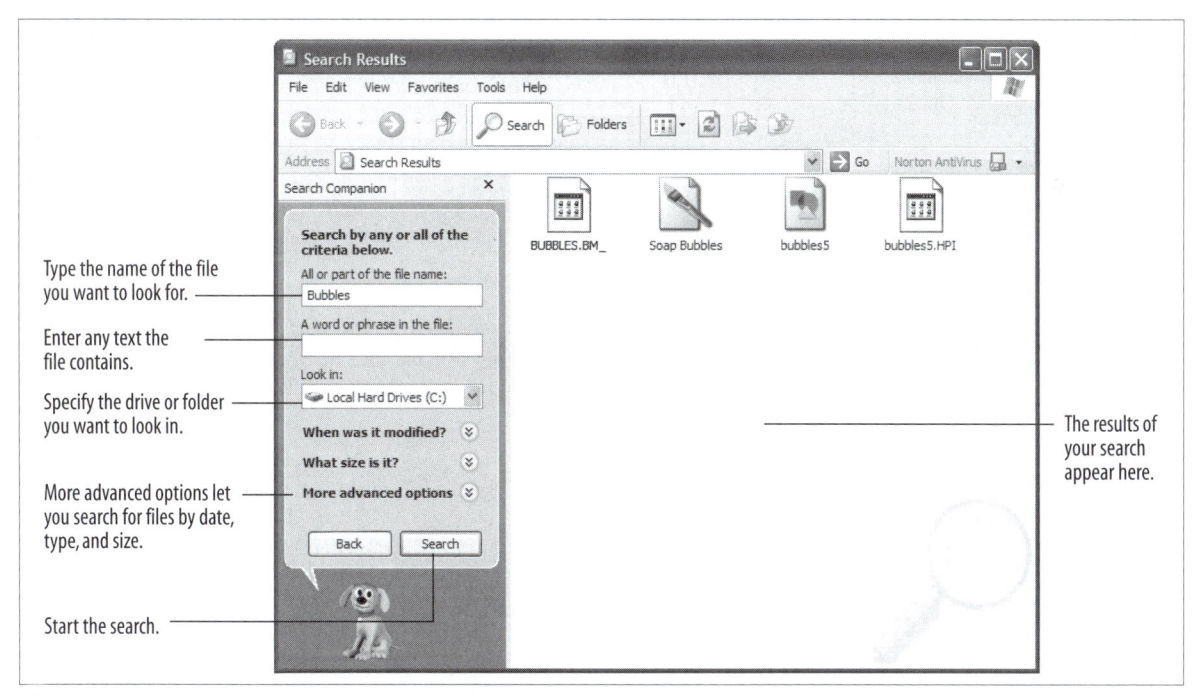

Figure 10-15. The Search Results window.

- Type the name of the file you want to look for.
- Enter any text the file contains.
- Specify the drive or folder you want to look in.
- More advanced options let you search for files by date, type, and size.
- Start the search.
- The results of your search appear here.

295

Lesson 10.6
File Properties and Finding a File

We'll cover two related topics in this lesson. The first topic is File Properties. Information about the size of a presentation, when it was created, when it was last modified, and who created it, can all be found with the File → Properties command. The File Properties dialog box also has custom fields, such as Subject and Category, so you can add your own information to your presentations.

The second topic covered in this lesson is how to find a file. It is just as easy to misplace and lose a file in your computer as it is to misplace your car keys—maybe easier! Luckily, Windows comes with a great Search feature that can track down your lost files, even if you can't remember their exact name or location.

1 Open the Lesson 4A presentation and select File → Properties from the menu, and click the General tab.

The General tab of the Properties dialog box appears, as shown in Figure 10-13. The General tab of the Properties dialog box tracks general information about the file, such as its size, location, when the file was created, and when it was last accessed or modified.

2 Click the Summary tab.

The Summary tab of the Properties dialog box lets you enter your own information to describe and summarize the file, such as the author, subject, keywords, and category. You can use the information in the Summary tab to help you search for files.

3 Close the Properties dialog box and exit PowerPoint without saving any of your changes.

You can find PowerPoint presentation files—or any other type of file for that matter—by using the Windows Search feature. Here's how:

4 Click the Start button at the bottom of your screen and select Search, then select All files and folders from the task pane.

The Search Results dialog box appears, as shown in Figure 10-15.

5 Type Homework in the All or part of the file name box, make sure the (C:) hard disk appears in the Look in box, and click the Search button.

This will search for any file that contains the words "Homework" such as "Homework 10", "Homework 3", etc. So, if you only know part of the file name, you can enter the part of the file name that you know.

A list of files that match the criteria you entered in the File name text box appear in the open dialog box.

6 Once the Homework 3 file appears in the window, click the Stop button to cancel the search.

7 Double-click the Homework 3 file located in your Practice folder or disk.

The Homework 3 presentation opens in Microsoft PowerPoint.

8 Close the Homework 3 file without saving any changes.

NOTE *File searches based on the text they contain are much slower than searches based on other criteria. Also, if you're searching for a file that contains a phrase, make sure you enter the exact sequence of the phrase. For example, if you're looking for a file that contains the phrase ACME Widget Company, and you tell Windows to search for a file containing the text ACME Company, Windows won't find the file because you didn't include the word Widget.*

You can cancel a search in progress, especially if you're getting too few or too many results, by clicking the Stop button at any time.

Chapter 10
Advanced Topics

QUICK REFERENCE

TO FIND A FILE:

1. CLICK THE **START BUTTON** AND SELECT **SEARCH**, THEN SELECT **ALL FILES AND FOLDERS** FROM THE TASK PANE.

2. ENTER PART OF THE FILE NAME IN THE **ALL OR PART OF THE FILE NAME** BOX. YOU CAN ALSO SEARCH FOR FILES USING OTHER CRITERIA, SUCH AS USING THE **A WORD OR PHRASE IN THE FILE** BOX OR BY CLICKING THE **MORE ADVANCED OPTIONS** LINK.

3. CLICK **SEARCH** TO START SEARCHING FOR THE FILE(S).

LESSON 10.7 Recording a Macro

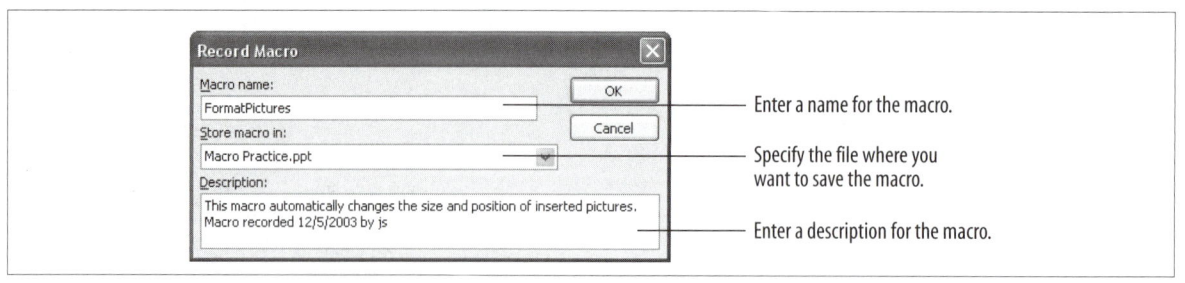

Figure 10-16. The Record Macro dialog box.

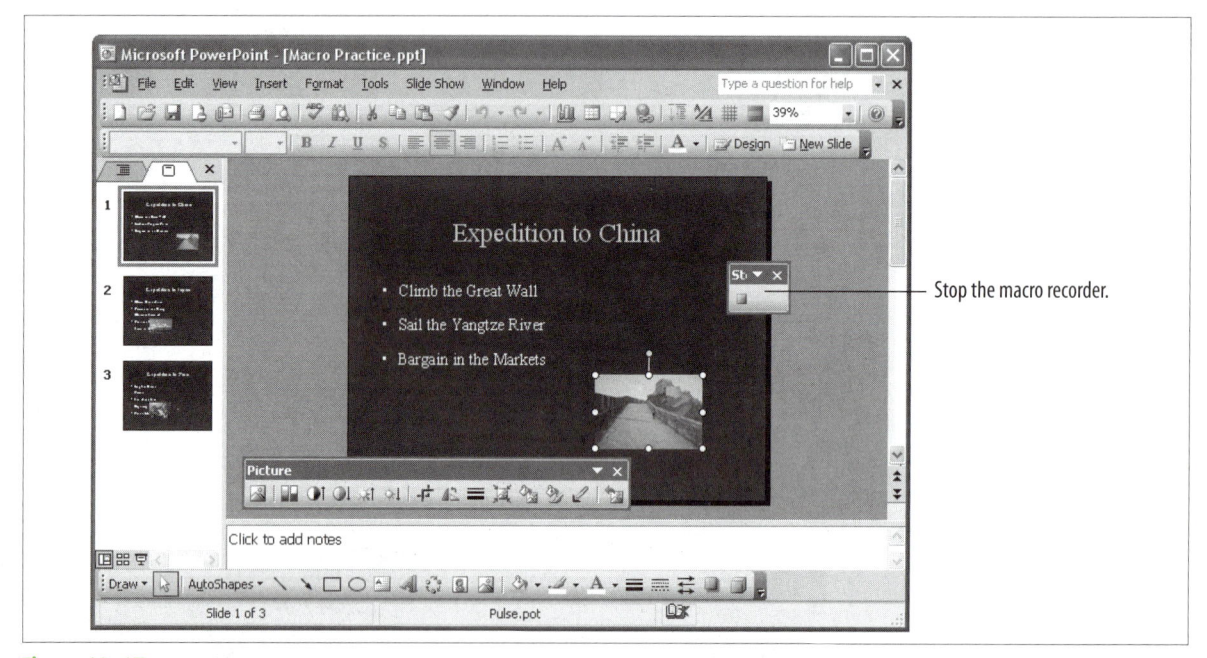

Figure 10-17. Recording a macro.

If you find yourself doing the same routine tasks over and over, you might be able to accomplish the same tasks much faster by creating a macro. A macro is a series of commands and instructions that are grouped together and executed as a single command. Instead of manually performing a series of time-consuming, repetitive actions in PowerPoint by yourself, you can create a macro to perform the task for you. There are two ways to create a macro: by recording them or by writing them in PowerPoint's built-in Visual Basic programming language. This lesson explains the easy way to create a macro—by recording the task(s) you want the macro to execute for you.

When you record a macro, imagine you're being videotaped: *everything* is recorded—all your commands, the data you enter, even any mistakes you make! Before you record a macro, you should write down a script that contains all the steps you want the macro to record. Practice or rehearse your script a couple of times, to make sure it works, before you actually record it. If you do make a mistake while recording a macro, don't worry—you can delete the existing macro and try again, or you can edit the macro's Visual Basic source code and fix the mistake (more on that later). Let's get started!

1 Open the presentation **Lesson 10** and save it as `Macro Practice`.

This slide show describes various travel promotions that North Shore Travel is offering. North Shore Travel's promotions change on a regular basis and so do the pictures in this presentation. After the pictures have been inserted, they must be updated so that they

Chapter 10
Advanced Topics

are all the same size and in the same position on each slide. Instead of having to manually size and position each inserted picture, you can record a macro to perform some of the repetitive work for you.

2 Click the Great Wall of China picture on Slide 1 to select it.

You need to enlarge the picture and move it to a better position on the slide, but first start the macro recorder to record your commands and actions. Here's how to record a macro:

3 Select Tools → Macro → Record New Macro from the menu.

The Record Macro dialog box appears, as shown in Figure 10-16. Here you must give your new macro a name and description.

4 In the Macro name text box, type FormatPictures.

Macro names can be no longer than 25 characters and cannot include spaces.

5 In the Description text box, type This macro automatically changes the size and position of inserted pictures.

6 Click OK.

The Stop Recording toolbar appears, indicating that PowerPoint is currently recording every command you issue into the "FormatPictures" macro. Do the next several steps very carefully—you don't want to make a mistake and record it in your macro!

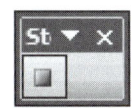

Stop Recording toolbar

7 Select Format → Picture from the menu.

The Format Picture dialog box appears.

8 Click the Size tab and make sure the Lock aspect ratio is checked.

You want every picture to be the same size—even if it causes some distortion. The Lock aspect ratio constrains the height and width of the selected object so that it maintains its original proportion.

9 In the Height box in the Size and rotate section, type 2.75.

You want every picture to be located in the same position so that the slides look similar.

10 Click the Position tab. In the Horizontal text box, type 5.17 and make sure the Top Left Corner option is selected in the From text box. In the Vertical text box, type 2.17 and again make sure the Top Left Corner option is selected in the From text box. Then click OK.

The Format Picture dialog box closes and the picture is resized and repositioned. This is the last step you want in the macro, so you can stop the macro recorder.

11 Click the Stop Recording button on the Stop Recording toolbar.

The Stop Recording toolbar closes, indicating that you are no longer recording a macro.

In the next lesson you will learn how to play the macro you just recorded.

Lesson 10.7
Recording a Macro

QUICK REFERENCE

TO RECORD A MACRO:

1. SELECT **TOOLS** → **MACRO** → **RECORD NEW MACRO** FROM THE MENU.
2. ENTER A NAME AND DESCRIPTION FOR THE MACRO.
3. CLICK **OK** AND CAREFULLY PERFORM THE ACTIONS YOU WANT TO INCLUDE IN YOUR MACRO.
4. CLICK THE **STOP RECORDING BUTTON** ON THE STOP RECORDING TOOLBAR WHEN YOU'RE FINISHED RECORDING YOUR MACRO.

LESSON 10.8

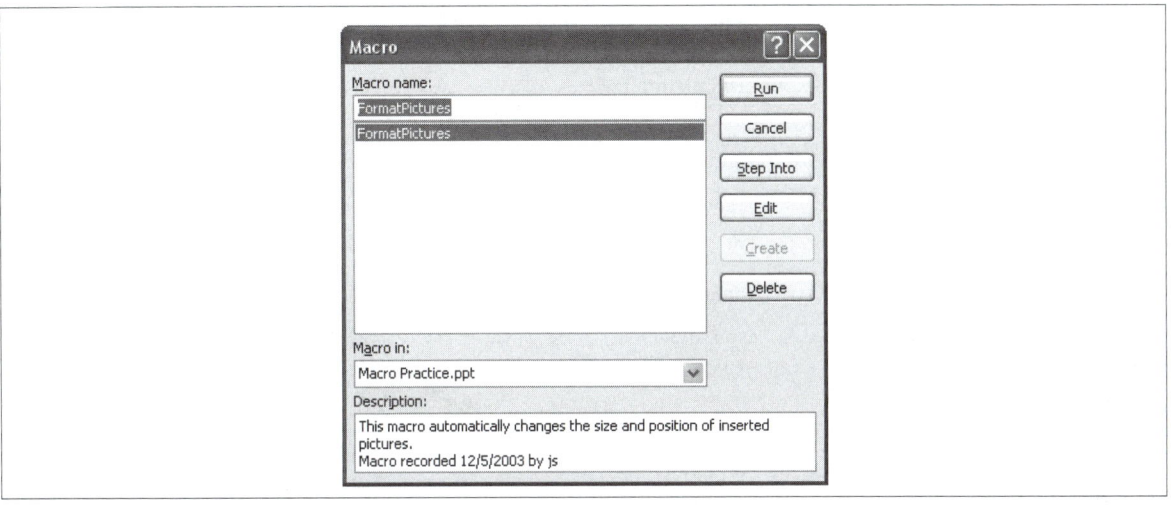

Playing and Editing a Macro

Figure 10-18. The Macro dialog box.

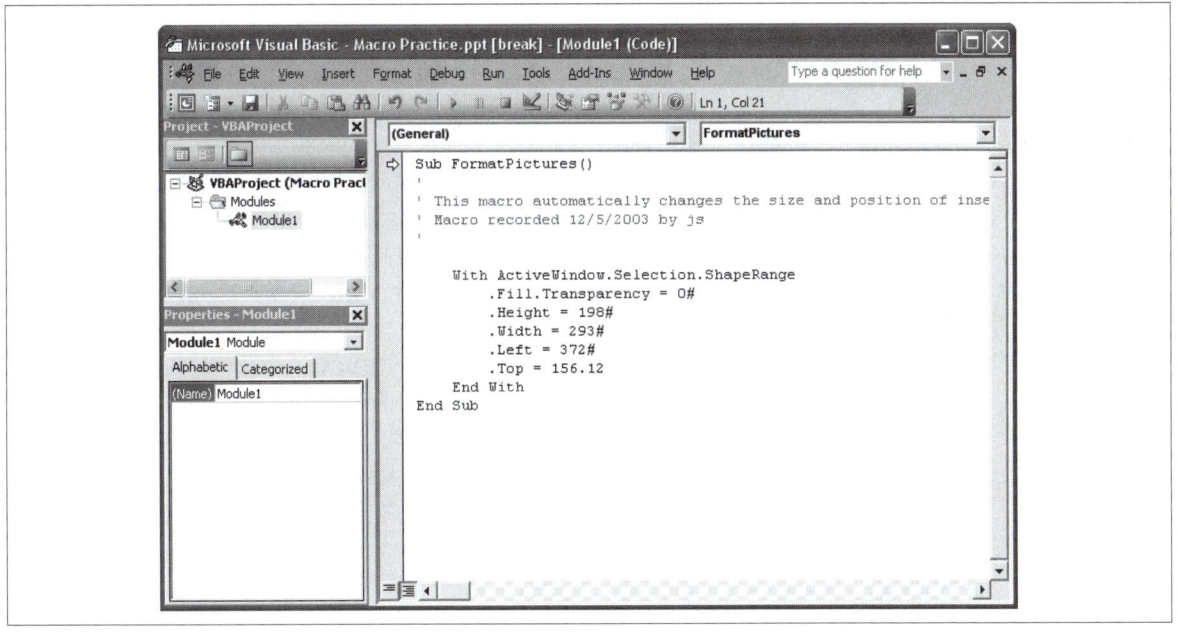

Figure 10-19. Editing a macro in the Microsoft Visual Basic Editor.

In this lesson you get to play the macro that you recorded in the previous lesson. Once you have created a macro, you can make it easily accessible by adding the macro as a button on a toolbar or by adding a new command for your macro under one of the menu options.

This lesson also introduces you to the Visual Basic (also called VB or VBA) programming language. Visual Basic is the code PowerPoint and other Microsoft Office programs use to record macros. If you're feeling adventurous, you can take a peek at or even attempt to edit the code that your macros are written in by opening the Microsoft Visual Basic Editor. Since PowerPoint is a pretty simple program, it's almost always easier to fix any mistakes in your macros by starting over and recording them from scratch.

301

Lesson 10.8
Playing and Editing a Macro

The following procedure describes how to run a macro:

1 Move to Slide 2 and click the Mount Fuji picture to select it.

We'll change the size and position of this picture using the macro we created instead of performing each step manually.

2 Select Tools → Macro → Macros from the menu.

The Macro dialog box appears, as shown in Figure 10-18. The Macro dialog box displays the available macros you can run.

3 In the Macro name list, click the FormatPictures macro and click Run.

The FormatPictures macro you recorded in the previous lesson runs, automatically changing the size and position of the selected picture.

Let's try it again.

4 Go to Slide 3, click on the picture to select it, and repeat Steps 2 and 3.

The FormatPictures macro works its magic and resizes and repositions the picture.

If you're feeling technical and have always wanted to see or even edit the Visual Basic code that macros are recorded in, here's how to edit a macro's code:

5 Select Tools → Macro → Macros from the menu.

The Macro dialog box appears.

6 Select the FormatPictures macro from the Macro name list and click Edit.

The Microsoft Visual Basic Editor program appears, as shown in Figure 10-19. Yikes! You're probably thinking, "What is all of that complex programming code doing on my screen?" Those funny-looking words aren't Hungarian, they're *Visual Basic*—the code, or language, the macro you recorded is written in. Whenever you record a macro, PowerPoint writes it and saves it in Visual Basic.

If you want, you can try editing some of a macro's Visual Basic code. Most of us have better things to do with our time than learning VBA, however, so…

7 Close the Visual Basic Editor by clicking the Close button in the top right corner of the screen.

Decide you don't need a macro anymore? Here's how to delete a macro:

8 Select Tools → Macro → Macros from the menu.

The Macro dialog box reappears.

9 Select the FormatPictures macro, click Delete, and click Delete to confirm the macro deletion.

PowerPoint deletes the FormatPictures macro.

10 Exit PowerPoint without saving your work.

QUICK REFERENCE

TO PLAY A MACRO:

1. SELECT TOOLS → MACRO → MACROS FROM THE MENU.

2. SELECT THE MACRO YOU WANT TO PLAY AND CLICK RUN.

TO EDIT A MACRO'S VISUAL BASIC CODE:

1. SELECT TOOLS → MACRO → MACROS FROM THE MENU.

2. SELECT THE MACRO AND CLICK EDIT.

3. EDIT THE MACRO!

4. WHEN YOU'RE FINISHED EDITING THE MACRO'S CODE, CLICK THE SAVE BUTTON, AND THEN CLOSE THE VISUAL BASIC EDITOR WINDOW.

TO DELETE A MACRO:

1. SELECT TOOLS → MACRO → MACROS FROM THE MENU.

2. SELECT THE MACRO, CLICK DELETE, AND CLICK DELETE TO CONFIRM THE DELETION.

Chapter Ten Review

Lesson Summary

Hiding, Displaying, and Moving Toolbars

To View or Hide a Toolbar: Select View → Toolbars from the menu and select the toolbar you want to display or hide, or right-click any toolbar or menu and select the toolbar you want to display or hide from the shortcut menu.

To Move a Toolbar to a New Location: Drag the toolbar by its move handle (if the toolbar is docked) or title bar (if the toolbar is floating) to the desired location.

Customizing PowerPoint's Toolbars

To Add a Button to a Toolbar: Select View → Toolbars → Customize from the menu and click the Commands tab. Select the command category from the Categories list, then find the desired command in the Commands list and drag the command to the toolbar.

To Remove a Button from a Toolbar: Select View → Toolbars → Customize from the menu and drag the button off the toolbar.

Sending Faxes

To Use the Fax Service: You must be signed up with a fax service provider, and you must have Word and Outlook 2003 installed on your computer.

To Send a Fax: Open the file you want to fax and select File → Send to → Recipient using Internet Fax Service from the menu. Enter the fax information: recipient name and fax number, and a subject. Choose the type of cover sheet you want to use in the Fax Service task pane and fill it out. Click the Send button.

To Preview the Fax: Click the Preview button in the Fax Service task pane.

To Calculate Cost of Fax: Click the Calculate Cost button in the Fax Service task pane.

To Fax Multiple Files: Click the Attach button in the fax message window and attach each file you want to fax.

Add Comments to a Slide

To Add a Comment to a Slide: Select Insert → Comment from the menu and type the note.

To Show or Hide Slide Comments: Click the Markup Button on the Reviewing toolbar or select View → Markup from the menu.

To Delete a Comment: Click the comment to select it then press the Delete key.

Customizing PowerPoint's Default Options

You can change PowerPoint's default options by selecting Tools → Options from the menu.

Finding a File

To Find a File: Click the Start button and select Search, then select All Files and Folders from the task pane. Enter part of the file name in the All or part of the file name box. You can also search for a file using other criteria—using the A word or phrase in the file box or by clicking the More advanced options link. Click Search to start searching for the file(s).

Recording a Macro

To Record a Macro: Select Tools → Macro → Record New Macro from the menu, enter a name and description for the macro, and click OK. Carefully perform the actions you want to include in your macro while the Macro Recorder records your every move. Click the Stop Recording button on the Stop Recording toolbar when you're finished recording your macro.

Playing and Editing a Macro

To Play a Macro: Select Tools → Macro → Macros from the menu, select the macro, and click Run.

To Edit a Macro's Visual Basic Code: Select Tools → Macro → Macros from the menu, select the macro, and click Edit. Edit the macro. When you're finished editing the macro's code, click the Save button and then close the Visual Basic Editor window.

To Delete a Macro: Select Tools → Macro → Macros from the menu, select the macro you want to delete, click Delete, and click Delete to confirm the deletion.

Chapter 10
Chapter Ten Review

Quiz

1. Which of the following statements is NOT true?

   A. You can change the position of a toolbar by dragging it by its move handle (if it's docked) or title bar (if it's floating).

   B. You can display a toolbar by selecting View → Toolbars and selecting the toolbar you want to display from the list.

   C. You can display a toolbar by clicking the Toolbar button on the Standard toolbar and selecting the toolbar you want to display from the list.

   D. Toolbars attach or "dock" to the sides of the program window.

2. Which of the following statements is NOT true?

   A. You can customize a toolbar by right-clicking any toolbar or menu and selecting Customize from the shortcut menu.

   B. You can customize a toolbar by selecting View → Toolbars → Customize from the menu.

   C. Once the Customize dialog box is open, you can add buttons to a toolbar by double-clicking on the toolbar where you want to insert the button.

   D. Once the Customize dialog box is open, you can add buttons to a toolbar by dragging them from the Commands list onto the toolbar.

3. You can modify PowerPoint's built-in toolbars, and you can create your own toolbars. (True or False?)

4. Which of the following statements is NOT true?

   A. You can begin to find a file by clicking the Windows Start button and selecting Search.

   B. Selecting File → Properties from the menu displays statistics on a file, such as its size and when it was last saved.

   C. Selecting Tools → Options from the menu opens the Options dialog box, which contains the default settings for PowerPoint.

   D. You can add a comment—an electronic Post-it® note—to your slide by switching to Notes view and typing the note.

5. Which of the following statements is NOT true?

   A. PowerPoint records macros in Visual Basic language.

   B. Macros names can be up to 25 characters long, including spaces.

   C. You start the macro recorder by selecting Tools → Macro → Record New Macro from the menu.

   D. When you record a macro, it records your every action—everything you type, every command you issue—even how you click and drag the mouse!

Homework

1. Start PowerPoint, select the Blank presentation option and click OK.

2. Insert a blank Title only slide.

3. Create a custom toolbar. Select Tools → Customize from the menu, click the Toolbars tab, and click New to create a new toolbar. Name the toolbar "My Commands." Click OK.

4. Click the Commands tab, browse through the various Categories and Commands, and drag the commands you think you will use most frequently onto the new My Commands toolbar.

5. Delete the My Commands toolbar when you're finished (click the Toolbars tab, select the My Commands toolbar and click Delete). Close the Customize dialog box.

6. Insert a comment on the current slide. Select Insert → Comment from the menu and type whatever you feel like on the note.

7. Hide the comment by selecting View → Markup from the menu.

Chapter 10
Advanced Topics

Quiz Answers

1. C. There isn't a Toolbar button in PowerPoint.

2. C. Once the Customize dialog box is open, you can add buttons to a toolbar by dragging commands from the commands list to the desired location on the toolbar—not by double-clicking.

3. True.

4. D. You *can* add notes to your slides in Notes view, but to insert a comment that actually appears on a slide, select Insert → Comment from the menu.

5. B. Macro names can't have spaces in them.

INDEX

Numbers

3-D effects, adding to objects, 163–165
90-degree increments, rotating objects in, 158

A

action buttons, 154, 272–274
   list of, 273
Action Settings dialog box, 273
adjustment handles
   on AutoShapes, 155
   on WordArt objects, 186
AIFF files, 245
aligning objects, 151–153
aligning paragraphs, 120
Animated GIF files, 250
animation, custom, 223–224
animation effects, 5
Animation Schemes, 5, 221
area charts, 202
Arial font, 101
arrowheads, removing from slides, 143
arrows, drawing, 135
ASCII files, importing outlines in, 268
assistants (subordinate boxes in organization charts), 207
AU files, 245
audio files (see sound files)
AutoContent Wizard, creating new presentations with, 25–27
AutoCorrect Options button, 89
automating multimedia in presentations, 252–254
AutoRecover feature, 92
AutoShapes, 154–156
   adding text to, 155
   creating action buttons, 273
   drawing, 155
AVI (windows video file) files, 250

B

background of slides
   changing, 115–117
   color of, 113, 143
bar charts, 201
basic shapes (AutoShapes category), 154
blank presentations, creating, 28
Blinds effect, applying to bulleted list, 224
block arrows (AutoShapes category), 154
BMP (bitmap) file format, 150
boldfacing text, 101
borders, adding to tables, 181
Bring Forward (layering command), 161
Bring to Front (layering command), 161
bulleted lists, 118
   adding custom animation to, 223
Bullets and Numbering dialog box, 119
buttons, adding to toolbars, 287

C

calculating cost of faxes, 290
callouts (AutoShapes category), 154
Cancel button, 16
CD Quality for recording, 247
CDs, packaging presentations to, 4, 234–235
center-aligning objects, 152
centered tab, 125
centering text, 121
CGM (Computer Graphics Metafile) file format, 150
Chart placeholder, 49, 195
Chart Type dialog box, 201
charts
   adding to presentations, 194–196
   formatting, 198
   resizing, 195
   selecting, 198
   types of, 200–202
check boxes, 15
checking your spelling, 64

Index

circles, drawing, 135
Clip Art
    inserting in slides, 145–147
    placeholder for, 50
Clipboard, 58
    collecting/pasting multiple items, 82–84
Close buttons on screen, 23
collapsing outlines, 68
color schemes, choosing, 112–114
colors
    adding shading to cells, 183
    applying to selected text, 104
    changing, for slide background, 115, 143
    in color schemes, changing, 113
    organization chart boxes, applying to, 210
column charts, 201
columns
    adjusting width of, 177
    inserting, 179
    selecting, 176
combo boxes, 15
Comic Sans MS font, 101
comments
    adding to slides, 291
    deleting from slides, 292
    showing/hiding, 292
connectors (AutoShapes category), 154
Contents placeholder, 49
context-sensitive shortcut menus, 17
context-sensitive smart tags, 4
continuous loop, playing movie clips in, 251
Copy command, 86
copying
    formatting, with Format Painter, 106
    multiple items with Office 2003 Clipboard, 82–84
    text, 59
correcting spelling errors, 64
Courier New font, 102
coworker boxes in organization charts, 207
Create Shortcut command, 86
creating new presentations, 13
    from blank presentations, 28
    from templates, 28
    with AutoContent Wizard, 25–27
cropping pictures, 149
Ctrl + B (toggles bold font), 18
Ctrl + C (copies text to clipboard), 18
Ctrl + End (moves insertion point to end), 18, 31
Ctrl + Home (moves insertion point to beginning), 18, 31
Ctrl + I (toggles italics font), 18
Ctrl + O (opens), 18
Ctrl + P (prints), 18
Ctrl + S (saves), 18
Ctrl + Spacebar (returns formatting to default), 18
Ctrl + U (toggles underlines), 18
Ctrl + V (pastes text from clipboard), 18
Ctrl + X (cuts text and puts on clipboard), 18
custom animation, adding to slides, 223–224
Custom Animation dialog box, 253
Custom Shows feature, 231
    adding/deleting slides, 232
Customize dialog box, 287
customizing
    default options, 293
    menus, 10
    toolbars, 287–288
Cut command, 86
cutting selected text, 58
cycle diagrams, 204

D

dates/times, adding to headers/footers, 123
decimal-aligned tab, 125
default options, customizing, 293
Define Custom Show dialog box, 231
Delete command, 86
deleting
    hyperlinks, 271
    macros, 302
    objects on slides, 140
    slides in Slide Sorter View, 76
    text in presentations, 53
    voice narration from slides, 248
demoting paragraphs, 51
deselecting text, 56
design templates
    applying to presentations, 108
    creating presentations from, 28
    more than one possible in presentation, 5
Diagram Gallery dialog box, 204
Diagram or Organizational Chart placeholder, 49
diagrams, types of, 204
dialog boxes, 15
    selecting multiple items from, 16
Display as icon option, 259
displaying hidden menu commands, 9
distributing selected objects, 152
docked vs. floating toolbars, 285
document outlines, importing into presentations, 267–269
Document Recovery feature, 5, 91–93
doodling on slides with electronic pen, 216
downward-pointing arrows
    in drop-down menus, 16
    on menus, clicking to display hidden commands, 9
drag and drop method
    moving objects on a slide, 140
    moving slides/paragraphs in outlines, 72
    rearranging organization charts, 207
Drawing toolbar, 7, 135–136
drop-down menus, 15

Index

E
Edit Hyperlink dialog box, 270
Edit menu, 10
editing Visual Basic code in macros, 302
electronic pen, doodling on slides with, 216
ellipses (…) in menus, 15
email, sending faxes via, 289
embedded vs. linked objects, 263
embedding
    Excel worksheets into slides, 260
    presentations into Word documents, 258
End (moves to end of line), 31
Excel charts (linked), inserting into presentations, 265
Excel worksheets
    embedded in slides, modifying, 262–264
    embedding into slides, 260
exiting PowerPoint 2003, 23
expanding outlines, 69

F
F1 key (Help key), 38
faxes
    calculating cost of, 290
    previewing, 290
    sending via email, 289
File menu, 10
File Properties dialog box, 296
files
    finding, 296
    managing in PowerPoint, 85–87
fill color
    of shapes, 113
        changing, 142
    of WordArt objects, changing, 188
Fill Color button, 183
fill effects for slide backgrounds, 115–117, 143
Find dialog box, 66
finding files, 296
flipping objects, 157–159
floating vs. docked toolbars, 285
flowcharts (AutoShapes category), 154
folders (special) in Open and Save As dialog boxes, 20
Font Color list, 113
Font dialog box, 15
    advanced font formatting with, 103–105
fonts
    formatting
        in text boxes, 137
        with Formatting toolbar, 100–102
    previewing settings, 104
    size of, changing, 101, 104, 138
    in tables, changing, 173
    type of, changing, 101, 103
footers, adding to presentations, 122

Format AutoShape dialog box, 143
    organization charts, formatting, 210
Format Data Series dialog box, 198
Format menu, 10
Format Painter, copying formatting with, 106
Format Table dialog box, 182
Format WordArt dialog box, 187–189
Formatting toolbar, 7, 12
    displaying with Standard toolbar, on one/two rows, 13
    formatting fonts with, 100–102
    using with tables, 176
full-screen mode
    displaying web-based presentations in, 278
    viewing movies in, 4, 251

G
getting help in PowerPoint, 38
Getting Started task pane, 4
GIF file format, 150
gradient fill effect, 115
    adding shading to cells, 184
graphics, inserting, 149
grayscale, changing color to, 149
grouping objects together, 152

H
Header and Footer dialog box, 122
headers, adding to presentations, 122
height of rows, adjusting, 177
Help buttons, 39
Help files for PowerPoint, 38
Help menu, 10
hiding
    menu commands, 9
    Office Assistant, 42
    toolbars, 284
Highlighter tool, 216
Home (moves to start of line), 31
Homework
    Chapter 1, 45
    Chapter 2, 97
    Chapter 3, 131
    Chapter 4, 169
    Chapter 5, 192
    Chapter 6, 213
    Chapter 7, 240
    Chapter 8, 256
    Chapter 9, 282
    Chapter 10, 304
horizontal scroll bars, 30
hyperlinks
    color of, 114
    inserting, 270–271
    removing, 271

Index

I

importing document outlines into presentations, 267–269
indents, adding to slides, 124–126
Insert CD Audio dialog box, 245
Insert Hyperlink dialog box, 271
Insert menu, 10
Insert Movie dialog box, 250
Insert Object dialog box, 260
Insert Outline dialog box, 268
Insert Picture dialog box, 149, 224
    options in, 146
Insert Shape button, inserting subordinates in organization charts, 206–208
Insert Sound dialog box, 244
Insert Table dialog box, 173
inserting
    columns/rows, 179
    Excel worksheets into slides, 260
    hyperlinks, 270–271
    presentations into Word documents, 258
    special characters/symbols, 73
    text in presentations, 53
    WordArt objects, 185
Internet
    web-based presentations, 275–277
        viewing, 278
italicizing text, 101

J

JPEG file format, 150

K

keyboard shortcuts
    commonly used, list of, 18
    issuing, 17
keystroke/mouse combinations, 140

L

landscape orientation, 127
layering objects, 160–162
layout of new slides, changing, 52
layout of organization charts, changing, 210
left mouse button, uses for, 17
left-aligned tab, 125
left-aligning text, 121
Lesson Summaries
    Chapter 1, 43
    Chapter 2, 94–96
    Chapter 3, 129
    Chapter 4, 166–167
    Chapter 5, 190
    Chapter 6, 212
    Chapter 7, 238
    Chapter 8, 255
    Chapter 9, 280
    Chapter 10, 303
levels of organization charts, 207
line charts, 201
line spacing of paragraphs, changing, 120
lines
    AutoShapes category, 154
    color of, changing, 143
    drawing, 135
    style of, changing, 143
Link to file option, 259
linked Excel charts, inserting into presentations, 265
linked vs. embedded objects, 263
list boxes, 15
Look In List control, 20, 23

M

Macro dialog box, 302
macros
    deleting, 302
    editing Visual Basic code in, 302
    playing, 301
    recording, 298–300
Make Available Offline command, 86
manager boxes in organization charts, 204
managing files in PowerPoint, 85–87
maximizing windows, 80
Media Clip placeholder, 50
memory usage by digital recordings, 248
menu bar, 7
menus, 9–11
    closing, 10
    customizing, 10
    opening, 9
microphones for recording voice narration, 247
Microsoft Clip Organizer, 250
Microsoft Graph program, 194–196
    types of charts/graphs, 200–202
Microsoft Internet Explorer, 276
Microsoft Organization Chart window, 204
Microsoft Word for Windows, importing outlines in, 267
MIDI files, 245
    adding sounds to slides, 244
minimizing windows, 81
Mouse Click/Mouse Over tabs in Action Settings dialog box, 273
Move Up/Move Down buttons on Outlining toolbar, 72
movie clips
    adding to slides, 250
    automating, 252–254
    moving around on slides, 250
    playing in continuous loop, 251
    viewing in full-screen mode, 4, 251
Movie Options dialog box, 251

Index

moving
    between slides in presentations, 30–32
    objects on slides, 140
    slides in Slide Sorter View, 76
    up/down in presentations, using scroll bars, 30
    WordArt objects, 186
MP3 files, 245
MPEG files, 250
multimedia, automating in presentations, 252–254
multiple presentations, working with, 79–81
music, adding to slides, 244–246

N

narrations
    adding to slides, 247
    deleting from slides, 248
    recording, 248
navigating through web-based presentations, 278
navigation tools for slide shows, 4
Netscape Navigator, 276
New command, 86
New Presentation task pane, 29
Next Slide button, 30
Normal View, 33–35
    tabs/indents, changing, 124
    working with animation in, 221
notes, adding to slides, 77, 217
Notes Page View, 35, 78, 217
Notes pane, 7
nudging objects with great precision, 140

O

Object dialog box, 259
Office 2003 Clipboard, collecting/pasting multiple items, 82–84
Office Assistant, 41
    hiding, 42
Office Online feature, 39
Offline Help feature, 39
OK button, 16
Open command, 86
Open dialog box, 19, 85–87
    special folders in, 20
Open With command, 86
opening presentations, 19–21
Options dialog box, 293
options in Print dialog box, 36
organization charts
    changing color of boxes in, 210
    changing layout of, 210
    creating, 203–205
    formatting, 210
    improvements to, 5

levels of, 207
    modifying, 206–208
orientation of pages, changing, 127
Outline pane, 51
    adding new slides in, 51
    collapsing outlines, 68
    expanding outlines, 69
    navigating through web-based presentations, 278
    rearranging contents of, 72
Outline tab, 7
outlines from documents, importing into presentations, 267–269
Outlining toolbar, 68
    buttons on, 69
ovals, drawing, 135
overlapping objects, layering, 160–162
overriding Slide Master, 111

P

Package for CD feature, 4, 234–235
packaged presentations, viewing, 236–237
packaging presentations to CDs/folders, 234–235
Page Down (moves to next slide), 31
Page Setup dialog box, 127
Page Up (moves to previous slide), 31
paragraphs
    aligning, 120
    demoting, 51
    line spacing, changing, 120
    promoting, 52
Paste Options button, 89
pasting
    multiple items with Office 2003 Clipboard, 82–84
    text, 59
pattern fill effect, 115
pen tool, doodling on slides with, 216
picture fill effect, 115
Picture toolbar, 149
pictures
    cropping, 149
    increasing size of, 139
    inserting in slides, 149–150, 224
    using as bullets, 119
pie charts, 201
placeholders in slides, 48–50
Play Sound dialog box, 253
playing macros, 301
portrait orientation, 127
PowerPoint 2003
    closing the program, 23
    default options, customizing, 293
    new features in, 4
    program screen, understanding, 6
    starting, 2

Index

PowerPoint Viewer program, 236–237
presentations
    action buttons in, 272–274
    charts, adding to, 194–196
    closing, 23
    creating, 13
        from blank presentations, 28
        from templates, 28
        with AutoContent Wizard, 25–27
    deleting text in, 53
    delivering on computer, 216–218
    design templates, applying to, 108
    editing text in, 53
    embedding into Word documents, 258
    finding and replacing information, 66
    headers/footers, adding to, 122
    hyperlinks in slides, 270–271
    importing document outlines into, 267–269
    inserting slides into, 48–50
    linked Excel charts, inserting, 265
    manually stepping through slides, 226
    movie clips, adding to, 250
    moving
        from slide to slide in, 30–32
        to end of, 51
    multiple, working with, 79–81
    music, adding to, 244–246
    opening, 19–21
    outlines of
        collapsing/expanding, 68–70
        rearranging, 72
    packaging to CDs/folders, 4, 234–235
    page setup, changing, 127
    printing, 36
    recovering, 91–93
    Rehearse Timings feature, 226
    saving
        as web pages, 275–277
        in same file, 23
        with new, different name, 22
    scroll bars, horizontal/vertical, 30
    selecting text in, 55–57
    self-running, creating, 229
    sounds, adding to, 244–246
    transition effects in slide shows, 219
    viewing, 33–35
    voice narration, adding to, 247–249
    web-based, 275–277
        viewing, 278
    zoom level in, changing, 34
preset colors, filling background with, 116
previewing
    faxes, 290
    font settings, 104
    new slide background, 116
    presentations before printing, 36
    web-based presentations, 278
Print command, 86
Print dialog box, options in, 36
printing presentations, 36
program screen, PowerPoint 2003, 6
promoting paragraphs, 52
Properties command, 86
Publish as Web Page dialog box, 276
pyramid diagrams, 204

Q

QuickTime files, 250
Quiz Answers
    Chapter 1, 46
    Chapter 2, 98
    Chapter 3, 132
    Chapter 4, 169
    Chapter 5, 192
    Chapter 6, 214
    Chapter 7, 241
    Chapter 8, 256
    Chapter 9, 282
    Chapter 10, 305
Quizzes
    Chapter 1, 45
    Chapter 2, 96
    Chapter 3, 130
    Chapter 4, 168
    Chapter 5, 191
    Chapter 6, 213
    Chapter 7, 239
    Chapter 8, 255
    Chapter 9, 281
    Chapter 10, 304

R

radial diagrams, 204
Radio Quality for recording, 247
rearranging outlines, 72
Record Macro dialog box, 299
Record Narration feature, 247–249
Record Sound dialog box, 248
recording macros, 298–300
recording quality, levels of, 247
recovering presentations, 5, 91–93
rectangles, drawing, 135
Redo command, 61
Rehearse Timings feature, 226
Rename command, 86
Repeat command, 62
Replace dialog box, 67
replacing selected text, 56
Research task pane, 4

resizing
    AutoShapes, 155
    charts, 195
    objects with AutoShape dialog box, 144
    pictures, 146
    text boxes, 138
    WordArt objects, 186
restoring windows, 80
Rich Text Format (RTF), importing outlines in, 267
right mouse button, bringing up shortcut menus with, 17
right-aligned tab, 125
right-clicking objects, 17
rotate handles, 158
rotate tool, 157
rotating objects, 157–159
rows
    adjusting height of, 177
    inserting, 179
    selecting, 175
rulers, setting tabs with, 124–126

S

Save As dialog box, 22
    special folders in, 20
Save dialog box, 85–87
saving presentations, 22
    as web pages, 275–277
Scan with Norton Antivirus command, 86
scatter charts, 201
ScreenTips, 13
scroll bars
    in list boxes, 15
    moving up/down in presentations, 30
Scroll Down button, 30
Search feature, 296
Search Results dialog box, 296
Select command, 86
selecting
    chart objects, 198
    columns in tables, 176
    objects to be aligned, 152
    rows in tables, 175
    text in presentations, 55–57
self-running presentations, creating, 229
Send Backward (layering command), 161
Send to Back (layering command), 161
Send To command, 86
Set Up Show dialog box, 226, 229
shading, adding to cells in a table, 183
Shadow Settings toolbar, 164
shadows
    adding behind text, 103
    adding to objects, 163–165
    color of, 113
shape of WordArt objects, changing, 188

Shift + Tab keys
    moving to previous cell in row, 173
    moving to previous option in dialog box, 15
    promoting paragraphs using, 52
shortcut menus, 17
    closing, 17
    commands for, 86
shortcuts
    for selecting text, 56
    using during slide shows, 217
Show command, 86
Show Large Previews option, 29
size of fonts, changing, 101, 104, 138
sizing handles, 139
    resizing pictures using, 146
Slide Design task pane, 108, 112
Slide Finder dialog box, 79
Slide Layout pane, 172, 203
slide layouts
    adjusting automatically, 5
    placeholders in, 48–50
Slide Master, setting appearance of slides with, 110–111
Slide pane, 7
Slide Show View, 33–35
    activating custom animation in, 224
    playing movie clips, 251
    rehearsing your timing in, 226
    self-running presentations, 230
slide shows
    creating custom shows, 231
    keystrokes for, 217
    navigation tools for, 4
Slide Sorter View, 33–35, 75–76
    using slide transitions in, 219, 229
    voice narrations in slides, 248
Slide Time box, 226
Slide Transition task pane, 220, 229
slides
    action buttons in, 272–274
    adding new slides in Outline pane, 51
    adding sounds from
        audio CDs, 245
        external files, 244
    adding tables to, 172–174
    adding text boxes to, 138
    adding text to, 49
    advancing to next, in Slide Show View, 216
    background of, 113, 115–117
    charts, adding to, 194–196
    comments
        adding, 291
        deleting from, 292
        showing/hiding, 292
    custom animation, adding to, 223–224
    duplicating in Slide Sorter View, 76
    embedded Excel worksheets, 260
        modifying, 262–264

Index

slides (*continued*)
    hyperlinks in, 270–271
    indents, adding to, 124–126
    inserting
        Clip Art in, 145–147
        into presentations, 48–50
        pictures in, 149–150, 224
    movie clips
        adding to, 250
        playing in continuous loop, 251
    moving from slide to slide in presentations, 30–32
    music, adding to, 244–246
    notes, adding to, 77, 217
    organization charts, creating, 203–205
    page orientation, changing, 127
    rearranging in Outline pane, 72
    Rehearse Timings feature, 226
    removing sounds from, 245
    selected, applying design templates to, 109
    special characters/symbols, inserting, 73
    tabs, adding to, 124–126
    thumbnails of, 5
    transition effects, adding to, 219
    voice narration
        adding to, 247
        deleting from, 248
Slides tab, 7
smart tags, 4, 88–90
sound files
    adding sounds from
        audio CDs, 245
        external files, 244
    automating, 252–254
    compatible with PowerPoint, 245
    removing sounds from slides, 245
Sound Selection dialog box, 247
special characters, adding to slides, 73
special folders in Open and Save As dialog boxes, 20
spell checking, 64
Standard toolbar, 7, 12
    displaying with Formatting toolbar, on one/two rows, 13
stars and banners (AutoShapes category), 154
starting PowerPoint 2003, 2
status bar, 7
Stop Recording toolbar, 299
style of lines, changing, 143
style of WordArt objects, changing, 188
subordinate boxes in organization charts, 204
    inserting, with Insert Shape button, 206–208
subscripts/superscripts, adding to text, 104
switching
    between open presentations, 79–81
    views in PowerPoint, 33
symbols, adding to slides, 73

T

Tab Alignment box, 125
Tab key
    adding new row to end of table, 179
    moving to next cell in row, 173
    moving to next option in dialog box, 15
    selecting slide objects with, 139
Table placeholder, 49, 173
tables
    borders, adding to, 181
    columns, selecting, 176
    creating, 172–174
    height of rows, adjusting, 177
    rows, selecting, 175
    shading, adding to cells, 183
    width of columns, adjusting, 177
Tables and Borders toolbar, 173, 182
tabs, adding to slides, 124–126
target diagrams, 204
Task pane, 5, 7
Telephone Quality for recording, 247
templates, design
    applying to presentations, 108
    creating presentations from, 28
    more than one possible in presentation, 5
text
    adding
        to AutoShapes, 155
        to slides, 49
    boldfacing, 101
    centering, 121
    color of, 113
    colors, applying to, 104
    copying, 59
    cutting, 58
    deleting in presentations, 53
    deselecting, 56
    editing in presentations, 53
    italicizing, 101
    left-aligning, 121
    pasting, 59
    selecting in presentations, 55–57
    spacing of WordArt objects, changing, 188
    subscripts/superscripts, adding to, 104
    underlining, adding to, 104
text boxes, 15
    adding to slides, 138
    formatting, 137
    resizing, 138
text files, importing outlines in, 268
Text placeholder, 49
text spacing of WordArt objects, changing, 188
texture fill effect, 115
thumbnails of slides, 5
    displaying, 7

Index

TIF file format, 150
Times New Roman font, 102
timing slide shows, rehearsing, 226
title bar, 7
Title Master, setting appearance of title slides with, 110–111
Title placeholder, 49
titles
    adding to slides, 194
    color of, 113
toolbar buttons
    displaying description of, 13
    how to use, 12
toolbars
    adding buttons to, 287
    customizing, 287–288
    docked vs. floating, 285
    hiding/displaying, 284
    moving to new location on screen, 284
Tools menu, 10
transition effects, adding to slides, 219
triggering sounds or events, 253
type of fonts, changing, 101, 103

U

underlined letters in menus, 9
underlining, adding to text, 104
Undo command, 61–63
ungrouping objects, 152
Up One Level button, 20, 23
user interface, streamlined, 4

V

Venn diagrams, 204
vertical scroll bars, 30
View buttons, 7
View menu, 10
Viewer program, PowerPoint, 236–237

viewing presentations, 33–35
views, switching in PowerPoint, 33
Visual Basic (VBA) code, editing in macros, 302
voice narrations
    adding to slides, 247
    deleting from slides, 248
    recording, 248

W

WAV files, 245
Web Options dialog box, 276
web-based presentations, 275–277
    viewing, 278
"What's This" button, 41
width of columns, adjusting, 177
Window menu, 10
    switching between open presentations, 79–81
windows
    maximizing, 80
    minimizing, 81
    multiple, working with, 79–81
    restoring, 80
Windows Clipboard, 58
Wingding font set, 119
WMA files, 245
WMF file format, 150
Word documents, embedding presentations into, 258
word wrapping text, 138
WordArt objects
    changing shape of, 188
    formatting, 188–189
    inserting, 185
    moving, 186
    resizing, 186

Z

zoom level in presentations, changing, 34

About CustomGuide, Inc.

CustomGuide, Inc. (*www.customguide.com*) is a leading provider of training materials and e-learning for organizations; their client list includes Harvard, Yale, and Oxford Universities. CustomGuide, Inc. was founded by a small group of instructors who were dissatisfied by the dry and technical nature of computer training materials available to trainers and educators. They decided to write their own series of courseware that would be fun and user-friendly; and best of all, they would license it in electronic format so instructors could print only the topics they needed for a class or training session. Later, they found themselves unhappy with the e-learning industry and decided to create a new series of online, interactive training that matched their courseware. Today employees, students, and instructors at more than 2,000 institutions worldwide use CustomGuide, Inc. courseware to help teach and learn about computers.

CustomGuide, Inc. Staff and Contributors

Jonathan High	President
Daniel High	Vice President of Sales and Marketing
Melissa Peterson	Senior Writer/Editor
Kitty Rogers	Writer/Editor
Kelly Waldrop	Writer/Editor
Steve Meinz	Writer/Editor
Stan Keathly	Senior Developer
Jeffery High	Developer
Chris Kannnenman	Developer
Jeremy Weaver	Senior Programmer
Luke Davidson	Programmer
Lisa Price	Director of Business Development
Soda Rajsombath	Office Manager and Sales Representative
Stan Guimont	Senior Sales Representative
Megan Diemand	Sales Representative
Hallie Stork	Sales Representative
Sarah Saeger	Sales Support
Julie Geisler	Narrator

Colophon

Our look is the result of reader comments, our own experimentation, and feedback from distribution channels. Distinctive covers complement our distinctive approach to technical topics, breathing personality and life into potentially dry subjects.

Marlowe Shaeffer was the production editor and proofreader for *PowerPoint 2003 Personal Trainer*. Mary Brady and Claire Cloutier provided quality control. Judy Hoer wrote the index.

The cover image of the comic book hero is an original illustration by Lou Brooks. The art of illustrator Lou Brooks has appeard on the covers of *Time* and *Newsweek* eight times, and his logo design for the game Monopoly is used throughout the world to this day. His work has also appeared in just about every major publication, and it has been animated for MTV, Nickelodeon, and HBO.

Emma Colby designed and produced the cover of this book with Adobe InDesign CS and Photoshop CS. The typefaces used on the cover are Base Twelve, designed by Zuzana Licko and issued by Emigre, Inc., and JY Comic Pro, issued by AGFA Monotype.

Melanie Wang designed the interior layout. David Futato designed the CD label. This book was converted by Andrew Savikas and Joe Wizda to FrameMaker 5.5.6 with a format conversion tool created by Erik Ray, Jason McIntosh, Neil Walls, and Mike Sierra that uses Perl and XML technologies. The typefaces are Minion, designed by Robert Slimbach and issued by Adobe Systems; Base Twelve and Base Nine; JY Comic Pro; and TheSansMono Condensed, designed by Luc(as) de Groot and issued by LucasFonts.

The technical illustrations that appear in the book were produced by Chris Reilley using Macromedia FreeHand MX and Adobe Photoshop CS.

Also Available

Windows XP Personal Trainer
By CustomGuide, Inc.
ISBN 0-596-00862-7, Includes CD-Rom
456 pages, **$29.95**

Excel 2003 Personal Trainer
By CustomGuide, Inc.
ISBN 0-596-00853-8, Includes CD-Rom
496 pages, **$29.95**

Coming Winter 2005

Access 2003 Personal Trainer, *ISBN 0-596-00937-2,* **$29.95**
Outlook 2003 Personal Trainer, *ISBN 0-596-00935-6,* **$29.95**
Word 2003 Personal Trainer, *ISBN 0-596-00936-4,* **$29.95**

**Windows XP Home Edition:
The Missing Manual,
2nd Edition**
By David Pogue
ISBN 0-596-00897-X
600 pages, **$24.95**

**Windows XP Pro:
The Missing Manual,
2nd Edition**
*By Craig Zacker, Linda Zacker
& David Pogue*
ISBN 0-596-00898-8
680 pages, **$29.95**

Better than e-books

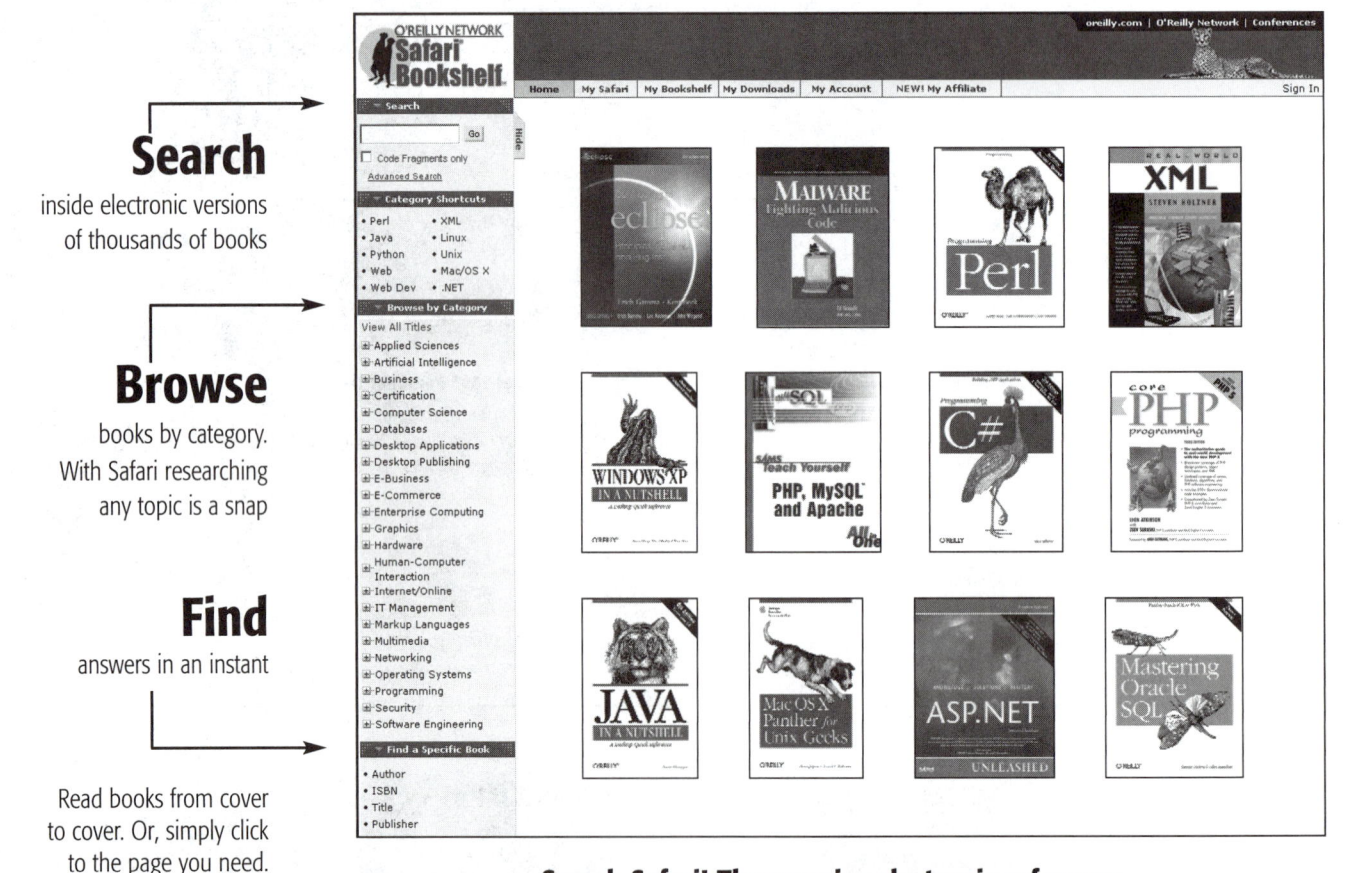

Try it FREE! Sign up today and get your first 14 days free. *safari.oreilly.com*

Search
inside electronic versions of thousands of books

Browse
books by category. With Safari researching any topic is a snap

Find
answers in an instant

Read books from cover to cover. Or, simply click to the page you need.

Search Safari! The premier electronic reference library for programmers and IT professionals

O'REILLY NETWORK Safari® Bookshelf

Addison Wesley · Sun Microsystems · Alpha · Java · Microsoft Press · Peachpit Press · O'Reilly · Que · Adobe Press · Sams · New Riders · Cisco Press · macromedia PRESS · Prentice Hall PTR

Related Titles Available from O'Reilly

Windows Users

Access Cookbook, *2nd Edition*

Access Database Design & Programming, *3rd Edition*

Excel Hacks

Excel Pocket Guide

Outlook 2000 in a Nutshell

Outlook Pocket Guide

PC Annoyances

Windows XP Annoyances

Windows XP Hacks

Windows XP Home Edition: The Missing Manual

Windows XP in a Nutshell

Windows XP Pocket Guide

Windows XP Power User

Windows XP Pro: The Missing Manual

Windows XP Unwired

Word Hacks

Word Pocket Guide, *2nd Edition*

O'REILLY®

Our books are available at most retail and online bookstores.
To order direct: 1-800-998-9938 • *order@oreilly.com* • *www.oreilly.com*
Online editions of most O'Reilly titles are available by subscription at *safari.oreilly.com*

Keep in touch with O'Reilly

1. Download examples from our books

To find example files for a book, go to:

www.oreilly.com/catalog

select the book, and follow the "Examples" link.

2. Register your O'Reilly books

Register your book at *register.oreilly.com*

Why register your books?
Once you've registered your O'Reilly books you can:

- Win O'Reilly books, T-shirts or discount coupons in our monthly drawing.
- Get special offers available only to registered O'Reilly customers.
- Get catalogs announcing new books (US and UK only).
- Get email notification of new editions of the O'Reilly books you own.

3. Join our email lists

Sign up to get topic-specific email announcements of new books and conferences, special offers, and O'Reilly Network technology newsletters at:

elists.oreilly.com

It's easy to customize your free elists subscription so you'll get exactly the O'Reilly news you want.

4. Get the latest news, tips, and tools

www.oreilly.com

- "Top 100 Sites on the Web"—PC Magazine
- CIO Magazine's Web Business 50 Awards

Our web site contains a library of comprehensive product information (including book excerpts and tables of contents), downloadable software, background articles, interviews with technology leaders, links to relevant sites, book cover art, and more.

5. Work for O'Reilly

Check out our web site for current employment opportunities:

jobs.oreilly.com

6. Contact us

O'Reilly & Associates
1005 Gravenstein Hwy North
Sebastopol, CA 95472 USA

TEL: 707-827-7000 or 800-998-9938
(6am to 5pm PST)

FAX: 707-829-0104

order@oreilly.com
For answers to problems regarding your order or our products. To place a book order online, visit:

www.oreilly.com/order_new

catalog@oreilly.com
To request a copy of our latest catalog.

booktech@oreilly.com
For book content technical questions or corrections.

corporate@oreilly.com
For educational, library, government, and corporate sales.

proposals@oreilly.com
To submit new book proposals to our editors and product managers.

international@oreilly.com
For information about our international distributors or translation queries. For a list of our distributors outside of North America check out:

international.oreilly.com/distributors.html

adoption@oreilly.com
For information about academic use of O'Reilly books, visit:

academic.oreilly.com

O'REILLY®

Our books are available at most retail and online bookstores.
To order direct: 1-800-998-9938 • *order@oreilly.com* • *www.oreilly.com*
Online editions of most O'Reilly titles are available by subscription at *safari.oreilly.com*